LANDMARKS IN RHETORIC
AND PUBLIC ADDRESS

LANDMARKS IN RHETORIC AND PUBLIC ADDRESS

David Potter, *General Editor*

Lectures

ON

RHETORIC AND BELLES LETTRES

BY

Hugh Blair, D.D.

VOLUME I

Edited by

HAROLD F. HARDING

Foreword by

DAVID POTTER

SOUTHERN ILLINOIS UNIVERSITY PRESS

CARBONDALE AND EDWARDSVILLE

Copyright © *1965,* by SOUTHERN ILLINOIS UNIVERSITY PRESS
Library of Congress Catalog Card No. 65–13061
Printed in the United States of America
DESIGNED BY ANDOR BRAUN

FOREWORD

By David Potter

ONE of the most highly regarded chairs at a British university is the Regius Professorship of Rhetoric and Belles Lettres at Edinburgh. It was established by King George III in 1762 and still exists. In the past century it has been graced by such names as Masson, Saintsbury, Grierson, and J. Dover Wilson. Of the long line, however, there is none whose lectures have been more widely read than those of the first occupant, Dr. Hugh Blair.

In 1783 Blair published under the title *Lectures on Rhetoric and Belles Lettres,* forty-seven lectures "read in the University of Edinburgh for twenty-four years." In the preface the writer states that the lectures were "originally designed for the initiation of Youth into the study of Belles Lettres, and of Composition" and that "the form of the Lectures, in which they were at first composed, is still retained. . . . He hopes, that to such as are studying to cultivate their Taste, to form their Style, or to prepare themselves for Public Speaking or Composition, his Lectures will afford a more comprehensive view of what relates to these subjects, than, as far as he knows, is to be received from any one Book in our Language."

Although, as Professor Harding indicates in his introduction, the *Lectures* have not always won critical acclaim, the reception by readers has long been extremely favorable. At least one hundred and thirty editions were issued, the last in 1911! It is not difficult to infer that few books in the area of rhetoric and criticism have had the continuous demand and acceptance of the *Lectures.* The established reputation of the Reverend Doctor Blair as a preacher might have prepared the contemporary audience. Samuel Johnson's endorsement certainly carried great weight. For students, the extensive use of British illustrative material contributed to the usefulness of the book. Whatever the reasons, only Blair's *Lectures* of all the important rhetorics of the eighteenth and early nineteenth centuries is still relatively available in the better second-hand book shops. Scores of thousands of copies were printed over scores of years.

Why, then, this edition? First, because the editions issued during the past hundred years are, in the main, abridged little volumes more suitable for convenience in carrying than for scholarly examination. Second, the few complete editions are usually bulky one-volume reprints, cracking apart with repeated handling and hard on tired eyes. Good editions are generally guarded in rare book rooms. Finally, no other edition available to today's student of rhetoric combines the readability and beauty of the first and complete London edition with a provocative, well-organized, and insightful introductory essay like the one which follows.

Professor Harold F. Harding, of the Department of Speech, the Ohio State University, has been a student of rhetorical theory since his seminar days at Cornell. He is the author of such important studies as "Quintilian's Witnesses," contributor to the three-volume *Literary History of the United States,* former Editor of *The Quarterly Journal of Speech,* and director of many doctoral dissertations in British and American Rhetoric and Public Address.

In addition to my indebtedness to the committee and Professor Harding, I am "beholden" to Vernon Sternberg, Ralph McCoy, Ferris Randall, and Ralph Bushee. Because of Mr. Sternberg's persuasiveness, a magnificent copy of the first London edition was purchased by the Southern Illinois University Library. The generosity and scholarly dedication of University Librarians McCoy, Randall, and Bushee permitted us to dismantle a superbly bound set of books so that a more readable and less expensive copy could be reprinted by photo-offset with a ten percent reduction of original page size. In so doing they have helped to restore Hugh Blair's rightful place in the history of rhetorical theory.

EDITOR'S INTRODUCTION

By Harold F. Harding

FOR well over a century beginning about 1760 Hugh Blair markedly influenced writers and speakers, teachers and students in Great Britain and in America. He was well known as a university lecturer on rhetoric and belles lettres, as a preacher to a fashionable Edinburgh congregation, as an editor and literary taste maker, and indeed as the shaper of the style of generations of readers. In republishing his *Lectures on Rhetoric and Belles Lettres,* it is fitting that we should appraise the man and his work in the light of what we of this generation know.

Although Blair's reputation today may have slipped from the high favor of the early nineteenth century it is still certain that he did more to interpret and make known the rhetorical theory of the ancients than any other British or American rhetorical writer. He was a conveyer of excellence in both written and spoken style. In fact, he wrote for his age the kind of a book Quintilian produced for the first century A.D. Blair selected and restated the teachings of writers like Aristotle, Longinus, Cicero, and Quintilian. He then exemplified their theories by the use of passages from English writers. These include among others Addison's *Spectator* papers, Swift's writings, and Bishop Atterbury's sermons.

Blair's *Lectures* has been alternately praised and scorned. The editor of the London, 1863 edition, Dr. Thomas Dale, Canon Residentiary of St. Paul's Cathedral felt impelled to warn that the work retained its "high position in popular esteem, notwithstanding the questionable character of some of the Author's canons of criticism, and the occasional contradiction of his own rules for style and structure in his own sentences." [1] Sir Richard C. Jebb, the classical scholar, states in his *Brittanica* article that "the popularity enjoyed by Blair's *Rhetoric* in the latter part of the 18th and the earlier part of the 19th century was merited rather by the form than by the matter." But when we now add up all the effects of Blair's precepts upon students, teachers, and preachers in Britain and in the colleges of the eastern United States it would seem that Blair's popularity was merited by both the form and the matter. His *Lectures* and his *Sermons* were widely published, read, and studied in ways that would make writers of today envious. In any history of rhetorical criticism they cannot be ignored.

BOSWELL ON BLAIR

THE best known portrayer of the literary activity of the time of Blair is his fellow Scotsman, James Boswell. His *Life of Johnson* and his *London Journal 1762–63* are full of references to the discussions about the writers, speakers, and actors of the day. Boswell reveals in lively style his own ambitions to speak and act. He carries on these conversations with Thomas and Frances Sheridan, David Garrick, Edmund Burke, David Hume, Lord Chesterfield, George Dempster, William Robertson, Blair, and others. The charm of Boswell's writing may indeed be due to his early study of rhetoric and criticism.

In the summer of 1761, Thomas Sheridan, father of Richard Brinsley Sheridan, came to Edinburgh to give a course of lectures on elocution. Boswell attended. He was twenty-one years old at the time. He had studied rhetoric with Adam Smith. He had already heard Dr. Blair preach and lecture. His literary aspirations were taking shape and he was cultivating those who could help him.

Henry Home, Lord Kames, author of the *Elements of Criticism,* 1762, was one of Boswell's friends. In the early fall of 1762 when young Boswell accompanied Lord and Lady Kames on a tour of Southern Scotland there must have been frequent conversation about authors and their merits.

By the time Boswell reached London in November 1762 to seek his fortune he already had a well stocked mind with ideas about taste, style, criticism, genius, and writing in general. He was becoming a man of discrimination.

Dr. Johnson and Boswell met for the first time on 16 May 1763. Some six or seven weeks before that event Dr. Blair came to visit in London. He had been appointed Regius Professor of Rhetoric and Belles Lettres at the University of Edinburgh in April of the year before. Boswell records how he and Blair dined together, took long walks, went to church, and engaged in serious talk. The *Journal* entry for 6 April 1763 reads as follows: "Blair is a very amiable man. In my earliest years I admired him while he was Minister in the Canongate. He is learned and ingenious, and has a degree of simplicity about him that is extremely engaging." [2]

BLAIR'S CAREER

THE foregoing quotation is a valuable appraisal made long before Blair became famous. It is well worth remembering as we proceed with more details about his qualifications as a teacher of eloquence and as an arbiter of taste. He was born in Edinburgh on 7 April 1718, the only child of John and Martha Blair. At 13 he matriculated at the University of Edinburgh. For nine years he studied the Humanities, Greek, Logic, and Natural Philosophy. He took his Master of Arts degree in 1739. It was probably Professor John Stevenson, his teacher of rhetoric, who shaped Blair's thinking and led him to the study of letters. One of Blair's classmates was John Witherspoon, author of a set of lectures on rhetoric and later president of what is now Princeton University, as well as a signer of the Declaration of Independence.

In October 1741 when Blair was twenty-three the Presbytery of Edinburgh licensed him to preach. A year later he was ordained and in February 1743 he was elected to preach at the Canongate Church in Edinburgh. He served there until 1754.

Blair's eight-volume edition of the *Works of Shakespear,* labored over in these formative years, came out in 1753 and also his edition of the *Sermons* of Frederick Carmichael, the preacher of New Greyfriars Church. His second call was to Lady Yester's Church where he preached for four years (1754–58). In this period and later Blair joined and took part in discussions of the Select Society, the St. Giles Society, and the *Belles Lettres* Society. In 1762 the celebrated literary group called the Poker Club was formed. The original members all became distinguished. They included Blair, Alexander Carlyle, Lord Kames, Adam Ferguson, and William John Stone.

In June 1757 the University of St. Andrews conferred on Blair the honorary Doctor of Divinity degree. A year later, at the age of forty, he became Minister of the High Church of St. Giles, the most influential in Edinburgh. It was while here that he attracted the favorable attention of the faculty of the University of Edinburgh. In December 1759 he began his Edinburgh lectures, at first sponsored by the town and held outside of campus grounds. For a dozen years ever since hearing Stevenson and Adam Smith (1748) lecture on rhetoric, Blair had been reading, taking notes, and reflecting on what should go into his own course of lectures. By 1762 his trial teaching had attained such a reputation that King George III created for him a Regius Professorship at an annual salary of £70. He distinguished himself in that chair until retirement in 1783. In that year he helped to found the Royal Society of Edinburgh and became one of the four chairmen of the literary section of the society. Blair's preaching and writing did not cease although his health gradually declined. Even in his final year, at the age of eighty-three, he was full of activity. Among other projects he recomposed a number of his sermons for a fifth volume, published in 1801.

Blair died on 27 December 1800. He lies buried near Greyfriars Church. As the plaque on the wall of the church states in Latin he was a good man, a loyal friend, a learned teacher and critic, and a bulwark of the University of Edinburgh for nearly sixty years.

BLAIR'S PURPOSE

IN the latter half of the eighteenth century more than fifty textbooks, essays, lectures, and treatises on rhetoric and literary criticism by thirty different writers were published in England, Ireland, and

Scotland.[3] Interest in literature and the teaching of writing and speaking ran high. As Blair noted: "Next to speech, writing is beyond doubt, the most useful art which men possess." He set about to help students become proficient in the art. He conceived his task to be that of "the initiation of youth into the Study of Belles Lettres, and of Composition. . . . He hopes that to such as are studying to cultivate their Taste, to form their Style, or to prepare themselves for Public Speaking or Composition, his Lectures will afford a more comprehensive view of what relates to these subjects, than, as far as he knows, is to be received from any one Book in our Language." [4]

The lectures of these two volumes were read continuously for twenty-four years. We can take Blair's word that he made few revisions before publication. If we remember this fact and think of the work as having been completed around 1760 we can discount the more common criticisms—about the author not being up to date, not sufficiently aware of later works on genius and taste, and often being too elementary in his outlook. Professor Blair knew he was speaking to college students, most of whom were lads of fifteen or a little older.

Conceptions of Rhetoric and Belles Lettres

In the preface, Blair admits his work is not wholly original, but it is not, he insists, a compilation from the writings of others. Indeed, on every topic he has thought for himself, consulting his own ideas and reflections.

The forty-seven lectures are of nearly equal length and closely retain the form and content of the course as delivered at the university. Blair, like Quintilian, was forced to publish, he says, because imperfect copies in note-form were circulating and being offered for sale in the bookstores of Parliament Close.[5]

Following the introductory lecture, we find four lectures on *Taste,* four on *Language,* fifteen on *Style,* and ten on *Eloquence.* The final thirteen lectures are devoted to a "critical examination of the most distinguished *species of composition* both in prose and verse." For students of speech and of rhetorical theory especially, some twenty lectures have most to offer: 10–19, dealing with Style, and 25–34, covering "Eloquence properly so called, or public speaking in its different kinds." Lectures 20–24 consist of critical examinations of certain of the *Spectator* papers and of a passage from Swift's "Proposal for correcting, improving, and ascertaining the English tongue." The last thirteen lectures, 35–47, concern criticism in the broadest scope. They touch upon historical writing, philosophical writing, poetry, tragedy, and comedy. These discourses represent Blair, the literary critic, as a judge of what he has chosen to call authors whose works exemplify taste and genius, or as in the case of Shakespeare of "genius shooting wild." [6]

We turn now to the early lectures to survey their main ideas. Taste, "the power of receiving pleasure from the beauties of nature and art," [7] is reducible to two characters, delicacy and correctness.[8] It is a faculty composed of "natural sensibility to beauty, and of improved understanding" [9] and may be greatly aided by exercise. Without an "internal sense of beauty" [10] however, study will avail little. There are, of course, "principles of reason and sound judgment" which can be applied to matters of taste.[11]

What is the standard for determining good taste? There can be but one court of appeal—universal acceptance of the past. "That which men concur the most in admiring must be held to be beautiful. His taste must be just and true which coincides with the general sentiments of men." [12]

Criticism is the habit of applying taste and good sense to the judging of the fine arts.[13] When we have accumulated data on a sufficient number of particular instances, we can then "ascend to general principles" of beauty as found in works of genius. Genius is a talent or aptitude for excelling that we inherit from nature. It may be improved but cannot be wholly acquired by art and study.[14]

There are, according to Addison, three primary sources of the pleasures of Taste: *beauty, grandeur,* and *novelty,*[15] and these qualities Blair adopts adding a fourth of his own, *imitation.* Melody, harmony, wit, humour, and ridicule also belong to Taste. Poetry, eloquence, and good writing receive their power not from any one of these pleasures, but from all.

The sublime in writing may be said to center upon vigorous

conciseness and simplicity.[16] We find the sources of the sublime "everywhere in nature." [17]

Language is the "expression of our ideas by certain articulate sounds, which are used as the signs of those ideas." [18] From the four lectures devoted to the rise and progress and the structure of language we derive what is the core of a main topic, the analysis of Style. Blair's definition of style is "the peculiar manner in which a man expresses his conceptions by means of Language." [19] Perspicuity and ornament are the two heads under which good style may be classified. In accordance with the dictum of Quintilian's *Institutio,* perspicuity is really the fundamental quality of the two. Again, following classical predecessors Blair discusses perspicuity with regard to words and phrases and concludes that three qualities are essential: purity, propriety, and precision.[20] In similar fashion, the demands of perfect sentence structure are four: clearness and precision, unity, strength, and harmony.[21] "The fundamental rule of the construction of Sentences, and into which all others might be resolved, undoubtedly is, to communicate in the clearest and most natural order, the ideas which we mean to transfuse into the minds of others." [22]

The ornamental feature of Blair's stylistic scheme rests almost entirely on a rather small number of figures, of which Metaphor, Hyperbole, Personification, Apostrophe, Comparison, and Antitheses are most important. Figures as a class are prompted either by the imagination or by the passions.[23]

In general, figures perform four functions: 1] they enrich language and make it more copious, 2] they confer dignity upon style, 3] as Aristotle points out, they let us see one thing in another, and 4] they give "us frequently a much clearer and more striking view of the principal object, than we could have if it were expressed in simple terms, and divested of the accessory idea." [24] In addition, we can always heighten the emotion by the figures we introduce.

Lectures 18 and 19 set forth the general characteristics of style. "The foundation of all good Style, is good sense accompanied with a lively imagination." [25] Among the practical directions that Blair offers for forming a proper style are: 1] study your material, 2] practice composing frequently, 3] read the best authors, 4] do not imitate servilely, 5] adapt according to the subject and the demands of hearers, 6] do not sacrifice clear thought to ornamental style.[26]

By "Eloquence" Blair means the art of persuasion.[27] It is therefore rhetoric in Cicero's [28] sense. But when Blair uses the term "rhetoric," he seems to have in mind written composition. Of the ten lectures (25–34) on eloquence, or public speaking, as he occasionally refers to the topic, two are devoted to the history of the subject, three to the different kinds of speaking: before popular assemblies, the bar, and the pulpit, two to the parts of the oration, and one to delivery. One lecture on means of improving in speech and another on the criticism of a sermon of Bishop Atterbury complete the section on style.

The purposes of eloquence are these: 1] to please, 2] "to inform, to instruct, to convince," [29] 3] to arouse the passions. If criticism is taste plus good sense, eloquence is good sense and solid thought.[30] And likewise, if good style is founded on perspicuity, "in all kinds of public speaking nothing is of greater consequence than a proper and clear method." [31]

We commonly think of the latter half of the eighteenth century as the beginning of a golden age of British eloquence, but it was far from that to Blair. England, he says, has the vital elements for great oratory: "free and bold genius of the country" and popular government, but where are the orators? Historians and poets there are of first rank, "but of orators and public speakers, how little have we to boast?" [32] As for good preaching, the practice then current, Blair declares, of reading sermons, has practically ruined the development of any great pulpit oratory.[33]

Throughout the lectures on speaking Blair repeatedly shows his dependence upon two classical sources, Cicero and especially Quintilian. But he refuses to use their classification of the kinds of oratory and prefers to base his discussion on what he terms "the great scenes of eloquence, popular assemblies, the bar, and the pulpit." [34] The summary of Blair's remarks on popular eloquence so accurately and concisely represents his philosophy of speech preparation and presentation as a whole that I shall give the excerpt in full:

The sum of what has been said is this: The end of Popular Speaking is persuasion; and this must be founded on conviction. Argument and reasoning must be the basis, if we would be Speakers of business, and not mere Declaimers. We should be engaged in earnest on the side which we espouse; and utter, as much as possible, our own, and not counterfeited Sentiments. The premeditation should be of things, rather than of words. Clear order and method should be studied: the manner and expression warm and animated; though still, in the midst of that vehemence, which may at times be suitable, carried on under proper restraints which regard to the audience, and to the decorum of character, ought to lay on every Public Speaker: the style free and easy; strong and descriptive, rather than diffuse; and the delivery determined and firm. To conclude this head, let every Orator remember, that the impression made by fine and artful speaking is momentary; that made of argument and good sense, is solid and lasting.[35]

This same set of directions holds true for eloquence at the bar (Lecture 28) and eloquence of the pulpit (Lecture 29). These particular observations may be added: forensic eloquence is founded on a lawyer's reputation and this in turn rests upon his own legal acumen.[36] Eloquence suitable for the bar whether in written brief or oral argument ought to be "of a calm and temperate kind and connected with close reasoning." [37] Distinctness is the advocate's greatest asset. It should show itself in the stating of the question, next in the statement of the issues, and finally in the order and arrangement of the parts of pleading.[38] In all speaking ethical appeal is paramount. Nothing can take the place of a speaker's reputation "of probity and honour." [39]

Persuasion is also the object of the pulpit orator. The preacher's aim should be "to persuade men to serve God and become better men" [40] and in so doing he may instruct, teach, reason, and argue. The preacher himself must always be a good man.[41] The two features which distinguish pulpit eloquence from other kinds of Public Speaking are gravity and warmth.[42] What are the characteristics of a good sermon? Five stand out: 1] unity, 2] particularizing of the subject, 3] selection of material, 4] adaptation to audience interest,

5] unwillingness to imitate the passing fashion in preaching.[43] Moreover, good preaching demands perspicuous style.[44] In general, a lively and animated style is well suited to the pulpit. The careful preacher never employs "strong figures or a pathetic style except in cases where the subject leads to them." [45] Whereas to Blair a French sermon is "a warm animated exhortation," an English sermon is "a piece of cool instructive reasoning." The perfect sermon, he thinks, would combine the qualities of the two types.[46]

Lecture 30 distinguishes the good and the bad in Bishop Atterbury's celebrated sermon on Praise and Thanksgiving. It is a critique of a preacher and his composition. The next two lectures take up in detail the "conduct of a discourse" or the parts of the oration from the introduction to the peroration. Throughout his treatment of this subject Blair restates classical precepts. Gain the good will of your hearers. Compose in an easy and natural style. See that the expression is correct. Be modest. Speak in a calm manner. Don't rush into your main topic. Such is the gist of the advice on the Introduction.[47] After you have stated the proposition, you may or may not "lay down heads," that is, reveal a division. In the case of sermon-writing Blair opposes the declaration of Fénelon in his *Dialogues on Eloquence* and commends the practice then current in British preaching of announcing heads.[48]

Logical and Emotional Appeals

IN treating the argumentative part of a discourse three things are necessary: the invention of the arguments, their disposition and arrangement, and last, clothing them in effective style.[49] Blair casts aside as too technical Aristotle's system of *Topoi* or Commonplaces and in their stead suggests two methods for reasoning: the Analytic, in which the orator builds up his proofs by successive points, and the Synthetic, when the point to be proved is announced and a series of arguments are arranged for its support.[50] This latter method is most suited "to the train of Popular Speaking."

For his discussion of the Pathetic, Blair again rejects Aristotle, or rather his treatment of the passions as found in Book 2 of the *Rhetoric,* and for practical reasons prefers to follow Quintilian's *Institutio,* Book 6.[51]

As for the Conclusion, the great rule is to place last whatever point will determine the balancing of a decision.[52]

Delivery

THE four chief requisites of good "Pronunciation, or Delivery" (Lecture 33) are: 1] proper loudness of voice, 2] distinctness, 3] slowness, and 4] propriety of pronunciation.[53] These matters are fundamental. Refinements of delivery focus on 1] proper emphasis, 2] pauses, 3] tones, and 4] gestures.[54] Of these, the study and exercise of good tone is probably the most important. And to this end Blair says, "the greatest and most material instruction which can be given . . . is to form the tones of Public Speaking upon the tones of sensible and animated conversation." [55] The same standard applies for action. "A public speaker must take that manner which is most natural to himself." [56] For specific advice on delivery the student is urged to consult the final chapter of the *Institutio,* Book 11. But even the rules there laid down, Blair believes, are of little use unless demonstrated in the presence of the student speaker.

Further Training

LECTURE 34 on Means of Improving in Eloquence is little more than a collection of Greek and Roman maxims on the speaker and the speech. The true orator is a virtuous man,[57] a man of generous sentiments and warm feelings,[58] endowed with a proper mixture of courage and modesty.[59] Next to these moral qualifications he must possess a fund of knowledge.[60] The aspiring speaker will not neglect the general circle of polite literature.[61] Study and enthusiastic application are always important.[62] Attention to the best models greatly aids improvement.[63] Frequent practice in composing and in speaking is necessary.[64] For gaining experience before audiences debating societies are excellent training places. Properly conducted they enable the student to acquire that *copia verborum* which the ancients deemed so vital in the equipment of the speaker.

Appraisal

WE have now scanned the twenty lectures that relate to rhetorical theory. One finds, of course, other places in the remaining twenty-seven lectures where Blair deals with speaking, but in these lectures he writes mainly as a critic and as a literary historian. His treatment of language in Lectures 6–9 is of interest to specialists in linguistics just as those on poetry, Lectures 38–47, have attraction for students of poetics.

Considering therefore the twenty lectures surveyed here, what special merit do they possess for the rhetorician and the student of eloquence? What is the reason for Blair's great vogue in his lifetime, and how do we account for the use of his book throughout most of the next century? A favorable or complimentary answer to the first part of that question should help to explain the second part.

Blair considers his lectures on oratory or public speaking to constitute a sort of system.[65] His main emphasis, more than half of his effort, goes to the details of Style. He is almost contemptuous of Invention and Disposition as set forth in Aristotle's *Rhetoric*. Memory is barely touched upon. Every speaker must decide for himself whether to memorize, read, or speak extempore. Delivery gets compressed into one lecture. It states in effect: follow nature, be earnest and occupied with your subject, and your previously formed habits will take care of everything.[66] And so, compared with any of the great classics, Aristotle's *Rhetoric*, Cicero's *De Oratore*, or Quintilian's *Institutio Oratoria*, Blair's "system" is a mere outline. What Blair has in fact done in his *Lectures* has been to digest and adapt some of the more important classical theories that applied to the needs of eighteenth-century speaking. He did not undertake the exhaustive cento of ancient rhetorical precepts that we find in John Ward's lectures. Blair was selective and discriminating. He emphasized what was important to him. Like every good teacher he had his students and their needs in mind.

After a restatement of Greek and Roman principles we find added the doctrine of "good sense." That expression is repeated at regular intervals throughout the work. Unfortunately, what is "good sense" in respect to style or taste in one generation is not always so in another. "Follow nature" is another of Blair's favorite injunctions —one that is generally more difficult to comply with than to write about. "Be clear" in meaning of words and in structure of sentences is also a main feature of Blair's teaching. In this respect he is repeating a leading precept of the *Institutio*. So we see, in matters of rhetorical theory, Blair may have, as he says, thought for himself, but in reality he is seldom original. He has, however, written understandingly and with an old-fashioned charm. His own long experience in the pulpit and his weekly exercise in composing sermons unquestionably gave to the *Lectures* a partical consideration they might not otherwise have had. When we read them we "listen" to a speaker and not a theorizer. We should put ourselves into the mental outlook of the college students of Scotland from about 1760 to 1784.

The Value of Blair's *Lectures*

WHAT was Blair's value in the latter half of the eighteenth century? How did it come, as a recent writer says, that "half the educated English-speaking world studied" [67] his famous book? The answer is found in Blair's reputation as a preacher. His church, the High Kirk, was the most prestigious in Edinburgh at the time.[68] His congregation was composed largely from the gentry and the learned community. His speaking style was unaffected. His sermons were thoughtful essays. He himself was a scholar, the friend of Hume, Ferguson, Alexander Carlyle, and Principal Robertson. In the pulpit Blair seems to have put into effect the theories of his classroom.[69] Dr. Samuel Johnson boasted that he was the first to give a stamp of approval to Blair's sermons.[70] That in itself was almost the acme of recognition. Once Blair's reputation as a preacher and later as a man of letters was created, its own momentum carried it along. Young authors brought him their manuscripts for criticism and he came to be regarded as "the literary accoucheur of Scotland." [71] Blair's *Critical Dissertation on the Poems of Ossian* (1763) made him a principal in the greatest literary controversy of the day. Strangely enough, Blair's own speech delivery did not seem to detract from his popularity. His platform manner is described as unforceful, his speech was said to be marked by a strong provincial dialect, and his general attitude indifferent.[72] But in spite of shortcomings Blair, the preacher, was a notable success. Judged by the sale of his *Lectures* and the size of his classes he was likewise a success as a writer on rhetoric. The man was heard and his books were read. What forms of acceptance are more convincing?

The Universities

WE cannot forget the high standards of the Scottish universities in the reign of George III. Their chairs were filled with first-rate scholars whose influence extended far beyond their classrooms.[73] Their glory and deserving fame is the more pronounced when the comparison is made with the low state of scholarship and teaching that prevailed at Oxford and Cambridge in the same period.[74] Besides the awakening at the Scottish universities there were many signs of a genuine revival of intellectual interest among the educated Scots classes. Ability to write and speak correct English, of a sort free from provincialisms, was earnestly sought by the cultivated. Beattie and Hume, for example, collaborated in compiling a list of Scotticisms to be carefully avoided.[75] In the process of helping their countrymen acquire "Received" English Blair and Campbell, Kames, and Monboddo had a significant part.

Blair as Professor

BLAIR's fame as a writer of sermons established and strengthened his reputation as a lecturer and writer on rhetoric. For this reason his lectures, both when delivered and when published, enjoyed a great patronage. The classes in rhetoric at the University of Edinburgh had been taught by the professor of logic from 1708 to 1760 and were seldom attended by more than a handful of students a year. But Blair had classes of 60 or more and when his successor, William Greenfield, took over in 1784 the attendance dwindled to twenty or less.[76] In his *Dictionary of Eminent Scotsmen* (1863) Robert Chambers tells us that so great was the interest aroused by Blair's lectures that impecunious students wrote out their notes and sold them to booksellers, who freely exhibited them for re-sale. These facts, supported by the scores of printings and editions for nearly a century after the two volumes of *Lectures* were first published in 1783, attest to the influence of Blair in his generation and afterwards. Judged by the standards of today, one may have to look hard to justify their high popularity. We can say, however, that before Campbell and Whately published their rhetorical works nothing as useful was available in English.

Blair's Sources

THERE is need for a word about Blair's sources. What writers did he rely upon? Were they ancient or modern? Are they mentioned or do we have to search for parallels? The problem is really not difficult. Blair is explicit. Quintilian, he says at the close of the section on eloquence "has digested into excellent order all the ancient ideas concerning rhetoric and is himself an eloquent writer." Few books, he continues, "abound more with good sense and discover a greater degree of just and accurate taste" than the *Institutio*.[77] Hence, that work has his highest approval. He cites it or borrows from it some fifty-odd times and more than from any other work. There are many more references to Quintilian than the Index lists. Next, in influence, comes Cicero. But Blair usually regards Cicero as an orator rather than as a writer on oratory and thus seems less indebted to him for theory. Aristotle has but slight appeal, although there is admission that in his *Rhetoric* he "laid the foundation for all that was afterwards written on the subject." [78] Plato's rhetorical dialogues are not mentioned and it can be argued that Blair owes little to the *Gorgias* or the *Phaedrus*. Among modern writers, Vossius is so full and ponderous that his work "is enough to disgust one with the study of eloquence." [79] Several French writers, Rollin, Batteaux, Crevier, Gibert and others, are mentioned, but Fénelon deserves special merit for his *Dialogues sur l'Eloquence*.[80] For his general ideas on taste Blair depended on the *Elements of Criticism* by Lord Kames. Actual citation of the book is limited to two instances,[81] but a comparison of the two authors reveals similarities in their conceptions of the elements of taste, the difficulty of analysis, and the standard for appeal. The Rev. Dr. George Campbell had published his *Philosophy of Rhetoric* in 1776, but Blair, as far as I can judge, uses that work in no substantial way.

James Burnett, Lord Monboddo, dealt with rhetoric at great length in his 6-volume work, *Of the Origin and Progress of Lan-*

guage, 1773–1792. But when we recall that Blair's lectures were largely finished in 1758–59 and not substantially changed when published in 1783, it is understandable why Monboddo is mentioned only in a footnote in Blair's *Lectures.* Blair was apparently not as interested in the judgments of his colleagues as modern scholars usually are. He was lecturing to college students and he was much more concerned with giving them what they needed to know to become good stylists.

Blair and Adam Smith

THE publication in 1963 of the notes of Adam Smith's *Lectures on Rhetoric and Belles Lettres* has revived the age-old controversy of the originality of Blair and how much he owed to others. Since we know that Blair attended Smith's lectures in Edinburgh (1748) and that he read Smith's notes before beginning his own course in 1759 there has been a presumption that Blair borrowed from Smith. John Rae, Smith's biographer, states: "The lectures Smith then delivered on English literature were burnt at his own request, shortly before his death. Blair, not only heard them at the time, but got the use of them, or at least part of them. . . . It has been suggested that they are practically reproduced in the lectures of Blair." Earlier Rae had said that Blair does not "seem to have borrowed anything but was the commonest property already" and then adds contemptuously "to borrow even a hat to any purpose, the two heads must be something of a size." The present editor of Smith's lecture notes, Professor Lothian aptly says, "with the discovery of Smith's lectures, it will now be possible to measure the two heads." [82]

I believe that Rae's insinuations of plagiarism by Blair are overdrawn. It is true that there are a number of points of similarity between the student's notes on Smith and Blair's *Lectures.* The two men touch upon many of the same subjects, they refer to several of the same authors as models of good form, and on the surface they appear to have the same standards of taste. But there are notable differences that should be explained. Here are a few:

1. The notes in Lothian's 1963 edition are oral remarks made in a classroom in 1762–63, long before accurate

reporting was in use. Even if they represent the gist of Smith's ideas we cannot be sure that they represent his actual sentences. They may or may not represent what Smith wanted to convey. "The writing, the gaps in the text, and the existence of certain comments, seem to suggest that these are the original notes written at speed in the lecture room, and not a fair copy." Most lecturers want to alter words and phrases or to delete before going into print. The fact that Smith ordered his notes destroyed would argue that he was unwilling to give them his unreserved approval.

2.   As the notes reveal, Smith is sketchy and suggestive. Blair is detailed and even discursive. He provides more than is needed and often repeats ideas. Whereas Blair's style is usually precise we have to compare it with a probably imperfect paraphrase of what Smith said. It is a case of lining up what one man wanted to say with what someone thought another man wanted to say. The comparison is to the disadvantage of Adam Smith.

3.   Blair was really interested in teaching students how to write (composition) and how to appreciate good literature (belles lettres). Practical speaking in the sense of pleading cases, presenting arguments in parliament, or delivering ceremonial addresses gets surprisingly little attention in either Smith or Blair. But Smith was mainly interested in style. "Indeed, in Smith style alone is the pressing concern of rhetoric and the area of greatest artistic latitude. His view is belletristic in that he extended the scope of rhetoric to literature and literary criticism, treating historical, didactic, and rhetorical composition as well as forensic, epideictic, and deliberative public address." Blair gives a broad treatment in his 47 lectures. They divide themselves, as he explains at the end of the first lecture, into five parts: 1] the Nature of Taste, 2] Consideration of language, 3] of style, 4] of eloquence, and 5] a critical examination of the species of composition. Smith's 29 lectures cannot be so easily classified. He gives headings to four and leaves the others untitled. Following the Introduction we find three lectures on language, three on words and figures of speech, and four on the style of Swift, Lucian, Addison, Lord Shaftesbury, and Virgil. Lectures 12 to 17 deal with composition, 18 to 20 with historians and their works. The poets are discussed in

Lecture 21. Lectures 22 to 24 concern various kinds of oratory. Invention and arrangement are combined in Lecture
25. The final five lectures, 26–30, touch upon the orations of
Cicero, Demosthenes, Thucydides, and a few British orators
before the bar.

It is clear that Smith neither covers the variety of topics
Blair does nor does he cover them as fully. Perhaps this is
because he refrained from using notes during the delivery of
his lectures. Perhaps, too, he regarded Rhetoric as an avoca-
tion and devoted his best scholarly efforts to Economics and
Jurisprudence.

4. Smith admired the Greek writers and referred to
them frequently. Blair, except for Demosthenes, seldom
does. Smith, however, does not seem to know Aristotle's
Rhetoric or Plato's rhetorical dialogues. He does not mention them. Blair relies heavily on Cicero and Quintilian.
Smith knows Cicero's orations but makes little use of the
De Oratore, Brutus, or *Orator.* His references to the *Institutio Oratoria* are so slight that we can only conclude that
Smith failed to discover the merits of Quintilian. In fact, the
differences in the attitudes of Smith and Blair towards
Quintilian may be their sharpest area of contrast. Blair has
several faults but a failure to appreciate the work of the first
Roman public professor of rhetoric is not one of them.

It is probably safe to say that Blair owes to Smith the idea of
combining the study of Belles Lettres with Rhetoric. He seems to
have followed Smith in his analysis of writers like Swift and Addison, Temple, Pope, Lord Clarendon and Lord Shaftesbury. Both
writers cite the orations of Demosthenes and Cicero as models for
study. Both are fond of the French writers. La Bruyère, Fénelon,
Rapin, and Voltaire. Like Smith, Blair refers several times to Diony-
sius of Halicarnassus, Lucian, Thucydides, Herodotus, Polybius,
Livy, and Caesar. Unlike Smith, Blair devotes several pages to
French preachers. He mentions Saurin, Bourdaloue, Massillon,
Bossuet, and Flechier.

It is easy to see broad topical similarities in the lectures of Blair
and the lecture-notes of Smith—especially in the way they treat in
detail the subjects of language, style, the writings of Swift, Demosthenes, Cicero, and the ancient historical writers.

It is not easy to prove that Blair adopted in wholesale fashion the ideas of Adam Smith. What each wrote had been commonly discussed in the Edinburgh literary clubs for years. Blair actually delivered a better set of lectures than his teacher delivered. But Smith, the versatile man and better scholar, was also interested in jurisprudence, ethics, and economics. We remember him today for the *Theory of Moral Sentiments* and his *Wealth of Nations* and not as a lecturer on rhetoric. Blair spent a lifetime teaching his subject, practicing it, and indeed, trying to save souls by it. It is natural, therefore, that his published lectures gained fame for him. Smith's unpublished notes come down to us two centuries later as a literary curiosity. They are like the first draft of a Greek tragedy. We see the power of the dramatist, we sense his abilities, we wish he could have completed his task.

SUMMARY AND CONCLUSION

IN the universities of Britain in the second half of the eighteenth century the rhetorical teachings of John Ward, Hugh Blair, and George Campbell predominated. For all three, style, of both written and spoken discourse, was most important. Although speaking *practice* both by the recitation of "elegant extracts" and by the giving of original declamations persisted in the schools and academies, it does not appear to have extended to the universities. Students may have gained practice at informal literary societies and debating clubs, as at Trinity College, Dublin, but it is doubtful if instruction in speaking with an instructor-critic in charge as we know it today was very prevalent. The evidence shows that Blair and his contemporary professors customarily read their lectures and then set their students adrift to gain practice by whatever means they could find.

This survey of Blair makes some conclusions apparent. As a writer on Rhetoric he was neither original, comprehensive, nor profound. His own style is clear, but not especially distinguished. He often becomes prolix and belabors the obvious. His principal contribution to the art of rhetoric seems to be in his classification of speeches—before the bar, at popular assemblies, and in the pulpit.

In the main Blair has adapted the tenets of the Scottish Common Sense School of Philosophy to the speaking situations of his time. He knows the ancient rhetorical lore, but believes it is too cumbersome and technical for his purposes. He is especially insistent that the classical devices for finding and stimulating ideas under Invention, *topoi* or *loci communes,* are not practical. They may, Blair believes, actually stifle ideas and curtail inventiveness. Likewise, Blair discounted the values of developing emotional appeals that Aristotle and other considered so fully.

Quintilian is clearly Blair's ideal and his master. He leaves no doubt about his high esteem for the *Institutio Oratoria.* That Blair's *Lecture*s continued to be published, imitated, praised, studied, condensed, and re-issued for several generations after his death is understandable.[83] The work is easy to grasp and immediately useful as a guide. It was written by a respected churchman whose sermons enjoyed the reputation of high excellence. College teachers, and especially those in the new colleges of the eastern United States, regarded Blair as scholarly and sound. His popularity in American classrooms continued unabated until the appearance of Whately's *Rhetoric* in 1828.[84]

Although in some respects Blair follows the strictly classical tradition laid down by John Ward in his *System of Oratory* (1759) in reality he goes beyond Ward in breadth of view and scope of generalization. Blair's chair at Edinburgh obliged him to pay more attention to criticism and the study of polite literature, or, as he says, to "distinguishing false ornament from true." His *Lectures* are the most detailed, suggestive, and helpful work on *belles lettres* which the group Bosker [85] calls "The Champions of Taste" produced. Blair's ambition to set forth a more comprehensive view of taste, style, public speaking, and composition than that found in any other one book does not fall so far short of its mark. Leslie Stephen, Edmund Gosse, and others have sneered at Blair for his lack of originality.[86] But that attitude is not entirely reasonable. The best of Blair's precepts have sound classical origins. What he says about composition is clearly stated and with the good sense of a man who knows from experience. In final judgment, Blair's reliance upon the practical wisdom of Quintilian saves him from the absurdities which less careful writers lapsed into in their efforts to be original.

A LIST OF REFERENCES

The most detailed bibliography of Blair and his works, his contemporaries, and his influence is that found in *Hugh Blair,* by Robert Morell Schmitz, King's Crown Press, New York, 1941, pp. 139–158. The following list giving only author or editor, title, place of publication, and year of publication contains items that have been most useful in the preparation of the Introduction to this edition. I am especially indebted to my former students, Professors Douglas Ehninger of the State University of Iowa and James L. Golden of Muskingum College for their generous assistance. Dr. Golden turned over to me his notes from the Huntington Library and elsewhere that were most valuable. Dr. Vincent M. Bevilacqua of the University of Virginia kindly let me read the manuscript of his essay, "Adam Smith's Lectures on Rhetoric and Belles Lettres," prior to its publication in *The Quarterly Journal of Speech* in 1965. To these persons and to the General Editor of this series, Dr. David Potter, I express my gratitude.

1. Allardyce, Alexander, Editor. *Scotland and Scotsmen in the Eighteenth Century.* (From the MSS. of John Ramsay of Ochtertyre) . 2 vols. Edinburgh and London, 1888.
2. Anderson, Dorothy S. "Edward T. Channing's Definition of Rhetoric." *Speech Monographs.* 14 (1947) . 80–92.
3. Bald, Marjory A. "The Pioneers of Anglicized Speech in Scotland." *The Scottish Historical Review.* 24 (1927) . 179–93.
4. Bate, Walter Jackson. *The Achievement of Samuel Johnson.* Oxford, 1955.
5. ———. *From Classic to Romantic: Premises of Taste in Eighteenth-century England.* Cambridge, Mass., 1946.
6. Beattie, James. *A Letter to the Rev. Hugh Blair, D. D. . . . on the Improvement of Psalmody in Scotland.* Edinburgh, 1829.
7. ———. *Essay on the Nature and Immutability of Truth.* London, 1770.
8. Bitzer, Lloyd F. "The Lively Idea: A Study of Hume's Influence

on George Campbell's *Philosophy of Rhetoric."* Unpublished
Ph.D. dissertation, State University of Iowa, 1962.

9. Blair, Hugh. *A Critical Edition of the Poems of Ossian, the son
of Fingal.* The first edition appeared anonymously in London,
1763. The second edition in 1765 bears Blair's name.

10. ———. *The British Poets.* 44 vols. Edinburgh, 1773.

11. ———. *Lectures on Rhetoric and Belles Lettres.* 2 vols. published
in London in June, 1783 and in Edinburgh in July, 1783. A
second edition with a few corrections appeared in 3 vols. in 1785.
See footnote 4 for a summary of others. A complete list with dates
is in Schmitz, *Hugh Blair,* p. 144.

12. ———. *Sermons,* Edinburgh and London, Vol. I, 1777. Vol. II,
1780. Vol. III, 1790. Vol. IV, 1794. Vol. V, 1801. James Finlayson
edited a five-volume set in 1801. Between 1777 and 1847 at least
75 editions of the *Sermons* appeared in the British Isles. In the
United States more than a dozen editions were published between
1790 and 1844.

13. ———. *The Works of Shakespear.* 8 vols., Edinburgh, 1753.
Other editions in 1761, 1769, 1771, 1795.

14. ———. Manuscript: Letters of Hugh Blair to Elizabeth Montagu.
Henry E. Huntington Library, San Marino, California.

15. ———. Manuscript: Hugh Blair to Dr. Percy. Pennsylvania
Historical Society, Philadelphia, Pennsylvania.

16. Bosker, A. *Literary Criticism in the Age of Johnson.* Groningen,
1930.

17. Boswell, James. *Boswelliana; The Commonplace Book of James
Boswell.* London, 1876.

18. ———. *Boswell's Journal of a Tour of the Hebrides with Samuel
Johnson,* LL.D. Edited by F. A. Pottle and C. H. Bennett. New
York, 1936.

19. ———. *Letters of James Boswell.* Edited by Chauncey B. Tinker.
2 vols. Oxford, 1924.

20. ———. *Boswell's Life of Johnson.* Edited by G. B. Hill, revised
by L. F. Powell. 6 vols. Oxford, 1934–50.

21. ———. *London Journal, 1762–1763.* Edited by F. A. Pottle. New
York, 1950.

22. ———. *Private Papers of James Boswell from Malahide Castle.*
18 vols. Mount Vernon, N. Y., 1928–1934.

23. Bower, Alexander. *The History of the University of Edinburgh.*
3 vols. Edinburgh, 1830.

24. Bray, J. W. *A History of English Critical Terms.* Boston, 1898.

25. Burns, Robert. *The Letters of Robert Burns.* Edited by J.
DeLancy Ferguson. Oxford, 1931.

26. Burnett, James (Lord Monboddo). *Of the Origin and Progress of Language.* 6 vols., Vol. 6 (1792) is devoted to Rhetoric. Edinburgh, 1773–1792.

27. Burton, John Hill. *Life and Correspondence of David Hume.* 2 vols. Edinburgh, 1846.

28. ———. *The History of Scotland.* 8 vols. New York, 1873.

29. Campbell, George. *A Dissertation on Miracles,* . . . 3rd edition. With a correspondence on the subject by Mr. Hume, Dr. Campbell, and Dr. Blair, 2 vols. Edinburgh, 1797.

30. ———. *Lectures on Pulpit Eloquence.* London, 1806.

31. ———. *The Philosophy of Rhetoric.* 2 vols. London, 1776. The most recent edition is that by Lloyd F. Bitzer in this series, 1963.

32. Carlyle, Alexander. *Autobiography of the Rev. Dr. Alexander Carlyle, Minister at Inveresk;* containing memorials of the men and events of his time. Edited by J. H. Burton. Boston, 1861.

33. Carmichael, Frederick. *Sermons on Several Important Subjects.* [Edited by Hugh Blair.] Edinburgh, 1757.

34. Carpenter, Richard. "Three Scottish Critics: An Essay in the History of Ideas." Unpublished Ph.D. dissertation, Boston University, 1951.

35. Chambers, Frank P. *The History of Taste.* Boston, 1932.

36. Chambers, Robert, ed. *A Biographical Dictionary of Eminent Scotsmen.* 4 vols. London, 1855.

37. ———. *Traditions of Edinburgh.* Edinburgh, 1825.

38. Chapman, R. W. "Blair on Ossian." *Review of English Studies.* 7 (1931) . 80–83.

39. Charvat, William. *The Origins of American Critical Thought, 1810–1835.* Philadelphia, 1936.

40. Clark, A. F. B. *Boileau and the French Classical Critics in England (1660–1830)* . Paris, 1925.

41. Cohen, Herman. "An Analysis of the Rhetoric of Hugh Blair." Unpublished Ph.D. dissertation, State University of Iowa, 1954.

42. ———. "Hugh Blair on Speech Education." *Southern Speech Journal.* 29 (1963) . 1–11.

43. ———. "Hugh Blair's Theory of Taste." *The Quarterly Journal of Speech.* 44 (1958) . 265–74.

44. Cowling, G. H. "The English Teaching of Dr. Hugh Blair." *Palaestra* 148 (Brandl Feltschrift, Band 110. 281–94) .

45. Cowper, William. *The Correspondence of William Cowper.* Edited by Thomas Wright. 2 vols. London, 1904.

46. ———. *Letters of William Cowper.* Edited by J. G. Frazer. 2 vols. London, 1912.

47. Crawford, John. "The Rhetoric of George Campbell." Unpublished Ph.D. dissertation, Northwestern University, 1947.

48. Dalzel, Andrew. *History of the University of Edinburgh from its foundation* (to *c.* 1772). 2 vols. Edinburgh, 1862.

49. Dargan, Edwin C. *A History of Preaching.* 2 vols. New York, 1911.

50. Edney, Clarence W. "George Campbell's Theory of Logical Truth." *Speech Monographs.* 15 (1948). 19–32.

51. ———. "George Campbell's Theory of Public Address." Unpublished Ph.D. dissertation, State University of Iowa, 1946.

52. Ehninger, Douglas. "Campbell, Blair, and Whately: Old Friends in a New Light." *Western Speech.* 19 (1955). 263–69.

53. ———. "Campbell, Blair, and Whately Revisited." *Southern Speech Journal.* 28 (1963). 169–82.

54. ———. "Dominant Trends in English Rhetorical Thought, 1750–1800." *Southern Speech Journal.* 18 (1952). 3–12.

55. ———. "George Campbell and the Revolution in Inventional Theory." *Southern Speech Journal.* 15 (1950). 270–76.

56. ———. "Selected Theories of *Inventio* in English Rhetoric, 1759–1828." Unpublished Ph.D. dissertation, Ohio State University, 1949.

57. ———. "John Ward and His Rhetoric." *Speech Monographs.* 18 (1951). 1–16.

58. ———. "Whately on Dispositio." *Quarterly Journal of Speech.* 40 (1954).

59. ——— and Golden, James L. "The Intrinsic Sources of Blair's Popularity." *Southern Speech Journal.* 22 (1956). 16–33.

60. ——— and Golden, James L. "The Intrinsic Sources of Blair's Popularity." *Southern Speech Journal.* 21 (1955). 12–30.

61. Elledge, Scott B. "The Background and Development in English Criticism of the Thesis of Generality and Particularity." *PMLA.* 62 (1947). 147–82.

62. ———. ed. *Eighteenth Century Critical Essays.* Ithaca, New York, 1961.

63. Elliot, Sir Gilbert. *Life and Letters of Sir Gilbert Elliot . . . from 1751 to 1806.* London, 1874.

64. Ewing, J. C. "Burns's Literary Correspondents, 1786–1796: with list of Letters addressed to the Poet." *Burns Chronicle,* Second Series, 8 (1933). 18–78.

65. Fay, G. R. *Adam Smith and the Scotland of His Day.* Cambridge, 1956.

105. Lee, Irving J. "A Study of Emotional Appeal in Rhetorical Theory." Unpublished Ph.D. dissertation, Northwestern University, 1939.

106. Lee, John. *The University of Edinburgh from its Foundation in 1583 to the Year 1839.* Edinburgh, 1884.

107. Légouis, Émile and Cazamian, Louis. *A History of English Literature.* New York, 1930.

108. Lockhart, John G. *The Life of. Robert Burns.* 2 vols. Liverpool, 1914.

109. Mason, John. *An Essay on Elocution.* London, 1748.

110. ———. *An Essay on the Action Proper for the Pulpit.* London, 1753.

111. Mathieson, William Law. *The Awakening of Scotland.* Glasgow, 1910.

112. Mays, Morley J. "Johnson and Blair on Addison's Prose Style." *Studies in Philology.* 39 (1942). 638–49.

113. McCosh, James. *Scottish Philosophy: Biographical, Expository, Critical from Hutcheson to Hamilton.* New York, 1875.

114. McDermott, Douglas. "George Campbell and the Classical Tradition." *The Quarterly Journal of Speech.* 49 (1963). 403–9.

115. McElroy D. D. "The Literary Clubs and Societies in Eighteenth Century Scotland." Unpublished Ph.D. dissertation, University of Edinburgh, 1952.

116. McKillop, Alan. *English Literature from Dryden to Burns.* New York, 1948.

117. Meikle, Henry W. "The Chair of Rhetoric and Belles Lettres at the University of Edinburgh." *University of Edinburgh Journal.* 13 (1946). 89–103.

118. Millar, John H. *A Literary History of Scotland.* New York, 1903.

119. ———. *The Mid-Eighteenth Century.* New York, 1902.

120. ———. *Scottish Prose of the Seventeenth and Eighteenth Centuries.* Glasgow, 1912.

121. Monk, Samuel H. *The Sublime: A Study of Critical Theories in XVIII-th Century England.* New York, 1935.

122. Ogilvie, John. *Philosopical and Critical Observations on the Nature, Characters, and Various Species of Composition.* 2 vols. London, 1774.

123. Perrin, Porter G. "The Teaching of Rhetoric in the American Colleges before 1750." Unpublished Ph.D. dissertation, University of Chicago, 1936.

124. Potter, Stephen. *The Muse in Chains.* London, 1937.

125. Pottle, F. A. *The Literary Career of James Boswell.* Oxford, 1929.

126. Priestley, Joseph. *A Course of Lectures on Oratory and Criticism.* London, 1777. Also Edited by Vincent Bevilacqua and Richard Murphy in this series, 1965.

127. Rae, John. *Life of Adam Smith.* London, 1895.

128. Randall, Helen Whitcomb. *The Critical Theory of Lord Kames.* Northampton, Mass., 1944.

129. Reid, Thomas. *Inquiry into the Human Mind on the Principles of Common Sense.* London, 1764.

130. Reid, W. H. "A Copious Account of the Life and Writings of the Author," as an introduction to *The Sentimental Beauties and Moral Delineations of the late Dr. Hugh Blair.* London, 1809.

131. Rollin, Charles. *The Method of Teaching and Studying the Belles Lettres.* 4 vols. London, 1737.

132. Saintsbury, George. *A History of Criticism and Literary Taste in Europe.* Second edition. 3 vols. New York, 1902.

133. Sandford, William P. *English Theories of Public Address, 1530–1828.* Columbus, Ohio, 1931.

134. Schmitz, Robert M. *Hugh Blair.* New York, 1948.

135. ———. "Dr. Johnson and Blair's Sermons." *Modern Language Notes.* 60 (1945) . 268–70.

136. ———. "Scottish Shakespeare." *The Shakespeare Association Bulletin.* 16 (1941) . 229–36.

137. Scott, W. R. *Adam Smith as Student and Professor.* Glasgow, 1937.

138. Smith, Adam. "Considerations concerning the First Formation of Languages," in *The Essays of Adam Smith,* 305–25, 1869.

139. ———. *Lectures on Rhetoric and Belles Lettres.* Edited by John M. Lothian. London, 1963.

140. Somerville, Thomas. *My Own Life and Times; 1741–1814.* Edinburgh, 1861.

141. ———. *History of English Thought in the Eighteenth Century.* London, 1876.

142. Sheridan, Thomas. *Lectures on Elocution.* London, 1762. Also edited by Frederick M. Haberman in this series, 1965.

143. ———. *British Education, or The Source of the Disorders of Great Britain.* London, 1756.

144. ———. *Lectures on the Art of Reading.* Dublin, 1775.

145. ———. *A Plan of Education for the Young Nobility and Gentry of Great Britain.* London, 1769.

146. ———. *A Discourse Being Introductory to a Course of Lectures on Elocution and the English Language.* London, 1759.

147. Stephen, Leslie. "Hugh Blair." In *Dictionary of National Biography.* London, 1882.

148. Swift, Jonathan. "Letter to a Young Clergyman." In vol. 8 of Swift, *Works,* arranged by Thomas Sheridan, 24 vols. New York, 1812.

149. Taylor, Harold. "Hume's Theory of Imagination." *University of Toronto Quarterly.* 12 (1942). 180–90.

150. Taylor, William M. *The Scottish Pulpit from the Reformation to the Present Day.* New York, 1887.

151. Tegg, Thomas. "Memoirs of the Rev. Hugh Blair." An Introduction to *The Beauties of Blair.* London, 1810.

152. Thomas, Ota Reynolds. "The Teaching of Rhetoric in the United States during the Classical Period of Education," in vol. 1 of *A History and Criticism of American Public Address.* Edited by W. N. Brigance, 2 vols. New York, 1943.

153. Thwing, Charles F. *A History of Higher Education in America.* New York, 1906.

154. Tytler, Alexander Fraser (Lord Woodhouselee). *Memoirs of the Life and Writings of the Honourable Henry Home of Kames,* Second edition. 3 vols. Edinburgh, 1814.

155. Ward, John. *A System of Oratory.* 2 vols. London, 1759.

156. Warr, Charles L. *The Presbyterian Tradition.* London, 1933.

157. Watt, Francis. *The Book of Edinburgh Anecdote.* New York, 1913.

158. Wilds, Elmer H. "Public Speaking in the Early Colleges and Schools." *The Quarterly Journal of Speech.* 2 (1916). 31–38.

159. Willey, Basil. *The Eighteenth Century Background: Studies in the Idea of Nature in the Thought of the Period.* New York, 1941.

160. Williams, A. M. "The Scottish School of Rhetoric." *Education.* 13 (1892–1893). 142–50, 220–27, 281–90, 344–54, 427–34, 488–96.

161. Wilson, John F. and Arnold, Carroll C. *Public Speaking as a Liberal Art.* Boston, 1964.

162. Witherspoon, John. *The Works of the Rev. John Witherspoon.* 4 vols. Philadelphia, 1800.

163. Whately, Richard. *Elements of Rhetoric.* London, 1828. Also edited by Douglas Ehninger in this series, 1963.

164. ———. *Elements of Logic.* London, 1826.

NOTES

1. Hugh Blair, *Lectures on Rhetoric and Belles Lettres,* Thomas Dale, ed. (London, 1863), p. vii.

2. James Boswell, *London Journal, 1762–63,* F. A. Pottle, ed. (New York, 1950), p. 234.

3. H. F. Harding, *English Rhetorical Theory, 1750–1800.* Unpublished Ph.D. dissertation, Cornell University, 1937.

4. Hugh Blair, *Lectures on Rhetoric and Belles Lettres,* 2 vols. (London, 1783), I, iv–v. Future references in this edition will be indicated in this fashion. Pages will follow the volume number. In his valuable book, *Hugh Blair* (New York, 1948), Robert M. Schmitz lists 26 British editions of the *Lectures on Rhetoric and Belles Lettres* published to 1863, two continental editions in English, 37 American editions between 1784 and 1853, 13 translations in French, Italian, Russian and Spanish between 1797 and 1855, and 52 Abridgments of the *Lectures* between 1787 and 1911. Schmitz also adds seven textbooks which use Blair's *Lectures* in part and two published "Questions for the Lectures." No other book on rhetoric in English approaches a record of this kind.

5. Blair, *Lectures,* I, iii.   6. *Ibid.,* II, 523.   7. *Ibid.,* I, 16.

8. *Ibid.,* I, 23.   9. *Ibid.,* I, 21.   10. *Ibid.,* I, 30.

11. *Ibid.,* I, 31.   12. *Ibid.,* I, 30.   13. *Ibid.,* I, 36.

14. *Ibid.,* I, 41.

15. *Ibid.,* referring to Addison's "Essay on the Pleasures of the Imagination" in Vol. 6 of the *Spectator.* I, 44.

16. *Ibid.,* I, 66, 70.   17. *Ibid.,* I, 75.   18. *Ibid.,* I, 98.

19. *Ibid.,* I, 183.   20. *Ibid.,* I, 186.   21. *Ibid.,* I, 209.

22. *Ibid.,* I, 245.   23. *Ibid.,* I, 275.   24. *Ibid.,* I, 287.

25. *Ibid.,* I, 402.   26. *Ibid.,* I, 402–7.

27. *Ibid.,* II, 3, 8. For other meanings of the term "eloquence," see J. W. Bray, *A History of Critical Terms* (Boston, 1898), p. 96.

28. *De Inventione,* I, 5, 6; *De Oratore,* I, 31, 138.

29. Blair, *Lectures,* II, 5.

30. *Ibid.,* II, 49. Compare II, 233: "Good sense and knowledge are the foundation of all good speaking."

31. *Ibid.,* II, 53.   32. *Ibid.,* II, 39.

33. *Ibid.,* II, 43. Also II, 118. At II, 102, Blair complains that "we have a great number of moderately good preachers, . . . but few who are singularly eminent."

34. *Ibid.,* II, 42.   35. *Ibid.,* II, 61.   36. *Ibid.,* II, 78.

37. *Ibid.,* II, 81.   38. *Ibid.,* II, 82–83.   39. *Ibid.,* II, 85.

40. *Ibid.,* II, 125.   41. *Ibid.,* II, 106.   42. *Ibid.,* II, 107.

43. *Ibid.,* II, 107–14.   44. *Ibid.,* II, 114.   45. *Ibid.,* II, 115.

46. *Ibid.,* II, 119.   47. *Ibid.,* II, 158–69.   48. *Ibid.,* II, 170.

49. *Ibid.,* II, 179–80.   50. *Ibid.,* II, 193–99.   51. *Ibid.,* II, 193–99.

52. *Ibid.,* II, 200.   53. *Ibid.,* II, 206.   54. *Ibid.,* II, 210–22.

55. *Ibid.,* II, 218.   56. *Ibid.,* II, 222.

57. *Ibid.,* II, 228. See also Herman Cohen, "Hugh Blair on Speech Education," *Southern Speech Journal,* 29 (1963), 1–11.

58. *Ibid.,* II, 232.   59. *Ibid.,* II, 232.   60. *Ibid.,* II, 233.

61. *Ibid.,* II, 237.   62. *Ibid.,* II, 236.   63. *Ibid.,* II, 236.

64. *Ibid.,* II, 239.   65. *Ibid.,* II, 246.   66. *Ibid.,* II, 246.

67. William Charvat, *The Origins of American Critical Thought, 1810–1835* (Philadelphia, 1936), p. 44.

68. H. G. Graham, *Scottish Men of Letters of the Eighteenth Century* (London, 1901), p. 121. Speaking of Blair's sermons as essays, composed by a professor of rhetoric to illustrate the principles of his art, see Leslie Stephen, *English Thought in the Eighteenth Century,* 2nd ed. (2 vols., London, 1881), II, 346. Elsewhere Stephen says Blair is like a "declaimer, whose rhetoric glides over the surface of things without bitting into the substance." *Ibid.,* II, 215. As a theologian Blair was "a mere washed out retailer of second-hand commonplaces who gave the impression that the real man had vanished and left nothing but a wig and gown." *Ibid.,* II, 347.

69. See James L. Golden, "Hugh Blair: Minister of St. Giles," *The Quarterly Journal of Speech,* 38 (1952), 155, 60. Also his 1948 Ohio State University Master's essay on Blair's practice in sermon writing.

70. Graham, p. 128. The sermons were published in five volumes from 1777–1801. Blair received £200 for the first volume, £200 for the second, and £600 for the third. When Lord Mansfield read selections from them to King George III, the King expressed a wish that every youth in Britain might own a copy of the Bible and of Blair. See Boswell's *Life,* Chap. 3, p. 104 where Johnson says: "Dr. Blair is printing some sermons. If they are all like the first, which I have read, they are *Sermones aurei, ac auro magis aurei.* It is excellently written as to doctrine and language." Also: "Please to return Dr. Blair thanks for his sermons. The Scotch write English wonderfully well." *Ibid.,* Chap. 3, p. 109.

71. Graham, p. 128.

72. Sir Alexander Grant, *The Story of the University of Edinburgh,* 2 vols. (London, 1884), I, 357. Quoting from Bower's *History University of Edinburgh,* Chap. 3, 17. Also Graham, p. 124.

73. J. H. Millar, *Scottish Prose of the Seventeenth and Eighteenth Centuries* (Glasgow, 1912), p. 177.

74. See A. D. Godley, *Oxford in the Eighteenth Century* (London, 1908), Chaps. 3 and 4; Christopher Wordsworth, *Scholae Academicae: Some Account of the Studies at the English Universities in the Eighteenth Century* (Cambridge, 1877).

75. See Hume's *Essays,* Green and Grove, eds. 4 vols. (London, 1874), II, 46.

76. Sir Alexander Grant, *The Story of the University of Edinburgh,* I, 350. At the request of Lord Kames, Adam Smith had given a course of lectures in rhetoric at the University of Edinburgh in 1750–51, I, 276. Blair tells us that he borrowed and studied Smith's manuscript notes. John Rae, *Life of Adam Smith* (London, 1895), p. 32. For the best recent account of Blair's life see Robert M. Schmitz, *Hugh Blair,* Chaps. 3–6. Also see John Hill, *An Account of the Life and Writings of Hugh Blair* (Edinburgh, 1807), and the biographical sketch by James Finlayson, in Blair's *Sermons* (London, 1826). See also Alexander Carlyle's *Autobiography,* 3rd ed. (London and Edinburgh, 1861), pp. 201–4 and *The European Magazine,* 4 (1783), 201–2.

77. Blair, *Lectures,* II, 244–45.   78. *Ibid.,* II, 242.

79. *Ibid.,* II, 243.   80. *Ibid.,* II, 242.   81. *Ibid.,* II, 243.

82. Adam Smith, *Lectures on Rhetoric and Belles Lettres,* John M. Lothian, ed. (London, 1963), p. xxi. Lothian uses the quotations from Rae's *Life of Adam Smith.*

83. See Charles A. Fritz, on "The Content of the Teaching of Speech in the American Colleges before 1850: With Special Reference to the Influence on the Current Theories." New York University Ph.D. dissertation, 1928; Donald Hayworth, "The Development of the Training of Public Speakers in America," *Quarterly Journal of Speech,* 14 (1928), 489–502; Warren Guthrie, "The Development of Rhetorical Theory in America, 1635–1850," *Speech Monographs,* 15 (1948), 61–71; William Charvat, *The Origins of American Critical Thought, 1810–1835* (Philadelphia, 1936).

84. For contemporary reviews of Blair's *Lectures,* see *The Monthly Review,* 68 (1783), 489–505; 69 (1783), 186–92; 70 (1784), 173–83; *The European Magazine,* 3 (1783), 433–35; 4 (1783), 33–34; 113–14; 197–202; *The English Review,* 2 (1783), 18–25; 81–95; *The Gentlemans Magazine,* 53 (1783), 684, 756.

85. A. Bosker, *Literary Criticism in the Age of Johnson* (Groningen, 1930).

86. Some seventeen adverse criticisms of Blair's *Lectures* have been assembled in the excellent monograph by Douglas Ehninger and James Golden, "The Intrinsic Sources of Blair's Popularity" in *Southern Speech Journal,* 21 (1955), 12–30. The authors give five good reasons for Blair's popularity. Their account should be read as the best modern explication of the *Lectures.* It serves to re-establish Blair's place in the history of rhetorical theory.

LECTURES

ON

RHETORIC

AND

BELLES LETTRES.

By HUGH BLAIR, D.D.

ONE OF THE MINISTERS OF THE HIGH CHURCH, AND
PROFESSOR OF RHETORIC AND BELLES LETTRES
IN THE UNIVERSITY, OF EDINBURGH.

IN TWO VOLUMES.

VOL. I.

LONDON:

PRINTED FOR W. STRAHAN; T. CADELL, IN THE STRAND;
AND W. CREECH, IN EDINBURGH.
MDCCLXXXIII.

PREFACE.

THE following Lectures were read in the Univerſity of Edinburgh, for Twenty-four years. The publication of them, at preſent, was not altogether a matter of choice. Imperfect Copies of them, in Manuſcript, from notes taken by Students who heard them read, were firſt privately handed about; and afterwards frequently expoſed to public ſale. When the Author ſaw them circulate ſo currently, as even to be quoted in print*, and found himſelf often threatened with ſurreptitious publications of them, he judged it to be high time that they ſhould proceed from his own hand, rather than come into public view under ſome very defective and erroneous form.

---

* Biographia Britannica. Article, ADDISON.

THEY

THEY were originally defigned for the initiation of Youth into the ftudy of Belles Lettres, and of Compofition. With the fame intention they are now publifhed; and, therefore, the form of Lectures, in which they were at firft compofed, is ftill retained. The Author gives them to the world, neither as a Work wholly original, nor as a Compilation from the Writings of others. On every fubject contained in them, he has thought for himfelf. He confulted his own ideas and reflections: and a great part of what will be found in thefe Lectures is entirely his own. At the fame time, he availed himfelf of the ideas and reflections of others, as far as he thought them proper to be adopted. To proceed in this manner, was his duty as a Public Profeffor. It was incumbent on him, to convey to his Pupils all the knowledge that could improve them; to deliver not merely what was new, but what might be ufeful, from whatever quarter it came. He hopes, that to fuch as are ftudying to cultivate their Tafte, to form their Style, or to prepare themfelves for Public Speaking or Compofition, his Lectures will

afford

afford a more comprehenſive view of what relates to theſe ſubjects, than, as far as he knows, is to be received from any one Book in our Language.

IN order to render his Work of greater ſervice, he has generally referred to the Books which he conſulted, as far as he remembers them; that the Readers might be directed to any farther illuſtration which they afford. But, as ſuch a length of time has elapſed ſince the firſt Compoſition of his Lectures, he may, perhaps, have adopted the ſentiments of ſome Author into whoſe Writings he had then looked, without now remembering whence he derived them.

IN the opinions which he has delivered concerning ſuch a variety of Authors, and of literary matters, as come under his conſideration, he cannot expect that all his Readers will concur with him. The ſubjects are of ſuch a nature, as allow room for much diverſity of taſte and ſentiment: and the Author will reſpectfully ſubmit to the judgment of the Public.

RETAINING

RETAINING the fimplicity of the Lecturing Style, as beft fitted for conveying inftruction, he has aimed, in his Language, at no more than perfpicuity. If, after the liberties which it was neceffary for him to take, in criticifing the Style of the moft eminent Writers in our language, his own Style fhall be thought open to reprehenfion, all that he can fay, is, that his Book will add one to the many proofs already afforded to the world, of its being much eafier to give inftruction, than to fet example.

CONTENTS

OF THE

FIRST VOLUME.

‡

L E C T U R E I.

I N T R O D U C T I O N.

ONE of the moſt diſtinguiſhed privileges which Providence has conferred upon mankind, is the power of
communicating their thoughts to one another. Deſtitute of this power, Reaſon would be a ſolitary, and, in ſome
meaſure, an unavailing principle. Speech is the great inſtrument by which man becomes beneficial to man: and it is to the
intercourſe and tranſmiſſion of thought, by means of ſpeech,
that we are chiefly indebted for the improvement of thought
itſelf. Small are the advances which a ſingle unaſſiſted individual can make towards perfecting any of his powers. What
we call human reaſon, is not the effort or ability of one, ſo
much as it is the reſult of the reaſon of many, ariſing from
lights mutually communicated, in conſequence of diſcourſe and
writing.

IT is obvious, then, that writing and diſcourſe are objects
intitled to the higheſt attention. Whether the influence of the

ſpeaker,

speaker, or the entertainment of the hearer, be confulted; whether utility or pleafure be the principal aim in view, we are prompted, by the ftrongeft motives, to ftudy how we may communicate our thoughts to one another with moft advantage. Accordingly we find, that in almoft every nation, as foon as language had extended itfelf beyond that fcanty communication which was requifite for the fupply of men's neceffities, the improvement of difcourfe began to attract regard. In the language even of rude uncultivated tribes, we can trace fome attention to the grace and force of thofe expreffions which they ufed, when they fought to perfuade or to affect. They were early fenfible of a beauty in difcourfe, and endeavoured to give it certain decorations which experience had taught them it was capable of receiving, long before the ftudy of thofe decorations was formed into a regular art.

BUT, among nations in a civilized ftate, no art has been cultivated with more care, than that of language, ftyle, and compofition. The attention paid to it may, indeed, be affumed as one mark of the progrefs of fociety towards its moft improved period. For, according as fociety improves and flourifhes, men acquire more influence over one another by means of reafoning and difcourfe; and in proportion as that influence is felt to enlarge, it muft follow, as a natural confequence, that they will beftow more care upon the methods of expreffing their conceptions with propriety and eloquence. Hence we find, that in all the polifhed nations of Europe, this ftudy has been treated as highly important, and has poffeffed a confiderable place in every plan of liberal education.

INDEED,

INDEED, when the arts of ſpeech and writing are mentioned, L E C T. I am ſenſible that prejudices againſt them are apt to riſe in the I. minds of many. A ſort of art is immediately thought of, that is oſtentatious and deceitful; the minute and trifling ſtudy of words alone; the pomp of expreſſion; the ſtudied fallacies of rhetoric; ornament ſubſtituted in the room of uſe. We need not wonder, that under ſuch imputations, all ſtudy of diſcourſe as an art, ſhould have ſuffered in the opinion of men of under-ſtanding: and I am far from denying, that rhetoric and criticiſm have ſometimes been ſo -managed as to tend to the corruption, rather than to the improvement, of good taſte and true elo-quence. But ſure it is equally poſſible to apply the princi-ples of reaſon and good ſenſe to this art, as to any other that is cultivated among men. If the following Lectures have any merit, it will conſiſt in an endeavour to ſubſtitute the applica-tion of theſe principles in the place of artificial and ſcholaſtic rhetoric; in an endeavour to explode falſe ornament, to direct attention more towards ſubſtance than ſhow, to recommend good ſenſe as the foundation of all good compoſition, and ſim-plicity as eſſential to all true ornament.

WHEN entering on the ſubject, I may be allowed, on this occaſion, to ſuggeſt a few thoughts concerning the importance and advantages of ſuch ſtudies, and the rank they are intitled to poſſeſs in academical education *. I am under no tempta-

---

* The Author was the firſt who read Lectures on this ſubject in the Univer-ſity of Edinburgh. He began with reading them in a private character in the year 1759. In the following year he was choſen Profeſſor of Rhetoric by the Magiſtrates and Town-council of Edinburgh: and, in 1762, his Majeſty was pleaſed to erect and endow a Profeſſion of Rhetoric and Belles Lettres in that Univerſity; and the Author was appointed the firſt Regius Profeſſor.

tion,

tion, for this purpose, of extolling their importance at the expence of any other department of science. On the contrary, the study of Rhetoric and Belles Lettres suppofes and requires a proper acquaintance with the reft of the liberal arts. It embraces them all within its circle, and recommends them to the higheft regard. The firft care of all fuch as wifh either to write with reputation, or to fpeak in public fo as to command attention, muft be, to extend their knowledge; to lay in a rich ftore of ideas relating to thofe fubjects of which the occafions of life may call them to difcourfe or to write. Hence, among the ancients, it was a fundamental principle, and frequently inculcated, " Quod omnibus difciplinis et artibus debet effe " inftructus orator;" that the orator ought to be an accomplifhed fcholar, and converfant in every part of learning. It is indeed impoffible to contrive an art, and very pernicious it were if it could be contrived, which fhould give the ftamp of merit to any compofition rich or fplendid in expreffion, but barren or erroneous in thought. They are the wretched attempts towards an art of this kind which have fo often difgraced oratory, and debafed it below its true ftandard. The graces of compofition have been employed to difguife or to fupply the want of matter; and the temporary applaufe of the ignorant has been courted, inftead of the lafting approbation of the difcerning. But fuch impofture can never maintain its ground long. Knowledge and fcience muft furnifh the materials that form the body and fubftance of any valuable compofition. Rhetoric ferves to add the polifh, and we know that none but firm and folid bodies can be polifhed well.

OF thofe who perufe the following Lectures, fome, by the profeffion to which they addict themfelves, or in confequence

of

of their prevailing inclination, may have the view of being employed in compofition, or in public fpeaking. Others, without any profpect of this kind, may wifh only to improve their tafte with refpect to writing and difcourfe, and to acquire principles which will enable them to judge for themfelves in that part of literature called the Belles Lettres.

WITH refpect to the former, fuch as may have occafion to communicate their fentiments to the Public, it is abundantly clear that fome preparation of ftudy is requifite for the end which they have in view. To fpeak or to write perfpicuoufly and agreeably, with purity, with grace and ftrength, are attainments of the utmoft confequence to all who purpofe, either by fpeech or writing, to addrefs the Public. For without being mafter of thofe attainments, no man can do juftice to his own conceptions ; but how rich foever he may be in knowledge and in good fenfe, will be able to avail himfelf lefs of thofe treafures, than fuch as poffefs not half his ftore, but who can difplay what they poffefs with more propriety. Neither are thefe attainments of that kind for which we are indebted to nature merely. Nature has, indeed, conferred upon fome a very favourable diftinction in this refpect, beyond others. But in thefe, as in moft other talents fhe beftows, fhe has left much to be wrought out by every man's own induftry. So confpicuous have been the effects of ftudy and improvement in every part of eloquence ; fuch remarkable examples have appeared of perfons furmounting, by their diligence, the difadvantages of the moft untoward nature, that among the learned it has long been a contefted, and remains ftill an undecided point, whether

nature

nature or art confer moſt towards excelling in writing and diſcourſe.

WITH reſpect to the manner in which art can moſt effectually furniſh aſſiſtance for ſuch a purpoſe, there may be diverſity
of opinions. I by no means pretend to ſay that mere rhetorical rules, how juſt ſoever, are ſufficient to form an orator.
Suppoſing natural genius to be favourable, more by a great
deal will depend upon private application and ſtudy, than upon
any ſyſtem of inſtruction that is capable of being publicly communicated. But at the ſame time, though rules and inſtruc-
tions cannot do all that is requiſite, they may, however, do
much that is of real uſe. They cannot, it is true, inſpire
genius ; but they can direct and aſſiſt it. They cannot remedy
barrenneſs ; but they may correct redundancy. They point
out proper models for imitation. They bring into view the
chief beauties that ought to be ſtudied, and the principal faults
that ought to be avoided; and thereby tend to enlighten taſte,
and to lead genius from unnatural deviations, into its proper
channel. What would not avail for the production of great
excellencies, may at leaſt ſerve to prevent the commiſſion of
conſiderable errors.

ALL that regards the ſtudy of eloquence and compoſition,
merits the higher attention upon this account, that it is intimately connected with the improvement of our intellectual
powers. For I muſt be allowed to ſay, that when we are
employed, after a proper manner, in the ſtudy of compoſition,
we are cultivating reaſon itſelf. True rhetoric and ſound logic

are

are very nearly allied. The ftudy of arranging and expreffing our thoughts with propriety, teaches to think, as well as to fpeak, accurately. By putting our fentiments into words, we always conceive them more diftinctly. Every one who has the flighteft acquaintance with compofition knows, that when he expreffes himfelf ill on any fubject, when his arrangement becomes loofe, and his fentences turn feeble, the defects of his ftyle can, almoft on every occafion, be traced back to his indiftinct conception of the fubject : fo clofe is the connection between thoughts and the words in which they are clothed.

THE ftudy of compofition, important in itfelf at all times, has acquired additional importance from the tafte and manners of the prefent age. It is an age wherein improvements, in every part of fcience, have been profecuted with ardour. To all the liberal arts much attention has been paid ; and to none more than to the beauty of language, and the grace and elegance of every kind of writing. The public ear is become refined. It will not eafily bear what is flovenly and incorrect. Every author muft afpire to fome merit in expreffion, as well as in fentiment, if he would not incur the danger of being neglected and defpifed.

I WILL not deny that the love of minute elegance, and attention to inferior ornaments of compofition, may at prefent have engroffed too great a degree of the public regard. It is indeed my opinion, that we lean to this extreme ; often more careful of polifhing ftyle, than of ftoring it with thought. Yet hence arifes a new reafon for the ftudy of juft and proper compofition. If it be requifite not to be deficient in elegance or

ornament

ornament in times when they are in fuch high eftimation, it is ftill more requifite to attain the power of diftinguifhing falfe ornament from true, in order to prevent our being carried away by that torrent of falfe and frivolous tafte, which never fails, when it is prevalent, to fweep along with it the raw and the ignorant. They who have never ftudied eloquence in its principles, nor have been trained to attend to the genuine and manly beauties of good writing, are always ready to be caught by the mere glare of language; and when they come to fpeak in public, or to compofe, have no other ftandard on which to form themfelves, except what chances to be fafhionable and popular, how corrupted foever, or erroneous, that may be.

But as there are many who have no fuch objeĉts as either compofition or public fpeaking in view, let us next confider what advantages may be derived by them, from fuch ftudies as form the fubjeĉt of thefe Leĉtures. To them, rhetoric is not fo much a praĉtical art as a fpeculative fcience; and the fame inftruĉtions which affift others in compofing, will affift them in judging of, and relifhing, the beauties of compofition. Whatever enables genius to execute well, will enable tafte to criticife juftly.

When we name criticifing, prejudices may perhaps arife, of the fame kind with thofe which I mentioned before with refpeĉt to rhetoric. As rhetoric has been fometimes thought to fignify nothing more than the fcholaftic ftudy of words, and phrafes, and tropes, fo criticifm has been confidered as merely the art of finding faults; as the frigid application of certain technical terms, by means of which perfons are taught to cavil

and

and cenfure in a learned manner. But this is the criticifm of pedants only. True criticifm is a liberal and humane art. It is the offspring of good fenfe and refined tafte. It aims at acquiring a juft difcernment of the real merit of authors. It promotes a lively relifh of their beauties, while it preferves us from that blind and implicit veneration which would confound their beauties and faults in our efteem. It teaches us, in a word, to admire and to blame with judgment, and not to follow the crowd blindly.

In an age when works of genius and literature are fo frequently the fubjects of difcourfe, when every one erects himfelf into a judge, and when we can hardly mingle in polite fociety without bearing fome fhare in fuch difcuffions; ftudies of this kind, it is not to be doubted, will appear to derive part of their importance from the ufe to which they may be applied in furnifhing materials for thofe fafhionable topics of difcourfe, and thereby enabling us to fupport a proper rank in focial life.

But I fhould be forry if we could not reft the merit of fuch ftudies on fomewhat of folid and intrinfical ufe independent of appearance and fhow. The exercife of tafte and of found criticifm, is in truth one of the moft improving employments of the underftanding. To apply the principles of good fenfe to compofition and difcourfe; to examine what is beautiful, and why it is fo; to employ ourfelves in diftinguifhing accurately between the fpecious and the folid, between affected and natural ornament, muft certainly improve us not a little in the moft valuable part of all philofophy, the philofophy of hu-

Vol. I.   C   man

man nature. For such disquisitions are very intimately connected with the knowledge of ourselves. They necessarily
lead us to reflect on the operations of the imagination, and
the movements of the heart; and increase our acquaintance
with some of the most refined feelings which belong to our
frame.

LOGICAL and Ethical disquisitions move in a higher sphere;
and are conversant with objects of a more severe kind; the progress of the understanding in its search after knowledge, and
the direction of the will in the proper pursuit of good. In
these they point out to man the improvement of his nature as
an intelligent being; and his duties as the subject of moral obli-
gation. Belles Lettres and criticism chiefly consider him as a
Being endowed with those powers of taste and imagination,
which were intended to embellish his mind, and to supply him
with rational and useful entertainment. They open a field of
investigation peculiar to themselves. All that relates to beauty,
harmony, grandeur, and elegance; all that can sooth the mind,
gratify the fancy, or move the affections, belongs to their pro-
vince. They present human nature under a different aspect
from that which it assumes to the view of other sciences. They
bring to light various springs of action which without their aid
might have passed unobserved; and which, though of a delicate
nature, frequently exert a powerful influence on several depart-
ments of human life.

SUCH studies have also this peculiar advantage, that they exercise our reason without fatiguing it. They lead to enquiries
acute, but not painful; profound, but not dry nor abstruse.

They

They ſtrew flowers in the path of ſcience; and while they keep the mind bent, in ſome degree, and active, they relieve it at the ſame time from that more toilſome labour to which it muſt ſubmit in the acquiſition of neceſſary erudition, or the inveſtigation of abſtract truth.

THE cultivation of taſte is farther recommended by the happy effects which it naturally tends to produce on human life. The moſt buſy man, in the moſt active ſphere, cannot be always occupied by buſineſs. Men of ſerious profeſſions cannot always be on the ſtretch of ſerious thought. Neither can the moſt gay and flouriſhing ſituations of fortune afford any man the power of filling all his hours with pleaſure. Life muſt always languiſh in the hands of the idle. It will frequently languiſh even in the hands of the buſy, if they have not ſome employment ſubſidiary to that which forms their main purſuit. How then ſhall theſe vacant ſpaces, thoſe unemployed intervals, which, more or leſs, occur in the life of every one, be filled up? How can we contrive to diſpoſe of them in any way that ſhall be more agreeable in itſelf, or more conſonant to the dignity of the human mind, than in the entertainments of taſte, and the ſtudy of polite literature? He who is ſo happy as to have acquired a reliſh for theſe, has always at hand an innocent and irreproachable amuſement for his leiſure hours, to ſave him from the danger of many a pernicious paſſion. He is not in hazard of being a burden to himſelf. He is not obliged to fly to low company, or to court the riot of looſe pleaſures, in order to cure the tediouſneſs of exiſtence.

PROVIDENCE

PROVIDENCE feems plainly to have pointed out this useful purpofe to which the pleafures of tafte may be applied, by interpofing them in a middle ftation between the pleafures of fenfe, and thofe of pure intellect. We were not defigned to grovel always among objects fo low as the former; nor are we capable of dwelling conftantly in fo high a region as the latter. The pleafures of tafte refrefh the mind after the toils of the intellect, and the labours of abftract ftudy; and they gradually raife it above the attachments of fenfe, and prepare it for the enjoyments of virtue.

So confonant is this to experience, that in the education of youth, no object has in every age appeared more important to wife men, than to tincture them early with a relifh for the entertainments of tafte. The tranfition is commonly made with eafe from thefe to the difcharge of the higher and more important duties of life. Good hopes may be entertained of thofe whofe minds have this liberal and elegant turn. Many virtues may be grafted upon it. Whereas to be entirely devoid of relifh for eloquence, poetry, or any of the fine arts, is juftly conftructed to be an unpromifing fymptom of youth; and raifes fufpicions of their being prone to low gratifications, or deftined to drudge in the more vulgar and illiberal purfuits of life.

THERE are indeed few good difpofitions of any kind with which the improvement of tafte is not more or lefs connected. A cultivated tafte increafes fenfibility to all the tender and humane paffions, by giving them frequent exercife; while it tends to weaken the more violent and fierce emotions.

———Ingenuas

——Ingenuas didiciffe fideliter artes
Emollit mores, nec finit effe feros *.

The elevated fentiments and high examples which poetry, eloquence and hiftory are often bringing under our view, naturally tend to nourifh in our minds publick fpirit, the love of
glory, contempt of external fortune, and the admiration of
what is truly illuftrious and great.

I will not go fo far as to fay that the improvement of tafte
and of virtue is the fame; or that they may always be expected to coexift in an equal degree. More powerful correctives
than tafte can apply, are neceffary for reforming the corrupt
propenfities which too frequently prevail among mankind.
Elegant fpeculations are fometimes found to float on the furface
of the mind, while bad paffions poffefs the interior regions of
the heart. At the fame time this cannot but be admitted, that
the exercife of tafte is, in its native tendency, moral and puri-
fying. From reading the moft admired productions of genius,
whether in poetry or profe, almoft every one rifes with fome
good impreffions left on his mind; and though thefe may not
always be durable, they are at leaft to be ranked among the
means of difpofing the heart to virtue. One thing is certain,
and I fhall hereafter have occafion to illuftrate it more fully,
that without poffeffing the virtuous affections in a ftrong degree, no man can attain eminence in the fublime parts of eloquence. He muft feel what a good man feels, if he expects
greatly to move or to intereft mankind. They are the ardent

* Thefe polifhed arts have humaniz'd mankind,
  Soften'd the rude, and calm'd the boift'rous mind.

7   fentiments

fentiments of honour, virtue, magnanimity, and publick fpirit, that only can kindle that fire of genius, and call up into the mind thofe high ideas, which attract the admiration of ages; and if this fpirit be neceffary to produce the moft diftinguifhed efforts of eloquence, it muft be neceffary alfo to our relifhing them with proper tafte and feeling.

On thefe general topics I fhall dwell no longer; but proceed directly to the confideration of the fubjects which are to employ the following Lectures. They divide themfelves into five parts. Firft, fome introductory differtations on the nature of tafte, and upon the fources of its pleafures. Secondly, the confideration of language: Thirdly, of ftyle: Fourthly, of eloquence properly fo called, or publick fpeaking in its different kinds. Laftly, a critical examination of the moft diftinguifhed fpecies of compofition, both in profe and verfe.

LECTURE

LECTURE II.

TASTE.

THE nature of the prefent undertaking leads me to begin with fome enquiries concerning Tafte, as it is this faculty which is always appealed to in difquifitions concerning the merit of difcourfe and writing.

THERE are few fubjects on which men talk more loofely and indiftinctly than on Tafte; few which it is more difficult to explain with precifion; and none which in this Courfe of Lectures will appear more dry or abftract. What I have to fay on the fubject fhall be in the following order. I fhall firft explain the Nature of Tafte as a power or faculty in the human mind. I fhall next confider how far it is an improveable faculty. I fhall fhew the fources of its improvement, and the characters of tafte in its moft perfect ftate. I fhall then examine the various fluctuations to which it is liable, and enquire whether there be any ftandard to which we can bring the different

taftes

taftes of men, in order to diftinguifh the corrupted from the true.

Taste may be defined " The power of receiving pleafure " from the beauties of nature and of art." The firft queftion that occurs concerning it is, whether it is to be confidered as an internal fenfe, or as an exertion of reafon? Reafon is a very general term; but if we underftand by it, that power of the mind which in fpeculative matters difcovers truth, and in prac- tical matters judges of the fitnefs of means to an end, I appre- hend the queftion may be eafily anfwered. For nothing can be more clear, than that tafte is not refolveable into any fuch operation of Reafon. It is not merely through a difcovery of the underftanding or a deduction of argument, that the mind receives pleafure from a beautiful profpect or a fine poem. Such objects often ftrike us intuitively, and make a ftrong impref- fion when we are unable to affign the reafons of our being pleafed. They fometimes ftrike in the fame manner the philo- fopher and the peafant; the boy and the man. Hence the faculty by which we relifh fuch beauties, feems more a-kin to a feeling of fenfe, than to a procefs of the underftanding: and accordingly from an external fenfe it has borrowed its name; that fenfe by which we receive and diftinguifh the pleafures of food having, in feveral languages, given rife to the word Tafte in the metaphorical meaning under which we now confider it. However, as in all fubjects which regard the operations of the mind, the inaccurate ufe of words is to be carefully avoid- ed, it muft not be inferred from what I have faid, that rea- fon is entirely excluded from the exertions of tafte. Though tafte, beyond doubt, be ultimately founded on a certain natural

and

and inftinctive fenfibility to beauty, yet reafon, as I fhall fhew
hereafter, affifts Tafte in many of its operations, and ferves to
enlarge its power*.

TASTE, in the fenfe in which I have explained it, is a faculty
common in fome degree to all men. Nothing that belongs to
human nature is more univerfal than the relifh of beauty of one
kind or other; of what is orderly, proportioned, grand, harmonious, new, or fprightly. In children, the rudiments of
Tafte difcover themfelves very early in a thoufand inftances; in
their fondnefs for regular bodies, their admiration of pictures
and ftatues, and imitations of all kinds; and their ftrong at-
tachment to whatever is new or marvellous. The moft ignorant
peafants are delighted with ballads and tales, and are ftruck
with the beautiful appearances of nature in the earth and
heavens. Even in the defarts of America, where human nature
fhews itfelf in its moft uncultivated ftate, the favages have their
ornaments of drefs, their war and their death fongs, their harangues, and their orators. We muft therefore conclude the
principles of Tafte to be deeply founded in the human
mind. It is no lefs effential to man to have fome difcernment
of beauty, than it is to poffefs the attributes of reafon and of
fpeech †.

BUT

* See Dr. Gerard's Effay on Tafte.—D'Alembert's Reflections on the ufe
and abufe of philofophy in matters which relate to Tafte.—Reflexions Critiques
fur la poëfie et fur la peinture, Tome II. ch. 22—31. Elements of Criticifm,
chap. 25.—Mr. Hume's Effay on the Standard of Tafte.—Introduction to the
Effay on the Sublime and Beautiful.

† On the fubject of Tafte confidered as a power or faculty of the mind, much
lefs is to be found among the antient, than among the modern rhetorical and
critical writers. The following remarkable paffage in Cicero ferves however to

But although none be wholly devoid of this faculty, yet the degrees in which it is poſſeſſed are widely different. In ſome men only the feeble glimmerings of Taſte appear; the beauties which they reliſh are of the coarſeſt kind; and of theſe they have but a weak and confuſed impreſſion: while in others, Taſte riſes to an acute diſcernment, and a lively enjoyment of the moſt refined beauties. In general, we may obſerve, that in the powers and pleaſures of Taſte, there is a more remarkable inequality among men than is uſually found in point of common ſenſe, reaſon, and judgment. The conſtitution of our nature in this, as in all other reſpects, diſcovers admirable wiſdom. In the diſtribution of thoſe talents which are neceſſary for man's well-being, Nature hath made leſs diſtinction among her children. But in the diſtribution of thoſe which belong only to the ornamental part of life, ſhe hath beſtowed her favours

ſhew, that his ideas on this ſubject agree perfectly with what has been ſaid above. He is ſpeaking of the beauties of ſtyle and numbers. " Illud autem nequis " admiretur quonam modo hæc vulgus imperitorum in audiendo, notet; cum in " omni genere, tum in hoc ipſo, magna quædam eſt vis, incredibiliſque naturæ. " Omnes enim tacito quodam ſenſu, ſine ulla arte aut ratione, quæ ſint in arti- " bus de rationibus recta et prava dijudicant: idque cum faciunt in picturis, et " in ſignis, et in aliis operibus, ad quorum intelligentiam a natura minus habent " inſtrumenti, tum multo oſtendunt magis in verborum, numerorum, vo- " cumque judicio; quod ea ſunt in communibus infixa ſenſibus; neque earum " rerum quenquam funditus natura voluit eſſe expertem." Cic. de Orat. lib. iii. cap. 50. Edit. Gruteri.——Quinctilian ſeems to include Taſte (for which, in the ſenſe which we now give to that word the antients appear to have had no diſtinct name) under what he calls judicium. " Locus de judicio, meâ quidem " opinione adeo partibus hujus operis omnibus connectus ac miſtus eſt, ut ne a " ſententiis quidem aut verbis ſaltem ſingulis poſſit ſeparari, nec magis arte tra- " ditur quam guſtus aut odor.——Ut contraria vitemus et communia, ne quid " in eloquendo corruptum obſcurumque ſit, referatur oportet ad ſenſus qui non " docentur." Inſtitut. lib. vi. cap. 3. Edit. Obrechti.

ſ   with

with more frugality. She hath both fown the feeds more
fparingly; and rendered a higher culture requifite for bringing
them to perfection.

THIS inequality of 'Tafte among men is owing, without
doubt, in part, to the different frame of their natures; to nicer
organs, and finer internal powers, with which fome are endowed
beyond others. But, if it be owing in part to nature, it is owing
to education and culture ftill more. The illuftration of this
leads to my next remark on this fubject, that Tafte is a moft
improveable faculty, if there be any fuch in human nature; a
remark which gives great encouragement to fuch a courfe of
ftudy as we are now propofing to purfue. Of the truth of this
affertion we may eafily be convinced, by only reflecting on that
immenfe fuperiority which education and improvement give to
civilized, above barbarous nations, in refinement of Tafte; and
on the fuperiority which they give in the fame nation to thofe
who have ftudied the liberal arts, above the rude and untaught
vulgar. The difference is fo great, that there is perhaps no one
particular in which thefe two claffes of men are fo far removed
from each other, as in refpect of the powers and the pleafures
of Tafte: and affuredly for this difference no other general caufe
can be affigned, but culture and education.—I fhall now proceed
to fhew what the means are, by which Tafte becomes fo remarkably fufceptible of cultivation and progrefs.

REFLECT firft upon that great law of our nature, that exercife is the chief fource of improvement in all our faculties.
This holds both in our bodily, and in our mental powers. It
holds even in our external fenfes; although thefe be lefs the fub-

D 2   ject

ject of cultivation than any of our other faculties. We fee how acute the fenfes become in perfons whofe trade or bufinefs leads to nice exertions of them. Touch, for inftance, becomes infinitely more exquifite in men whofe employment requires them to examine the polifh of bodies, than it is in others. They who deal in microfcopical obfervations, or are accuftomed to engrave on precious ftones, acquire furprifing accuracy of fight in difcerning the minuteft objects; and practice in attending to different flavours and taftes of liquors, wonderfully improves the power of diftinguifhing them, and of tracing their compofition. Placing internal Tafte therefore on the footing of a fimple fenfe, it cannot be doubted that frequent exercife, and curious attention to its proper objects, muft greatly heighten its power. Of this we have one clear proof in that part of Tafte, which is called an ear for mufic. Experience every day fhews, that nothing is more improveable. Only the fimpleft and plaineft compofitions are relifhed at firft; ufe and practice extend our pleafure; teach us to relifh finer melody, and by degrees enable us to enter into the intricate and compounded pleafures of harmony. So an eye for the beauties of painting is never all at once acquired. It is gradually formed by being converfant among pictures, and ftudying the works of the beft mafters.

PRECISELY in the fame manner, with refpect to the beauty of compofition and difcourfe, attention to the moft approved models, ftudy of the beft authors, comparifons of lower and higher degrees of the fame beauties, operate towards the refinement of Tafte. When one is only beginning his acquaintance with works of genius, the fentiment which attends them is

4   obfcure

obſcure and confuſed. He cannot point out the ſeveral excellencies or blemiſhes of a performance which he peruſes; he is
at a loſs on what to reſt his judgment; all that can be expected
is, that he ſhould tell in general whether he be pleaſed or not.
But allow him more experience in works of this kind, and his
Taſte becomes by degrees more exact and enlightened. He
begins to perceive not only the character of the whole, but the
beauties and defects of each part; and is able to deſcribe the-
peculiar qualities which he praiſes or blames. The miſt diſſi-
pates which ſeemed formerly to hang over the object; and he
can at length pronounce firmly, and without heſitation, concerning it. Thus in Taſte, conſidered as mere ſenſibility, exerciſe opens a great ſource of improvement.

But although Taſte be ultimately founded on ſenſibility, it
muſt not be conſidered as inſtinctive ſenſibility alone. Reaſon
and good ſenſe, as I before hinted, have ſo extenſive an influence
on all the operations and deciſions of Taſte, that a thorough
good Taſte may well be conſidered as a power compounded of
natural ſenſibility to beauty, and of improved underſtanding.
In order to be ſatisfied of this, let us obſerve, that the greater
part of the productions of genius are no other than imitations of
nature; repreſentations of the characters, actions, or manners
of men. The pleaſure we receive from ſuch imitations or repreſentations is founded on mere Taſte: but to judge whether
they be properly executed, belongs to the underſtanding, which
compares the copy with the original.

In reading, for inſtance, ſuch a poem as the Æneid, a great
part of our pleaſure ariſes from the plan or ſtory being well
conducted,

L E C T.
II.

conducted, and all the parts joined together with probability and due connexion ; from the characters being taken from nature, the fentiments being fuited to the characters, and the ftyle to the fentiments. The pleafure which arifes from a poem fo conducted, is felt or enjoyed by Tafte as an internal fenfe; but the difcovery of this conduct in the poem is owing to reafon; and the more that reafon enables us to difcover fuch propriety in the conduct, the greater will be our pleafure. We are pleafed, through our natural fenfe of beauty. Reafon fhews us why, and upon what grounds, we are pleafed. Wherever in works of Tafte, any refemblance to nature is aimed at; wherever there is any reference of parts to a whole, or of means to an end, as there is indeed in almoft every writing and difcourfe, there the underftanding muft always have a great part to act.

HERE then is a wide field for reafon's exerting its powers in relation to the objects of Tafte, particularly with refpect to compofition, and works of genius; and hence arifes a fecond and a very confiderable fource of the improvement of Tafte, from the application of reafon and good fenfe to fuch productions of genius. Spurious beauties, fuch as unnatural characters, forced fentiments, affected ftyle, may pleafe for a little; but they pleafe only becaufe their oppofition to nature and to good fenfe has not been examined, or attended to. Once fhew how nature might have been more juftly imitated or reprefented; how the writer might have managed his fubject to greater advantage; the illufion will prefently be diffipated, and thofe falfe beauties will pleafe no more.

FROM

FROM thefe two fources then, firft, the frequent exercife of Tafte, and next the application of good fenfe and reafon to the objects of Tafte, Tafte as a power of the mind receives its improvement. In its perfect ftate, it is undoubtedly the refult both of nature and of art. It fuppofes our natural fenfe of beauty to be refined by frequent attention to the moft beautiful objects, and at the fame time to be guided and improved by the light of the underftanding.

I MUST be allowed to add, that as a found head, fo likewife a good heart, is a very material requifite to juft Tafte. The moral beauties are not only in themfelves fuperiour to all others, but they exert an influence, either more near or more remote, on a great variety of other objects of Tafte. Wherever the affections, characters, or actions of men are concerned (and thefe certainly afford the nobleft fubjects to genius), there can be neither any juft or affecting defcription of them, nor any thorough feeling of the beauty of that defcription, without our poffeffing the virtuous affections. He whofe heart is indelicate or hard, he who has no admiration of what is truly noble or praifeworthy, nor the proper fympathetic fenfe of what is foft and tender, muft have a very imperfect relifh of the higheft beauties of eloquence and poetry.

THE characters of Tafte when brought to its moft perfect ftate are all reducible to two, Delicacy and Correctnefs.

DELICACY of Tafte refpects principally the perfection of that natural fenfibility on which Tafte is founded. It implies thofe finer organs or powers which enable us to difcover beauties

that

that lie hid from a vulgar eye. One may have ſtrong ſenſibi-lity, and yet be deficient in delicate Taſte. He may be deeply impreſſed by ſuch beauties as he perceives; but he perceives only what is in ſome degree coarſe, what is bold and palpable; while chaſter and ſimpler ornaments eſcape his notice. In this ſtate Taſte generally exiſts among rude and unrefined nations. But a perſon of delicate Taſte both feels ſtrongly, and feels ac-curately. He ſees diſtinctions and differences where others ſee none; the moſt latent beauty does not eſcape him, and he is ſenſible of the ſmalleſt blemiſh. Delicacy of Taſte is judged of by the ſame marks that we uſe in judging of the delicacy of an external ſenſe. As the goodneſs of the palate is not tried by ſtrong flavours, but by a mixture of ingredients, where, not-withſtanding the confuſion, we remain ſenſible of each; in like manner delicacy of internal Taſte appears, by a quick and lively ſenſibility to its fineſt, moſt compounded, or moſt latent objects.

CORRECTNESS of Taſte reſpects chiefly the improvement which that faculty receives through its connexion with the un-derſtanding. A man of correct Taſte is one who is never im-poſed on by counterfeit beauties; who carries always in his mind that ſtandard of good ſenſe which he employs in judging of every thing. He eſtimates with propriety the comparative merit of the ſeveral beauties which he meets with in any work of genius; refers them to their proper claſſes; aſſigns the prin-ciples, as far as they can be traced, whence their power of pleaſing us flows; and is pleaſed himſelf preciſely in that degree in which he ought, and no more.

IT

IT is true that thefe two qualities of Tafte, Delicacy and Cor-rectnefs, mutually imply each other. No Tafte can be exquifitely delicate without being correct; nor can be thoroughly correct without being delicate. But ftill a predominancy of one or other quality in the mixture is often vifible. The power of Delicacy is chiefly feen in difcerning the true merit of a work; the power of Correctnefs, in rejecting falfe pretenfions to merit. Delicacy leans more to feeling; Correctnefs more to reafon and judgment. The former is more the gift of nature; the latter, more the product of culture and art. Among the antient critics, Longinus poffeffed moft Delicacy; Ariftotle, moft Correctnefs. Among the moderns, Mr. Addifon is a high example of delicate Tafte; Dean Swift, had he written on the fubject of criticifm, would perhaps have afforded the example of a correct one.

HAVING viewed Tafte in its moft improved and perfect ftate, I come next to confider its deviations from that ftate, the fluctuations and changes to which it is liable; and to en-quire whether, in the midft of thefe, there be any means of diftinguifhing a true from a corrupted Tafte. This brings us to the moft difficult part of our tafk. For it muft be acknow-ledged, that no principle of the human mind is, in its opera-tions, more fluctuating and capricious than Tafte. Its varia-tions have been fo great and frequent, as to create a fufpicion with fome, of its being merely arbitrary; grounded on no foundation, afcertainable by no ftandard, but wholly dependent on changing fancy; the confequence of which would be, that all ftudies or regular enquiries concerning the objects of Tafte were vain. In architecture, the Grecian models were long efteemed the moft perfect. In fucceeding ages, the Gothic

VOL. I.   E   architecture

architecture alone prevailed, and afterwards the Grecian Tafte revived in all its vigour, and engroffed the public admiration. In eloquence and poetry, the Afiatics at no time relifhed any thing but what was full of ornament, and fplendid in a degree that we would denominate gawdy; whilft the Greeks admired only chafte and fimple beauties, and defpifed the Afiatic oftentation. In our own country, how many writings that were greatly extolled two or three centuries ago, are now fallen into entire difrepute and oblivion? Without going back to remote inftances, how very different is the tafte of poetry which prevails in Great Britain now, from what prevailed there no longer ago than the reign of king Charles II. which the authors too of that time deemed an Auguftan age: when nothing was in vogue but an affected brilliancy of wit; when the fimple majefty of Milton was overlooked, and Paradife Loft almoft entirely unknown; when Cowley's laboured and unnatural conceits were admired as the very quinteffence of genius; Waller's gay fprightlinefs was miftaken for the tender fpirit of Love poetry; and fuch writers as Suckling and Etheridge were held in efteem for dramatic compofition?

THE queftion is, what conclufion we are to form from fuch inftances as thefe? Is there any thing that can be called a ftandard of Tafte, by appealing to which we may diftinguifh between a good and a bad Tafte? Or, is there in truth no fuch diftinction; and are we to hold that, according to the proverb, there is no difputing of Taftes; but that whatever pleafes is right, for that reafon that it does pleafe? This is the queftion, and a very nice and fubtile one it is, which we are now to difcufs,

7

I BEGIN

I BEGIN by obferving, that if there be no fuch thing as any ftandard of Tafte, this confequence muft immediately follow, that all Taftes are equally good; a pofition, which though it may pafs unnoticed in flight matters, and when we fpeak of the leffer differences among the Taftes of men, yet when we apply it to the extremes, its abfurdity prefently becomes glaring. For is there any one who will ferioufly maintain that the Tafte of a Hottentot or a Laplander is as delicate and as correct as that of a Longinus or an Addifon? or, that he can be charged with no defect or incapacity who thinks a common news-writer as excellent an Hiftorian as Tacitus? As it would be held down-right extravagance to talk in this manner, we are led unavoidably to this conclufion, that there is fome foundation for the prefer-ence of one man's Tafte to that of another; or, that there is a good and a bad, right and a wrong in Tafte, as in other things.

BUT to prevent miftakes on this fubject, it is neceffary to obferve next, that the diverfity of Taftes which prevails among mankind, does not in every cafe infer corruption of Tafte, or oblige us to feek for fome ftandard in order to determine who are in the right. The Taftes of men may differ very confider-ably as to their object, and yet none of them be wrong. One man relifhes Poetry moft; another takes pleafure in nothing but Hiftory. One prefers Comedy; another, Tragedy. One admires the fimple; another, the ornamented ftyle. The young are amufed with gay and fprightly compofitions. The elderly are more entertained with thofe of a graver caft. Some nations delight in bold pictures of manners, and ftrong reprefentations

of

of paſſion. Others incline to more correct and regular elegance both in deſcription and ſentiment. Though all differ, yet all pitch upon ſome one beauty which peculiarly ſuits their turn of mind ; and therefore no one has a title to condemn the reſt. It is not in matters of Taſte, as in queſtions of mere reaſon, where there is but one concluſion that can be true, and all the reſt are erroneous. Truth, which is the object of reaſon, is one ; Beauty, which is the object of Taſte, is manifold. Taſte therefore admits of latitude and diverſity of objects, in ſufficient conſiſtency with goodneſs or juſtneſs of Taſte.

But then, to explain this matter thoroughly, I muſt obſerve farther, that this admiſſible diverſity of Taſtes can only have place where the objects of Taſte are different. Where it is with reſpect to the ſame object that men diſagree, when one condemns that as ugly, which another admires as highly beautiful ; then it is no longer diverſity, but direct oppoſition of Taſte that takes place ; and therefore one muſt be in the right, and another in the wrong, unleſs that abſurd paradox were allowed to hold, that all Taſtes are equally good and true. One man prefers Virgil to Homer. Suppoſe that I, on the other hand, admire Homer more than Virgil. I have as yet no reaſon to ſay that our Taſtes are contradictory. The other perſon is moſt ſtruck with the elegance and tenderneſs which are the characteriſtics of Virgil ; I, with the ſimplicity and fire of Homer. As long as neither of us deny that both Homer and Virgil have great beauties, our difference falls within the compaſs of that diverſity of Taſtes, which I have ſhewed to be natural and allowable. But if the other man ſhall aſſert that Homer has no beauties

ties

ties whatever; that he holds him to be a dull and fpiritlefs writer, and that he would as foon perufe any old legend of Knight-Errantry as the Iliad; then I exclaim, that my anta-gonift either is void of all Tafte, or that his Tafte is corrupted in a miferable degree; and I appeal to whatever I think the ftan-dard of Tafte, to fhew him that he is in the wrong.

WHAT that ftandard is, to which, in fuch oppofition of Taftes, we are obliged to have recourfe, remains to be traced. A ftandard properly fignifies, that which is of fuch undoubted authority as to be the teft of other things of the fame kind. Thus a ftandard weight or meafure, is that which is appointed by law to regulate all other meafures and weights. Thus the court is faid to be the ftandard of good breeding; and the fcrip-ture, of theological truth.

WHEN we fay that nature is the ftandard of Tafte, we lay down a principle very true and juft, as far as it can be applied. There is no doubt, that in all cafes where an imitation is in-tended of fome object that exifts in nature, as in reprefenting human characters or actions, conformity to nature affords a full and diftinct criterion of what is truly beautiful. Reafon hath in fuch cafes full fcope for exerting its authority; for approving or condemning; by comparing the copy with the original. But there are innumerable cafes in which this rule cannot be at all applied; and conformity to nature, is an expreffion frequently ufed, without any diftinct or deter-minate meaning. We muft therefore fearch for fomewhat that can be rendered more clear and precife, to be the ftandard of Tafte.

TASTE,

TASTE, as I before explained it, is ultimately founded on an internal fenfe of beauty, which is natural to men, and which, in its application to particular objects, is capable of being guided and enlightened by reafon. Now, were there any one perfon who poffeffed in full perfection all the powers of human nature, whofe internal fenfes were in every inftance exquifite and juft, and whofe reafon was unerring and fure, the determinations of fuch a perfon concerning beauty, would, beyond doubt, be a perfect ftandard for the Tafte of all others. Whereever their Tafte differed from his, it could be imputed only to fome imperfection in their natural powers. But as there is no fuch living ftandard, no one perfon to whom all mankind will allow fuch fubmiffion to be due, what is there of fufficient authority to be the ftandard of the various and oppofite Taftes of men? Moft certainly there is nothing but the Tafte, as far as it can be gathered, of human nature. That which men concur the moft in admiring, muft be held to be beautiful. His Tafte muft be efteemed juft and true, which coincides with the general fentiments of men. In this ftandard we muft reft. To the fenfe of mankind the ultimate appeal muft ever lie, in all works of Tafte. If any one fhould maintain that fugar was bitter and tobacco was fweet, no reafonings could avail to prove it. The Tafte of fuch a perfon would infallibly be held to be difeafed, merely becaufe it differed fo widely from the Tafte of the fpecies to which he belongs. In like manner, with regard to the objects of fentiment or internal Tafte, the common feelings of men carry the fame authority, and have a title to regulate the Tafte of every individual.

BUT

But have we then, it will be faid, no other criterion of what is beautiful, than the approbation of the majority? Muft we collect the voices of others, before we form any judgment for ourfelves, of what deferves applaufe in Eloquence or Poetry? By no means; there are principles of reafon and found judgment which can be applied to matters of Tafte, as well as to the fubjects of fcience and philofophy. He who admires or cenfures any work of genius, is always ready, if his Tafte be in any degree improved, to affign fome reafons of his decifion. He appeals to principles, and points out the grounds on which he proceeds. Tafte is a fort of compound power, in which the light of the underftanding always mingles, more or lefs, with the feelings of fentiment.

But, though reafon can carry us a certain length in judging concerning works of Tafte, it is not to be forgotten that the ultimate conclufions to which our reafonings lead, refer at laft to fenfe and perception. We may fpeculate and argue concerning propriety of conduct in a Tragedy, or an Epic Poem. Juft reafonings on the fubject will correct the caprice of unenlightened Tafte, and eftablifh principles for judging of what deferves praife. But, at the fame time, thefe reafonings appeal always, in the laft refort, to feeling. The foundation upon which they reft, is what has been found from experience to pleafe mankind moft univerfally. Upon this ground we prefer a fimple and natural, to an artificial and affected ftyle; a regular and well-connected ftory, to loofe and fcattered narratives; a cataftrophe which is tender and pathetic, to one which leaves us unmoved. It is from confulting our own imagination and heart, and from

attending

L E C T.
   II.
attending to the feelings of others, that any principles are formed which acquire authority in matters of Taste *.

WHEN we refer to the concurring sentiments of men as the ultimate test of what is to be accounted beautiful in the arts, this is to be always understood of men placed in such situations as are favourable to the proper exertions of Taste. Every one must perceive, that among rude and uncivilized nations, and during the ages of ignorance and darkness, any loose notions that are entertained concerning such subjects carry no authority. In those states of society, Taste has no materials on which to operate. It is either totally suppressed, or appears in its lowest and most imperfect form. We refer to the sentiments of mankind in polished and flourishing nations; when arts are

---

* The difference between the authors who found the standard of Taste upon the common feelings of human nature ascertained by general approbation, and those who found it upon established principles which can be ascertained by reason, is more an apparent than a real difference. Like many other literary controversies, it turns chiefly on modes of expression. For they who lay the greatest stress on sentiment and feeling, make no scruple of applying argument and reason to matters of Taste. They appeal, like other writers, to established principles, in judging of the excellencies of Eloquence or Poetry; and plainly shew, that the general approbation to which they ultimately recur, is an approbation resulting from discussion as well as from sentiment. They, on the other hand, who in order to vindicate Taste from any suspicion of being arbitrary, maintain that it is ascertainable by the standard of reason, admit nevertheless, that what pleases universally, must on that account be held to be truly beautiful; and that no rules or conclusions concerning objects of Taste, can have any just authority, if they be found to contradict the general sentiments of men. These two systems, therefore, differ in reality very little from one another. Sentiment and Reason enter into both; and by allowing to each of these powers its due place, both systems may be rendered consistent. Accordingly, it is in this light that I have endeavoured to place the subject.

cultivated

cultivated and manners refined; when works of genius are fubjected to free difcuffion, and Tafte is improved by Science and
philofophy.

EVEN among nations, at fuch a period of fociety, I admit,
that accidental caufes may occafionally warp the proper operations of Tafte ; fometimes the ftate of religion, fometimes the
form of government, may for a while pervert it ; a licentious
court may introduce a tafte for falfe ornaments, and diffolute
writings. The ufage of one admired genius may procure approbation for his faults, and even render them fafhionable.
Sometimes envy may have power to bear down, for a little,
productions of great merit; while popular humour, or party
fpirit, may, at other times, exalt to a high, though fhort-lived, reputation, what little deferved it. But though fuch cafual circumftances give the appearance of caprice to the judgments of
Tafte, that appearance is eafily corrected. In the courfe of
time, the genuine tafte of human nature never fails to difclofe
itfelf, and to gain the afcendant over any fantaftic and corrupted
modes of Tafte which may chance to have been introduced.
Thefe may have currency for a while, and miflead fuperficial
judges ; but being fubjected to examination, by degrees they
pafs away ; while that alone remains which is founded on found
reafon, and the native feelings of men.

I BY no means pretend, that there is any ftandard of Tafte,
to which, in every particular inftance, we can refort for clear
and immediate determination. Where, indeed, is fuch a ftandard to be found for deciding any of thofe great controverfies in
reafon and philofophy, which perpetually divide mankind ? In

the prefent cafe, there was plainly no occafion for any fuch
ftrict and abfolute provifion to be made.   In order to judge of
what is morally good or evil, of what man ought, or ought
not in duty to do, it was fit that the means of clear and precife
determination fhould be afforded us.   But to afcertain in every
cafe with the utmoft exactnefs what is beautiful or elegant, was
not at all neceffary to the happinefs of man.   And therefore
fome diverfity in feeling was here allowed to take place;
and room was left for difcuffion and debate, concerning the
degree of approbation to which any work of genius is entitled.

THE conclufion, which it is fufficient for us to reft upon,
is, that Tafte is far from being an arbitrary principle, which
is fubject to the fancy of every individual, and which admits
of no criterion for determining whether it be falfe or true.
Its foundation is the fame in all human minds.   It is built
upon fentiments and perceptions which belong to our nature;
and which, in general, operate with the fame uniformity as our
other intellectual principles. When thefe fentiments are perverted
by ignorance and prejudice, they are capable of being rectified
by reafon.   Their found and natural ftate is ultimately determined, by comparing them with the general Tafte of mankind.   Let men declaim as much as they pleafe, concerning
the caprice and the uncertainty of Tafte, it is found, by experience, that there are beauties, which, if they be difplayed in a
proper light, have power to command lafting and general admiration.   In every compofition, what interefts the imagination,
and touches the heart, pleafes all ages and all nations.   There is
a certain ftring, which, being properly ftruck, the human heart is
fo made as to anfwer to it.

HENCE

HENCE the univerfal teftimony which the moft improved nations of the earth have confpired, throughout a long tract of ages, to give to fome few works of genius ; fuch as the Iliad of Homer, and the Æneid of Virgil. Hence the authority which fuch works have acquired, as ftandards in fome degree of poetical compofition ; fince from them we are enabled to collect what the fenfe of mankind is, concerning thofe beauties which give them the higheft pleafure, and which therefore poetry ought to exhibit. Authority or prejudice may, in one age or country, give a temporary reputation to an indifferent poet, or a bad artift ; but when foreigners, or when pofterity examine his works, his faults are difcerned, and the genuine Tafte of human nature appears. " Opinionum commenta delet dies ; naturæ judicia " confirmat." Time overthrows the illufions of opinion, but eftablifhes the decifions of nature.

LECTURE

LECTURE III.

TASTE, Criticifm, and Genius, are words currently
employed, without diftinct ideas annexed to them. In
beginning a courfe of Lectures where fuch words muft often
occur, it is neceffary to afcertain their meaning with fome precifion. Having in the laft Lecture treated of Tafte, I proceed
to explain the nature and foundation of Criticifm. True Criticifm is the application of Tafte and of good fenfe to the feveral
fine arts. The object which it propofes is, to diftinguifh what
is beautiful and what is faulty in every performance ; from
particular inftances to afcend to general principles; and fo to
form rules or conclufions concerning the feveral kinds of beauty
in works of Genius.

THE rules of Criticifm are not formed by any induction, *à
priori*, as it is called ; that is, they are not formed by a train of
abftract

abstract reasoning, independent of facts and observations. Criticism is an art founded wholly on experience; on the observation of such beauties as have come nearest to the standard which I before established.: that is, of such beauties as have been found to please mankind most generally. For example; Aristotle's rules concerning the unity of action in dramatic and epic composition, were not rules first discovered by logical reasoning, and then applied to poetry; but they were drawn from the practice of Homer and Sophocles: they were founded upon observing the superior pleasure which we receive from the relation of an action which is one and entire, beyond what we receive from the relation of scattered and unconnected facts. Such observations taking their rise at first from feeling and experience, were found on examination to be so consonant to reason, and to the principles of human nature, as to pass into established rules, and to be conveniently applied for judging of the excellency of any performance. This is the most natural account of the origin of Criticism.

A MASTERLY genius, it is true, will of himself, untaught, compose in such a manner as shall be agreeable to the most material rules of Criticism; for as these rules are founded in nature, nature will often suggest them in practice. Homer, it is more than probable, was acquainted with no systems of the art of poetry. Guided by genius alone, he composed in verse a regular story, which all posterity has admired. But this is no argument against the usefulness of Criticism as an art. For as no human genius is perfect, there is no writer but may receive assistance from critical observations upon the beauties and faults of those who have gone before him. No observations

or

or rules can indeed fupply the defect of genius, or infpire it where it is wanting. But they may often direct it into its proper channel; they may correct its extravagancies, and point out to it the moft juft and proper imitation of nature. Critical rules are defigned chiefly to fhew the faults that ought to be avoided. To nature we muft be indebted for the production of eminent beauties.

FROM what has been faid, we are enabled to form a judgment concerning thofe complaints which it has long been fafhionable for petty authors to make againft Critics and Criticifm. Critics have been reprefented as the great abridgers of the native liberty of genius; as the impofers of unnatural fhackles and bonds upon writers, from whofe cruel perfecution they muft fly to the Public, and implore its protection. Such fupplicatory prefaces are not calculated to give very favourable ideas of the genius of the author. For every good writer will be pleafed to have his work examined by the principles of found underftanding, and true Tafte. The declamations againft Criticifm commonly proceed upon this fuppofition, that Critics are fuch as judge by rule, not by feeling; which is fo far from being true, that they who judge after this manner are pedants, not Critics. For all the rules of genuine Criticifm I have fhewn to be ultimately founded on feeling; and Tafte and Feeling are neceffary to guide us in the application of thefe rules to every particular inftance. As there is nothing in which all forts of perfons more readily affect to be judges than in works of Tafte, there is no doubt that the number of incompetent Critics will always be great. But this affords no more foundation for a general invective againft Criticifm, than the number

of

of bad philofophers or reafoners affords againft reafon and philofophy.

An objection more plaufible may be formed againft Criticifm, from the applaufe that fome performances have received from the Public, which, when accurately confidered, are found to contradict the rules eftablifhed by Criticifm. Now, according to the principles laid down in the laft Lecture, the Public is the fupreme judge to whom the laft appeal muft be made in every work of Tafte; as the ftandard of Tafte is founded on the fentiments that are natural and common to all men. But with refpect to this we are to obferve, that the fenfe of the Public is often too haftily judged of. The genuine public Tafte does not always appear in the firft applaufe given upon the publication of any new work. There are both a great vulgar and a fmall, apt to be catched and dazzled by very fuperficial beauties, the admiration of which in a little time paffes away: and fometimes a writer may acquire great temporary reputation merely by his compliance with the paffions or prejudices, with the party-fpirit or fuperftitious notions, that may chance to rule for a time almoft a whole nation. In fuch cafes, though the Public may feem to praife, true Criticifm may with reafon condemn; and it will in progrefs of time gain the afcendant: for the judgment of true Criticifm, and the voice of the Public, when once become unprejudiced and difpaffionate, will ever coincide at laft.

Instances, I admit, there are, of fome works that contain grofs tranfgreffions of the laws of Criticifm, acquiring, neverthelefs, a general, and even a lafting admiration. Such are the

the plays of Shakefpeare, which, confidered as dramatic poems, are irregular in the higheft degree. But then we are to remark, that they have gained the public admiration, not by their being irregular, not by their tranfgreffions of the rules of art, but in fpite of fuch tranfgreffions. They poffefs other beauties which are conformable to juft rules; and the force of thefe beauties has been fo great as to overpower all cenfure, and to give the Public a degree of fatisfaction fuperior to the difguft arifing from their blemifhes. Shakefpeare pleafes, not by his bringing the tranfactions of many years into one play; not by his grotefque mixtures of Tragedy and Comedy in one piece, nor by the ftrained thoughts, and affected witticifms, which he fometimes employs. Thefe we confider as blemifhes, and impute them to the grofsnefs of the age in which he lived. But he pleafes by his animated and mafterly reprefentations of characters, by the livelinefs of his defcriptions, the force of his fentiments, and his poffeffing, beyond all writers, the natural language of paffion: Beauties which true Criticifm no lefs teaches us to place in the higheft rank, than nature teaches us to feel.——This much it may fuffice to have faid concerning the origin, office, and importance of Criticifm.

I proceed next to explain the meaning of another term, which there will be frequent occafion to employ in thefe Lectures; that is, *Genius*.

Taste and Genius are two words frequently joined together; and therefore, by inaccurate thinkers, confounded. They fignify however two quite different things. The difference between them can be clearly pointed out; and it is of importance

to.

to remember it. Tafte confifts in the power of judging: Genius, in the power of executing. One may have a confiderable degree of Tafte in Poetry, Eloquence, or any of the fine arts, who has little or hardly any Genius for compofition or execution in any of thefe arts: But Genius cannot be found without including Tafte alfo. Genius, therefore, deferves to be confidered as a higher power of the mind than Tafte. Genius always imports fomething inventive or creative; which does not reft in mere fenfibility to beauty where it is perceived, but which can, moreover, produce new beauties, and exhibit them in fuch a manner as ftrongly to imprefs the minds of others. Refined Tafte forms a good critic; but Genius is farther neceffary to form the poet, or the orator.

IT is proper alfo to obferve, that Genius is a word, which, in common acceptation, extends much farther than to the objects of Tafte. It is ufed to fignify that talent or aptitude which we receive from nature, for excelling in any one thing whatever. Thus we fpeak of a Genius for mathematics, as well as a Genius for poetry; of a Genius for war, for politics, or for any mechanical employment.

THIS talent or aptitude for excelling in fome one particular, is, I have faid, what we receive from nature. By art and ftudy, no doubt, it may be greatly improved; but by them alone it cannot be acquired. As Genius is a higher faculty than Tafte, it is ever, according to the ufual frugality of nature, more limited in the fphere of its operations. It is not uncommon to meet with perfons who have an excellent Tafte in feveral of the polite arts, fuch as mufic, poetry, painting, and eloquence, altogether: But, to find one who is an excellent performer in all thefe arts, is much more rare; or rather, indeed, fuch an one is not to be looked for. A fort of Univerfal Genius, or one who is equally and indifferently turned towards feveral different profeffions and arts, is not likely to excel in any. Although there may be fome few exceptions, yet in general it holds, that when the bent of the mind is wholly directed towards fome one object, exclufive, in a manner, of others, there is the faireft profpect of eminence in that, whatever it be. The rays muft converge to a point, in order to glow intenfely. This remark I here chufe to make, on account of its great importance to young people; in leading them to examine with care, and to purfue with ardour, the current and pointing of nature towards thofe exertions of Genius in which they are moft likely to excel.

A GENIUS for any of the fine arts, as I before obferved, always fuppofes Tafte; and it is clear, that the improvement of Tafte will ferve both to forward and to correct the operations of Genius. In proportion as the Tafte of a poet, or orator, becomes more refined with refpect to the beauties of compofition, it will certainly affift him to produce the more finifhed beauties in his work. Genius, however, in a Poet or Orator, may fometimes exift in a higher degree than Tafte; that is, Genius may be bold and ftrong, when Tafte is neither very delicate, nor very correct. This is often the cafe in the infancy of arts; a period, when Genius frequently exerts itfelf with great vigour, and executes with much warmth; while Tafte, which requires experience, and improves by flower degrees, hath not yet attained its full growth. Homer and Shakefpear

are

are proofs of what I now affert; in whofe admirable writings are found inftances of rudenefs and indelicacy, which the more refined Tafte of later writers, who had far inferior Genius to them, would have taught them to avoid. As all human perfection is limited, this may very probably be the law of our nature, that it is not given to one man to execute with vigour and fire, and, at the fame time, to attend to all the leffer and more refined graces that belong to the exact perfection of his work: While, on the other hand, a thorough Tafte for thofe inferior graces, is, for the moft part, accompanied with a diminution of fublimity and force.

HAVING thus explained the nature of Tafte, the nature and importance of Criticifm, and the diftinction between Tafte and Genius; I am now to enter on confidering the fources of the Pleafures of Tafte. Here opens a very extenfive field; no lefs than all the pleafures of the imagination, as they are commonly called, whether afforded us by natural objects, or by the imitations and defcriptions of them. But it is not neceffary to the purpofe of my Lectures, that all thefe fhould be examined fully; the pleafure which we receive from difcourfe, or writing, being the main object of them. All that I purpofe is, to give fome openings into the Pleafures of Tafte in general; and to infift, more particularly, upon Sublimity and Beauty.

WE are far from having yet attained to any fyftem concerning this fubject. Mr. Addifon was the firft who attempted a regular enquiry, in his Effay on the Pleafures of the Imagina-

G 2

tion,

tion, publifhed in the fixth volume of the Spectator. He has reduced thefe Pleafures under three heads ; Beauty, Grandeur, and Novelty. His fpeculations on this fubject, if not exceedingly profound, are, however, very beautiful and entertaining ; and he has the merit of having opened a tract, which was before unbeaten. The advances made fince his time in this curious part of philofophical Criticifm, are not very confiderable ;, though fome ingenious writers have purfued the fubject. This is owing, doubtlefs, to that thinnefs and fubtility which are found to be properties of all the feelings of Tafte. They are engaging objects ; but when we would lay firm hold of them, and fubject them to a regular difcuffion, they are always ready to elude our grafp. It is difficult to make a full enumeration of the feveral objects that give pleafure to Tafte ; it is more difficult to define all thofe which have been difcovered, and to reduce them under proper claffes ; and, when we would go farther, and inveftigate the efficient caufes of the pleafure which we receive from fuch objects, here, above all, we find ourfelves at a lofs. For inftance ; we all learn by experience, that certain figures of bodies appear to us more beautiful than others. On enquiring farther, we find that the regularity of fome figures, and the graceful variety of others, are the foundation of the beauty which we difcern in them ; but when we attempt to go a ftep beyond this, and enquire what is the caufe of regularity and variety producing in our minds the fenfation of Beauty, any reafon we can affign is extremely imperfect. Thofe firft principles of internal fenfation, nature feems to have covered with an impenetrable veil.

I⊤

IT is fome comfort, however, that although the efficient caufe be obfcure, the final caufe of thofe fenfations lies in many cafes more open : And, in entering on this fubject, we cannot avoid taking notice of the ftrong impreffion which the powers of Tafte and Imagination are calculated to give us of the benignity of our Creator. By endowing us with fuch powers, he hath widely enlarged the fphere of the pleafures of human life ; and thofe, too, of a kind the moft pure and innocent. The neceffary purpofes of life might have been abundantly anfwered, though our fenfes of feeing and hearing had only ferved to diftinguifh external objects, without conveying to us any of thofe refined and delicate fenfations of Beauty and Grandeur, with which we are now fo much delighted. This additional embellifhment and glory, which, for promoting our entertainment, the Author of nature hath poured forth upon his works, is one ftriking teftimony, among many others, of benevolence and goodnefs. This thought, which Mr. Addifon firft ftarted, Dr. Akenfide, in his Poem on the Pleafures of the Imagination, has happily purfued.

> ————— Not content
> With every food of life to nourifh man,
> By kind illufions of the wondering fenfe,
> Thou mak'ft all nature, Beauty to his eye,
> Or Mufic to his ear.——

I SHALL begin with confidering the Pleafure which arifes from Sublimity or Grandeur, of which I propofe to treat at fome length ; both, as this has a character more precife and diftinctly marked, than any other, of the Pleafures of the Imagination,

tion, and as it coincides more directly with our main subject. For the greater distinctness I shall, first, treat of the Grandeur or Sublimity of external objects themselves, which will employ the rest of this Lecture ; and, afterwards, of the description of such objects, or, of what is called the Sublime in Writing, which shall be the subject of a following Lecture.   I distinguish these two things from one another, the Grandeur of the objects themselves when they are presented to the eye, and the description of that Grandeur in discourse or writing ; though most Critics, inaccurately I think, blend them together ; and I consider Grandeur and Sublimity as terms synonymous, or nearly so. If there be any distinction between them, it arises from Sublimity's expressing Grandeur in its highest degree *.

It is not easy to describe, in words, the precise impression which great and sublime objects make upon us, when we behold them ; but every one has a conception of it. It consists in a kind of admiration and expansion of the mind ; it raises the mind much above its ordinary state ; and fills it with a degree of wonder and astonishment, which it cannot well express.   The emotion is certainly delightful ; but it is altogether of the serious kind : a degree of awfulness and solemnity, even approaching to severity, commonly attends it when at its height ; very distinguishable from the more gay and brisk emotion raised by beautiful objects.

The simplest form of external Grandeur appears in the vast and boundless prospects presented to us by nature ; such as

* See a Philosophical Inquiry into the Origin of our Ideas of the Sublime and Beautiful. Dr. Gerard on Taste, Section II. Elements of Criticism, Chap. IV.

wide

wide extended plains, to which the eye can fee no limits ; the firmament of Heaven ; or the boundlefs expanfe of the Ocean. All vaftnefs produces the impreffion of Sublimity. It is to be remarked, however, that fpace, extended in length, makes not fo ftrong an impreffion as height or depth. Though a boundlefs plain be a grand object, yet a high mountain, to which we look up, or an awful precipice or tower whence we look down on the objects which lie below, is ftill more fo. The exceffive Grandeur of the firmament arifes from its height, joined to its boundlefs extent ; and that of the ocean, not from its extent alone, but from the perpetual motion and irrefiftible force of that mafs of waters. Wherever fpace is concerned, it is clear, that amplitude or greatnefs of extent, in one dimenfion or other, is neceffary to Grandeur. Remove all bounds from any object, and you prefently render it fublime. Hence infinite fpace, endlefs numbers, and eternal duration, fill the mind with great ideas.

FROM this fome have imagined, that vaftnefs, or amplitude of extent, is the foundation of all Sublimity. But I cannot be of this opinion, becaufe many objects appear fublime which have no relation to fpace at all. Such, for inftance, is great loudnefs of found. The burft of thunder or of cannon, the roaring of winds, the fhouting of multitudes, the found of vaft cataracts of water, are all inconteftibly grand objects. " I heard the " voice of a great multitude, as the found of many waters, and " of mighty thunderings, faying Allelujah." In general we may obferve, that great power and force exerted, always raife fublime ideas : and perhaps the moft copious fource of thefe is derived from this quarter. Hence the grandeur of earthquakes

and

and burning mountains; of great conflagrations; of the ftormy ocean, and overflowing waters; of tempefts of wind; of thunder and lightning; and of all the uncommon violence of the elements. Nothing is more fublime than mighty power and ftrength. A ftream that runs within its banks, is a beautiful object; but when it rufhes down with the impetuofity and noife of a torrent, it prefently becomes a fublime one. From lions, and other animals of ftrength, are drawn fublime comparifons in poets. A race horfe is looked upon with pleafure; but it is the war-horfe, " whofe neck is clothed with thunder," that carries grandeur in its idea. The engagement of two great armies, as it is the higheft exertion of human might, combines a variety of fources of the Sublime; and has accordingly been always confidered as one of the moft ftriking and magnificent fpectacles that can be either prefented to the eye, or exhibited to the imagination in defcription.

For the farther illuftration of this fubject, it is proper to remark, that all ideas of the folemn and awful kind, and even bordering on the terrible, tend greatly to affift the Sublime; fuch as darknefs, folitude, and filence. What are the fcenes of nature that elevate the mind in the higheft degree, and produce the fublime fenfation? Not the gay landfcape, the flowery field, or the flourifhing city; but the hoary mountain, and the folitary lake; the aged foreft, and the torrent falling over the rock. Hence too, night-fcenes are commonly the moft fublime. The firmament when filled with ftars, fcattered in fuch vaft numbers, and with fuch magnificent profufion, ftrikes the imagination with a more awful grandeur, than when we view it enlightened by all the fplendour of the Sun. The deep found

I

of

of a great bell, or the ſtriking of a great clock, are at any time grand; but, when heard amid the ſilence and ſtillneſs of the night, they become doubly ſo. Darkneſs is very commonly applied for adding ſublimity to all our ideas of the Deity. " He maketh darkneſs his pavilion; he dwelleth in the thick " cloud." So Milton

> ——————How oft, amidſt
> Thick clouds and dark, does Heaven's all-ruling Sire
> Chuſe to reſide, his glory unobſcured,
> And, with the Majeſty of darkneſs, round
> Circles his throne——   Book II. 263.

Obſerve, with how much art Virgil has introduced all thoſe ideas of ſilence, vacuity, and darkneſs, when he is going to intro- duce his Hero to the infernal regions, and to diſcloſe the ſecrets of the great deep.

> Dii quibus imperium eſt animarum, umbræque ſilentes,
> Et Chaos, et Phlegethon, loca noĉte ſilentia latè,
> Sit mihi fas audita loqui; ſit numine veſtro
> Pandere res altâ terrâ, & caligine merſas.
> Ibant obſcuri, ſola ſub noĉte, per umbram,
> Perque domos Ditis vacuos, et inania regna;
> Quale per incertam lunam, ſub luce maligna
> Eſt iter in ſylvis—— *.
>   Theſe

---

* Ye ſubterranean Gods, whoſe awful ſway
The gliding ghoſts and ſilent ſhades obey;
O Chaos, hear! and Phlegethon profound!
Whoſe ſolemn empire ſtretches wide around!
Give me, ye great tremendous powers! to tell
Of ſcenes and wonders in the depths of Hell;

Give

Thefe paffages I quote at prefent, not fo much as inftances of Sublime Writing, though in themfelves they truly are fo, as to fhew, by the effect of them, that the objects which they prefent to us, belong to the clafs of fublime ones.

OBSCURITY, we are farther to remark, is not unfavourable to the Sublime. Though it render the object indiftinct, the impreffion, however, may be great; for, as an ingenious Author has well obferved, it is one thing to make an idea clear, and another to make it affecting to the imagination; and the imagination may be ftrongly affected, and, in fact, often is fo, by objects of which we have no clear conception. Thus we fee, that almoft all the defcriptions given us of the appearances of fupernatural Beings, carry fome Sublimity, though the conceptions which they afford us be confufed and indiftinct. Their Sublimity arifes from the ideas, which they always convey, of fuperior power and might, joined with an awful obfcurity. We may fee this fully exemplified in the following noble paffage of the book of Job. " In thoughts from the " vifions of the night, when deep fleep falleth upon men, " fear came upon me, and trembling, which made all my bones " to fhake. Then a fpirit paffed before my face; the hair of " my flefh ftood up: it ftood ftill; but I could not difcern

---

Give me your mighty fecrets to difplay,
From thofe black realms of darknefs to the day.

　　　　　　　　　　　　　　　　　　　　　PITT.

Obfcure they went; through dreary fhades, that led
Along the wafte dominions of the dead ;
As wander travellers in woods by night,
By the moon's doubtful and malignant light.

　　　　　　　　　　　　　　　　　　　　　DRYDEN.

" the

" the form thereof; an image was before mine eyes; there was
" filence; and I heard a voice——Shall mortal man be more
" juft than God*?" (Job, iv. 15.) No ideas, it is plain, as
are fo fublime as thofe taken from the Supreme Being; the moft
unknown, but the greateft of all objects; the infinity of whofe
nature, and the eternity of whofe duration, joined with the
omnipotence of his power, though they furpafs our conceptions,
yet exalt them to the higheft. In general, all objects that are
greatly raifed above us, or far removed from us, either in
fpace or in time, are apt to ftrike us as great. Our viewing
them, as through the mift of diftance or antiquity, is favourable to the impreffions of their Sublimity.

As obfcurity, fo diforder too, is very compatible with grandeur; nay, frequently heightens it. Few things that are
ftrictly regular, and methodical, appear fublime. We fee the
limits on every fide; we feel ourfelves confined; there is no
room for the mind's exerting any great effort. Exact proportion of parts, though it enters often into the beautiful, is much
difregarded in the Sublime. A great mafs of rocks, thrown

* The picture which Lucretius has drawn of the dominion of fuperftition
over mankind, reprefenting it as a portentous fpectre fhowing its head from the
clouds, and difmaying the whole human race with its countenance, together
with the magnanimity of Epicurus in raifing himfelf up againft it, carries all
the grandeur of a fublime, obfcure, and awful image.

> Humana ante oculos fœde cum vita jaceret
> In terris, oppreffa gravi fub religione,
> Quæ caput a cœli regionibus oftendebat,
> Horribili fuper afpectu mortalibus inftans,
> Primum Graius homo mortales tollere contra
> Eft oculos aufus.——   Lib. I.

H 2

together

together by the hand of nature with wildnefs and confufion, ftrike the mind with more grandeur, than if they had been adjufted, to each other with the moft accurate fymmetry.

IN the feeble attempts, which human art can make towards producing grand objects (feeble, I mean, in comparifon with the powers of nature), greatnefs of dimenfions always conftitutes a principal part. No pile of building can convey any idea of Sublimity, unlefs it be ample and lofty. There is, too, in architecture, what is called Greatnefs of manner; which feems chiefly to arife, from prefenting the object to us in one full point of view; fo that it fhall make its impreffion whole, entire, and undivided, upon the mind. A Gothic cathedral raifes ideas of grandeur in our minds, by its fize, its height, its awful obfcurity, its ftrength, its antiquity, and its durability.

THERE ftill remains to be mentioned one clafs of Sublime objects; what may be called the moral, or fentimental Sublime; arifing from certain exertions of the human mind; from certain affections, and actions, of our fellow-creatures. Thefe will be found to be all, or chiefly, of that clafs, which comes under the name of Magnanimity or Heroifm; and they produce an effect extremely fimilar to what is produced by the view of grand objects in nature; filling the mind with admiration, and elevating it above itfelf. A noted inftance of this, quoted by all the French Critics, is the celebrated *Qu'il, Mourut* of Corneille, in the Tragedy of Horace. In the famous combat betwixt the Horatii and the Curiatii, the old Horatius, being informed, that two of his fons are flain, and that the third had betaken himfelf to flight, at firft will not believe the report;

but

but being thoroughly affured of the fact, is fired with all the fentiments of high honour and indignation at this fuppofed unworthy behaviour of his furviving fon. He is reminded, that his fon ftood alone againft three, and afked what he would have had him to have done ?—" To have died,"—he anfwers. In the fame manner Porus, taken prifoner by Alexander, after a gallant defence, and afked in what manner he would be treated ? anfwering, " Like a king ;" and Cæfar chiding the pilot who was afraid to fet out with him in a ftorm, " Quid times? " Cæfarem vehis ;" are good inftances of this fentimental fublime. Wherever, in fome critical and high fituation, we behold a man uncommonly intrepid, and refting upon himfelf ; fuperior to paffion and to fear ; animated by fome great principle to the contempt of popular opinion, of felfifh intereft, of dangers, or of death ; there we are ftruck with a fenfe of the Sublime*.

* The Sublime, in natural and in moral objects, is brought before us in one view, and compared together, in the following beautiful paffage of Akenfide's Pleafures of the Imagination :

Look then abroad through nature ; to the range
Of planets, funs, and adamantine fpheres,
Wheeling, unfhaken, thro' the void immenfe ;
And fpeak, O man ! does this capacious fcene,
With half that kindling majefty, dilate
Thy ftrong conception, as when Brutus rofe,
Refulgent, from the ftroke of Cæfar's fate,
Amid the crowd of patriots ; and his arm
Aloft extending, like eternal Jove,
When guilt brings down the thunder, call'd aloud
On Tully's name, and fhook his crimfon fteel,
And bade the father of his country hail !
For lo ! the tyrant proftrate on the duft ;
And Rome again is free.——— BOOK I.

HIGH

HIGH virtue is the most natural and fertile source of this moral Sublimity. However, on some occasions, where Virtue either has no place, or is but imperfectly displayed, yet if extraordinary vigour and force of mind be discovered, we are not insensible to a degree of grandeur in the character; and from the splendid conqueror, or the daring conspirator, whom we are far from approving, we cannot with-hold our admiration *.

I HAVE now enumerated a variety of instances, both in inanimate objects and in human life, wherein the Sublime appears. In all these instances, the emotion raised in us is of the same kind, although the objects that produce the emotion be of widely different kinds. A question next arises, whether we are able to discover some one fundamental quality in which all these different objects agree, and which is the cause of

---

* Silius Italicus has studied to give an august idea of Hannibal, by representing him as surrounded with all his victories, in the place of guards. One who had formed a design of assassinating him in the midst of a feast, is thus addressed :

Fallit te, mensas inter quod credis inermem ;
Tot bellis quæsita viro, tot cœdibus, armat
Majestas æterna ducem. Si admoveris ora
Cannas, & Trebiam ante oculos, Trasymenaque busta
Et Pauli stare ingentem miraberis umbram.

A thought somewhat of the same nature occurs in a French author, " Il se " cache ; mais sa reputation le decouvre : Il marche sans suite & sans equipage ; " mais chacun, dans son esprit, le met sur un char de triomphe. On compte, en " le voiant, les ennemis qu'il a vaincus, non pas les serviteurs qui le suivent. " Tout seul qu'il est, on se figure, autour de lui, ses vertus, & ses victoires que " l'accompagnent. Moins il est superbe, plus il devient venerable." Oraison funebre de M. de Turenne, par M. Flechier.—Both these passages are splendid, rather than sublime. In the first, there is a want of justness in the thought ; in the second, of simplicity in the expression.

their

their producing an emotion of the fame nature in our minds? Various hypothefes have been formed concerning this; but, as far as appears to me, hitherto unfatisfactory. Some have imagined that amplitude, or great extent, joined with fimplicity, is either immediately, or remotely, the fundamental quality of whatever is fublime; but we have feen that amplitude is confined to one fpecies of Sublime Objects; and cannot, without violent ftraining, be applied to them all. The Author of " a Phi- " lofophical Enquiry into the Origin of our Ideas of the Sublime " and Beautiful," to whom we are indebted for feveral ingenious and original thoughts upon this fubject, propofes a formal theory upon this foundation, That terror is the fource of the Sublime, and that no objects have this character, but fuch as produce impreffions of pain and danger. It is indeed true, that many terrible objects are highly fublime; and that grandeur does not refufe an alliance with the idea of danger. But though this is very properly illuftrated by the Author (many of whofe fentiments on that head I have adopted), yet he feems to ftretch his theory too far, when he reprefents the Sublime as confifting wholly in modes of danger, or of pain. For the proper fenfation of Sublimity, appears to be very diftinguifhable from the fenfation of either of thofe; and, on feveral occafions, to be entirely feparated from them. In many grand objects, there is no coincidence with terror at all; as in the magnificent profpect of wide extended plains, and of the ftarry firmament; or in the moral difpofitions and fentiments, which we view with high admiration ; and in many painful and terrible objects alfo, it is clear, there is no fort of grandeur. The amputation of a limb, or the bite of a fnake, are exceedingly terrible ; but are deftitute of all claim whatever to Sublimity. I am inclined to

hink,

think, that mighty force or power, whether accompanied with terror or not, whether employed in protecting, or in alarming us, has a better title, than any thing that has yet been mentioned, to be the fundamental quality of the Sublime; as, after the review which we have taken, there does not occur to me any Sublime Object, into the idea of which, power, strength, and force, either enter not directly, or are not, at least, intimately associated with the idea, by leading our thoughts to some astonishing power, as concerned in the production of the object. However, I do not insist upon this as sufficient to found a general theory: It is enough, now, to have given this view of the nature and different kinds of Sublime Objects; by which I hope to have laid a proper foundation for discussing, with greater accuracy, the Sublime in Writing and Composition.

LECTURE

LECTURE IV.

THE SUBLIME IN WRITING.

HAVING treated of Grandeur or Sublimity in external objects, the way seems now to be cleared, for treating, with more advantage, of the description of such objects; or, of what is called the Sublime in Writing. Though it may appear early to enter on the consideration of this subject; yet, as the Sublime is a species of Writing which depends less than any other on the artificial embellishments of rhetoric, it may be examined with as much propriety here, as in any subsequent part of the Lectures.

MANY critical terms have unfortunately been employed, in a sense too loose and vague; none more so, than that of the Sublime. Every one is acquainted with the character of Cæsar's Commentaries, and of the style in which they are written; a style remarkably pure, simple, and elegant; but the most remote from the Sublime, of any of the classical authors. Yet this author has a German critic, Johannes Gulielmus Bergerus, who wrote no longer ago than the year 1720, pitched upon as the perfect model of the Sublime, and has compofed a quarto volume, entitled, *De naturali pulchritudine Orationis;* the exprefs intention of which, is to fhew, that Cæfar's Commentaries contain the moft complete exemplification of all Longinus's rules relating to Sublime Writing. This I mention as a ftrong proof of the confufed ideas which have prevailed, concerning this fubject. The true fenfe of Sublime Writing, undoubtedly, is fuch a defcription of objects, or exhibition of fentiments, which are in themfelves of a Sublime nature, as fhall give us ftrong impreffions of them. But there is another very indefinite, and therefore very improper, fenfe, which has been too often put upon it; when it is applied to fignify any remarkable and diftinguifhing excellency of compofition; whether it raife in us the ideas of grandeur, or thofe of gentlenefs, elegance, or any other fort of beauty. In this fenfe, Cæfar's Commentaries may, indeed, be termed Sublime, and fo may many Sonnets, Paftorals, and Love Elegies, as well as Homer's Iliad. But this evidently confounds the ufe of words; and marks no one fpecies, or character, of compofition whatever.

I AM forry to be obliged to obferve, that the Sublime is too often ufed in this laft and improper fenfe, by the celebrated critic Longinus, in his treatife on this fubject. He fets out, indeed, with defcribing it in its juft and proper meaning; as fomething that elevates the mind above itfelf, and fills it with high conceptions, and a noble pride. But from this view of it he frequently departs; and fubftitutes in the place of it, whatever, in any ftrain of compofition, pleafes highly. Thus, many of

the

the paffages which he produces as inftances of the Sublime, are merely elegant, without having the moft diftant relation to proper Sublimity; witnefs Sappho's famous Ode, on which he defcants at confiderable length. He points out five fources of the Sublime. The firft is, Boldnefs or Grandeur in the Thoughts; the fecond is, the Pathetic; the third, the proper application of Figures; the fourth, the ufe of Tropes and beautiful Expreffions; the fifth, Mufical Structure and Arrangement of Words. This is the plan of one who was writing a treatife of rhetoric, or of the beauties of Writing in general; not of the Sublime in particular. For of thefe five heads, only the two firft have any peculiar relation to the Sublime; Boldnefs and Grandeur in the Thoughts, and, in fome inftances, the Pathetic, or ftrong exertions of Paffion: The other three, Tropes, Figures, and Mufical Arrangement, have no more relation to the Sublime, than to other kinds of good Writing; perhaps lefs to the Sublime than to any other fpecies whatever; becaufe it requires lefs the affiftance of ornament. From this it appears, that clear and precife ideas on this head are not to be expected from that writer. I would not, however, be underftood, as if I meant, by this cenfure, to reprefent his treatife as of fmall value. I know no critic, antient or modern, that difcovers a more lively relifh of the beauties of fine writing, than Longinus; and he has alfo the merit of being himfelf an excellent, and, in feveral paffages, a truly Sublime, writer. But, as his work has been generally confidered as a ftandard on this fubject, it was incumbent on me to give my opinion concerning the benefit to be derived from it. It deferves to be confulted, not fo much for diftinct inftruction concerning the Sub-

lime,

LECT.
IV.

lime, as for excellent general ideas concerning beauty in writing.

I RETURN now to the proper and natural idea of the Sublime in compofition. The foundation of it muft always be laid in the nature of the object defcribed. Unlefs it be fuch an object as, if prefented to our eyes, if exhibited to us in reality, would raife ideas of that elevating, that awful, and magnificent kind, which we call Sublime; the defcription, however finely drawn, is not entitled to come under this clafs. This excludes all objects that are merely beautiful, gay, or elegant. In the next place, the object muft not only, in itfelf, be Sublime, but it muft be fet before us in fuch a light as is moft proper to give us a clear and full impreffion of it; it muft be defcribed with ftrength, with concifenefs, and fimplicity. This depends, principally, upon the lively impreffion which the poet, or orator has of the object which he exhibits; and upon his being deeply affected, and warmed, by the Sublime idea which he would convey. If his own feeling be languid, he can never infpire us with any ftrong emotion. Inftances, which are extremely neceffary on this fubject, will clearly fhow the importance of all thofe requifites which I have juft now mentioned.

IT is, generally fpeaking, among the moft antient authors, that we are to look for the moft ftriking inftances of the Sublime. I am inclined to think, that the early ages of the world, and the rude unimproved ftate of fociety, are peculiarly favourable to the ftrong emotions of Sublimity. The genius of men is then

much

much turned to admiration and aftonifhment. Meeting with many objects, to them new and ftrange, their imagination is kept glowing, and their paffions are often raifed to the utmoft. They think, and exprefs themfelves boldly, and without reftraint. In the progrefs of fociety, the genius and manners of men undergo a change more favourable to accuracy, than to ftrength or Sublimity.

Of all writings, antient or modern, the Sacred Scriptures afford us the higheft inftances of the Sublime. The defcriptions of the Deity, in them, are wonderfully noble; both from the grandeur of the object, and the manner of reprefenting it. What an affemblage, for inftance, of awful and fublime ideas is prefented to us, in that paffage of the XVIIIth Pfalm, where an appearance of the Almighty is defcribed? " In my diftrefs " I called upon the Lord; he heard my voice out of his temple, " and my cry came before him. Then, the earth fhook and " trembled; the foundations alfo of the hills were moved; be- " caufe he was wroth. He bowed the heavens, and came " down, and darknefs was under his feet; and he did ride " upon a Cherub, and did fly; yea, he did fly upon the wings " of the wind. He made darknefs his fecret place; his pavilion " round about him were dark waters, and thick clouds of the " fky." Here, agreeably to the principles eftablifhed in the laft Lecture, we fee, with what propriety and fuccefs the circumftances of darknefs and terror are applied for heightening the Sublime. So, alfo, the prophet Habakkuk, in a fimilar paffage: " He ftood, and meafured the earth; he beheld, and " drove afunder the nations. The everlafting mountains were " fcattered; the perpetual hills did bow; his ways are everlaft-
" ing.

" ing. The mountains faw thee; and they trembled. The
" overflowing of the water paffed by. The deep uttered his
" voice, and lifted up his hands on high."

THE noted inftance, given by Longinus, from Mofes, " God
" faid, let there be light; and there was light," is not liable to
the cenfure which I paffed on fome of his inftances, of being
foreign to the fubject. It belongs to the true Sublime, and the
Sublimity of it arifes from the ftrong conception it gives, of an
exertion of power, producing its effect with the utmoft fpeed
and facility. A thought of the fame kind is magnificently
amplified in the following paffage of Ifaiah (chap. xxiv. 24.
27, 28.): " Thus faith the Lord, thy Redeemer, and he that
" formed thee from the womb: I am the Lord that maketh all
" things, that.ftretcheth forth the heavens alone, that fpreadeth
" abroad the earth by myfelf——that faith to the deep, Be
" dry, and I will dry up thy rivers; that faith of Cyrus, He
" is my fhepherd, and fhall perform all my pleafure; even, fay-
" ing to Jerufalem, Thou fhalt be built; and to the Temple,
" Thy foundation fhall be laid." There is a paffage in the
Pfalms, which deferves to be mentioned under this head;
" God," fays the Pfalmift, " ftilleth the noife of the feas, the
" noife of their waves, and the tumults of the people." The
joining together two fuch grand objects, as the ragings of the
waters, and the tumults of the people, between which there is
fo much refemblance as to form a very natural affociation
in the fancy, and the reprefenting them both as fubject, at
one 'moment, to the command of God, produces a noble
effect.

HOMER

HOMER is a poet, who, in all ages, and by all critics, has been greatly admired for Sublimity; and he owes much of his grandeur to that native and unaffected simplicity which characterises his manner. His descriptions of hosts engaging; the animation, the fire, and rapidity, which he throws into his battles, present to every reader of the Iliad, frequent instances of Sublime Writing. His introduction of the Gods, tends often to heighten, in a high degree, the majesty of his warlike scenes. Hence Longinus bestows such high and just commendations on that passage, in the XVth book of the Iliad, where Neptune, when preparing to issue forth into the engagement, is described as shaking the mountains with his steps, and driving his chariot along the ocean. Minerva, arming herself for fight in the Vth book; and Apollo, in the XVth, leading on the Trojans, and flashing terror with his Ægis on the face of the Greeks, are similar instances of great Sublimity added to the description of battles, by the appearances of those celestial beings. In the XXth book, where all the Gods take part in the engagement, according as they severally favour either the Grecians, or the Trojans, the poet seems to put forth one of his highest efforts, and the description rises into the most awful magnificence. All nature is represented as in commotion. Jupiter thunders in the heavens; Neptune strikes the earth with his Trident; the ships, the city, and the mountains shake; the earth trembles to its centre; Pluto starts from his throne, in dread left the secrets of the infernal region should be laid open to the view of mortals. The passage is worthy of being inserted.

Αὐτὰρ ἐπεὶ μεθ᾽ ὁμιλον Ὀλύμπιοι ἤλυθεν ἀνδρῶν,
Ὦρτο δ᾽ Ἔρις κρατερὴ, λαοσσοὸς αὖε δ᾽ Ἀθηνη,——

Αὖε

Αὖε δ' Ἄρης ἑτέρωθεν, ἐρεμνῇ λαίλαπ ἴσος,——
Ὡς τὲς ἀμφωτέρες μάκαρες θεοὶ ὀτρυνον]ες,
Σύμβαλον, ἐν δ' αὐτοῖς ἔριδα ῥήγνυντο βαρεῖαν·
Δεινὸν δ' ἐβρόντησε πατὴρ ἀνδρῶν τε θεῶν τε
Ὑψόθεν· αὐτὰρ ἔνερθε Ποσειδάων ἐτίναξε
Γαῖαν ἀπειρεσίην, ὀρέων τ' αἰπεινὰ κάρηνα.
Πάντες δ' ἐσσείοντο πόδες πολυπιδάκε Ἴδης,
Καὶ κορυφαὶ, Τρώων τε πόλις, καὶ νῆες Ἀχαιῶν.
Ἔδδεισεν δ' ὑπένερθεν ἄναξ ἐνέρων, Ἀϊδωνεὺς,
Δείσας δ' ἐκ θρόνε ἆλ]ο, καὶ ἴαχε· μὴ οἱ ὕπερθε
Γαῖαν ἀναρρήξειε Ποσειδάων ἐνοσίχθων,
Οἰκία δε θνητοῖσι καὶ ἀθανάτοισι φανείη
Σμερδαλέ, εὐρώεντα, τά τε ςυγέεσι θεοί περ'
Τόσσος ἄρα κτύπος ὦρτο θεῶν ἔριδι ξυνιόντων *.

Iliad, 20. 47. &c.

THE

---

* But when the powers defcending fwelled the fight,
Then tumult rofe, fierce rage, and pale affright ;
Now through the trembling fhores Minerva calls,
And now fhe thunders from the Grecian walls.
Mars, hov'ring o'er his Troy, his terror fhrouds
In gloomy tempefts, and a night of clouds ;
Now through each Trojan heart he fury pours,
With voice divine, from Ilion's topmoft towers——
Above, the Sire of Gods his thunder rolls,
And peals on peals redoubled rend the poles ;
Beneath, ftern Neptune fhakes the folid ground,
The forefts wave, the mountains nod around ;
Through all her fummits tremble Ida's woods,
And from their fources boil her hundred floods :
Troy's turrets totter on the rocking plain,
And the tofs'd navies beat the heaving main:

Deep

THE works of Offian (as I have elfewhere fhewn) abound with examples of the Sublime. The fubjects of that Author, and the manner in which he writes, are particularly favourable to it. He poffeffes all the plain and venerable manner of the antient times. He deals in no fuperfluous or gaudy ornaments; but throws forth his images with a rapid concifenefs, which enable them to ftrike the mind with the greateft force. Among poets of more polifhed times, we are to look for the graces of correct writing, for juft proportion of parts, and fkilfully conducted narration. In the midft of fmiling fcenery and pleafurable themes, the gay and the beautiful will appear, undoubtedly, to more advantage. But amidft the rude fcenes of nature and of fociety, fuch as Offian defcribes; amidft rocks, and torrents, and whirlwinds, and battles, dwells the Sublime; and naturally affociates itfelf with that grave and folemn fpirit which diftinguifhes the Author of Fingal. " As autumn's dark ftorms pour from two echoing " hills, fo toward each other approached the heroes. As two " dark ftreams from high rocks meet and mix, and roar on " the plain; loud, rough, and dark, in battle, met Lochlin " and Inisfail; chief mixed his ftrokes with chief, and man with " man. Steel clanging founded on fteel. Helmets are cleft " on high; blood burfts, and fmokes around. As the troubled

---

Deep in the difmal region of the dead,
Th' infernal monarch rear'd his horrid head,
Leapt from his throne, left Neptune's arm fhould lay
His dark dominions open to the day;
And pour in light on Pluto's drear abodes,
Abhorr'd by men, and dreadful ev'n to Gods.
Such wars th' immortals wage; fuch horrors rend
The world's vaft concave, when the Gods contend.   POPE.

" noife

LECT.
IV.

" noife of the ocean when roll the waves on high; as the laft
" peal of the thunder of heaven; fuch is the noife of battle.
" The groan of the people fpread over the hills. It was like
" the thunder of night, when the cloud burfts on Cona, and
" a thoufand ghofts fhriek at once on the hollow wind."
Never were images of more awful Sublimity employed to
heighten the terror of battle.

I HAVE produced thefe inftances, in order to demonftrate
how effential concifenefs and fimplicity are to Sublime Writing.
Simplicity, I place in oppofition to ftudied and profufe ornament ; and concifenefs, to fuperfluous expreffion. The reafon
why a defect, either in concifenefs or fimplicity, is hurtful in a
peculiar manner to the Sublime, I fhall endeavour to explain.
The emotion occafioned in the mind by fome great or noble
object, raifes it confiderably above its ordinary pitch. A fort
of enthufiafm is produced, extremely agreeable while it lafts ;
but from which the mind is tending every moment to fall
down into its ordinary fituation. Now, when an author has
brought us, or is attempting to bring us, into this ftate ; if he
multiplies words unneceffarily, if he decks the Sublime object
which he prefents to us, round and round, with glittering
ornaments ; nay, if he throws in any one decoration that finks
in the leaft below the capital image, that moment he alters the
key ; he relaxes the tenfion of the mind ; the ftrength of the
feeling is emafculated ; the Beautiful may remain, but the Sublime is gone.——When Julius Cæfar faid to the Pilot who was
afraid to put to fea with him in a ftorm, " Quid times? Cæfarem
" vehis;" we are ftruck with the daring magnanimity of one rely-
ing with fuch confidence on his caufe and his fortune. Thefe few
words

words convey every thing neceſſary to give us the impreſſion L E C T.
IV.
full. Lucan reſolved to amplify and adorn the thought. Obſerve how every time he twiſts it round, it departs farther
from the Sublime, till it end at laſt in tumid declamation.

Sperne minas, inquit, pelagi, ventoque furenti
Trade ſinum : Italiam, ſi, cœlo auctore, recuſas,
Me, pete. Sola tibi cauſa hæc eſt juſta timoris
Victorem non noſſe tuum ; quem numina nunquam
Deſtituunt ; de quo male tunc Fortuna meretur
Cum poſt vota venit. Medias perrumpe procellas
Tutelâ ſecure meâ. Cœli iſti fretique
Non puppis noſtræ labor eſt. Hanc Cæſare preſſam
A fluctu defendet onus ; nam proderit undis
Iſte ratis.————Quid tanta ſtrage paratur
Ignoras ? quærit pelagi cœlique tumultu
Quid præſtet fortuna mihi *.————
Phars. V. 578.
On

---

* But Cæſar ſtill ſuperior to diſtreſs,
  Fearleſs, and confident of ſure ſucceſs,
  Thus to the pilot loud :——The ſeas deſpiſe,
  And the vain threat'ning of the noiſy ſkies ;
  Though Gods deny thee yon Auſonian ſtrand,
  Yet go, I charge you, go, at my command.
  Thy ignorance alone can cauſe thy fears,
  'Thou know'ſt not what a freight thy veſſel bears ;
  Thou know'ſt not I am he to whom 'tis given,
  Never to want the care of watchful heaven.
  Obedient fortune waits my humble thrall,
  And always ready, comes before I call.
  Let winds, and ſeas, loud wars at freedom wage,
  And waſte upon themſelves their empty rage,
  A ſtronger, mightier Dæmon is thy friend,

K 2
Thou

On account of the great importance of fimplicity and concifenefs, I conceive rhyme, in Englifh verfe, to be, if not inconfiftent
with the Sublime, at leaft very unfavourable to it. The conftrained
elegance of this kind of verfe, and ftudied fmoothnefs of the
founds, anfwering regularly to each other at the end of the
line, though they be quite confiftent with gentle emotions, yet
weaken the native force of Sublimity; befides, that the fuperfluous words which the poet is often obliged to introduce, in
order to fill up the rhyme, tend farther to enfeeble it. Homer's
defcription of the nod of Jupiter, as fhaking the heavens, has
been admired, in all ages, as highly Sublime. Literally tranflated, it runs thus : " He fpoke, and bending his fable brows,
" gave the awful nod; while he fhook the celeftial locks of his
" immortal head, all Olympus was fhaken." Mr. Pope tranf-
lates it thus :

> He fpoke ; and awful bends his fable brows,
> Shakes his ambrofial curls, and gives the nod,
> The ftamp of fate, and fanction of a God.
> High Heaven with trembling the dread fignal took,
> And all Olympus to its centre fhook.

The image is fpread out, and attempted to be beautified; but
it is, in truth, weakened. The third line—" The ftamp of
" fate,

> Thou, and thy bark, on Cæfar's fate depend.
> Thou ftand'ft amaz'd to view this dreadful fcene,
> And wonder'ft what the Gods and Fortune mean;
> But artfully their bounties thus they raife,
> And from my danger arrogate new praife :
> Amidft the fears of death they bid me live,
> And ftill enhance what they are fure to give.   Rowe.

" fate, and fanction of a God," is merely expletive ; and introduced for no other reafon but to fill up the rhyme; for it in-
terrupts the defcription, and clogs the image. For the fame
reafon, out of mere compliance with the rhyme, Jupiter is reprefented as fhaking his locks before he gives the nod ;—
" Shakes his ambrofial curls, and gives the nod," which is trifling, and without meaning. Whereas, in the original, the
hair of his head fhaken, is the effect of his nod, and makes a
happy picturefque circumftance in the defcription *.

THE boldnefs, freedom, and variety of our blank verfe, is
infinitely more favourable than rhyme, to all kinds of Sublime
poetry. The fulleft proof of this is afforded by Milton; an
author, whofe genius led him eminently to the Sublime. The
whole firft and fecond books of Paradife Loft, are continued
inftances of it. Take only, for an example, the following
noted defcription of Satan, after his fall, appearing at the head
of the infernal hofts :

———————————He, above the reft,
In fhape and gefture proudly eminent,
Stood like a tower : his form had not yet loft
All her original brightnefs, nor appeared
Lefs than archangel ruined ; and the excefs
Of glory obfcured : As when the fun, new rifen,
Looks through the horizontal mifty air,
Shorn of his beams ; or, from behind, the moon,
In dim eclipfe, difaftrous twilight fheds
On half the nations, and with fear of change

Perplexes

* See Webb on the Beauties of Poetry.

Perplexes monarchs.   Darken'd fo, yet fhone
Above them all th' Archangel.——

Here concur a variety of fources of the Sublime: The principal object eminently great; a high fuperior nature, fallen indeed, but erecting itfelf againft diftrefs; the grandeur of the
principal object heightened, by affociating it with fo noble an
idea as that of the fun fuffering an eclipfe; this picture fhaded
with all thofe images of change and trouble, of darknefs and
terror, which coincide fo finely with the Sublime emotion;
and the whole expreffed in a ftyle and verfification, eafy, natural, and fimple, but magnificent.

I HAVE fpoken of fimplicitity and concifenefs, as effential to
Sublime Writing.   In my general defcription of it, I mentioned Strength, as another neceffary requifite.   The Strength of
defcription arifes, in a great meafure, from a fimple concifenefs; but, it fuppofes alfo fomething more; namely, a proper
choice of circumftances in the defcription, fo as to exhibit the
object in its full and moft ftriking point of view.   For every
object has feveral faces, fo to fpeak, by which it may be prefented to us, according to the circumftances with which we
furround it; and it will appear eminently Sublime, or not, in
proportion as all thefe circumftances are happily chofen, and of
a Sublime kind.   Here lies the great art of the writer; and
indeed, the great difficulty of Sublime defcription.   If the defcription be too general, and divefted of circumftances, the object appears in a faint light; it makes a feeble impreffion, or no
impreffion at all, on the reader.   At the fame time, if any trivial
or improper circumftances are mingled, the whole is degraded.

A STORM

A storm or tempeſt, for inſtance, is a Sublime objeċt in nature. But, to render it Sublime in deſcription, it is not enough, either to give us mere general expreſſions concerning the violence of the tempeſt, or to deſcribe its common, vulgar effeċts, in overthrowing trees and houſes. It muſt be painted with ſuch circumſtances as fill the mind with great and awful ideas. This is very happily done by Virgil, in the following paſſage :

> Ipſe Pater, media nimborum in noċte, coruſcâ
> Fulmina molitur dextrâ ; quo maxima motu
> Terra tremit; fugere feræ; & mortalia corda,
> Per gentes humilis ſtravit pavor : Ille, flagranti
> Aut Atho, aut Rhodopen, aut alta Ceraunia telo
> Dejicit *.——— ——— GEORG. I.

Every circumſtance in this noble deſcription is the produċtion of an imagination heated and aſtoniſhed with the grandeur of the objeċt. If there be any defeċt, it is in the words immediately

---

* The Father of the Gods his glory ſhrouds,
  Involv'd in tempeſts, and a night of clouds ;
  And from the middle darkneſs flaſhing out,
  By fits he deals his fiery bolts about.
  Earth feels the motions of her angry God,
  Her intrails tremble, and her mountains nod, }
  And flying beaſts in foreſts ſeek abode.
  Deep horror ſeizes every human breaſt ;
  Their pride is humbled, and their fears confeſt ;
  While he, from high his rolling thunders throws,
  And fires the mountains with repeated blows ;
  The rocks are from their old foundations rent ;
  The winds redouble, and the rains augment. DRYDEN.

diately following thofe I have quoted; " Ingeminant Auftri,
" et denfiffimus imber ;" where the tranfition is made too
haftily, I am afraid, from the preceding Sublime images,
to a thick fhower, and the blowing of the fouth wind ; and
fhews how difficult it frequently is, to defcend with grace, without feeming to fall.

THE high importance of the rule which I have been now
giving, concerning the proper choice of circumftances, when
defcription is meant to be Sublime, feems to me not to
have been fufficiently attended to. It has, however,
fuch a foundation in nature, as renders the leaft deflexion
from it fatal. When a writer is aiming at the beautiful only,
his defcriptions may have improprieties in them, and yet be
beautiful ftill. Some trivial, or misjudged circumftances, can
be overlooked by the reader ; they make only the difference of
more or lefs; the gay, or pleafing emotion, which he has raifed,
fubfifts ftill. But the cafe is quite different with the Sublime.
There, one trifling circumftance, one mean idea, is fufficient to
deftroy the whole charm. This is owing to the nature of the
emotion aimed at by Sublime defcription, which admits of no
mediocrity, and cannot fubfift in a middle ftate ; but muft either
highly tranfport us, or, if unfuccefsful in the execution, leave
us greatly difgufted, and difpleafed. We attempt to rife along
with the writer; the imagination is awakened, and put upon the
ftretch ; but it requires to be fupported ; and if, in the midft
of its effort, you defert it unexpectedly, down it comes with a
painful fhock. When Milton, in his battle of the angels,
defcribes them as tearing up the mountains, and throwing
them at one another ; there are, in his defcription, as Mr. Ad-

                              2   difon

difon has obferved, no circumftances but what are properly Sublime :

> From their foundations loos'ning to and fro,
> They plucked the feated hills, with all their load,
> Rocks, waters, woods; and by the fhaggy tops
> Uplifting, bore them in their hands.——

Whereas Claudian, in a fragment upon the war of the giants, has contrived to render this idea of their throwing the mountains, which is in itfelf fo grand, burlefque and ridiculous; by this fingle circumftance, of one of his giants with the mountain Ida upon his fhoulders, and a river, which flowed from the mountain, running down along the giant's back, as he held it up in that pofture. There is a defcription too in Virgil, which, I think, is cenfurable, though more flightly, in this refpect. It is that of the burning mountain Ætna; a fubject certainly very proper to be worked up by a poet into a Sublime defcription :

> ————Horrificis juxta tonat Ætna ruinis.
> Interdumque atram prorumpit ad æthera nubem,
> Turbine fumantem piceo, & candente favilla ;
> Attollitque globos flammarum, & fidera lambit.
> Interdum fcopulos, avulfaque vifcera montis
> Erigit eructans, liquefactaque faxa fub auras
> Cum gemitu glomerat, fundoque exæftuat imo *. Æn.III. 571.

Here, after feveral magnificent images, the Poet concludes with perfonifying the mountain under this figure, " eructans
" vifcera

---

* The port capacious, and fecure from wind,
  Is to the foot of thundering Ætna joined,

" vifcera cum gemitu," belching up its bowels with a
groan; which, by likening the mountain to a fick, or drunk
perfon, degrades the majefty of the defcription. It is to no
purpofe to tell us, that the Poet here alludes to the fable of the
gaint Enceladus lying under mount Ætna; and that he fuppofes his motions and toffings to have occafioned the fiery
eruptions. He intended the defcription of a Sublime object;
and the natural ideas, raifed by a burning mountain, are infinitely more lofty, than the belchings of any giant, how huge
foever. The debafing effect of the idea which is here prefented,
will appear in a ftronger light, by feeing what figure it makes
in a poem of Sir Richard Blackmore's, who, through a mon-
ftrous perverfity of tafte, had chofen this for the capital circumftance in his defcription, and thereby (as Dr. Arbuthnot
humoroufly obferves, in his Treatife on the Art of Sinking)
had reprefented the mountain as in a fit of the cholic.

> Ætna, and all the burning mountains find
> Their kindled ftores with inbred ftorms of wind
> Blown up to rage, and roaring out complain,
> As torn with inward gripes and torturing pain;
> Labouring, they caft their dreadful vomit round,
> And with their melted bowels fpread the ground.

Such

> By turns a pitchy cloud fhe rolls on high,
> By turns hot embers from her entrails fly,
> And flakes of mounting flames that lick the fky.
> Oft from her bowels maffy rocks are thrown,
> And fhivered by the force, come piece-meal down.
> Oft liquid lakes of burning fulphur flow,
> Fed from the fiery fprings that boil below.   DRYDEN.

In this tranflation of Dryden's, the debafing circumftance to which I object
in the original, is, with propriety, omitted.

*

Such inftances fhew how much the Sublime depends upon a juft felection of circumftances; and with how great care every circumftance muft be avoided, which, by bordering in the leaft upon the mean, or even upon the gay or the trifling, alters the tone of the emotion.

IF it fhall now be enquired, What are the proper fources of the Sublime? My anfwer is, That they are to be looked for every where in nature. It is not by hunting after tropes, and figures, and rhetorical affiftances, that we can expect to produce it. No: it ftands clear, for the moft part, of thefe laboured refinements of art. It muft come unfought, if it come at all; and be the natural offspring of a ftrong imagination.

Eft Deus in nobis; agitante calefcimus illo.

Wherever a great and awful object is prefented in nature, or a very magnanimous and exalted affection of the human mind is difplayed; thence, if you can catch the impreffion ftrongly, and exhibit it warm and glowing, you may draw the Sublime. Thefe are its only proper fources. In judging of any ftriking beauty in compofition, whether it is, or is not, to be referred to this clafs, we muft attend to the nature of the emotion which it raifes; and only, if it be of that elevating, folemn, and awful kind, which diftinguifhes this feeling, we can pronounce it Sublime.

FROM the account which I have given of the nature of the Sublime, it clearly follows, that it is an emotion which can never be long protracted. The mind, by no force of genius, can be kept, for any confiderable time, fo far raifed above its common tone; but will, of courfe, relax into its ordinary fitua-

tion.

tion. Neither are the abilities of any human writer fufficient to fupply a continued run of unmixed Sublime conceptions. The utmoft we can expect is, that this fire of imagination fhould fometimes flafh upon us like lightning from heaven, and then difappear. In Homer and Milton, this effulgence of genius breaks forth more frequently, and with greater luftre than in moft authors. Shakefpeare alfo rifes often into the true Sublime. But no author whatever is Sublime throughout. Some, indeed, there are, who, by a ftrength and dignity in their conceptions, and a current of high ideas that runs through their whole compofition, preferve the reader's mind always in a tone nearly allied to the Sublime ; for which reafon they may, in a limited fenfe, merit the name of continued Sublime writers ; and, in this clafs, we may juftly place Demofthenes and Plato.

As for what is called the Sublime ftyle, it is, for the moft part, a very bad one ; and has no relation whatever to the real Sublime. Perfons are apt to imagine, that magnificent words, accumulated epithets, and a certain fwelling kind of expreffion, by rifing above what is ufual or vulgar, contributes to, or even forms, the Sublime. Nothing can be more falfe. In all the inftances of Sublime Writing, which I have given, nothing of this kind appears. " God faid, Let there be light, and there " was light." This is ftriking and Sublime. But put it into what is commonly called the Sublime ftyle : " The Sovereign " Arbiter of nature, by the potent energy of a fingle word, " commanded the light to exift;" and, as Boileau has well obferved, the ftyle indeed is raifed, but the thought is fallen. In general, in all good writing, the Sublime lies in the thought, not in the words; and when the thought is truly noble, it will,

for

for the moſt part, clothe itſelf in a native dignity of language. The Sublime, indeed, rejects mean, low, or trivial expreſſions; but it is equally an enemy to ſuch as are turgid. The main ſecret of being Sublime, is to ſay great things in few and plain words. It will be found to hold, without exception, that the moſt Sublime authors are the ſimpleſt in their ſtyle; and wherever you find a writer, who affects a more than ordinary pomp and parade of words, and is always endeavouring to magnify his ſubject by epithets, there you may immediately ſuſpect, that, feeble in ſentiment, he is ſtudying to ſupport himſelf by mere expreſſion.

THE ſame unfavourable judgment we muſt paſs, on all that laboured apparatus with which ſome writers introduce a paſſage, or deſcription, which they intend ſhall be Sublime; calling on their readers to attend, invoking their Muſe, or breaking forth into general, unmeaning exclamations, concerning the greatneſs, terribleneſs, or majeſty of the object, which they are to deſcribe. Mr. Addiſon, in his Campaign, has fallen into an error of this kind, when about to deſcribe the battle of Blenheim.

> But O! my Muſe! what numbers wilt thou find
> To ſing the furious troops in battle joined?
> Methinks, I hear the drum's tumultuous ſound,
> The victor's ſhouts, and dying groans, confound; &c.

Introductions of this kind, are a forced attempt in a writer, to ſpur up himſelf, and his reader, when he finds his imagination flagging in vigour. It is like taking artificial ſpirits in order to ſupply the want of ſuch as are natural. By this obſervation, how-

4

ever I do not mean to pass a general censure on Mr. Addison's Campaign, which, in several places, is far from wanting merit ; and in particular, the noted comparison of his hero to the angel who rides in the whirlwind and directs the storm, is a truly Sublime image.

THE faults opposite to the Sublime are chiefly two ; the Frigid, and the Bombast. The Frigid consists, in degrading an object, or sentiment, which is Sublime in itself, by our mean conception of it ; or by our weak, low, and childish description of it. This betrays entire absence, or at least great poverty of genius. Of this, there are abundance of examples, and these commented upon with much humour, in the Treatise on the Art of Sinking, in Dean Swift's works ; the instances taken chiefly from Sir Richard Blackmore. One of these, I had occasion already to give, in relation to mount Ætna, and it were needless to produce any more. The Bombast lies, in forcing an ordinary or trivial object out of its rank, and endeavouring to raise it into the Sublime ; or, in attempting to exalt a Sublime object beyond all natural and reasonable bounds. Into this error, which is but too common, writers of genius may sometimes fall, by unluckily losing sight of the true point of the Sublime. This is also called Fustian, or Rant. Shakespeare, a great, but incorrect genius, is not unexceptionable here. Dryden and Lee, in their tragedies, abound with it.

THUS far of the Sublime ; of which I have treated fully, because it is so capital an excellency in fine writing, and because clear and precise ideas on this head are, as far as I know, not to be met with in critical writers.

BEFORE

BEFORE concluding this Lecture, there is one obfervation which I chufe to make at this time; I fhall make it once for all, and hope it will be afterwards remembered. It is with refpect to the inftances of faults, or rather blemifhes and imperfections, which, as I have done in this Lecture, I fhall hereafter continue to take, when I can, from writers of reputation. I have not the leaft intention thereby to difparage their character in the general. I fhall have other occafions of doing equal juftice to their beauties. But it is no reflection on any human per- formance, that it is not abfolutely perfect. The tafk would be much eafier for me, to collect inftances of faults from bad writers. But they would draw no attention, when quoted from books which nobody reads. And I conceive, that the method which I follow, will contribute more to make the beft authors be read with pleafure, when one properly diftinguifhes their beauties from their faults; and is led to imitate and admire only what is worthy of imitation and admiration.

L E C T U R E   V.

BEAUTY, AND OTHER PLEASURES OF TASTE.

AS Sublimity conftitutes a particular character of compofition, and forms one of the higheft excellencies of eloquence and of poetry, it was proper to treat of it at fome length.
It will not be neceffary to difcufs fo particularly all the other
pleafures that arife from Tafte, as fome of them have lefs relation
to our main fubject. On Beauty only I fhall make feveral obfervations, both as the fubject is curious, and as it tends to
improve Tafte, and to difcover the foundation of feveral of the
graces of defcription and of poetry *.

BEAUTY, next to Sublimity, affords, beyond doubt, the
higheft pleafure to the imagination. The emotion which it

* See Hutchinfon's Enquiry concerning Beauty and Virtue.—Gerard on
Tafte, chap. iii.—Enquiry into the Origin of the Ideas of the Sublime and
Beautiful.—Elements of Criticifm, chap. iii.—Spectator, vol. vi. Effay on the
Pleafures of Tafte.

raifes,

raifes, is very diftinguifhable from that of Sublimity.   It is of
a calmer kind; more gentle and foothing; does not elevate
the mind fo much, but produces an agreeable ferenity.   Sublimity raifes a feeling, too violent, as I fhowed, to be lafting;
the pleafure arifing from Beauty admits of longer continuance.
It extends alfo to a much greater variety of objeƈts than Sublimity; to a variety indeed fo great, that the feelings which
Beautiful objeƈts produce, differ confiderably, not in degree
only, but alfo in kind, from one another.   Hence, no word in
the language is ufed in a more vague fignification than Beauty.
It is applied to almoft every external objeƈt that pleafes the eye,
or the ear; to a great number of the graces of writing; to
many difpofitions of the mind; nay, to feveral objeƈts of mere
abftraƈt fcience.   We talk currently of a beautiful tree or flower;
a beautiful poem; a beautiful charaƈter; and a beautiful
theorem in mathematics.

HENCE we may eafily perceive, that, among fo great a variety of objeƈts, to find out fome one quality in which they all
agree, and which is the foundation of that agreeable fenfation
they all raife, muft be a very difficult, if not, more probably,
a vain attempt.   Objeƈts, denominated Beautiful, are fo different, as to pleafe, not in virtue of any one quality common to
them all, but by means of feveral different principles in human
nature.   The agreeable emotion which they all raife, is fomewhat of the fame nature; and, therefore, has the common
name of Beauty given to it; but it is raifed by different caufes.

HYPOTHESES, however, have been framed by ingenious
men, for affigning the fundamental quality of Beauty in all

objects. In particular, Uniformity amidst Variety, has been insisted on as this fundamental quality. For the Beauty of many figures, I admit that this accounts in a satisfying manner. But when we endeavour to apply this principle to Beautiful objects of some other kind, as to Colour for instance, or Motion, we shall soon find that it has no place. And even in external figured objects, it does not hold, that their Beauty is in proportion to their mixture of Variety with Uniformity; seeing many please us as highly beautiful, which have almost no variety at all; and others, which are various to a degree of intricacy. Laying systems of this kind, therefore, aside, what I now propose is, to give an enumeration of several of those classes of objects in which Beauty most remarkably appears; and to point out, as far as I can, the separate principles of Beauty in each of them.

COLOUR affords, perhaps, the simplest instance of Beauty, and therefore the fittest to begin with. Here, neither Variety, nor Uniformity, nor any other principle that I know, can be assigned, as the foundation of Beauty. We can refer it to no other cause but the structure of the eye, which determines us to receive certain modifications of the rays of light with more pleasure than others. And we see accordingly, that, as the organ of sensation varies in different persons, they have their different favourite colours. It is probable, that association of ideas has influence, in some cases, on the pleasure which we receive from colours. Green, for instance, may appear more beautiful, by being connected in our ideas with rural prospects and scenes; white, with innocence; blue, with the serenity of the sky. Independent of associations of this kind, all that we

can

can farther obferve concerning colours is, that thofe chofen for
Beauty are, generally, delicate, rather than glaring.   Such
are thofe paintings with which nature hath ornamented fome of
her works, and which art ftrives in vain to imitate; as the
feathers of feveral kinds of birds, the leaves of flowers, and the
fine variation of colours exhibited by the fky at the rifing and
fetting of the fun.   Thefe prefent to us the higheft inftances of
the Beauty of colouring; and have accordingly been the
favourite fubjects of poetical defcription in all countries.

FROM Colour we proceed to Figure, which opens to us
forms of Beauty more complex and diverfified.   Regularity
firft occurs to be noticed as a fource of Beauty.   By a regular
figure, is meant, one which we perceive to be formed according to fome certain rule, and not left arbitrary, or loofe,
in the conftruction of its parts.   Thus, a circle, a fquare, a
triangle, or a hexagon, pleafe the eye, by their regularity, as
beautiful figures.   We muft not, however, conclude, that all
figures pleafe in proportion to their regularity; or that regularity is the fole, or the chief, foundation of Beauty in figure.
On the contrary, a certain graceful variety is found to be a
much more powerful principle of Beauty; and is therefore
ftudied a great deal more than regularity, in all works that are
defigned merely to pleafe the eye.   I am, indeed, inclined to
think, that regularity appears beautiful to us, chiefly, if not
only, on account of its fuggefting the ideas of fitnefs, propriety, and ufe, which have always a greater connection with
orderly and proportioned forms, than with thofe which appear
not conftructed according to any certain rule.   It is clear, that
nature, who is undoubtedly the moft graceful artift, hath, in

M 2   all

all her ornamental works, purfued variety, with an apparent neglect of regularity. Cabinets, doors, and windows, are made after a regular form, in cubes and parallelograms, with exact proportion of parts; and by being fo formed they pleafe the eye; for this good reafon, that, being works of ufe, they are, by fuch figures, the better fuited to the ends for which they were defigned. But plants, flowers, and leaves are full of variety and diverfity. A ftraight canal is an infipid figure, in comparifon of the mæanders of rivers. Cones and pyramids are beautiful; but trees growing in their natural wildnefs, are infinitely more beautiful than when trimmed into pyramids and cones. The apartments of a houfe muft be regular in their difpofition, for the conveniency of its inhabitants; but a garden, which is defigned merely for Beauty, would be exceedingly difgufting, if it had as much uniformity and order in its parts as a dwelling-houfe.

MR. HOGARTH, in his Analyfis of Beauty, has obferved, that figures bounded by curve lines are, in general, more beautiful than thofe bounded by ftraight lines and angles. He pitches upon two lines, on which, according to him, the Beauty of figure principally depends; and he has illuftrated, and fupported his doctrine, by a furprifing number of inftances. The one is the Waving Line, or a curve bending backwards and forwards, fomewhat in the form of the letter S. This he calls the Line of Beauty; and fhews how often it is found in fhells, flowers, and fuch other ornamental works of nature; as is common alfo in the figures defigned by painters and fculptors, for the purpofe of decoration. The other Line, which he calls the Line of Grace, is the former waving curve, twifted round

fome

fome folid body. The curling worm of a common jack is one of the inftances he gives of it. Twifted pillars, and twifted horns, alfo exhibit it. In all the inftances which he mentions, Variety plainly appears to be fo material a principle of Beauty, that he feems not to err much when he defines the art of drawing pleafing forms, to be the art of varying well. For the curve line, fo much the favourite of painters, derives, according to him, its chief advantage, from its perpetual bending and variation from the ftiff regularity of the ftraight line.

MOTION furnifhes another fource of Beauty, diftinct from Figure. Motion of itfelf is pleafing ; and bodies in motion are, " cæteris paribus," preferred to thofe in reft. It is, however, only gentle motion that belongs to the Beautiful ; for when it is very fwift, or very forcible, fuch as that of a torrent, it partakes of the Sublime. The motion of a bird gliding through the air, is extremely Beautiful ; the fwiftnefs with which lightning darts through the heavens, is magnificent and aftonifhing. And here, it is proper to obferve, that the fenfations of Sublime and Beauful are not always diftinguifhed by very diftant boundaries ; but are capable, in feveral inftances, of approaching towards each other. Thus, a fmooth running ftream, is one of the moft beautiful objects in nature : as it fwells gradually into a great river, the beautiful, by degrees, is loft in the Sublime. A young tree is a beautiful object ; a fpreading antient oak, is a venerable and a grand one. The calmnefs of a fine morning is beautiful ; the univerfal ftillnefs of the evening is highly Sublime. But to return to the Beauty of motion, it will be found, I think, to hold very generally, that motion in a ftraight line is not fo beautiful as in an undulating waving direction ; and mo-

tion

tion upwards is, commonly too, more agreeable than motion downwards. The eafy curling motion of flame and fmoke to be inftanced, as an object fingularly agreeable: and here Mr. Hogarth's waving line recurs upon us as a principle of Beauty. That artift obferves very ingenioufly, that all the common and neceffary motions for the bufinefs of life, are performed by men in ftraight or plain lines; but that all the graceful and ornamental movements are made in waving lines: an obfervation not unworthy of being attended to, by all who ftudy the grace of gefture and action.

THOUGH Colour, Figure, and Motion, be feparate principles of Beauty; yet in many beautiful objects they all meet, and thereby render the Beauty both greater, and more complex. Thus, in flowers, trees, animals, we are entertained at once with the delicacy of the colour, with the gracefulnefs of the figure, and fometimes alfo with the motion of the object. Although each of thefe produce a feparate agreeable fenfation, yet they are of fuch a fimiliar nature, as readily to mix and blend in one general perception of Beauty, which we afcribe to the whole object as its caufe: For Beauty is always conceived by us, as fomething refiding in the object which raifes the pleafant fenfation; a fort of glory which dwells upon, and invefts it. Perhaps the moft complete affemblage of beautiful objects that can any where be found, is prefented by a rich natural landfcape, where there is a fufficient variety of objects: fields in verdure, fcattered trees and flowers, running water, and animals grazing. If to thefe be joined, fome of the productions of art, which fuit fuch a fcene; as a bridge with arches over a river, fmoke rifing from cottages in the midft of trees, and the diftant

6 view

view of a fine building feen by the rifing fun; we then enjoy, in the higheſt perfection, that gay, cheerful, and placid fenſation which characterifes Beauty. To have an eye and a taſte formed for catching the peculiar Beauties of ſuch ſcenes as theſe, is a neceſſary requifite for all who attempt poetical defcription.

THE Beauty of the human countenance is more complex than any that we have yet confidered. It includes the Beauty of colour, arifing from the delicate ſhades of the complexion ; and the Beauty of figure, arifing from the lines which form the different features of the face. But the chief Beauty of the countenance depends upon a myſterious expreſſion, which it conveys of the qualities of the mind ; of good fenfe, or good humour ; of ſprightlinefs, candour, benevolence, fenſibility, or other amiable difpofitions. How it comes to paſs, that a certain conformation of features is connected in our idea with certain moral qualities ; whether we are taught by inſtinct, or by ex- perience, to form this connection, and to read the mind in the countenance ; belongs not to us now to enquire, nor is indeed eafy to refolve. The fact is certain, and acknowledged, that what gives the human countenance its moſt diſtinguiſhing Beauty, is what is called its expreſſion ; or an image, which it is conceived to ſhew of internal moral difpofitions.

THIS leads to obſerve, that there are certain qualities of the mind which, whether expreſſed in the countenance, or by words, or by actions, always raife in us a feeling fimilar to that of Beauty. There are two great claſſes of moral qualities ; one is of the high and the great virtues, which require extra- ordinary efforts, and turn upon dangers and ſufferings ; as

heroifm,

heroifm, magnaninity, contempt of pleafures, and contempt of death. Thefe, as I have obferved in a former Lecture, excite in the fpectator an emotion of Sublimity and Grandeur. The other clafs is generally of the focial virtues, and fuch as are of a fofter and gentler kind; as compaffion, mildnefs, friendfhip, and generofity. Thefe raife in the beholder a fenfation of pleafure, fo much akin to that produced by Beautiful external objects, that, though of a more dignified nature, it may, without impropriety, be claffed under the fame head.

A SPECIES of Beauty, diftinct from any I have yet mentioned, arifes from defign or art; or, in other words, from the perception of means being adapted to an end; or the parts of any thing being well fitted to anfwer the defign of the whole. When, in confidering the ftructure of a tree or a plant, we obferve, how all the parts, the roots, the ftem, the bark, and the leaves, are fuited to the growth and nutriment of the whole: much more when we furvey all the parts and members of a living animal; or when we examine any of the curious works of art; fuch as a clock, a fhip, or any nice machine; the pleafure which we have in the furvey, is wholly founded on this fenfe of Beauty. It is altogether different from the perception of Beauty produced by colour, figure, variety, or any of the caufes formerly mentioned. When I look at a watch, for inftance, the cafe of it, if finely engraved, and of curious workmanfhip, ftrikes me as beautiful in the former fenfe; bright colour, exquifite polifh, figures finely raifed and turned. But when I examine the conftruction of the fpring and the wheels, and praife the Beauty of the internal machinery; my pleafure then arifes wholly from the view of that admirable

art,

art, with which fo many various and complicated parts are made
to unite for one purpofe.

THIS fenfe of Beauty, in fitnefs and defign, has an extenfive
influence over many of our ideas. It is the foundation of the
Beauty which we difcover in the proportion of doors, windows,
arches, pillars, and all the orders of architecture. Let the
ornaments of a building be ever fo fine and elegant in themfelves, yet if they interfere with this fenfe of fitnefs and defign,
they lofe their Beauty, and hurt the eye, like difagreeable objects. Twifted columns, for inftance, are undoubtedly ornamental ; but as they have an appearance of weaknefs, they
always difpleafe when they are made ufe of to fupport any part
of a building that is maffy, and that feemed to require a more
fubftantial prop. We cannot look upon any work whatever,
without being led, by a natural affociation of ideas, to think of
its end and defign, and of courfe to examine the propriety of
its parts, in relation to this defign and end. When their propriety is clearly difcerned, the work feems always to have fome
Beauty ; but when there is a total want of propriety, it never
fails of appearing deformed. Our fenfe of fitnefs and defign,
therefore, is fo powerful, and holds fo high a rank among our
perceptions, as to regulate, in a great meafure, our other ideas
of Beauty : An obfervation which I the rather make, as it is of
the utmoft importance, that all who ftudy compofition fhould
carefully attend to it. For, in an epic poem, a hiftory, an oration, or any work of genius, we always require, as we do in
other works, a fitnefs, or adjuftment of means, to the end
which the author is fuppofed to have in view. Let his defcriptions be ever fo rich, or his figures ever fo elegant, yet, if they

are out of place, if they are not proper parts of that whole, if they fuit not the main defign, they lofe all their Beauty; nay, from Beauties they are converted into Deformities. Such power has our fenfe of fitnefs and congruity, to produce a total transformation of an object whofe appearance otherwife would have been Beautiful.

After having mentioned fo many various fpecies of Beauty, it now only remains to take notice of Beauty as it is applied to writing or difcourfe; a term commonly ufed in a fenfe altogether loofe and undetermined. For it is applied to all that pleafes, either in ftyle or in fentiment, from whatever principle that pleafure flows; and a Beautiful poem or oration means, in common language, no other than a good one, or one well compofed. In this fenfe, it is plain, the word is altogether indefinite, and points at no particular fpecies or kind of Beauty. There is, however, another fenfe, fomewhat more definite, in which Beauty of writing characterifes a particular manner; when it is ufed to fignify a certain grace and amænity in the turn either of ftyle or fentiment, for which fome authors have been peculiarly diftinguifhed. In this fenfe, it denotes a manner neither remarkably fublime, nor vehemently paffionate, nor uncommonly fparkling; but fuch as raifes in the reader an emotion of the gentle placid kind, fimilar to what is raifed by the contemplation of beautiful objects in nature; which neither lifts the mind very high, nor agitates it very much, but diffufes over the imagination an agreeable and pleafing ferenity. Mr. Addifon is a writer altogether of this character; and is one of the moft proper and precife examples that can be given of it. Fenelon, the author of the Adventures of Telemachus, may be

given

given as another example. Virgil too, though very capable of rifing on occafions into the Sublime, yet, in his general manner, is diftinguifhed by the character of Beauty and Grace rather than of Sublimity. Among orators, Cicero has more of the Beautiful than Demofthenes, whofe genius led him wholly towards vehemence and ftrength.

THIS much it is fufficient to have faid upon the fubject of Beauty. We have traced it through a variety of forms; as next to Sublimity, it is the moft copious fource of the Pleafures of Tafte; and as the confideration of the different appearances, and principles of Beauty, tends to the improvement of Tafte in many fubjects.

BUT it is not only by appearing under the forms of Sublime or Beautiful, that objects delight the imagination. From feveral other principles alfo, they derive their power of giving it pleafure.

NOVELTY, for inftance, has been mentioned by Mr. Addifon, and by every writer on this fubject. An object which has no merit to recommend it, except its being uncommon or new, by means of this quality alone, produces in the mind a vivid and an agreeable emotion. Hence that paffion of curiofity, which prevails fo generally among mankind. Objects and ideas which have been long familiar, make too faint an impreffion to give an agreeable exercife to our faculties. New and ftrange objects roufe the mind from its dormant ftate, by giving it a quick and pleafing impulfe. Hence, in a great meafure, the entertainment afforded us by fiction and romance. The

N 2

emotion

emotion raifed by Novelty is of a more lively and pungent nature, than that produced by Beauty; but much fhorter in its
continuance.   For if the object have in itfelf no charms to hold
our attention, the fhining glofs thrown upon it by Novelty foon
wears off.

BESIDES Novelty, Imitation is another fource of Pleafure to
Tafte. This gives rife to what Mr. Addifon terms, the Secondary
Pleafures of Imagination; which form, doubtlefs, a very extenfive clafs.   For all Imitation affords fome pleafure; not only
the Imitation of beautiful or great objects, by recalling the original ideas of Beauty or Grandeur which fuch objects themfelves
exhibited; but even objects which have neither Beauty nor
Grandeur, nay, fome which are terrible or deformed, pleafe us
in a fecondary or reprefented view.

THE Pleafures of Melody and Harmony belong alfo to Tafte.
There is no agreeable fenfation we receive, either from Beauty
or Sublimity, but what is capable of being heightened by the
power of mufical found.   Whence the delight of poetical numbers; and even of the more concealed and loofer meafures of
profe. Wit, Humour, and Ridicule likewife open a variety of
pleafures to Tafte, quite diftinct from any that we have yet
confidered.

AT prefent it is not neceffary to purfue any farther the fubject of the Pleafures of Tafte.   I have opened fome of the
general principles; it is time now to make the application to
our chief fubject.   If the queftion be put, To what clafs of thofe
Pleafures of Tafte which I have enumerated, that Pleafure is

                                                                    to

to be referred, which we receive from poetry, eloquence, or
fine writing? My anfwer is, Not to any one, but to them all.
This fingular advantage, writing and difcourfe poffefs, that they
encompafs fo large and rich a field on all fides, and have power
to exhibit, in great perfection, not a fingle fet of objects only,
but almoft the whole of thofe which give Pleafure to Tafte and
Imagination; whether that Pleafure arife from Sublimity, from
Beauty in its different forms, from Defign and Art, from Moral
Sentiment, from Novelty, from Harmony, from Wit, Humour
and Ridicule. To whichfoever of thefe the peculiar bent of
a perfon's Tafte lies, from fome writer or other, he has it always in his power to receive the gratification of it.

Now this high power which eloquence and poetry poffefs, of
fupplying Tafte and Imagination with fuch a wide circle of pleafures, they derive altogether from their having a greater capacity of Imitation and Defcription than is poffeffed by any other
art. Of all the means which human ingenuity has contrived
for recalling the images of real objects, and awakening, by
reprefentation, fimilar emotions to thofe which are raifed by the
original, none is fo full and extenfive as that which is executed
by words and writing. Through the affiftance of this happy
invention, there is nothing, either in the natural or moral
world, but what can be reprefented and fet before the mind, in
colours very ftrong and lively. Hence it is ufual among critical
writers, to fpeak of Difcourfe as the chief of all the imitative or
mimetic arts; they compare it with painting and with fculpture,
and in many refpects prefer it juftly before them.

THIS

THIS ftyle was firft introduced by Ariftotle in his Poetics; and fince his time, has acquired a general currency among modern authors. But, as it is of confequence to introduce as much precifion as poffible into critical language, I muft obferve, that this manner of fpeaking is not accurate. Neither difcourfe in general, nor poetry in particular, can be called altogether imitative arts. We muft diftinguifh betwixt Imitation and Defcription, which are ideas that fhould not be confounded. Imitation is performed by means of fomewhat that has a natural likenefs and refemblance to the thing imitated, and of confequence is underftood by all; fuch are ftatues and pictures. Defcription, again, is the raifing in the mind the conception of an object by means of fome arbitrary or inftituted fymbols, underftood only by thofe who agree in the inftitution of them; fuch are words and writing. Words have no natural refemblance to the ideas or objects which they are employed to fignify; but a ftatue or a picture has a natural likenefs to the original. And therefore Imitation and Defcription differ confiderably in their nature from each other.

As far, indeed, as a poet or a hiftorian introduces into his work perfons actually fpeaking; and, by the words which he puts into their mouths, reprefents the difcourfe which they might be fuppofed to hold; fo far his art may more accurately be called Imitative: and this is the cafe in all dramatic compofition. But in Narrative or Defcriptive works, it can with no propriety be called fo. Who, for inftance, would call Virgil's Defcription of a tempeft, in the firft Æneid, an Imitation of a ftorm? If we heard of the Imitation of a battle, we might naturally think of fome mock fight, or reprefentation of a battle

on

on the ftage, but would never apprehend, that it meant one of Homer's Defcriptions in the Iliad. I admit, at the fame time, that Imitation and Defcription agree in their principal effect, of recalling, by external figns, the ideas of things which we do not fee. But though in this they coincide, yet it fhould not be forgotten, that the terms themfelves are not fynonymous; that they import different means of effecting the fame end; and of courfe make different impreffions on the mind *.

* Though, in the execution of particular parts, Poetry is certainly Defcriptive rather than Imitative, yet there is a qualified fenfe in which Poetry, in the general, may be termed an Imitative art. The fubject of the poet (as Dr. Gerard has fhown in the Appendix to his Effay on Tafte) is intended to be an Imitation, not of things really exifting, but of the courfe of nature; that is, a feigned reprefentation of fuch events, or fuch fcenes, as though they never had a being, yet might have exifted; and which, therefore, by their probability, bear a refemblance to nature. It was probably, in this fenfe, that Ariftotle termed Poetry a mimetic art. How far either the Imitation or the Defcription which Poetry employs, is fuperior to the imitative powers of Painting and Mufic, is well fhown by Mr. Harris, in his Treatife on Mufic, Painting, and Poetry. The chief advantage which Poetry, or Difcourfe in general enjoys is, that whereas, by the nature of his art, the Painter is confined to the reprefentation of a fingle moment, writing and difcourfe can trace a tranfaction through its whole progrefs. That moment, indeed, which the painter pitches upon for the fubject of his picture, he may be faid to exhibit with more advantage than the poet or the orator; inafmuch as he fets before us, in one view, all the minute concurrent circumftances of the event which happen in one individual point of time, as they appear in nature; while Difcourfe is obliged to exhibit them in fucceffion, and by means of a detail, which is in danger of becoming tedious, in order to be clear; or if not tedious, is in danger of being obfcure. But to that point of time which he has chofen, the painter being entirely confined, he cannot exhibit various ftages of the fame action or event; and he is fubject to this farther defect, that he can only exhibit objects as they appear to the eye, and can very imperfectly delineate characters and fentiments, which are the nobleft fubjects of Imitation or Defcription. The power of reprefenting thefe with full advantage, gives a high fuperiority to Difcourfe and Writing above all other imitative arts.

WHETHER

WHETHER we confider Poetry in particular, and Difcourfe in general, as Imitative or Defcriptive; it is evident, that their whole power, in recalling the impreffions of real objects, is derived from the fignificancy of words. As their excellency flows altogether from this fource, we muft, in order to make way for further enquiries, begin at this fountain head. I fhall, therefore, in the next Lecture, enter upon the confideration of Language: of the origin, the progrefs, and conftruction of which, I purpofe to treat at fome length.

LECTURE VI.

RISE AND PROGRESS OF LANGUAGE.

HAVING finifhed my obfervations on the Pleafures of Tafte, which were meant to be introductory to the principal fubject of thefe Lectures, I now begin to treat of Language; which is the foundation of the whole power of eloquence. This will lead to a confiderable difcuffion; and there are few fubjects belonging to polite literature, which more merit fuch a difcuffion. I fhall firft give a Hiftory of the Rife and Progrefs of Language in feveral particulars, from its early to its more advanced periods; which fhall be followed by a fimilar Hiftory of the Rife and Progrefs of Writing. I fhall next give fome account of the Conftruction of Language, or the Principles of Univerfal Grammar; and fhall, laftly, apply thefe obfervations more particularly to the Englifh Tongue *.

LANGUAGE,

* See Dr. Adam Smith's Differtation on the Formation of Languages. — Treatife of the Origin and Progrefs of Language, in 3 vols.—Harris's Hermes, or,

LANGUAGE, in general, fignifies the expreffion of our ideas by certain articulate founds, which are ufed as the figns of thofe ideas. By articulate founds, are meant thofe modulations of fimple voice, or of found emitted from the thorax, which are formed by means of the mouth and its feveral organs, the teeth, the tongue, the lips, and the palate. How far there is any natural connexion between the ideas of the mind and the founds emitted, will appear from what I am afterwards to offer. But as the natural connexion can, upon any fyftem, affect only a fmall part of the fabric of Language; the connexion between words and ideas may, in general, be confidered as arbitrary and conventional, owing to the agreement of men among themfelves; the clear proof of which is, that different nations have different Languages, or a different fet of articulate founds, which they have chofen for communicating their ideas.

THIS artificial method of communicating thought, we now behold carried to the higheft perfection. Language is become a vehicle by which the moft delicate and refined emotions of one mind can be tranfmitted, or, if we may fo fpeak, transfufed into another. Not only are names given to all objects around us, by which means an eafy and fpeedy intercourfe is carried

---

a Philofophical Enquiry concerning Language and Univerfal Grammar.—Effai fur l'Origine des Connoiffances Humaines, par L'Abbé Condillac.—Principes de Grammaire, par Marfais.—Grammaire Generale & Raifonnée.—Traité de la Formation Mechanique des Langues, par le Prefident de Broffes.—Difcours fur l'Inegalité parmi les Hommes, par Rouffeau.—Grammaire Generale, par Beauzce.—Principes de la Traduction, par Batteux.—Warburton's Divine Legation of Mofes, vol. iii.—Sanctii Minerva, cum notis Perizonii.—Les Vrais Principes de la I angue Françoife, par l'Abbé Girard.

on

on for providing the neceffaries of life, but all the relations
and differences among thefe objects are minutely marked, the invifible fentiments of the mind are defcribed, the moft abftract notions and conceptions are rendered intelligible; and all the ideas which fcience can difcover, or imagination create, are known by their proper names. Nay, Language has been carried fo far, as to be made an inftrument of the moft refined luxury. Not refting in mere perfpicuity, we require ornament alfo; not fatisfied with having the conceptions of others made known to us, we make a farther demand, to have them fo decked and adorned as to entertain our fancy; and this demand, it is found very poffible to gratify. In this ftate, we now find Language. In this ftate, it has been found among many nations for fome thoufand years. The object is become familiar; and, like the expanfe of the firmament, and other great objects, which we are accuftomed to behold, we behold it without wonder.

But carry your thoughts back to the firft dawn of Language among men. Reflect upon the feeble beginnings from which it muft have arifen, and upon the many and great obftacles which it muft have encountered in its progrefs; and you will find reafon for the higheft aftonifhment, on viewing the height which it has now attained. We admire feveral of the inventions of art; we plume ourfelves on fome difcoveries which have been made in latter ages, ferving to advance knowledge, and to render life comfortable; we fpeak of them as the boaft of human reafon. But certainly no invention is entitled to any fuch degree of admiration as that of Language; which, too,

muft

muft have been the product of the firft and rudeft ages, if indeed it can be confidered as a human invention at all.

THINK of the circumftances of mankind when Languages
began to be formed. They were a wandering fcattered race;
no fociety among them except families; and the family fociety
too very imperfect, as their method of living by hunting or
pafturage muft have feparated them frequently from one
another. In this fituation, when fo much divided, and their
intercourfe fo rare, How could any one fet of founds, or words,
be generally agreed on as the figns of their ideas? Suppofing
that a few, whom chance or neceffity threw together, agreed by
fome means upon certain figns, yet by what authority could
thefe be propagated among other tribes or families, fo as to
fpread and grow up into a Language? One would think, that
in order to any Language fixing and extending itfelf, men muft
have been previoufly gathered together in confiderable numbers; fociety muft have been already far advanced; and yet,
on the other hand, there feems to have been an abfolute neceffity
for Speech, previous to the formation of Society. For, by
what bond could any multitude of men be kept together, or be
made to join in the profecution of any common intereft, until
once, by the intervention of Speech, they could communicate
their wants and intentions to each other? So that, either how
Society could form itfelf, previoufly to Language; or how
words could rife into a Language, previoufly to Society formed,
feem to be points attended with equal difficulty. And when we
confider farther, that curious analogy which prevails in the
conftruction of almoft all Languages, and that deep and fubtile
logic on which they are founded, difficulties increafe fo much

upon

upon us, on all hands, that there feems to be no fmall reafon for referring the firft origin of all Language to divine teaching or infpiration.

BUT fuppofing Language to have a Divine original, we cannot, however, fuppofe, that a perfect fyftem of it was all at once given to man. It is much more natural to think, that God taught our firft parents only fuch Language as fuited their prefent occafions; leaving them, as he did in other things, to enlarge and improve it as their future neceffities fhould require. Confequently, thofe firft rudiments of Speech muft have been poor and narrow; and we are at full liberty to enquire in what manner, and by what fteps, Language advanced to the ftate in which we now find it. The hiftory which I am to give of this progrefs, will fuggeft feveral things, both curious in themfelves, and ufeful in our future difquifitions.

IF we fhould fuppofe a period before any words were invented or known, it is clear, that men could have no other method of communicating to others what they felt, than by the cries of paffion, accompanied with fuch motions and geftures as were farther expreffive of paffion. For thefe are the only figns which nature teaches all men, and which are underftood by all. One who faw another going into fome place where he himfelf had been frightened, or expofed to danger, and who fought to warn his neighbour of the danger, could contrive no other way of doing fo, than by uttering thofe cries, and making thofe geftures, which are the figns of fear: juft as two men, at this day, would endeavour to make themfelves be underftood by each other, who fhould be thrown together on a

defolate

defolate ifland, ignorant of one another's Language. Thofe exclamations, therefore, which by Grammarians are called Interjections, uttered in a ftrong and paffionate manner, were, beyond doubt, the firft elements or beginnings of Speech.

WHEN more enlarged communication became neceffary, and names began to be affigned to objects, in what manner can we fuppofe men to have proceeded in this affignation of names, or invention of words? Undoubtedly, by imitating, as much as they could, the nature of the object which they named, by the found of the name which they gave to it. As a Painter, who would reprefent grafs, muft employ a green colour; fo, in the beginnings of Language, one giving a name to any thing harfh or boifterous, would of courfe employ a harfh or boifterous found. He could not do otherwife, if he meant to excite in the hearer the idea of that thing which he fought to name. To fuppofe words invented, or names given, to things, in a manner purely arbitrary, without any ground or reafon, is to fuppofe an effect without a caufe. There muft have always been fome motive which led to the affignation of one name rather than another; and we can conceive no motive which would more univerfally operate upon men in their firft efforts towards Language, than a defire to paint by Speech, the objects which they named, in a manner more or lefs complete, according as the vocal organs had it in their power to effect this imitation.

WHEREVER objects were to be named, in which found, noife, or motion were concerned, the imitation by words was abundantly obvious. Nothing was more natural, than to imitate, by the found of the voice, the quality of the found or noife which

4   any

any external object made; and to form its name accordingly. Thus, in all Languages, we find a multitude of words that are evidently conſtructed upon this principle. A certain bird is termed the Cuckoo, from the ſound which it emits. When one ſort of wind is ſaid to *whiſtle*, and another to *roar*; when a ſerpent is ſaid to *hiſs*; a fly to *buz*, and falling timber to *craſh*; when a ſtream is ſaid to *flow*, and hail to *rattle*; the analogy between the word and the thing ſignified is plainly diſcernible.

In the names of objects which addreſs the ſight only, where neither noiſe nor motion are concerned, and ſtill more in the terms appropriated to moral ideas, this analogy appears to fail. Many learned men, however, have been of opinion, that though, in ſuch caſes, it becomes more obſcure, yet it is not altogether loſt; but that throughout the radical words of all Languages, there may be traced ſome degree of correſpondence with the object ſignified. With regard to moral and intellectual ideas, they remark, that, in every Language, the terms ſigniſicant of them, are derived from the names of ſenſible objects to which they are conceived to be analogous; and with regard to ſenſible objects pertaining merely to ſight, they remark, that their moſt diſtinguiſhing qualities have certain radical ſounds appropriated to the expreſſion of them, in a great variety of Languages. Stability, for inſtance, fluidity, hollowneſs, ſmoothneſs, gentleneſs, violence, &c. they imagine to be painted by the ſound of certain letters or ſyllables, which have ſome relation to thoſe different ſtates of viſible objects, on account of an obſcure reſemblance which the organs of voice are capable of aſſuming to ſuch external qualities. By this natural

mechaniſm,

mechanifm, they imagine all Languages to have been at firft conftructed, and the roots of their capital words formed *.

As far as this fyftem is founded in truth, Language appears to be not altogether arbitrary in its origin. Among the ancient Stoic and Platonic Philofophers, it was a queftion much agitated,

* The Author, who has carried his fpeculations on this fubject the fartheft, is the Prefident Des Broffes, in his " Traité de la Formation Mechanique " des Langues." Some of the radical letters or fyllables which he fuppofes to carry this expreffive power in moft known Languages are, St, to fignify ftability or reft; Fl, to denote fluency; Cl, a gentle defcent; R, what relates to rapid motion; C, to cavity or hollownefs, &c. A century before his time, Dr. Wallis, in his Grammar of the Englifh Language, had taken notice of thefe fignificant roots, and reprefented it as a peculiar excellency of our Tongue, that, beyond all others, it expreffed the nature of the objects which it names, by employing founds fharper, fofter, weaker, ftronger, more obfcure, or more ftridulous, according as the idea which is to be fuggefted requires. He gives various examples. Thus; words formed upon St, always denote firmnefs and ftrength, analogous to the Latin *fto*; as, ftand, ftay, ftaff, ftop, ftout, fteady, ftake, ftamp, ftallion, ftately, &c. Words beginning with Str, intimate violent force, and energy, analogous to the Greek στρωννυμι; as, ftrive, ftrength, ftrike, ftripe, ftrefs, ftruggle, ftride, ftretch, ftrip, &c. Thr, implies forcible motion; as, throw, throb, thruft, through, threaten, thraldom. Wr, obliquity or diftortion; as, wry, wreft, wreath, wreftle, wring, wrong, wrangle, wrath, wrack, &c. Sw, filent agitation, or lateral motion; as, fway, fwing, fwerve, fweep, fwim. Sl, a gentle fall or lefs obfervable motion; as, flide, flip, fly, flit, flow, flack, fling. Sp, diffipation or expanfion; as, fpread, fprout, fprinkle, fplit, fpill, fpring. Terminations in Afh, indicate fomething acting nimbly and fharply; as, crafh, gafh, rafh, flafh, lafh, flafh. Terminations in Ufh, fomething acting more obtufely and dully; as, crufh, brufh, hufh gufh, blufh. The learned Author produces a great many more examples of the fame kind, which feem to leave no doubt, that the analogies of found have had fome influence on the formation of words. At the fame time, in all fpeculations of this kind, there is fo much room for fancy to operate, that they ought to be adopted with much caution in forming any general theory.

2   " Utrum

"Utrum nomina rerum fint naturâ, an impofitione?" φυσει
ή θεσί'; by which they meant, Whether words were merely
conventional fymbols; of the rife of which no account could
be given, except the pleafure of the firft inventors of Language? or, Whether there was fome principle in nature that
led to the affignation of particular names to particular objects;
and thofe of the Platonic fchool favoured the latter opinion*?

THIS principle, however, of a natural relation between
words and objects, can only be applied to Language in its moft
fimple and primitive ftate. Though, in every Tongue, fome
remains of it, as I have fhown above, can be traced, it were
utterly in vain to fearch for it throughout the whole conftruction of any modern Language. As the multitude of terms increafe in every nation, and the immenfe field of Language is
filled up, words, by a thoufand fanciful and irregular methods
of derivation and compofition, come to deviate widely from the

* Vid. Plat. in Cratylo. "Nomina verbaque non pofita fortuito, fed qua-
"dam vi & ratione naturæ facta effe, P. Nigidius in Grammaticis Commen-
"tariis docet; rem fane in philofophiæ differtationibus celebrem. In eam
"rem multa argumenta dicit, cur videri poffint verba effe naturalia, magis
"quàm arbitraria, *Vos*, inquit, cum dicimus, motu quodam oris conveniente,
"cum ipfius verbi demonftratione utimur, & labias fenfim primores emove-
"mus, ac fpiritum atque animam porro verfum, & ad eos quibus confermoci-
"namur intendimus. At contra cum dicimus *Nos*, neque profufo intentoque
"flatu vocis, neque projectis labiis pronunciamus; fed et fpiritum et labias
"quafi intra nofmet ipfos coërcemus. Hoc fit idem et in eo quod dicimus,
"*tu*, & *ego*, & *mihi*, & *tibi*. Nam ficuti cum adnuimus & abnuimus,
"motus quodam illo vel capitis, vel oculorum, a natura rei quam fignificat,
"non abhorret, ita in his vocibus quafi geftus quidam oris & fpiritus naturalis
"eft. Eadem ratio eft in Græcis quoque vocibus quam effe in noftris
"animadvertimus." A. GELLIUS, Noct. Atticæ, lib. x. cap. 4.

primitive

primitive character of their roots, and to lose all analogy or resemblance in sound to the things signified. In this state we now find Language. Words, as we now employ them, taken in the general, may be confidered as symbols, not as imitations; as arbitrary, or instituted, not natural signs of ideas. But there can be no doubt, I think, that Language, the nearer we remount to its rise among men, will be found to partake more of a natural expression. As it could be originally formed on nothing but imitation, it would, in its primitive state, be more picturesque; much more barren indeed, and narrow in the circle of its terms, than now; but so far as it went, more expressive by sound of the thing signified. This, then, may be assumed as one character of the first state, or beginnings, of Language, among every savage tribe.

A SECOND character of Language, in its early state, is drawn from the manner in which words were at first pronounced, or uttered, by men. Interjections, I showed, or passionate exclamations, were the first elements of Speech. Men laboured to communicate their feelings to one another, by those expressive cries and gestures which nature taught them. After words, or names of objects, began to be invented, this mode of speaking, by natural signs, could not be all at once disused. For Language, in its infancy, must have been extremely barren; and there certainly was a period, among all rude nations, when conversation was carried on by a very few words, intermixed with many exclamations and earnest gestures. The small stock of words which men as yet possessed, rendered those helps absolutely necessary for explaining their conceptions; and rude, uncultivated men, not having always at hand even

the

the few words which they knew, would naturally labour to make themfelves underftood, by varying their tones of voice, and accompanying their tones with the moft fignificant gefticulations they could make. At this day, when perfons attempt to fpeak in any Language which they poffefs imperfectly, they have recourfe to all thefe fupplemental methods, in order to render themfelves more intelligible. The plan too, according to which I have fhown, that Language was originally conftructed, upon refemblance or analogy, as far as was poffible, to the thing fignified, would naturally lead men to utter their words with more emphafis and force, as long as Language was a fort of painting by means of found. For all thofe reafons this may be affumed as a principle, that the pronunciation of the earlieft Languages was accompanied with more gefticulation, and with more and greater inflexions of voice, than what we now ufe; there was more action in it; and it was more upon a crying or finging tone.

To this manner of fpeaking, neceffity firft gave rife. But we muft obferve, that, after this neceffity had, in a great meafure, ceafed, by Language becoming, in procefs of time, more extenfive and copious, the antient manner of Speech ftill fubfifted among many nations; and what had arifen from neceffity, continued to be ufed for ornament. Wherever there was much fire and vivacity in the genius of nations, they were naturally inclined to a mode of converfation which gratified the imagination fo much; for, an imagination which is warm, is always prone to throw both a great deal of action, and a variety of tones, into difcourfe. Upon this principle, Dr.

P 2　　　　　　　　　　　Warburton

Warburton accounts for fo much fpeaking by action, as we find among the Old Teftament Prophets; as when Jeremiah breaks the potter's veffel, in fight of the people; throws a book into the Euphrates; puts on bonds and yokes; and carries out his houfehold ftuff; all which, he imagines, might be fignificant modes of expreffion, very natural in thofe ages, when men were accuftomed to explain themfelves fo much by actions and geftures. In like manner, among the Northern American tribes, certain motions and actions were found to be much ufed as explanatory of their meaning, on all their great occafions of intercourfe with each other; and by the belts and ftrings of wampum, which they gave and received, they were ac-cuftomed to declare their meaning, as much as by their dif-courfes.

WITH regard to inflexions of voice, thefe are fo natural, that, to fome nations, it has appeared eafier to exprefs different ideas, by varying the tone with which they pronounced the fame word, than to contrive words for all their ideas. This is the practice of the Chinefe in particular. The number of words in their Language is faid not to be great; but, in fpeaking, they vary each of their words on no lefs than five different tones, by which they make the fame word fignify five different things. This muft give a great appearance of mufic or finging to their Speech. For thofe inflexions of voice which, in the infancy of Language, were no more than harfh or diffonant cries, muft, as Language gradually polifhes, pafs into more fmooth and mufical founds: and hence is formed, what we call, the Profody of a Language.

It

It is remarkable, and deferves attention, that, both in the Greek and Roman Languages, this mufical and gefticulating pronunciation was retained in a very high degree. Without having attended to this, we will be at a lofs in underftanding feveral paffages of the Claffics, which relate to the public fpeaking, and the theatrical entertainments, of the antients. It appears, from many circumftances, that the profody both of the Greeks and Romans, was carried much farther than ours; or that they fpoke with more, and ftronger, inflexions of voice than we ufe. The quantity of their fyllables was much more fixed than in any of the modern Languages, and rendered much more fenfible to the ear in pronouncing them. Befides quantities, or the difference of fhort and long, accents were placed upon moft of their fyllables, the acute, grave, and circumflex; the ufe of which accents we have now entirely loft, but which, we know, determined the fpeaker's voice to rife or fall. Our modern pronunciation muft have appeared to them a lifelefs monotony. The declamation of their orators, and the pronunciation of their actors upon the ftage, approached to the nature of recitative in mufic ; was capable of being marked in notes, and fupported with inftruments; as feveral learned men have fully proved. And if this was the cafe, as they have fhown, among the Romans, the Greeks, it is well known, were ftill a more mufical people than the Romans, and carried their attention to tone and pronunciation much farther in every public exhibition. Ariftotle, in his Poëtics, confiders the mufic of Tragedy as one of its chief and moft effential parts.

The cafe was parallel with regard to geftures : for ftrong tones, and animated geftures, we may obferve, always go to-

3   gether.

gether. Action is treated of by all the antient critics, as the chief quality in every public fpeaker. The action, both of the orators and the players in Greece and Rome, was far more vehement than what we are accuftomed to. Rofcius would have feemed a madman to us. Gefture was of fuch confequence upon the antient ftage, that there is reafon for believing, that, on fome occafions, the fpeaking and the acting part were divided, which, according to our ideas, would form a ftrange exhibition ; one player fpoke the words in the proper tones, while another performed the correfponding motions and geftures. We learn from Cicero, that it was a conteft between him and Rofcius, whether he could exprefs a fentiment in a greater variety of phrafes, or Rofcius in a greater variety of intelligible fignificant geftures. At laft, gefture came to engrofs the ftage wholly ; for, under the reigns of Auguftus and Tiberius, the favourite entertainment of the Public was the pantomime, which was carried on entirely by mute gefticulation. The people were moved, and wept at it, as much as at tragedies ; and the paffion for it became fo ftrong, that laws were obliged to be made, for reftraining the Senators from ftudying the pantomime art. Now, though in declamations and theatrical exhibitions, both tone and gefture were, doubtlefs, carried much farther than in common difcourfe ; yet public fpeaking, of any kind, muft, in every country, bear fome proportion to the manner that is ufed in converfation ; and fuch public entertainments as I have now mentioned, could never have been relifhed by a nation, whofe tones and geftures, in difcourfe, were as languid as ours.

I   WHEN

WHEN the Barbarians fpread themfelves over the Roman Empire, thefe more phlegmatic nations did not retain the accents, the tones and geftures, which neceffity at firft introduced, and cuftom and fancy afterwards fo long fupported, in the Greek and Roman Languages. As the Latin Tongue was loft in their idioms, fo the character of fpeech and pronunciation began to be changed throughout Europe. Nothing of the fame attention was paid to the mufic of Language, or to the pomp of declamation, and theatrical action. Both converfation and public fpeaking became more fimple and plain; fuch as we now find it; without that enthufiaftic mixture of tones and geftures, which diftinguifhed the antient nations. At the reftoration of letters, the genius of Language was fo much altered, and the manners of the people become fo different, that it was no eafy matter to underftand what the Antients had faid, concerning their declamations and public fpectacles. Our plain manner of fpeaking, in thefe northern countries, expreffes the paffions with fufficient energy, to move thofe who are not accuftomed to any more vehement manner. But, undoubtedly, more varied tones, and more animated motions, carry a natural expreffion of warmer feelings. Accordingly, in different modern Languages, the profody of Speech partakes more of mufic, in proportion to the livelinefs and fenfibility of the people. A Frenchman both varies his accents, and gefticulates while he fpeaks, much more than an Englifhman. An Italian, a great deal more than either. Mufical pronunciation and expreffive gefture are, to this day, the diftinction of Italy.

FROM the pronunciation of Language, let us proceed, in the third place, to confider of the Style of Language in its moft

early

early ſtate, and of its progreſs in this reſpect alſo. As the manner in which men at firſt uttered their words, and maintained converſation, was ſtrong and expreſſive, enforcing their imperfectly expreſſed ideas by cries and geſtures ; ſo the Language which they uſed, could be no other than full of figures and metaphors, not correct indeed, but forcible and picturefque.

We are apt, upon a ſuperficial view, to imagine, that thoſe modes of expreſſion which are called Figures of Speech, are among the chief refinements of Speech, not invented till after Language had advanced to its later periods, and mankind were brought into a poliſhed ſtate ; and that, then, they were deviſed by Orators and Rhetoricians. The quite contrary of this is the truth. Mankind never employed ſo many figures of Speech, as when they had hardly any words for expreſſing their meaning.

For firſt, the want of proper names for every object, obliged them to uſe one name for many ; and, of courſe, to expreſs themſelves by compariſons, metaphors, alluſions, and all thoſe ſubſtituted forms of Speech which render Language figurative. Next, as the objects with which they were moſt converſant, were the ſenſible, material objects around them, names would be given to thoſe objects long before words were invented for ſignifying the diſpoſitions of the mind, or any ſort of moral and intellectual ideas. Hence, the early Language of men being entirely made up of words deſcriptive of ſenſible objects, it became, of neceſſity, extremely metaphorical. For, to ſignify any deſire or paſſion, or any act or feeling of the mind,

mind, they had no precife expreffion which was appropriated to that purpofe, but were under a neceffity of painting the emotion, or paffion, which they felt, by allufion to thofe fenfible objects which had moft relation to it, and which could render it, in fome fort, vifible to others.

But it was not neceffity alone, that gave rife to this figured ftyle. Other circumftances alfo, at the commencement of Language, contributed to it. In the infancy of all focieties, men are much under the dominion of imagination and paffion. They live fcattered and difperfed; they are unacquainted with the courfe of things; they are, every day, meeting with new and ftrange objects. Fear and furprife, wonder and aftonifhment, are their moft frequent paffions. Their Language will neceffarily partake of this character of their minds. They will be prone to exaggeration and hyperbole. They will be given to defcribe every thing with the ftrongeft colours, and moft vehement expreffions; infinitely more than men living in the advanced and cultivated periods of Society, when their imagination is more chaftened, their paffions are more tamed, and a wider experience has rendered the objects of life more familiar to them. Even the manner in which I before fhowed that the firft tribes of men uttered their words, would have confiderable influence on their ftyle. Wherever ftrong exclamations, tones, and geftures, enter much into converfation, the imagination is always more exercifed; a greater effort of fancy and paffion is excited. Confequently, the fancy kept awake, and rendered more fprightly by this mode of utterance, operates upon ftyle, and enlivens it more.

THESE reafonings are confirmed by undoubted facts. The
ftyle of all the moft early Languages, among nations who are
in the firft and rude periods of Society, is found, without exception, to be full of figures; hyperbolical and picturefque in
a high degree. We have a ftriking inftance of this in the
American Languages, which are known, by the moft authentic
accounts, to be figurative to excefs. The Iroquois and Illinois,
carry on their treaties and public tranfactions with bolder metaphors, and greater pomp of ftyle, than we ufe in our poetical
productions *.

ANOTHER remarkable inftance is, the ftyle of the Old
Teftament, which is carried on by conftant allufions to fenfible

---

* Thus, to give an inftance of the fingular ftyle of thefe nations, the Five
Nations of Canada, when entering on a treaty of peace with us, expreffed
themfelves by their Chiefs, in the following Language : " We are happy in
" having buried under ground the red axe, that has fo often been dyed with the
" blood of our brethren. Now, in this fort, we inter the axe, and plant the
" tree of Peace. We plant a tree, whofe top will reach the Sun ; and its
" branches fpread abroad, fo that it fhall be feen afar off. May its growth
" never be ftifled and choked ; but may it fhade both your country and ours
" with its leaves ! Let us make faft its roots, and extend them to the utmoft
" of your colonies. If the French fhould come to fhake this tree, we would
" know it by the motion of its roots reaching into our country. May the
" Great Spirit allow us to reft in tranquillity upon our matts, and never again
" dig up the axe to cut down the tree of Peace ! Let the earth be trod hard
" over it, where it lies buried. Let a ftrong ftream run under the pit, to wafh
" the evil away out of our fight and remembrance.—The fire that had long
" burned in Albany is extinguifhed. The bloody bed is wafhed clean, and
" the tears are wiped from our eyes. We now renew the covenant chain of
" friendfhip. Let it be kept bright and clean as filver, and not fuffered to
" contract any ruft. Let not any one pull away his arm from it." Thefe
paffages are extracted from Cadwallader Colden's Hiftory of the Five Indian
Nations ; where it appears, from the authentic documents he produces, that
fuch is their genuine ftyle.

I   objects.

objects. Iniquity, or guilt, is expreſſed by " a ſpotted garment;" miſery, by " drinking the cup of aſtoniſhment ;" vain purſuits, by " feeding on aſhes ;" a ſinful life, by " a crooked path ;" proſperity, by " the candle of the Lord ſhining on our head ;" and the like, in innumerable inſtances. Hence, we have been accuſtomed to call this ſort of ſtyle, the Oriental Style ; as fancying it to be peculiar to the nations of the Eaſt : Whereas, from the American Style, and from many other inſtances, it plainly appears not to have been peculiar to any one region or climate ; but to have been common to all nations, in certain periods of Society and Language.

HENCE, we may receive ſome light concerning that ſeeming paradox, that Poetry is more antient than Proſe. I ſhall have occaſion to diſcuſs this point fully hereafter, when I come to treat of the Nature and Origin of Poetry. At preſent, it is ſufficient to obſerve, that, from what has been ſaid it plainly appears, that the ſtyle of all Language muſt have been originally poetical ; ſtrongly tinctured with that enthuſiaſm, and that deſcriptive, metaphorical expreſſion, which diſtinguiſhes Poetry.

As Language, in its progreſs, began to grow more copious, it gradually loſt that figurative ſtyle, which was its early character. When men were furniſhed with proper and familiar names for every object, both ſenſible and moral, they were not obliged to uſe ſo many circumlocutions. Style became more preciſe, and, of courſe, more ſimple. Imagination too, in proportion as Society advanced, had leſs influence over mankind. The vehement manner of ſpeaking by tones and

Q 2 geſtures,

gestures, became not so universal. The understanding was more exercised; the fancy, less. Intercourse among mankind becoming more extensive and frequent, clearness of style, in signifying their meaning to each other, was the chief object of attention. In place of Poets, Philosophers became the instructors of men; and, in their reasonings on all different subjects, introduced that plainer and simpler style of composition, which we now call Prose. Among the Greeks, Pherecydes of Scyros, the master of Pythagoras, is recorded to have been the first, who, in this sense, composed any writing in prose. The antient metaphorical and poetical dress of Language, was now laid aside from the intercourse of men, and reserved for those occasions only, on which ornament was professedly studied.

THUS I have pursued the History of Language through some of the variations it has undergone: I have considered it, in the first structure, and composition, of words; in the manner of uttering or pronouncing words; and in the style and character of Speech. I have yet to consider it in another view, respecting the order and arrangement of words; when we shall find a progress to have taken place, similar to what I have been now illustrating.

L E C T U R E VII.

RISE and PROGRESS of LANGUAGE, AND of WRITING.

WHEN we attend to the order in which words are arranged in a fentence, or fignificant propofition, we find a very remarkable difference between the antient and the modern Tongues. The confideration of this will ferve to unfold farther the genius of Language, and to fhow the caufes of thofe alterations, which it has undergone, in the progrefs of Society.

IN order to conceive diftinctly the nature of that alteration of which I now fpeak, let us go back, as we did formerly, to the moft early period of Language. Let us figure to ourfelves a Savage, who beholds fome object, fuch as fruit, which raifes his defire, and who requefts another to give it to him. Suppofing our Savage to be unacquainted with words, he would,

in

in that cafe, labour to make himfelf be underftood, by pointing earneftly at the object which he defired, and uttering at the fame time a paffionate cry. Suppofing him to have acquired words, the firft word which he uttered would, of courfe, be the name of that object. He would not exprefs himfelf, according to our Englifh order of conftruction, " Give me fruit;" but according to the Latin order, " Fruit give me;" " Fructum " da mihi:" For this plain reafon, that his attention was wholly directed towards fruit, the defired object. This was the exciting idea; the object which moved him to fpeak; and, of courfe, would be the firft named. Such an arrangement is precifely putting into words the gefture which nature taught the Savage to make, before he was acquainted with words; and therefore it may be depended upon as certain, that he would fall moft readily into this arrangement.

Accustomed now to a different method of ordering our words, we call this an inverfion, and confider it as a forced and unnatural order of Speech. But though not the moft logical, it is, however, in one view, the moft natural order; becaufe, it is the order fuggefted by imagination and defire, which always impel us to mention their object in the firft place. We might therefore conclude, *a priori*, that this would be the order in which words were moft commonly arranged at the beginnings of Language; and accordingly we find, in fact, that, in this order, words are arranged in moft of the antient Tongues; as in the Greek and the Latin; and it is faid alfo, in the Ruffian, the Sclavonic, the Gaëlic, and feveral of the American Tongues.

                                                              In

In the Latin Language, the arrangement which moſt commonly obtains, is, to place firſt, in the ſentence, that word which expreſſes the principal object of the diſcourſe, together with its circumſtances; and afterwards, the perſon, or the thing, that acts upon it. Thus Salluſt, comparing together the mind and the body; " Animi imperio, corporis ſervitio, magis utimur ;" which order certainly renders the ſentence more lively and ſtriking, than when it is arranged according to our Engliſh conſtruction; " We make moſt uſe of the direction of the ſoul, " and of the ſervice of the body." The Latin order gratifies more the rapidity of the imagination, which naturally runs firſt to that which is its chief object; and having once named it, carries it in view throughout the reſt of the ſentence. In the ſame manner in poetry :

> Juſtum & tenacem propoſiti virum,
> Non civium ardor prava jubentium,
> Non vultus inſtantis tyranni,
> Mente quatit ſolida.————

Every perſon of taſte muſt be ſenſible, that here the words are arranged with a much greater regard to the figure which the ſeveral objects make in the fancy, than our Engliſh conſtruction admits ; which would require the " Juſtum & tenacem " propoſiti virum," though, undoubtedly, the capital object in the ſentence, to be thrown into the laſt place.

I HAVE ſaid, that, in the Greek and Roman Languages, the moſt common arrangement is, to place that firſt which ſtrikes the imagination of the ſpeaker moſt. I do not, however, pretend,

tend, that this holds without exception. Sometimes regard to the harmony of the period requires a different order; and in Languages fusceptible of fo much mufical beauty, and pronounced with fo much tone and modulation as were ufed by thofe nations, the harmony of periods was an object carefully ftudied. Sometimes too, attention to the perfpicuity, to the force, or to the artful fufpenfion of the fpeaker's meaning, alter this order; and produce fuch varieties in the arrangement, that it is not eafy to reduce them to any one principle. But, in general, this was the genius and character of moft of the antient Languages, to give fuch full liberty to the collocation of words, as allowed them to affume whatever order was moft agreeable to the fpeaker's imagination. The Hebrew is, indeed, an exception: which, though not altogether without inverfions, yet employs them lefs frequently, and approaches nearer to the Englifh conftruction, than either the Greek or the Latin.

ALL the modern Languages of Europe have adopted a different arrangement from the antient. In their profe compofitions, very little variety is admitted in the collocation of words; they are moftly fixed to one order; and that order is, what may be called, the Order of the Underftanding. They place firft in the fentence, the perfon or thing which fpeaks or acts; next, its action; and laftly, the object of its action. So that the ideas are made to fucceed to one another, not according to the degree of importance which the feveral objects carry in the imagination, but according to the order of nature and of time.

AN

An Englifh writer, paying a compliment to a great man, would fay thus: " It is impoffible for me to pafs over, in " filence, fuch remarkable mildnefs, fuch fingular and unheard- " of clemency, and fuch unufual moderation, in the exercife of " fupreme power." Here we have, firft prefented to us, the the perfon who fpeaks. " It is impoffible for *me* ;" next, what that perfon is to do, " impoffible for him *to pafs over in filence*;" and laftly, the object which moves him fo to do, " the mild- " nefs, clemency, and moderation of his patron." Cicero, from whom I have tranflated thefe words, juft reverfes this order; beginning with the object, placing that firft which was the exciting idea in the fpeaker's mind, and ending with the fpeaker and his action. " Tantam manfuetudinem, tam in- " ufitatam inauditamque clementiam, tantumque in fumma " poteftate rerum omnium modum, tacitus multo modo præ- " terire poffum." (Orat. pro Marcell.)

The Latin order is more animated ; the Englifh, more clear and diftinct. The Romans generally arranged their words according to the order in which the ideas rofe in the fpeaker's imagination. We arrange them according to the order in which the underftanding directs thofe ideas to be exhibited, in fucceffion, to the view of another. Our arrangement, therefore, appears to be the confequence of greater refinement in the art of Speech ; as far as clearnefs in communication is underftood to be the end of Speech.

In poetry, where we are fuppofed to rife above the ordinary ftyle, and to fpeak the Language of fancy and paffion, our arrangement is not altogether fo limited ; but fome greater liberty is allowed for tranſpoſition, and inverſion. Even there, however, that liberty is confined within narrow bounds, in compariſon of the Antient Languages. The different modern Tongues vary from one another, in this reſpect. The French Language is, of them all, the moſt determinate in the order of its words, and admits the leaſt of inverſion, either in proſe or poetry. The Engliſh admits it more. But the Italian retains the moſt of the antient tranſpoſitive character; though one is apt to think, at the expence of a little obſcurity in the ſtyle of ſome of their authors, who deal moſt in theſe tranſ-poſitions.

It is proper, next, to obſerve, that there is one circumſtance in the ſtructure of all the modern Tongues, which, of ne-ceſſity, limits their arrangement, in a great meaſure, to one fixed and determinate train. We have difuſed thoſe differences of termination, which, in the Greek and Latin, diſtinguiſhed the ſeveral caſes of nouns, and tenſes of verbs; and which, thereby, pointed out the mutual relation of the ſeveral words in a ſentence to one another, though the related words were disjoined, and placed in different parts of the ſentence. This is an alteration in the ſtructure of Language, of which I ſhall have occaſion to ſay more in the next Lecture. One ob-vious effect of it is, that we have now, for the moſt part, no way left us to ſhew the cloſe relation of any two words to one another in meaning, but by placing them cloſe to one another in the period. For inſtance; the Romans could, with propriety, expreſs themſelves thus;

> Extinctum nymphæ crudeli funere Daphnim
> Flebant.————— ——— ———

Becauſe

Becaufe " Extinctum & Daphnim," being both in the accufative cafe, this fhowed, that the adjective and the fubftantive were related to each other, though placed at the two extremities of the line; and that both were governed by the active verb " Flebant," to which " nymphæ" plainly appeared to be the nominative. The different terminations here reduced all into order, and made the connection of the feveral words perfectly clear. But let us tranflate thefe words literally into Englifh, according to the Latin arrangement; " Dead the " nymphs by a cruel fate Daphnis lamented;" and they become a perfect riddle, in which it is impoffible to find any meaning.

IT was by means of this contrivance, which obtained in almoft all the antient Languages, of varying the termination of nouns and verbs, and thereby pointing out the concordance, and the government of the words, in a fentence, that they enjoyed fo much liberty of tranfpofition, and could marfhal and arrange their words in any way that gratified the imagination, or pleafed the ear. When Language came to be modelled by the northern nations who overran the empire, they dropped the cafes of nouns, and the different termination of verbs, with the more eafe, becaufe they placed no great value upon the advantages arifing from fuch a ftructure of Language. They were attentive only to clearnefs, and copioufnefs of expreffion. They neither regarded much the harmony of found, nor fought to gratify the imagination by the collocation of words. They ftudied folely to exprefs themfelves in fuch a manner as fhould exhibit their ideas to others in the moft diftinct and intelligible order. And hence, if our Language, by reafon of

the

the simple arrangement of its words, possesses less harmony, less beauty, and less force, than the Greek or Latin; it is, however, in its meaning, more obvious and plain.

THUS I have shewn what the natural Progress of Language has been, in several material articles; and this account of the Genius and Progress of Language, lays a foundation for many observations, both curious and useful. From what has been said, in this, and the preceding Lecture, it appears, that Language was, at first, barren in words, but descriptive by the sound of these words; and expressive in the manner of uttering them, by the aid of significant tones and gestures: Style was figurative and poetical: arrangement was fanciful and lively. It appears, that, in all the successive changes which Language has undergone, as the world advanced, the understanding has gained ground on the fancy and imagination. The Progress of Language, in this respect, resembles the progress of age in man. The imagination is most vigorous and predominant in youth; with advancing years, the imagination cools, and the understanding ripens. Thus Language, proceeding from sterility to copiousness, hath, at the same time, proceeded from vivacity to accuracy; from fire and enthusiasm, to coolness and precision. Those characters of early Language, descriptive sound, vehement tones and gestures, figurative style, and inverted arrangement, all hang together, have a mutual influence on each other; and have all gradually given place, to arbitrary sounds, calm pronunciation, simple style, plain arrangement. Language is become, in modern times, more correct, indeed, and accurate; but, however, less striking and animated: In its

antient

antient ſtate, more favourable to poetry and oratory; in its preſent, to reaſon and philoſophy.

HAVING finiſhed my account of the Progreſs of Speech, I proceed to give an account of the Progreſs of Writing, which next demands our notice; though it will not require ſo full a diſcuſſion as the former ſubject.

NEXT to Speech, Writing is, beyond doubt, the moſt uſeful art of which men are poſſeſſed. It is plainly an improvement upon Speech, and therefore muſt have been poſterior to it in order of time. At firſt, men thought of nothing more than communicating their thoughts to one another, when preſent, by means of words, or ſounds, which they uttered. Afterwards, they deviſed this further method, of mutual communication with one another, when abſent, by means of marks or characters preſented to the eye, which we call Writing.

WRITTEN characters are of two ſorts. They are either ſigns for things, or ſigns for words. Of the former ſort, ſigns of things, are the pictures, hieroglyphics, and ſymbols, employed by the antient nations; of the latter ſort, ſigns for words, are the alphabetical characters, now employed by all Europeans. Theſe two kinds of Writing are generically, and eſſentially, diſtinct.

PICTURES were, undoubtedly, the firſt eſſay towards Writing. Imitation is ſo natural to man, that, in all ages, and among all nations, ſome methods have obtained, of copying or tracing the likeneſs of ſenſible objects. Thoſe methods would

foon

3

LECT.
VII.

foon be employed by men for giving fome imperfect information to others, at a diftance, of what had happened; or, for
preferving the memory of facts which they fought to record.
Thus, to fignify that one man had killed another, they drew the
figure of one man ftretched upon the earth, and of another
ftanding by him with a deadly weapon in his hand. We find,
in fact, that, when America was firft difcovered, this was the
only fort of Writing known in the kingdom of Mexico. By
hiftorical pictures, the Mexicans are faid to have tranfmitted the
memory of the moft important tranfactions of their empire. Thefe,
however, muft have been extremely imperfect records; and the
nations who had no other, muft have been very grofs and rude.
Pictures could do no more than delineate external events. They
could neither exhibit the connections of them, nor defcribe fuch
qualities as were not vifible to the eye, nor convey any idea of
the difpofitions, or words, of men.

To fupply, in fome degree, this defect, there arofe, in procefs of time, the invention of what are called, Hieroglyphical
Characters; which may be confidered as the fecond ftage of the
Art of Writing. Hieroglyphics confift in certain fymbols,
which are made to ftand for invifible objects, on account of an
analogy or refemblance which fuch fymbols were fuppofed to bear
to the objects. Thus, an eye, was the hieroglyphical fymbol
of knowledge; a circle, of eternity, which has neither beginning, nor end. Hieroglyphics, therefore, were a more refined and extenfive fpecies of painting. Pictures delineated the
refemblance of external vifible objects. Hieroglyphics painted
invifible objects, by analogies taken from the external world.

AMONG

AMONG the Mexicans, were found fome traces of hierogly- phical characters, intermixed with their hiftorical pictures. But Egypt was the country where this fort of Writing was moft ftudied, and brought into a regular art. In hieroglyphics, was conveyed all the boafted wifdom of their priefts. Ac- cording to the properties which they afcribed to animals, or the qualities with which they fuppofed natural objects to be en- dowed, they pitched upon them to be the emblems, or hiero- glyphics, of moral objects; and employed them in their Writ- ing for that end. Thus, ingratitude was denominated by a viper; imprudence, by a fly; wifdom, by an ant; victory, by a hawk; a dutiful child, by a ftork; a man univerfally fhunned, by an eel, which they fuppofed to be found in company with no other fifh. Sometimes they joined together two or more of thefe hieroglyphical characters; as, a ferpent with a hawk's head; to denote nature, with God prefiding over it. But, as many of thofe properties of objects which they affumed for the foundation of their hieroglyphics, were merely imaginary, and the allufions drawn from them were forced and ambiguous; as the conjunction of their characters rendered them ftill more obfcure, and muft have expreffed very indiftinctly the connec- tions and relations of things; this fort of Writing could be no other than ænigmatical, and confufed, in the higheft degree; and muft have been a very imperfect vehicle of knowledge of any kind.

IT has been imagined, that hieroglyphics were an invention of the Egyptian priefts, for concealing their learning from com- mon view; and that, upon this account, it was preferred by them to the alphabetical method of Writing. But this is

certainly

certainly a miſtake. Hieroglyphics were, undoubtedly, employed, at firſt, from neceſſity, not from choice or refinement;
and would never have been thought of, if alphabetical characters
had been known. The nature of the invention plainly ſhows
it to have been one of thoſe groſs and rude eſſays towards Writing, which were adopted in the early ages of the world; in
order to extend ſome farther the firſt method which they had
employed of ſimple pictures, or repreſentations of viſible objects. Indeed, in after-times, when alphabetical Writing was
introduced into Egypt, and the hieroglyphical was, of courſe,
fallen into diſuſe, it is known, that the prieſts ſtill employed
the hieroglyphical characters, as a ſacred kind of Writing, now
become peculiar to themſelves, and ſerving to give an air of
myſtery to their learning and religion. In this ſtate, the Greeks
found hieroglyphical Writing, when they began to have intercourſe with Egypt; and ſome of their writers miſtook this uſe,
to which they found it applied, for the cauſe that had given
riſe to the invention.

As Writing advanced, from pictures of viſible objects, to
hieroglyphics, or ſymbols of things inviſible; from theſe latter,
it advanced, among ſome nations, to ſimple arbitrary marks
which ſtood for objects, though without any reſemblance or
analogy to the objects ſignified. Of this nature was the method
of Writing practiſed among the Peruvians. They made uſe of
ſmall cords, of different colours; and by knots upon theſe, of
various ſizes, and differently ranged, they contrived ſigns for
giving information, and communicating their thoughts to one
another.

Of

OF this nature alſo, are the written characters, which are ufed to this day, throughout the great empire of China. The Chineſe have no alphabet of letters, or ſimple ſounds, which compoſe their words. But every ſingle character which they uſe in Writing, is ſignificant of an idea; it is a mark which ſtands for ſome one thing, or object. By conſequence, the number of theſe characters muſt be immenſe. It muſt correſpond to the whole number of objects, or ideas, which they have occaſion to expreſs; that is, to the whole number of words which they employ in Speech: nay, it muſt be greater than the number of words; one word, by varying the tone, with which it is ſpoken, may be made to ſignify ſeveral different things. They are ſaid to have ſeventy thouſand of thoſe written characters. To read and write them to perfection, is the ſtudy of a whole life; which ſubjects learning, among them, to infinite diſadvantage; and muſt have greatly retarded the progreſs of all ſcience.

LECT. VII.

CONCERNING the origin of theſe Chineſe characters, there have been different opinions, and much controverſy. According to the moſt probable accounts, the Chineſe Writing began, like the Egyptian, with pictures, and hieroglyphical figures. Theſe figures being, in progreſs, abbreviated in their form, for the ſake of writing them eaſily, and greatly enlarged in their number, paſſed, at length, into thoſe marks or characters which they now uſe, and which have ſpread themſelves through ſeveral nations of the Eaſt. For we are informed, that the Japaneſe, the Tonquineſe, and the Corœans, who ſpeak different languages from one another, and from the inhabitants of China, uſe, however, the ſame written characters with them;

and, by this means, correfpond intelligibly with each other in Writing, though ignorant of the Language fpoken in their feveral countries; a plain proof, that the Chinefe characters are, like hieroglyphics, independent of Language; are figns of things, not of words.

WE have one inftance of this fort of Writing in Europe. Our cyphers, as they are called, or arithmetical figures, 1, 2, 3, 4, &c. which we have derived from the Arabians, are fignificant marks, precifely of the fame nature with the Chinefe characters. They have no dependence on words; but each figure reprefents an object; reprefents the number for which it ftands; and, accordingly, on being prefented to the eye, is equally underftood by all the nations who have agreed in the ufe of thefe cyphers; by Italians, Spaniards, French, and Englifh, however different the Languages of thofe nations are from one another, and whatever different names they give, in their refpective Languages, to each numerical cypher.

As far, then, as we have yet advanced, nothing has appeared which refembles our letters, or which can be called Writing, in the fenfe we now give to that term. What we have hitherto feen, were all direct figns for things, and made no ufe of the medium of found, or words; either figns by reprefentation, as the Mexican pictures; or figns by analogy, as the Egyptian hieroglyphics; or figns by inftitution, as the Peruvian knots, the Chinefe characters, and the Arabian cyphers.

AT length, in different nations, men became fenfible of the imperfection, the ambiguity, and the tedioufnefs of each of thefe

methods

methods of communication with one another. They began to consider, that by employing signs which should stand not directly for things, but for the words which they used in Speech for naming these things, a considerable advantage would be gained. For they reflected farther, that though the number of words in every Language be, indeed, very great, yet the number of articulate sounds, which are used in composing these words, is comparatively small. The same simple sounds are continually recurring and repeated; and are combined together, in various ways, for forming all the variety of words which we utter. They bethought themselves, therefore, of inventing signs, not for each word, by itself, but for each of those simple sounds which we employ in forming our words; and, by joining together a few of those signs, they saw that it would be practicable to express, in Writing, the whole combinations of sounds which our words require.

THE first step, in this new progress, was the invention of an alphabet of syllables, which probably preceded the invention of an alphabet of letters, among some of the antient nations; and which is said to be retained, to this day, in Æthiopia, and some countries of India. By fixing upon a particular mark, or character, for every syllable in the Language, the number of characters, necessary to be used in Writing, was reduced within a much smaller compass than the number of words in the Language. Still, however, the number of characters was great; and must have continued to render both reading and writing very laborious arts. Till, at last, some happy genius arose; and tracing the sounds made by the human voice, to their most simple elements, reduced them to a very few vowels and con-

S 2　　　　　　　　　　sonants;

fonants; and, by affixing to each of thefe the figns which we now call Letters, taught men how, by their combinations, to put into Writing all the different words, or combinations of found, which they employed in Speech. By being reduced to this fimplicity, the art of Writing was brought to its higheft ftate of perfection; and, in this ftate, we now enjoy it in all the countries of Europe.

To whom we are indebted for this fublime and refined difcovery, does not appear. Concealed by the darknefs of remote antiquity, the great inventor is deprived of thofe honours which would ftill be paid to his memory, by all the lovers of knowledge and learning. It appears from the books which Mofes has written, that, among the Jews, and probably among the Egyptians, letters had been invented prior to his age. The univerfal tradition among the antients is, that they were firft imported into Greece by Cadmus the Phœnician; who, according to the common fyftem of chronology, was contemporary with Jofhua; according to Sir Ifaac Newton's fyftem, contemporary with King David. As the Phœnicians are not known to have been the inventors of any art or fcience, though, by means of their extenfive commerce, they propagated the difcoveries made by other nations, the moft probable and natural account of the origin of alphabetical characters is, that they took rife in Egypt, the firft civilized kingdom of which we have any authentic accounts, and the great fource of arts and polity among the antients. In that country, the favourite ftudy of hieroglyphical characters, had directed much attention to the art of Writing. Their hieroglyphics are known to have been intermixed with abbreviated fymbols, and arbi-

trary

trary marks; whence, at laſt, they caught the idea of contriving marks, not for things merely, but for ſounds. Accordingly, Plato (in Phœdro) expreſsly attributes the invention of letters to Theuth, the Egyptian, who is ſuppoſed to have been the Hermes, or Mercury, of the Greeks. Cadmus himſelf, though he paſſed from Phœnicia to Greece, yet is affirmed, by ſeveral of the antients, to have been originally of Thebes in Egypt. Moſt probably, Moſes carried with him the Egyptian letters into the land of Canaan; and there being adopted by the Phœnicians, who inhabited part of that country, they were tranſmitted into Greece.

THE alphabet which Cadmus brought into Greece was imperfect, and is ſaid to have contained only ſixteen letters. The reſt were afterwards added, according as ſigns for proper ſounds were found to be wanting. It is curious to obſerve, that the letters which we uſe at this day, can be traced back to this very alphabet of Cadmus. The Roman alphabet, which obtains with us, and with moſt of the European nations, is plainly formed on the Greek, with a few variations. And all learned men obſerve, that the Greek characters, eſpecially according to the manner in which they are formed in the oldeſt inſcriptions, have a remarkable conformity with the Hebrew or Samaritan characters, which, it is agreed, are the ſame with the Phœnician, or the alphabet of Cadmus. Invert the Greek characters from left to right, according to the Phœnician and Hebrew manner of Writing, and they are nearly the ſame. Beſides the conformity of figure, the names or denominations of the letters, alpha, beta, gamma, &c. and the order in which the letters are arranged, in all the ſeveral alpha-

3

bets,

bets, Phœnician, Hebrew, Greek, and Roman, agree ſo much, as amounts to a demonſtration, that they were all derived originally from the ſame ſource. An invention ſo uſeful and ſimple, was greedily received by mankind, and propagated with ſpeed and facility through many different nations.

THE letters were, originally, written from the right hand towards the left; that is, in a contrary order to what we now practiſe. This manner of Writing obtained among the Aſſyrians, Phœnicians, Arabians, and Hebrews; and from ſome very old inſcriptions, appears to have obtained alſo among the Greeks. Afterwards, the Greeks adopted a new method, writing their lines alternately from the right to the left, and from the left to the right, which was called *Bouſtrophedon* ; or, writing after the manner in which oxen plow the ground. Of this, ſeveral ſpecimens ſtill remain ; particularly, the inſcription on the famous Sigæan monument ; and down to the days of Solon, the legiſlator of Athens, this continued to be the common method of Writing. At length, the motion from the left hand to the right being found more natural and commodious, the practice of Writing, in this direction, prevailed throughout all the countries of Europe.

WRITING was long a kind of engraving. Pillars, and tables of ſtone, were firſt employed for this purpoſe, and afterwards, plates of the ſofter metals, ſuch as lead. In proportion as Writing became more common, lighter and more portable ſubſtances were employed. The leaves, and the bark of certain trees, were uſed in ſome countries ; and in others,

tablets

tablets of wood, covered with a thin coat of foft wax, on L E C T. which the impreffion was made with a ftylus of iron. In VII. later times, the hides of animals, properly prepared and polifhed into parchment, were the moft common materials. Our prefent method of writing on paper, is an invention of no greater antiquity than the fourteenth century.

Thus I have given fome account of the Progrefs of thefe two great arts, Speech and Writing ; by which men's thoughts are communicated, and the foundation laid for all knowledge and improvement. Let us conclude the fubject, with comparing, in a few words, fpoken Language, and written Language ; or words uttered in our hearing, with words reprefented to the eye ; where we fhall find feveral advantages and difadvantages to be balanced on both fides.

The advantages of Writing above Speech are, that Writing is both a more extenfive, and a more permanent method of communication. More extenfive ; as it is not confined within the narrow circle of thofe who hear our words, but, by means of written characters, we can fend our thoughts abroad, and propagate them through the world ; we can lift our voice, fo as to fpeak to the moft diftant regions of the earth. More permanent alfo ; as it prolongs this voice to the moft diftant ages ; it gives us the means of recording our fentiments to futurity, and of perpetuating the inftructive memory of paft tranfactions. It likewife affords this advantage to fuch as read, above fuch as hear, that, having the written characters before their eyes, they can arreft the fenfe of the writer. They can paufe, and revolve, and compare, at their leifure, one paffage

with

with another; whereas, the voice is fugitive and paffing; you muft catch the words the moment they are uttered, or you lofe them for ever.

But, although thefe be fo great advantages of written Language, that Speech, without Writing, would have been very inadequate for the inftruction of mankind; yet we muft not forget to obferve, that fpoken Language has a great fuperiority over written Language, in point of energy or force. The voice of the living Speaker, makes an impreffion on the mind, much ftronger than can be made by the perufal of any Writing. The tones of voice, the looks and gefture, which accompany difcourfe, and which no Writing can convey, render difcourfe, when it is well managed, infinitely more clear, and more expreffive, than the moft accurate Writing. For tones, looks, and geftures, are natural interpreters of the fentiments of the mind. They remove ambiguities; they enforce impreffions; they operate on us by means of fympathy, which is one of the moft powerful inftruments of perfuafion. Our fympathy is always awakened more, by hearing the Speaker, than by reading his works in our clofet. Hence, though Writing may anfwer the purpofes of mere inftruction, yet all the great and high efforts of eloquence muft be made, by means of fpoken, not of written, Language.

LECTURE VIII.

STRUCTURE OF LANGUAGE.

AFTER having given an account of the Rife and Progrefs of Language, I proceed to treat of its Structure, or of General Grammar. The Structure of Language is extremely artificial; and there are few fciences, in which a deeper, or more refined logic, is employed, than in Grammar. It is apt to be flighted by fuperficial thinkers, as belonging to thofe rudiments of knowledge, which were inculcated upon us in our earlieft youth. But what was then inculcated before we could comprehend its principles, would abundantly repay our ftudy in maturer years; and to the ignorance of it, muft be attributed many of thofe fundamental defects which appear in writing.

FEW authors have written with philofophical accuracy on the principles of General Grammar; and, what is more to be regretted, fewer ftill have thought of applying thofe principles to the

VOL. I.   T   Englifh

Englifh Language.   While the French Tongue has long been
an object of attention to many able and ingenious writers of
that nation, who have confidered its conftruction, and determined its propriety with great accuracy, the Genius and
Grammar of the Englifh, to the reproach of the country, have
not been ftudied with equal care, or afcertained with the fame
precifion.   Attempts have been made, indeed, of late, towards
fupplying this defect; and fome able writers have entered on
the fubject; but much remains yet to be done.

I DO not propofe to give any fyftem, either of Grammar
in general, or of Englifh Grammar in particular.   A minute
difcuffion of the niceties of Language would carry us too
much off from other objects, which demand our attention in
this courfe of Lectures.   But I propofe to give a general view
of the chief principles relating to this fubject, in obfervations
on the feveral parts of which Speech or Language is compofed;
remarking, as I go along, the peculiarities of our own Tongue.
After which, I fhall make fome more particular remarks on
the Genius of the Englifh Language.

THE firft thing to be confidered, is, the divifion of the feveral
parts of Speech.   The effential parts of Speech are the fame
in all Languages.   There muft always be fome words which
denote the names of objects, or mark the fubject of difcourfe;
other words, which denote the qualities of thofe objects, and
exprefs what we affirm concerning them; and other words,
which point out their connections and relations.   Hence, fubftantives, pronouns, adjectives, verbs, prepofitions, and conjunctions, muft neceffarily be found in all Languages.   The
moft

moſt ſimple and comprehenſive diviſion of the parts of Speech
is, into ſubſtantives, attributives, and connectives *. Sub-
ſtantives, are all the words which expreſs the names of objects,
or the ſubjects of diſcourſe; attributives, are all the words
which expreſs any attribute, property, or action of the former;
connectives, are what expreſs the connections, relations, and
dependencies, which take place among them. The common
grammatical diviſion of Speech into eight parts; nouns, pronouns, verbs, participles, adverbs, prepoſitions, interjections,
and conjunctions, is not very logical, as might be eaſily ſhewn;
as it comprehends, under the general term of nouns, both
ſubſtantives and adjectives, which are parts of Speech generically and eſſentially diſtinct; while it makes a ſeparate part of
ſpeech of participles, which are no other than verbal adjectives.
However, as theſe are the terms to which our ears have been
moſt familiariſed, and, as an exact logical diviſion is of no
great conſequence to our preſent purpoſe, it will be better to
make uſe of theſe known terms than of any other.

WE are naturally led to begin with the conſideration of ſubſtantive nouns, which are the foundation of all Grammar, and

---

* Quinctilian informs us, that this was the moſt antient diviſion. " Tum
" videbit quot & quæ ſunt partes orationis. Quanquam de numero parum
" convenit. Veteres enim, quorum fuerant Ariſtoteles atque Theodictes,
" verba modo, & nomina, & convinctiones tradiderunt. Videlicet, quod in
" verbis vim ſermonis, in nominibus materiam (quia alterum eſt quod
" loquimur, alterum de quo loquimur), in convinctionibus autem com-
" plexum eorum eſſe judicarunt; quas conjunctiones a pleriſque dici ſcio;
" ſed hæc videtur ex συνδεσμω magis propria tranſlatio. Paulatim a philo-
" ſophicis ac maximè a ſtoicis, auctus eſt numerus; ac primùm con-
" vinctionibus articuli adjecti; poſt præpoſitiones; nominibus, appellatio,
" deinde pronomen; deinde miſtum verbo participium; ipſis verbis, ad-
" verbia." Lib. I. cap. iv.

T 2

may

L E C T. may be confidered as the moſt antient part of Speech.   For,
VIII.   aſſuredly, as ſoon as men had got beyond ſimple interjections, or
exclamations of paſſion, and began to communicate themſelves
by diſcourſe, they would be under a neceſſity of aſſigning names
to the objects they ſaw around them ; which, in Grammatical
Language, is called, the Invention of ſubſtantive nouns *.
And here, at our firſt ſetting out, ſomewhat curious occurs.
The individual objects which ſurround us, are infinite in number.   A ſavage, wherever he looked, beheld foreſts and trees.

* I do not mean to aſſert, that, among all nations, the firſt invented words
were ſimple and regular ſubſtantive nouns.   Nothing is more difficult and uncertain, than to aſcertain the preciſe ſteps by which men proceeded in the formation of Language.   Names for objects muſt, doubtleſs, have ariſen in the
moſt early ſtages of Speech.   But, it is probable, as the learned author of the
Treatiſe, *On the Origin and Progreſs of Language,* has ſhown (vol. i. p. 371.
395.), that, among ſeveral ſavage tribes, ſome of the firſt articulate ſounds
that were formed, denoted a whole ſentence rather than the name of a particular object ; conveying ſome information, or expreſſing ſome deſires or fears,
ſuited to the circumſtances in which that tribe was placed, or relating to the
buſineſs they had moſt frequent occaſion to carry on ; as, the lion is coming,
the river is ſwelling, &c. Many of their firſt words, it is likewiſe probable,
were not ſimple ſubſtantive nouns, but ſubſtantives, accompanied with ſome
of thoſe attributes, in conjunction with which they were moſt frequently accuſtomed to behold them ; as, the great bear, the little hut, the wound made by
the hatchet, &c. Of all which, the Author produces inſtances from ſeveral of the
American Languages ; and it is, undoubtedly, ſuitable to the natural courſe
of the operations of the human mind, thus to begin with particulars the moſt
obvious to ſenſe, and to proceed, from theſe, to more general expreſſions.
He likewiſe obſerves, that the words of thoſe primitive tongues are far from
being, as we might ſuppoſe them, rude and ſhort, and crowded with conſonants ; but, on the contrary, are, for the moſt part, long words, and full of
vowels. This is the conſequence of their being formed upon the natural ſounds
which the voice utters with moſt eaſe, a little varied and diſtinguiſhed by ar-
ticulation ; and he ſhows this to hold, in fact, among moſt of the barbarous
Languages which are known.

To

To give feparate names to every one of thofe trees, would have been an endlefs and impracticable undertaking. His firft object was, to give a name to that particular tree, whofe fruit relieved his hunger, or whofe fhade protected him from the fun. But obferving, that though other trees were diftinguifhed from this by peculiar qualities of fize or appearance, yet, that they alfo agreed and refembled one another, in certain common qualities, fuch as fpringing from a root, and bearing branches and leaves, he formed, in his mind, fome general idea of thofe common qualities, and ranging all that poffeffed them under one clafs of objects, he called that whole clafs, *a tree*. Longer experience taught him to fubdivide this genus into the feveral fpecies of oak, pine, afh, and the reft, according as his obfervation extended to the feveral qualities in which thefe trees agreed or differed.

But, ftill, he made ufe only of general terms in Speech. For the oak, the pine, and the afh, were names of whole claffes of objects; each of which included an immenfe number of undiftinguifhed individuals. Here then, it appears, that though the formation of abftract, or general conceptions, is fuppofed to be a difficult operation of the mind; fuch conceptions muft have entered into the very firft formation of Language. For, if we except only the proper names of perfons, fuch as Cæfar, John, Peter, all the other fubftantive nouns which we employ in difcourfe, are the names, not of individual objects, but of very extenfive genera, or fpecies of objects; as, man, lion, houfe, river, &c. We are not, however, to imagine, that this invention of general, or abftract terms, requires any great exertion of metaphyfical capacity: For, by whatever fteps the

mind.

mind proceeds in it, it is certain, that, when men have once obferved refemblances among objects, they are naturally inclined to call all thofe which refemble one another, by one common name ; and of courfe, to clafs them under one fpecies. We may daily obferve this practifed by children, in their firft attempts towards acquiring Language.

BUT now, after Language had proceeded as far as I have defcribed, the notification which it made of objects was ftill very imperfect : For, when one mentioned to another, in difcourfe, any fubftantive noun; fuch as, man, lion, or tree, how was it to be known which man, which lion, or which tree he meant, among the many comprehended under one name ? Here occurs a very curious, and a very ufeful contrivance for fpecifying the individual object intended, by means of that part of Speech called, the Article.

THE force of the Article confifts, in pointing, or fingling out from the common mafs, the individual of which we mean to fpeak.   In Englifh, we have two Articles, *a* and *the*; *a* is more general and unlimited; *the* more definite and fpecial. *A* is much the fame with *one*, and marks only any one individual of a fpecies ; that individual being either unknown, or left undetermined ; as, a lion, a king.   *The*, which poffeffes more properly the force of the Article, afcertains fome known or determined individual of the fpecies ; as, the lion, the king.

ARTICLES are words of great ufe in Speech.   In fome Languages, however, they are not found.   The Greeks have but one Article, ὁ ἡ το, which anfwers to our definite, or proper

4

Article,

Article, *the*. They have no word which anſwers to our Article *a*; but they ſupply its place by the abſence of their Article: Thus, Βασιλευς ſignifies, *a* king; ὁ Βασιλευς, *the* king. The Latins have no Article. In the room of it, they employ pronouns, as, hic, ille, iſte, for pointing out the objects which they want to diſtinguiſh. "Noſter ſermo," ſays Quinctilian, "articulos non deſiderat, ideoque in alias partes orationis ſpar-" guntur." This, however, appears to me a defect in the Latin tongue; as Articles contribute much to the clearneſs and preciſion of Language.

In order to illuſtrate this, remark, what difference there is in the meaning of the following expreſſions in Engliſh, depending wholly on the different employment of the Articles: "The ſon of a king.—The ſon of the king—A ſon of the "king's." Each of theſe three phraſes has an entirely different meaning, which I need not explain, becauſe any one who underſtands the Language, conceives it clearly at firſt hearing, through the different application of the Articles, *a* and *the*. Whereas, in Latin, "Filius regis," is wholly undetermined; and to explain, in which of theſe three ſenſes it is to be underſtood, for it may bear any of them, a circumlocution of ſeveral words muſt be uſed. In the ſame manner, "Are you "*a* king?" "Are you *the* king?" are queſtions of quite ſeparate import; which, however, are confounded together in the Latin phraſe, "eſne tu rex?" "Thou art *a* man," is a very general and harmleſs poſition; but, "thou art *the* man," is an aſſertion, capable, we know, of ſtriking terror and remorſe into the heart. Theſe obſervations illuſtrate the force and importance of Articles: And, at the ſame time, I gladly

lay

lay hold of any opportunity of fhowing the advantages of our own Language.

BESIDES this quality of being particularifed by the Article, three affections belong to fubftantive nouns, number, gender, and cafe, which require our confideration.

NUMBER diftinguifhes them as one, or many, of the fame kind, called the Singular and Plural; a diftinction found in all Languages, and which muft, indeed, have been coëval with the very infancy of Language; as there were few things which men had more frequent occafion to exprefs, than the difference between one and many. For the greater facility of expreffing it, it has, in all Languages, been marked by fome variation made upon the fubftantive noun; as we fee, in Englifh, our plural is commonly formed by the addition of the letter S. In the Hebrew, Greek, and fome other antient Languages, we find, not only a plural, but a dual number; the rife of which may very naturally be accounted for, from feparate terms of numbering not being yet invented, and one, two, and many, being all, or, at leaft, the chief numeral diftinctions which men, at firft, had any occafion to take notice of.

GENDER, is an affection of fubftantive nouns, which will lead us into more difcuffion than number. Gender, being founded on the diftinction of the two fexes, it is plain, that, in a proper fenfe, it can only find place in the names of living creatures, which admit the diftinction of male and female; and, therefore, can be ranged under the mafculine or feminine genders. All other fubftantive nouns ought to belong, to what

2

gramma-

grammarians call, the Neuter Gender, which is meant to imply the negation of either fex. But, with refpect to this diftribution, fomewhat fingular hath obtained in the ftructure of Language. For, in correfpondence to that diftinction of male and female fex, which runs through all the claffes of animals, men have, in moft Languages, ranked a great number of inanimate objects alfo, under the like diftinctions of mafculine and feminine. Thus we find it, both in the Greek and Latin Tongues. *Gladius*, a fword, for inftance, is mafculine ; *fagitta*, an arrow, is feminine ; and this affignation of fex to inanimate objects, this diftinction of them into mafculine and feminine, appears often to be entirely capricious ; derived from no other principle than the cafual ftructure of the Language, which refers to a certain gender, words of a certain termination. In the Greek and Latin, however, all inanimate objects are not diftributed into mafculine and feminine ; but many of of them are alfo claffed, where all of them ought to have been, under the neuter gender ; as, *templum*, a church ; *fedile*, a feat.

But the genius of the French and Italian Tongues differs, in this refpect, from the Greek and Latin. In the French and Italian, from whatever caufe it has happened, fo it is, that the neuter gender is wholly unknown, and that all their names of inanimate objects are put upon the fame footing with living creatures ; and diftributed, without exception, into mafculine and feminine. The French have two articles, the mafculine *le*, and the feminine *la* ; and one or other of thefe is prefixed to all fubftantive nouns in the Language, to denote their gender. The Italians make the fame univerfal ufe of their articles *il* and *lo*, for the mafculine ; and *la*, for the feminine.

IN the Englifh Language, it is remarkable that there obtains a peculiarity quite oppofite. In the French and Italian, there is no neuter gender. In the Englifh, when we ufe common difcourfe, all fubftantive nouns, that are not names of living creatures, are neuter, without exception. *He*, *fhe*, and *it*, are the marks of the three genders; and we always ufe *it*, in fpeaking of any object where there is no fex, or where the fex is not known. The Englifh is, perhaps, the only Language in the known world (except the Chinefe, which is faid to agree with it in this particular), where the diftinction of gender is properly and philofophically applied in the ufe of words, and confined, as it ought to be, to mark the real diftinctions of male and female.

HENCE arifes a very great and fignal advantage of the Englifh Tongue, which it is of confequence to remark *. Though in common difcourfe, as I have already obferved, we employ only the proper and literal diftinction of fexes; yet the genius of the Language permits us, whenever it will add beauty to our difcourfe, to make the names of inanimate objects mafculine or feminine in a metaphorical fenfe; and when we do fo, we are underftood to quit the literal ftyle, and to ufe one of the figures of difcourfe.

FOR inftance; if I am fpeaking of virtue, in the courfe of ordinary converfation, or of ftrict reafoning, I refer the word to no fex or gender; I fay, " Virtue is its own reward;" or, " it is the law of our nature." But if I chufe to rife into a

---

* The following obfervations on the metaphorical ufe of genders, in the Englifh Language, are taken from Mr. Harris's Hermes.

higher

higher tone; if I feek to embellifh and animate my difcourfe, I give a fex to virtue; I fay, " She defcends from Heaven;" " fhe alone confers true honour upon man;" " her gifts are " the only durable rewards." By this means, we have it in our power to vary our ftyle at pleafure. By making a very flight alteration, we can perfonify any objeƈt that we chufe to introduce with dignity; and by this change of manner, we give warning, that we are paffing from the ftriƈt and logical, to the ornamented and rhetorical ftyle.

THIS is an advantage which, not only every poet, but every good writer and fpeaker in profe, is, on many occafions, glad to lay hold of, and improve: and it is an advantage peculiar to our Tongue; no other Language poffeffes it. For, in other Languages, every word has one fixed gender, mafculine, feminine, or neuter, which can, upon no occafion, be changed; αρετη, for inftance, in Greek, *virtus* in Latin, and *la vertu* in French, are uniformly feminine. *She*, muft always be the pronoun anfwering to the word, whether you be writing in poetry or profe, whether you be ufing the ftyle of reafoning, or that of declamation: whereas, in Englifh, we can either exprefs ourfelves with the philofophical accuracy of giving no gender to things inanimate; or by giving them gender, and transforming them into perfons, we adapt them to the ftyle of poetry, and, when it is proper, we enliven profe.

IT deferves to be further remarked on this fubjeƈt, that, when we employ that liberty which our Language allows, of afcribing fex to any inanimate objeƈt, we have not, however, the liberty of making it of what gender we pleafe, mafculine

U 2

or

or feminine; but are, in general, fubjected to fome rule of gender which the currency of Language has fixed to that object. The foundation of that rule is imagined, by Mr. Harris, in his "Philofophical Enquiry into the Principles of Grammar," to be laid in a certain diftant refemblance, or analogy, to the natural diftinction of the two fexes.

THUS, according to him, we commonly give the mafculine gender to thofe fubftantive nouns ufed figuratively, which are confpicuous for the attributes of imparting, or communicating; which are by nature ftrong and efficacious, either to good or evil; or which have a claim to fome eminence, whether laudable or not. Thofe again, he imagines, to be generally made feminine, which are confpicuous for the attributes of containing, and of bringing forth; which have more of the paffive in their nature, than the active; which are peculiarly beautiful, or amiable; or which have refpect to fuch exceffes as are rather feminine than mafculine. Upon thefe principles he takes notice, that the fun is always put in the mafculine gender with us; the moon in the feminine, as being the receptacle of the fun's light. The earth is, univerfally, feminine. A fhip, a country, a city, are likewife made feminine, as receivers, or containers. God, in all Languages, is mafculine. Time, we make mafculine, on account of its mighty efficacy; virtue, feminine, from its beauty, and its being the object of love. Fortune is always feminine. Mr. Harris imagines, that the reafons which determine the gender of fuch capital words as thefe, hold in moft other Languages, as well as the Englifh. This, however, appears doubtful. A variety of circumftances, which feem cafual to us, becaufe we cannot reduce

them

them to principles, muſt, unqueſtionably, have influenced the
original formation of Languages; and in no article whatever
does Language appear to have been more capricious, and to
have proceeded leſs according to fixed rule, than in the impoſi-
tion of gender upon things inanimate; eſpecially among ſuch
nations as have applied the diſtinction of maſculine and feminine
to all ſubſtantive nouns.

HAVING diſcuſſed gender, I proceed, next, to another remarkable peculiarity of ſubſtantive nouns, which, in the ſtyle
of grammar, is called, their declenſion by caſes. Let us, firſt,
conſider what caſes ſignify. In order to underſtand this, it is
neceſſary to obſerve, that, after men had given names to external objects, had particulariſed them by means of the article,
and diſtinguiſhed them by number and gender, ſtill their Language remained extremely imperfect, till they had deviſed ſome
method of expreſſing the relations which thoſe objects bore, one
towards another. They would find it of little uſe to have a
name for man, lion, tree, river, without being able, at the
ſame time, to ſignify how theſe ſtood with reſpect to each
other; whether, as approaching to, receding from, joined
with, and the like. Indeed, the relations which objects bear
to one another, are immenſely numerous; and therefore, to
deviſe names for them all, muſt have been among the laſt and
moſt difficult refinements of Language. But, in its moſt early
periods, it was abſolutely neceſſary to expreſs, in ſome way or
other, ſuch relations as were moſt important, and as occurred
moſt frequently in common Speech. Hence the genitive,
dative, and ablative caſes of nouns, which expreſs the noun
itſelf, together with thoſe relations, *of, to, from, with,* and *by*;

3

the

the relations which, of all others, we have the moſt frequent occaſion to mention. The proper idea then of caſes in declenſion, is no other than an expreſſion of the ſtate, or relation, which one objeƈt bears to another, denoted by ſome variation made upon the name of that objeƈt; moſt commonly in the final letters, and by ſome Languages, in the initial.

ALL Languages, however, do not agree in this mode of expreſſion. The Greek, Latin, and ſeveral other Languages, uſe declenſion. The Engliſh, French, and Italian, do not; or, at moſt, uſe it very imperfeƈtly. In place of the variations of caſes, theſe modern Tongues expreſs the relations of objeƈts, by means of the words called Prepoſitions, which are the names of thoſe relations, prefixed to the name of the objeƈt. Engliſh nouns have no caſe whatever, except a ſort of genitive, commonly formed by the addition of the letter s to the noun; as when we ſay " Dryden's Poems," meaning the Poems of Dryden. Our perſonal pronouns have alſo a caſe, which anſwers to the aceuſative of the Latin, *I, me,*—*he, him,*—*who, whom.* There is nothing, then, or at leaſt very little, in the Grammar of our Language, which correſponds to declenſion in the antient Languages.

Two queſtions, reſpeƈting this ſubjeƈt, may be put. Firſt, Which of theſe methods of expreſſing relations, whether that by declenſion, or that by prepoſitions, was the moſt antient uſage in Language? And next, Which of them has the beſt effeƈt? Both methods, it is plain, are the ſame as to the ſenſe, and differ only in form. For the ſignificancy of the Roman Language would not have been altered, though the nouns,

!   like

like ours, had been without cafes, provided they had employed prepofitions ; and though, to exprefs a difciple of Plato, they had faid, " Difcipulus de Plato," like the modern Italians, in place of " Difcipulus Platonis."

Now, with refpect to the antiquity of cafes, although they may, on firft view, feem to conftitute a more artificial method than the other, of denoting relations, yet there are ftrong rea-fons for thinking that this was the earlieft method practifed by men. We find, in fact, that declenfions and cafes are ufed in moft of what are called the Mother Tongues, or Original Lan-guages, as well as in the Greek and Latin. And a very natural and fatisfying account can be given why this ufage fhould have early obtained. Relations are the moft abftract and metaphyfical ideas of any which men have occafion to form, when they are confidered by themfelves, and feparated from the related object. It would puzzle any man, as has been well obferved by an Author on this fubject, to give a diftinct account of what is meant by fuch a word as *of*, or *from*, when it ftands by itfelf, and to explain all that may be included under it. The firft rude inventors of Language, therefore, would be long of arriving at fuch general terms. In place of confidering any relation in the abftract, and de-vifing a name for it, they would much more eafily conceive it in conjunction with a particular object ; and they would ex--prefs their conceptions of it, by varying the name of that object through all the different cafes ; *hominis*, of a man ; *homini*, to a man ; *homine*, with a man, &c.

BUT,

BUT, though this method of declenſion was, probably, the only method which men employed, at firſt, for denoting relations, yet, in progreſs of time, many other relations being obſerved, beſides thoſe which are ſignified by the caſes of nouns, and men alſo becoming more capable of general and metaphyſical ideas, ſeparate names were gradually invented for all the relations which occurred, forming that part of Speech which we now call Prepoſitions. Prepoſitions being once introduced, they were found to be capable of ſupplying the place of caſes, by being prefixed to the nominative of the noun. Hence, it came to paſs, that, as nations were intermixed by migrations and conqueſts, and were obliged to learn, and adopt the Languages of one another, prepoſitions ſupplanted the uſe of caſes and declenſions. When the Italian Tongue, for inſtance, ſprung out of the Roman, it was found more eaſy and ſimple, by the Gothic nations, to accommodate a few prepoſitions to the nominative of every noun, and to ſay, *di Roma, al Roma, di Carthago, al Carthago*, than to remember all the variety of terminations, *Romæ, Romam, Carthaginis, Carthaginem*, which the uſe of declenſions required in the antient nouns. By this progreſs we can give a natural account how nouns, in our modern Tongues, come to be ſo void of declenſion: A progreſs which is fully illuſtrated in Dr. Adam Smith's ingenious Diſſertation on the Formation of Languages.

WITH regard to the other queſtion on this ſubject, Which of theſe two methods is of the greateſt utility and beauty? we ſhall find advantages and diſadvantages to be balanced on both ſides. There is no doubt that, by aboliſhing caſes, we have

rendered

rendered the ſtructure of modern Languages more ſimple. We have diſembarraſſed it of all the intricacy which aroſe from the different forms of declenſion, of which the Romans had no fewer than five; and from all the irregularities in theſe ſeveral declenſions. We have thereby rendered our Languages more eaſy to be acquired, and leſs ſubject to the perplexity of rules. But, though the ſimplicity and eaſe of Language be great and eſtimable advantages, yet there are alſo ſuch diſadvantages attending the modern method, as leave the balance, on the whole, doubtful, or rather incline it to the ſide of antiquity.

FOR, in the firſt place, by our conſtant uſe of prepoſitions for expreſſing the relations of things, we have filled Language with a multitude of thoſe little words, which are eternally occurring in every ſentence, and may be thought thereby to have encumbered Speech, by an addition of terms; and by rendering it more prolix, to have enervated its force. In the ſecond place, we have certainly rendered the ſound of Language leſs agreeable to the ear, by depriving it of that variety and ſweetneſs, which aroſe from the length of words, and the change of terminations, occaſioned by the caſes in the Greek and Latin. But, in the third place, the moſt material diſadvantage is, that, by this abolition of caſes, and by a ſimilar alteration, of which I am to ſpeak in the next Lecture, in the conjugation of verbs, we have deprived ourſelves of that liberty of tranſpoſition in the arrangement of words, which the Antient Languages enjoyed.

IN the Antient Tongues, as I formerly obſerved, the different terminations, produced by declenſion and conjugation,

VOL. I.   X   pointed

pointed out the reference of the feveral words of a fentence to one another, without the aid of juxtapofition; fuffered them to be placed, without ambiguity, in whatever order was moft fuited to give emphafis to the meaning, or harmony to the found. But now, having none of thofe marks of relation incorporated with the words themfelves, we have no other way left us, of fhowing what words in a fentence are moft clofely connected in meaning, than that of placing them clofe by one another in the period. The meaning of the fentence is brought out in feparate members and portions; it is broken down and divided. Whereas the ftructure of the Greek and Roman fentences, by the government of their nouns and verbs, prefented the meaning fo interwoven and compounded in all its parts, as to make us perceive it in one united view. The clofing words of the period afcertained the relation of each member to another; and all that ought to be connected in our idea, appeared connected in the expreffion. Hence, more brevity, more vivacity, more force. That luggage of particles (as an ingenious Author happily expreffes it), which we are obliged always to carry along with us, both clogs ftyle, and enfeebles fentiment *.

PRONOUNS

---

* " The various terminations of the fame word, whether verb or noun, " are always conceived to be more intimately connected with the term " which they ferve to lengthen, than the additional, detached, and in them- " felves, infignificant particles, which we are obliged to employ as connectives " to our fignificant words. Our method gives almoft the fame expofure to " the one as to the other, making the fignificant parts, and the infignificant, " equally confpicuous; theirs, much oftener finks, as it were, the former into " the latter, at once preferving their ufe, and hiding their weaknefs. Our modern " Languages may, in this refpect, be compared to the art of the carpenter in " its rudeft ftate; when the union of the materials, employed by the artifan,

" could

PRONOUNS are the claſs of words moſt nearly related to ſubſtantive nouns; being, as the name imports, repreſentatives, or ſubſtitutes, of nouns. *I, thou, he, ſhe,* and *it,* are no other than an abridged way of naming the perſons, or objects, with which we have immediate intercourſe, or to which we are obliged frequently to refer in diſcourſe. Accordingly, they are ſubject to the ſame modifications with ſubſtantive nouns, of number, gender, and caſe. Only, with reſpect to gender, we may obſerve, that the pronouns of the firſt and ſecond perſon, as they are called, *I* and *thou,* do not appear to have had the diſtinctions of gender given them in any Language; for this plain reaſon, that, as they always refer to perſons who are preſent to each other, when they ſpeak, their ſex muſt appear, and therefore needs not be marked by a maſculine or feminine pronoun. But, as the third perſon may be abſent, or unknown, the diſtinction of gender there becomes neceſſary; and accordingly, in Engliſh, it hath all the three genders belonging to it; *he, ſhe, it.* As to caſes; even thoſe Languages which have dropped them in ſubſtantive nouns, ſometimes retain more of them in pronouns, for the ſake of the greater readineſs in expreſſing relations; as pronouns are words of ſuch frequent occurrence in diſcourſe. In Engliſh, moſt of our grammarians hold the perſonal pronouns to have two caſes,

---

" could be effected only by the help of thoſe external and coarſe implements,
" pins, nails, and cramps. The antient Languages reſemble the ſame art
" in its moſt improved ſtate, after the invention of dovetail joints, grooves, and
" mortices; when thus all the principal junctions are effected, by forming
" properly, the extremities, or terminations, of the pieces to be joined. For,
" by means of theſe, the union of the parts is rendered cloſer; while that by
" which that union is produced, is ſcarcely perceivable." The Philoſophy of
Rhetoric. By Dr. Campbell, vol. ii. p. 412.

beſides

befides the nominative; a genitive, and an accufative,—*I, mine,
me;—thou, thine, thee;—he, his, him;—who, whofe, whom.*

In the firft ftage of Speech, it is probable that the
places of thofe pronouns were fupplied, by pointing to the
objeƈt when prefent, and naming it when abfent.   For one can
hardly think that pronouns were of early invention; as they
are words of fuch a particular and artificial nature.   *I, thou,
he, it,* it is to be obferved, are not names peculiar to any fingle
objeƈt, but fo very general, that they may be applied to all
perfons, or objeƈts, whatever, in certain circumftances.   *It,* is
the moft general term that can poffibly be conceived, as it may
ftand for any one thing in the univerfe, of which we fpeak.
At the fame time, thefe pronouns have this quality, that, in
the circumftances in which they are applied, they never denote
more than one precife individual; which they afcertain, and
fpecify, much in the fame manner as is done by the article.
So that pronouns are, at once, the moft general, and the moft
particular words in Language.   They are commonly the moft
irregular and troublefome words to the learner, in the Grammar of all Tongues; as being the words moft in common
ufe, and fubjeƈted thereby to the greateft varieties.

Adjectives; or terms of quality, fuch as, *great, little,
black, white, yours, ours,* are the plaineft and fimpleft of all
that clafs of words which are termed attributive.   They are
found in all Languages; and, in all Languages, muft have
been very early invented; as objeƈts could not be diftinguifhed
from each other, nor any intercourfe be carried on concerning them, till once names were given to their different
qualities.

                                        I HAVE

I HAVE nothing to obferve in relation to them, except that fingularity which attends them in the Greek and Latin, of having the fame form given them with fubftantive nouns; being declined, like them, by cafes, and fubjected to the like diftinctions of number and gender. Whence it has happened, that grammarians have made them to belong to the fame part of Speech, and divided the noun into fubftantive and adjective; an arrangement, founded more on attention to the external form of words, than to their nature and force. For adjectives, or terms of quality, have not, by their nature, the leaft refemblance to fubftantive nouns, as they never exprefs any thing which can poffibly fubfift by itfelf; which is the very effence of the fubftantive noun. They are, indeed, more a-kin to verbs, which, like them, exprefs the attribute of fome fubftance.

IT may, at firft view, appear fomewhat odd and fantaftic, that adjectives fhould, in thefe antient Languages, have affumed fo much the form of fubftantives; fince neither number, nor gender, nor cafes, nor relations, have any thing to do, in a proper fenfe, with mere qualities, fuch as, *good* or *great*, *foft* or *hard*. And yet *bonus*, and *magnus*, and *tener*, have their fingular and plural, their mafculine and feminine, their genitives and datives, like any of the names of fubftances, or perfons. But this can be accounted for, from the genius of thofe Tongues. They avoided, as much as poffible, confidering qualities feparately, or in the abftract. They made them a part, or appendage, of the fubftance which they ferved to diftinguifh; they made the adjective depend on its fubftantive, and refemble it in termination, in number, and gender, in order

that

that the two might coalefce the more intimately, and be joined in the form of expreffion, as they were in the nature of things. The liberty of tranfpofition, too, which thofe Languages indulged, required fuch a method as this to be followed. For, allowing the related words of a fentence to be placed at a diftance from each other, it required the relation of adjectives to their proper fubftantives to be pointed out, by fuch fimilar circumftances of form and termination, as, according to the grammatical ftyle, fhould fhow their concordance. When I fay, in Englifh, the " Beautiful wife of a brave man," the juxtapofition of the words prevents all ambiguity. But when I fay, in Latin, " Formofa fortis viri uxor;" it is only the agreement, in gender, number, and cafe, of the adjective " *formofa*," which is the firft word of the fentence, with the fubftantive " *uxor*," which is the laft word that declares the meaning.

LECTURE IX.

STRUCTURE OF LANGUAGE.
ENGLISH TONGUE.

OF the whole clafs of words that are called attributive, indeed, of all the parts of Speech, the moft complex, by far, is the verb. It is chiefly in this part of Speech, that the fubtile and profound metaphyfic of Language appears; and, therefore, in examining the nature and different variations of the verb, there might be room for ample difcuffion. But as I am fenfible that fuch grammatical difcuffions, when they are purfued far, become intricate and obfcure, I fhall avoid dwelling any longer on this fubject, than feems abfolutely neceffary.

THE verb is fo far of the fame nature with the adjective, that it expreffes, like it, an attribute, or property, of fome perfon or thing. But it does more than this. For, in all verbs, in every Language, there are no lefs than three things

4   implied

implied at once; the attribute of some substantive, an affirma-tion concerning that attribute, and time. Thus, when I say, " the sun shineth." Shining, is the attribute ascribed to the sun; the present time is marked; and an affirmation is in-cluded, that this property of shining belongs, at that time, to the sun. The participle, " shining," is merely an adjective, which denotes an attribute, or property, and also expresses time; but carries no affirmation. The infinitive mood, " to " shine," may be called the name of the verb; it carries nei-ther time nor affirmation; but simply expresses that attribute, action, or state of things, which is to be the subject of the other moods and tenses. Hence the infinitive is often a-kin to a substantive noun; and, both in English and Latin, is sometimes constructed as such. As, " Scire tuum nihil est." " Dulce et decorum est pro patria mori." And, in English, in the same manner. " To write well is difficult; to speak " eloquently is still more difficult." But as, through all the other tenses and moods, the affirmation runs, and is essential to them; " the sun shineth, was shining, shone, will shine, " would have shone," &c. the affirmation seems to be that which chiefly distinguishes the verb from the other parts of Speech, and gives it its most conspicuous power. Hence there can be no sentence, or complete proposition, without a verb either expressed or implied. For, whenever we speak, we always mean to assert, that something is, or is not; and the word which carries this assertion, or affirmation, is a verb. From this sort of eminence belonging to it, this part of Speech hath received its name; verb, from the Latin, *verbum*, or *the word*, by way of distinction.

✝

VERBS,

VERBS, therefore, from their importance and neceffity in Speech, muft have been coëval with men's firft attempts towards the formation of Language : Though, indeed, it muft have been the work of long time, to rear them up to that accurate and complex ftructure, which they now poffefs. It feems very probable, as Dr. Smith hath fuggefted, that the radical verb, or the firft form of it, in moft Languages, would be, what we now call, the Imperfonal Verb. " It rains; it " thunders; it is light; it is agreeable;" and the like ; as this is the very fimpleft form of the verb, and merely affirms the exiftence of an event, or of a ftate of things. By degrees, after pronouns were invented, fuch verbs became perfonal, and were branched out into all the variety of tenfes and moods.

THE tenfes of the verb are contrived to imply the feveral diftinctions of time. Of thefe, I muft take fome notice, in order to fhow the admirable accuracy with which Language is conftructed. We think, commonly, of no more than the three great divifions of time, into the paft, the prefent, and the future : and we might imagine, that if verbs had been fo contrived, as fimply to exprefs thefe, no more was needful. But Language proceeds with much greater fubtilty. It fplits time into its feveral moments. It confiders time as never ftanding ftill, but always flowing; things paft, as more or lefs perfectly completed ; and things future, as more or lefs remote, by different gradations. Hence the great variety of tenfes in moft Tongues.

THE prefent may, indeed, be always confidered as one indivifible point, fufceptible of no variety. " I write, or, I am

VOL. I.   Y   " writing;

" writing; *fcribo*." But it is not fo with the paft. There is no Language fo poor, but it hath two or three tenfes to exprefs the varieties of it. Ours hath no fewer than four. 1. A paft action may be confidered as left unfinifhed; which makes the imperfect tenfe, " I was writing; *fcribebam*." 2. As juft now finifhed. This makes the proper perfect tenfe, which, in Englifh, is always expreffed by the help of the auxiliary verb, " I have written." 3. It may be confidered as finifhed fome time ago; the particular time left indefinite. " I wrote; " *fcripfi*;" which may either fignify, " I wrote yefterday, or I " wrote a twelvemonth ago." This is what grammarians call an aörift, or indefinite paft. 4. It may be confidered as finifhed before fomething elfe, which is alfo paft. This is the plufquamperfect. " I had written; *fcripferam*. I had " written before I received his letter."

HERE we obferve, with fome pleafure, that we have an advantage over the Latins, who have only three varieties upon the paft time. They have no proper perfect tenfe, or one which diftinguifhes an action juft now finifhed, from an action that was finifhed fome time ago. In both thefe cafes, they muft fay, " *fcripfi*." Though there be a manifeft difference in the tenfes, which our Language expreffes, by this varia-tion, " I have written," meaning, I have juft now finifhed writing; and, " I wrote," meaning at fome former time, fince which, other things have intervened. This difference the Romans have no tenfe to exprefs; and, therefore, can only do it by a circumlocution.

THE

THE chief varieties in the future time are two; a fimple or indefinite future : " I fhall write; *fcribam :*" And a future, relating to fomething elfe, which is alfo future. " I fhall " have written; *fcripfero.*" I fhall have written before he arrives *.

BESIDES tenfes, or the power of expreffing time, verbs admit the diftinction of Voices, as they are called, the active and the paffive; according as the affirmation refpects fomething that is done, or fomething that is fuffered; " I love, or I am " loved." They admit alfo the diftinction of moods, which are defigned to exprefs the affirmation, whether active or paf-five, under different forms. The indicative mood, for inftance, fimply declares a propofition, " I write; I have written;" the imperative requires, commands, threatens, " write thou; " let him write." The fubjunctive expreffes the propofition under the form of a condition, or in fubordination to fome other thing, to which a reference is made, " I might write, " I could write, I fhould write, if the cafe were fo and fo." This manner of expreffing an affirmation, under fo many dif-ferent forms, together alfo with the diftinction of the three perfons, *I, thou,* and *he,* conftitutes what is called, the conju-gation of verbs, which makes fo great a part of the grammar of all Languages.

IT now clearly appears, as I before obferved, that, of all the parts of Speech, verbs are, by far, the moft artificial and com-

LECT. IX.

---

* On the tenfes of verbs, Mr. Harris's Hermes may be confulted, by fuch as defire to fee them fcrutinized with metaphyfical accuracy ; and alfo, the Treatife on the Origin and Progrefs of Language, Vol. ii. p. 125.

plex.

plex. Confider only, how many things are denoted by this single Latin word " *amaviſſem*, I would have loved." Firſt, The perſon who ſpeaks, " I." Secondly, An attribute, or action of that perſon, " loving." Thirdly, An affirmation concerning that action. Fourthly, The paſt time denoted in that affirmation, " have loved :" and, Fifthly, A condition on which the action is ſuſpended, " would have loved." It appears curious and remarkable, that words of this complex import, and with more or leſs of this artificial ſtructure, are to be found, as far as we know, in all Languages of the world.

INDEED, the form of conjugation, or the manner of expreſſing all theſe varieties in the verb, differs greatly in different Tongues. Conjugation is eſteemed moſt perfect in thoſe Languages, which, by varying either the termination or the initial ſyllable of the verb, expreſs the greateſt number of important circumſtances, without the help of auxiliary words. In the Oriental Tongues, the verbs are ſaid to have few tenſes, or expreſſions of time ; but then their moods are ſo contrived, as to expreſs a great variety of circumſtances and relations. In the Hebrew, for inſtance, they ſay, in one word, without the help of any auxiliary, not only " I have taught," but, " I " have taught exactly, or often ; I have been commanded to " teach ; I have taught myſelf." The Greek, which is the moſt perfect of all the known Tongues, is very regular and complete in all the tenſes and moods. The Latin is formed on the ſame model, but more imperfect ; eſpecially in the paſſive voice, which forms moſt of the tenſes by the help of the auxiliary " *ſum*."

IN all the modern European Tongues, conjugation is very defective. They admit few varieties in the termination of the verb itfelf; but have almoft conftant recourfe to their auxiliary verbs, throughout all the moods and tenfes, both active and paffive. Language has undergone a change in conjugation, perfectly fimilar to that which, I fhowed in the laft Lecture, it underwent with refpect to declenfion. As prepofitions, prefixed to the noun, fuperfeded the ufe of cafes; fo the two great auxiliary verbs, to *have*, and to *be*, with thofe other auxiliaries which we ufe in Englifh, *do, fhall, will, may*, and *can*, prefixed to the participle, fuperfede, in a great meafure, the different terminations of moods and tenfes, which formed the antient conjugations.

THE alteration, in both cafes, was owing to the fame caufe, and will be eafily underftood, from reflecting on what was formerly obferved. The auxiliary verbs are like prepofitions, words of a very general and abftract nature. They imply the different modifications of fimple exiftence, confidered alone, and without reference to any particular thing. In the early ftate of Speech, the import of them would be incorporated, fo to fpeak, with every particular verb in its tenfes and moods, long before words were invented for denoting fuch abftract conceptions of exiftence, alone, and by themfelves. But after thofe auxiliary verbs came, in the progrefs of Language, to be invented and known, and to have tenfes and moods given to them like other verbs; it was found, that as they carried in their nature the force of that affirmation which diftinguifhes the verb, they might, by being joined with the participle which gives the meaning of the verb, fupply the place of moft

of

of the moods and tenfes. Hence, as the modern Tongues began to rife out of the ruins of the antient, this method eftablifhed itfelf in the new formation of Speech. Such words, for inftance; as, *am, was, have, fhall,* being once familiar, it appeared more eafy to apply thefe to any verb whatever; as, *I am loved*; *I was loved*; *I have loved;* than to remember that variety of terminations which were requifite in conjugating the antient verbs, *amor, amabar, amavi,* &c. Two or three varieties only, in the termination of the verb, were retained, as, *love, loved, loving;* and all the reft were dropt. The confequence, however, of this practice, was the fame as that of abolifhing declenfions. It rendered Language more fimple and eafy in its ftructure; but withal, more prolix, and lefs graceful. This finifhes all that feemed moft neceffary to be obferved with refpect to verbs.

THE remaining parts of Speech, which are called the indeclinable parts, or that admit of no variations, will not detain us long.

ADVERBS are the firft that occur. Thefe form a very numerous clafs of words in every Language, reducible, in general, to the head of attributives; as they ferve to modify, or to denote fome circumftance of an action, or of a quality, relative to its time, place, order, degree, and the other properties of it, which we have occafion to fpecify. They are, for the moft part, no more than an abridged mode of Speech, expreffing, by one word, what might, by a circumlocution, be refolved into two or more words belonging to the other parts of Speech. " Exceedingly," for inftance, is the fame as, " in

9

" a high

" a high degree ;" " bravely," the fame as, " with bravery or
" valour ;" " here," the fame as, " in this place ;" " often,
" and feldom," the fame as, " for many and for few times :"
and fo of the reft. Hence, adverbs may be conceived as of lefs
neceffity, and of later introduction into the fyftem of Speech,
than many other claffes of words ; and, accordingly, the great
body of them are derived from other words formerly eftablifhed
in the Language.

PREPOSITIONS and conjunctions, are words more effential
to difcourfe than the greateft part of adverbs. They form
that clafs of words, called Connectives, without which there
could be no Language ; ferving to exprefs the relations which
things bear to one another, their mutual influence, dependencies, and coherence ; thereby joining words together into
intelligible and fignificant propofitions. Conjunctions are
generally employed for connecting fentences, or members of
fentences ; as, *and*, *becaufe*, *although*, and the like. Prepofitions are employed for connecting words, by fhowing the relation which one fubftantive noun bears to another ; as, *of*, *from*,
to, *above*, *below*, &c. Of the force of thefe I had occafion
to fpeak before, when treating of the cafes and declenfions of
fubftantive nouns.

IT is abundantly evident, that all thefe connective particles
muft be of the greateft ufe in Speech ; feeing they point out
the relations and tranfitions by which the mind paffes from
one idea to another. They are the foundation of all reafoning,
which is no other thing than the connection of thoughts. And,
therefore, though among barbarous nations, and in the rude
uncivilifed

LECT.
IX.
uncivilifed ages of the world, the ftock of thefe words might be fmall, it muft always have increafed, as mankind advanced in the arts of reafoning and reflection. The more any nation is improved by fcience, and the more perfect their Language becomes, we may naturally expect, that it will abound the more with connective particles; expreffing relations of things, and tranfitions of thought, which had efcaped a groffer view. Accordingly, no Tongue is fo full of them as the Greek, in confequence of the acute and fubtile genius of that refined people. In every Language, much of the beauty and ftrength of it depends on the proper ufe of conjunctions, prepofitions, and thofe relative pronouns, which alfo ferve the fame purpofe of connecting the different parts of difcourfe. It is the right, or wrong management of thefe, which chiefly makes difcourfe appear firm and compacted, or disjointed and loofe ; which caufes it to march with a fmooth and even pace, or with gouty and hobbling fteps.

I SHALL dwell no longer on the general conftruction of Language. Allow me, only, before I difmifs the fubject, to obferve, that dry and intricate as it may feem to fome, it is, however, of great importance, and very nearly connected with the philofophy of the human mind. For, if Speech be the vehicle, or interpreter of the conceptions of our minds, an examination of its Structure and Progrefs cannot but unfold many things concerning the nature and progrefs of our conceptions themfelves, and the operations of our faculties; a fubject that is always inftructive to man. " Nequis," fays Quinctilian, an author of excellent judgment, " nequis tan-
!   " quam

" quam parva faſtidiat grammatices elementa. Non quia
" magnæ ſit operæ conſonantes a vocalibus diſcernere, eaſque
" in ſemivocalium numerum, mutarumque partiri, ſed quia
" interiora velut ſacri hujus adeuntibus, apparebit multa
" rerum ſubtilitas, quæ non modo acuere ingenia puerilia,
" ſed exercere altiſſimam quoque eruditionem ac ſcientiam
" poſſit *." 1. 4.

LET us now come nearer to our own Language. In this,
and the preceding Lecture, ſome obſervations have already been
made on its Structure. But it is proper, that we ſhould be a
little more particular in the examination of it.

THE Language which is, at preſent, ſpoken throughout
Great Britain, is neither the antient primitive Speech of the
iſland, nor derived from it; but is altogether of foreign origin. The Language of the firſt inhabitants of our iſland,
beyond doubt, was the Celtic, or Gaelic, common to them
with Gaul; from which country, it appears, by many circumſtances, that Great Britain was peopled. This Celtic
Tongue, which is ſaid to be very expreſſive and copious, and
is, probably, one of the moſt antient Languages in the world,
obtained once in moſt of the weſtern regions of Europe. It
was the Language of Gaul, of Great Britain, of Ireland,

---

* " Let no man deſpiſe, as inconſiderable, the elements of grammar, be-
" cauſe it may ſeem to him a matter of ſmall conſequence, to ſhow the diſtinc-
" tion between vowels and conſonants, and to divide the latter into liquids and
" mutes. But they who penetrate into the innermoſt parts of this temple of
" ſcience, will there diſcover ſuch refinement and ſubtility of matter, as is not
" only proper to ſharpen the underſtandings of young men, but ſufficient to
" give exerciſe for the moſt profound knowledge and erudition."

and, very probably, of Spain alfo; till, in the courfe of thofe revolutions, which, by means of the conquefts, firft, of the Romans, and afterwards, of the northern nations, changed the government, fpeech, and, in a manner, the whole face of Europe, this Tongue was gradually obliterated: and now fubfifts only in the mountains of Wales, in the Highlands of Scotland, and among the wild Irifh. For the Irifh, the Welch, and the Erfe, are no other than different dialeɛts of the fame Tongue, the antient Celtic.

THIS, then, was the Language of the primitive Britons, the firft inhabitants, that we know of, in our ifland; and continued fo till the arrival of the Saxons in England, in the year of our Lord 450; who, having conquered the Britons, did not intermix with them, but expelled them from their habitations, and drove them, together with their Language, into the mountains of Wales. The Saxons were one of thofe northern nations that overran Europe; and their Tongue, a dialeɛt of the Gothic or Teutonic, altogether diftinɛt from the Celtic, laid the foundation of the prefent Englifh Tongue. With fome intermixture of Danifh, a Language, probably, from the fame root with the Saxon, it continued to be fpoken throughout the fouthern part of the Ifland, till the time of William the Conqueror. He introduced his Norman or French as the Language of the court, which made a confiderable change in the Speech of the nation; and the Englifh, which was fpoken afterwards, and continues to be fpoken now, is a mixture of the antient Saxon, and this Norman French, together with fuch new and foreign words as commerce and learning have, in progrefs of time, gradually introduced.

THE

THE hiſtory of the Engliſh Language can, in this manner, be clearly traced. The Language ſpoken in the low countries of Scotland, is now, and has been for many centuries, no other than a dialect of the Engliſh. How, indeed, or by what ſteps, the antient Celtic Tongue came to be baniſhed from the Low Country in Scotland, and to make its retreat into the Highlands and Iſlands, cannot be ſo well pointed out, as how the like revolution was brought about in England. Whether the ſouthernmoſt part of Scotland was once ſubject to the Saxons, and formed a part of the kingdom of Northumberland ; or, whether the great number of Engliſh exiles that retreated into Scotland, upon the Norman conqueſt, and upon other occaſions, introduced into that country their own Language, which afterwards, by the mutual intercourſe of the two nations, prevailed over the Celtic, are uncertain and conteſted points, the diſcuſſion of which would lead us too far from our ſubject.

FROM what has been ſaid, it appears, that the Teutonic dialect is the baſis of our preſent Speech. It has been imported among us in three different forms, the Saxon, the Daniſh, and the Norman ; all which have mingled together in our Language. A very great number of our words too, are plainly derived from the Latin. Theſe, we had not directly from the Latin, but moſt of them, it is probable, entered into our Tongue through the channel of that Norman French, which William the Conqueror introduced. For, as the Romans had long been in full poſſeſſion of Gaul, the Language ſpoken in that country, when it was invaded by the Franks and Normans, was a ſort of corrupted Latin, mingled with

Celtic,

Celtic, to which was given the name of Romanſhe: and as the Franks and Normans did not, like the Saxons in England, expel the inhabitants, but, after their victories, mingled with them; the Language of the country became a compound of the Teutonic dialect imported by theſe conquerors, and of the former corrupted Latin. Hence, the French Language has always continued to have a very conſiderable affinity with the Latin; and hence, a great number of words of Latin origin, which were in uſe among the Normans in France, were introduced into our Tongue at the conqueſt; to which, indeed, many have ſince been added, directly from the Latin, in conſequence of the great diffuſion of Roman literature throughout all Europe.

FROM the influx of ſo many ſtreams, from the junction of ſo many diſſimilar parts, it naturally follows, that the Engliſh, like every compounded Language, muſt needs be ſomewhat irregular. We cannot expect from it that correſpondence of parts, that complete analogy in ſtructure, which may be found in thoſe ſimpler Languages, which have been formed in a manner within themſelves, and built on one foundation. Hence, as I before ſhowed, it has but ſmall remains of conjugation or declenſion; and its ſyntax is narrow, as there are few marks in the words themſelves that can ſhow their relation to each other, or, in the grammatical ſtyle, point out either their concordance, or their government, in the ſentence. Our words having been brought to us from ſeveral different regions, ſtraggle, if we may ſo ſpeak, aſunder from each other; and do not coaleſce ſo naturally in the ſtructure of a ſentence, as the words in the Greek and Roman Tongues.

BUT

BUT thefe difadvantages, if they be fuch, of a compound Language, are balanced by other advantages that attend it; particularly, by the number and variety of words with which fuch a Language is likely to be enriched. Few Languages are, in fact, more copious than the Englifh. In all grave fubjects efpecially, hiftorical, critical, political, and moral, no writer has the leaft reafon to complain of the barrennefs of our Tongue. The ftudious reflecting genius of the people, has brought together great ftore of expreffions, on fuch fubjects, from every quarter. We are rich too in the Language of poetry. Our poetical ftyle differs widely from profe, not in point of numbers only, but in the very words themfelves; which fhows what a ftock and compafs of words we have it in our power to felect and employ, fuited to thofe different occafions. Herein we are infinitely fuperior to the French, whofe poetical Language, if it were not diftinguifhed by rhyme, would not be known to differ from their ordinary profe.

IT is chiefly, indeed, on grave fubjects, and with refpect to the ftronger emotions of the mind, that our Language difplays its power of expreffion. We are faid to have thirty words, at leaft, for denoting all the varieties of the paffion of anger *. But, in defcribing the more delicate fentiments and emotions, our Tongue is not fo fertile. It muft be confeffed, that the

---

* Anger, wrath, paffion, rage, fury, outrage, fiercenefs, fharpnefs, animofity, choler, refentment, heat, heart-burning; to fume, ftorm, inflame, be incenfed; to vex, kindle, irritate, enrage, exafperate, provoke, fret; to be fullen, hafty, hot, rough, four, peevifh, &c.

Preface to Greenwood's Grammar.

French.

French Language furpaffes ours, by far, in expreffing the nicer fhades of character; efpecially thofe varieties of manner, temper, and behaviour, which are difplayed in our focial intercourfe with one another. Let any one attempt to tranflate, into Englifh, only a few pages of one of Marivaux's Novels, and he will foon be fenfible of our deficiency of expreffion on thefe fubjects. Indeed, no Language is fo copious as the French for whatever is delicate, gay, and amufing. It is, perhaps, the happieft Language for converfation in the known world; but, on the higher fubjects of compofition, the Englifh may be juftly efteemed to excel it confiderably.

LANGUAGE is generally underftood to receive its predominant tincture from the national character of the people who fpeak it. We muft not, indeed, expect, that it will carry an exact and full impreffion of their genius and manners; for, among all nations, the original ftock of words which they received from their anceftors, remain as the foundation of their Speech throughout many ages, while their manners undergo, perhaps, very great alterations. National character will, however, always have fome perceptible influence on the turn of Language; and the gaiety and vivacity of the French, and the gravity and thoughtfulnefs of the Englifh, are fufficiently impreffed on their refpective Tongues.

FROM the genius of our Language, and the character of thofe who fpeak it, it may be expected to have ftrength and energy. It is, indeed, naturally prolix; owing to the great number of particles and auxiliary verbs which we are obliged conftantly to employ; and this prolixity muft, in fome degree,

enfeeble

enfeeble it. We feldom can exprefs fo much by one word as was done by the verbs, and by the nouns, in the Greek and Roman Languages. Our ftyle is lefs compact; our conceptions being fpread out among more words, and fplit, as it were, into more parts, make a fainter impreffion when we utter them. Notwithftanding this defect, by our abounding in terms for expreffing all the ftrong emotions of the mind, and by the liberty which we enjoy, in a greater degree than moft nations, of compounding words, our Language may be efteemed to poffefs confiderable force of expreffion; comparatively, at leaft, with the other modern Tongues, though much below the antient. The Style of Milton alone, both in poetry and profe, is a fufficient proof, that the Englifh Tongue is far from being deftitute of nerves and energy.

THE flexibility of a Language, or its power of accommodation to different ftyles and manners, fo as to be either grave and ftrong, or eafy and flowing, or tender and gentle, or pompous and magnificent, as occafions require, or as an author's genius prompts, is a quality of great importance in fpeaking and writing. It feems to depend upon three things; the copioufnefs of a Language; the different arrangements of which its words are fufceptible; and the variety and beauty of the found of thofe words, fo as to correfpond to many different fubjects. Never did any Tongue poffefs this quality fo eminently as the Greek, which every writer of genius could fo mould, as to make the ftyle perfectly expreffive of his own manner and peculiar turn. It had all the three requifites, which I have mentioned, as neceffary for this purpofe. It joined to thefe the graceful variety of its different dialects; and thereby readily

affumed

aſſumed every ſort of charaƈter which an author could wiſh, from the moſt ſimple and moſt familiar, up to the moſt majeſtic. The Latin, though a very beautiful Language, is inferior, in this reſpeƈt, to the Greek. It has more of a fixed charaƈter of ſtatelineſs and gravity. It is always firm and maſculine in the tenor of its ſound; and is ſupported by a certain ſenatorial dignity, of which it is difficult for a writer to diveſt it wholly, on any occaſion. Among the modern Tongues, the Italian poſſeſſes a great deal more of this flexibility than the French. By its copiouſneſs, its freedom of arrangement, and the great beauty and harmony of its ſounds, it ſuits itſelf very happily to moſt ſubjeƈts, either in proſe or in poetry; is capable of the auguſt and the ſtrong, as well as the tender; and ſeems to be, on the whole, the moſt perfeƈt of all the modern dialeƈts which have ariſen out of the ruins of the antient. Our own Language, though not equal to the Italian in flexibility, yet is not deſtitute of a conſiderable degree of this quality. If any one will conſider the diverſity of ſtyle which appears in ſome of our claſſics; that great difference of manner, for inſtance, which is marked by the Style of Lord Shafteſbury, and that of Dean Swift; he will ſee, in our Tongue, ſuch a circle of expreſſion, ſuch a power of accommodation to the different taſte of writers, as redounds not a little to its honour.

WHAT the Engliſh has been moſt taxed with, is its deficiency in harmony of ſound. But though every native is apt to be partial to the ſounds of his own Language, and may, therefore, be ſuſpeƈted of not being a fair judge in this point; yet, I imagine, there are evident grounds on which it may be

ſhown,

shown, that this charge against our Tongue has been carried too far. The melody of our versification, its power of supporting poetical numbers, without any assistance from rhyme, is alone a sufficient proof that our Language is far from being unmusical. Our verse is, after the Italian, the most diversified and harmonious of any of the modern dialects; unquestionably far beyond the French verse, in variety, sweetness, and melody. Mr. Sheridan has shown, in his Lectures, that we abound more in vowel and diphthong sounds, than most Languages; and these too, so divided into long and short, as to afford a proper diversity in the quantity of our syllables. Our consonants, he observes, which appear so crowded to the eye on paper, often form combinations not disagreeable to the ear in pronouncing; and, in particular, the objection which has been made to the frequent recurrence of the hissing consonant s in our Language, is unjust and ill-founded. For, it has not been attended to, that very commonly, and in the final syllables especially, this letter loses altogether the hissing sound, and is transformed into a z, which is one of the sounds on which the ear rests with pleasure; as in *has*, *these*, *those*, *loves*, *hears*, and innumerable more, where, though the letter s be retained in writing, it has really the power of z, not of the common s.

AFTER all, however, it must be admitted, that smoothness, or beauty of sound, is none of the distinguishing properties of the English Tongue. Though not incapable of being formed into melodious arrangements, yet strength and expressiveness, more than grace, form its character. We incline, in general, to a short pronunciation of our words, and have shortened the quantity of most of those which we borrow from the Latin, as

VOL. I.   A a   *orator,*

orator, *ſpectacle*, *theatre*, *liberty*, and ſuch like. Agreeable to this, is a remarkable peculiarity of Engliſh pronunciation, the throwing the accent farther back, that is, nearer the beginning of the word, than is done by any other nation. In Greek and Latin, no word is accented farther back than the third ſyllable from the end, or what is called the antepenult. But, in Engliſh, we have many words accented on the fourth, ſome on the fifth ſyllable from the end, as, *mémorable*, *convéniency*, *ámbulatory*, *prófitableneſs*. The general effect of this practice of haſtening the accent, or placing it ſo near the beginning of a word, is to give a briſk and a ſpirited, but at the ſame time, a rapid and hurried, and not very muſical, tone to the whole pronunciation of a people.

THE Engliſh Tongue poſſeſſes, undoubtedly, this property, of being the moſt ſimple in its form and conſtruction, of all the European dialects. It is free from all intricacy of caſes, declenſions, moods and tenſes. Its words are ſubject to fewer variations from their original form than thoſe of any other Language. Its ſubſtantives have no diſtinction of gender, except what nature has made, and but one variation in caſe. Its adjectives admit of no change at all, except what expreſſes the degree of compariſon. Its verbs, inſtead of running through all the varieties of antient conjugation, ſuffer no more than four or five changes in termination. By the help of a few prepoſitions and auxiliary verbs, all the purpoſes of ſignificancy in meaning are accompliſhed; while the words, for the moſt part, preſerve their form unchanged. The diſadvantages in point of elegance, brevity, and force, which follow from this ſtructure of our Language, I have before pointed out. But,

at

at the fame time, it muft be admitted, that fuch a ftructure contributes to facility. It renders the acquifition of our Language lefs laborious, the arrangement of our words more plain and obvious, the rules of our fyntax fewer and more fimple.

I AGREE, indeed, with Dr. Lowth (preface to his Grammar), in thinking that this very fimplicity and facility of our Language proves a caufe of its being frequently written and fpoken with lefs accuracy. It was neceffary to ftudy Languages, which were of a more complex and artificial form, with greater care. The marks of gender and cafe, the varieties of conjugation and declenfion, the multiplied rules of fyntax, were all to be attended to in Speech. Hence Language became more an object of art. It was reduced into form ; a ftandard was eftablifhed ; and any departures from the ftandard became confpicuous. Whereas, among us, Language is hardly confidered as an object of grammatical rule. We take it for granted, that a competent fkill in it may be acquired without any ftudy ; and that, in a fyntax fo narrow and confined as ours, there is nothing which demands attention. Hence arifes the habit of writing in a loofe and inaccurate manner.

I ADMIT, that no grammatical rules have fufficient authority to controul the firm and eftablifhed ufage of Language. Eftablifhed cuftom, in fpeaking and writing, is the ftandard to which we muft at laft refort for determining every controverted point in Language and Style. But it will not follow from this, that grammatical rules are fuperfeded as ufelefs. In every Language, which has been in any degree cultivated, there prevails a certain ftructure and analogy of parts, which

is

is underſtood to give foundation to the moſt reputable uſage of Speech ; and which, in all caſes, when uſage is looſe or dubious, poſſeſſes conſiderable authority. In every Language, there are rules of ſyntax which muſt be inviolably obſerved by all who would either write or ſpeak with any propriety. For ſyntax is no other than that arrangement of words, in a ſentence, which renders the meaning of each word, and the relation of all the words to one another, moſt clear and intelligible.

ALL the rules of Latin ſyntax, it is true, cannot be applied to our Language. Many of thoſe rules aroſe from the particular form of their Language, which occaſioned verbs or prepoſitions to govern, ſome the genitive, ſome the dative, ſome the accuſative or ablative caſe. But, abſtracting from theſe peculiarities, it is to be always remembered, that the chief and fundamental rules of ſyntax are common to the Engliſh as well as the Latin Tongue ; and, indeed, belong equally to all Languages. For, in all Languages, the parts which compoſe Speech are eſſentially the ſame ; ſubſtantives, adjectives, verbs, and connecting particles : And wherever theſe parts of Speech are found, there are certain neceſſary relations among them, which regulate their ſyntax, or the place which they ought to poſſeſs in a ſentence. Thus, in Engliſh, juſt as much as in Latin, the adjective muſt, by poſition, be made to agree with its ſubſtantive ; and the verb muſt agree with its nominative in perſon and number; becauſe, from the nature of things, a word, which expreſſes either a quality or an action, muſt correſpond as cloſely as poſſible with the name of that thing whoſe quality, or whoſe action, it expreſſes. Two or more ſubſtantives, joined by a copulative, muſt always require the verbs or pro-

6

nouns,

nouns, to which they refer, to be placed in the plural number;
otherwife, their common relation to thefe verbs or pronouns is not pointed out. An active verb muft, in every Language, govern the accufative; that is, clearly point out fome fubftantive noun, as the object to which its action is directed. A relative pronoun muft, in every form of Speech, agree with its antecedent in gender, number, and perfon; and conjunctions, or connecting particles, ought always to couple like cafes and moods; that is, ought to join together words which are of the fame form and ftate with each other. I mention thefe, as a few exemplifications of that fundamental regard to fyntax, which, even in fuch a Language as ours, is abfolutely requifite for writing or fpeaking with any propriety.

WHATEVER the advantages, or defects of the Englifh Language be, as it is our own Language, it deferves a high degree of our ftudy and attention, both with regard to the choice of words which we employ, and with regard to the fyntax, or the arrangement of thefe words in a fentence. We know how much the Greeks and the Romans, in their moft polifhed and flourifhing times, cultivated their own Tongues. We know how much ftudy both the French, and the Italians, have beftowed upon theirs. Whatever knowledge may be acquired by the ftudy of other Languages, it can never be communicated with advantage, unlefs by fuch as can write and fpeak their own Language well. Let the matter of an author be ever fo good and ufeful, his compofitions will always fuffer in the public efteem, if his expreffion be deficient in purity and propriety. At the fame time, the attainment of a correct and elegant ftyle, is an object which demands application and labour.

If

LECT.
IX.

If any imagine they can catch it merely by the ear, or acquire it by a flight perufal of fome of our good authors, they will find themfelves much difappointed. The many errors, even in point of grammar, the many offences againft purity of Language, which are committed by writers who are far from being contemptible, demonftrate, that a careful ftudy of the Language is previoufly requifite, in all who aim at writing it properly *.

* On this fubject, the Reader ought to perufe Dr. Lowth's Short Introduction to Englifh Grammar, with Critical Notes; which is the grammatical performance of higheft authority that has appeared in our time, and in which he will fee, what I have faid concerning the inaccuracies in Language of fome of our beft writers, fully verified. In Dr. Campbell's Philofophy of Rhetoric, he will likewife find many acute and ingenious obfervations, both on the Englifh Language, and on Style in general. And Dr. Prieftley's Rudiments of Englifh Grammar will alfo be ufeful, by pointing out feveral of the errors into which writers are apt to fall.

LECTURE X.

STYLE——PERSPICUITY AND PRECISION.

HAVING finifhed the fubjeƈ of Language, I now enter on the confideration of Style, and the rules that relate to it.

IT is not eafy to give a precife idea of what is meant by Style. The beft definition I can give of it, is, the peculiar manner in which a man expreffes his conceptions, by means of Language. It is different from mere Language or words. The words, which an author employs, may be proper and faultlefs; and his Style may, neverthelefs, have great faults; it may be dry, or ftiff, or feeble, or affeƈed. Style has always fome reference to an author's manner of thinking. It is a piƈure of the ideas which rife in his mind, and of the manner in which they rife there; and, hence, when we are examining an author's compofition, it is, in many cafes, extremely difficult to

feparate

separate the Style from the fentiment. No wonder thefe two fhould be fo intimately connected, as Style is nothing elfe, than that fort of expreffion which our thoughts moft readily affume. Hence, different countries have been noted for peculiarities of Style, fuited to their different temper and genius. The eaftern nations animated their Style with the moft ftrong and hyperbolical figures. The Athenians, a polifhed and acute people, formed a Style accurate, clear, and neat. The Afiatics, gay and loofe in their manners, affected a Style florid and diffufe. The like fort of characteriftical differences are commonly remarked in the Style of the French, the Englifh, and the Spaniards. In giving the general characters of Style, it is ufual to talk of a nervous, a feeble, or a fpirited Style; which are plainly the characters of a writer's manner of thinking, as well as of expreffing himfelf: So difficult it is to feparate thefe two things from one another. Of the general characters of Style, I am afterwards to difcourfe; but it will be neceffary to begin with examining the more fimple qualities of it; from the affemblage of which, its more complex denominations, in a great meafure, refult.

ALL the qualities of a good Style may be ranged under two heads, Perfpicuity and Ornament. For all that can poffibly be required of Language, is, to convey our ideas clearly to the minds of others, and, at the fame time, in fuch a drefs, as by pleafing and interefting them, fhall moft effectually ftrengthen the impreffions which we feek to make. When both thefe ends are anfwered, we certainly accomplifh every purpofe for which we ufe Writing and Difcourfe.

PERSPICUITY

PERSPICUITY, it will be readily admitted, is the fundamental quality of Style*; a quality so essential in every kind of writing, that, for the want of it, nothing can atone. Without this, the richest ornaments of Style only glimmer through the dark; and puzzle, instead of pleasing, the reader. This, therefore, must be our first object, to make our meaning clearly and fully understood, and understood without the least difficulty. " Oratio," says Quinctilian, " debet negligenter " quoque audientibus esse aperta; ut in animum audientis, " sicut sol in oculos, etiamsi in eum non intendatur, occurrat. " Quare, non solum ut intelligere possit, sed ne omnino possit " non intelligere curandum †." If we are obliged to follow a writer with much care, to pause, and to read over his sentences a second time, in order to comprehend them fully, he will never please us long. Mankind are too indolent to relish so much labour. They may pretend to admire the author's depth, after they have discovered his meaning; but they will seldom be inclined to take up his work a second time.

AUTHORS sometimes plead the difficulty of their subject, as an excuse for the want of Perspicuity. But the excuse can rarely, if ever, be sustained. For whatever a man conceives

* " Nobis prima sit virtus, perspicuitas, propria verba, rectus ordo, non " in longum dilata conclusio; nihil neque desit, neque superfluat."

QUINCTIL. lib. viii.

† " Discourse ought always to be obvious, even to the most careless and " negligent hearer; so that the sense shall strike his mind, as the light of the " sun does our eyes, though they are not directed upwards to it. We must " study, not only that every hearer may understand us, but that it shall be impossible for him not to understand us."

clearly, that, it is in his power, if he will be at the trouble, to put into diſtinct propoſitions, or to expreſs clearly to others: and upon no ſubject ought any man to write, where he cannot think clearly. His ideas, indeed, may, very excuſably, be on ſome ſubjects incomplete or inadequate; but ſtill, as far as they go, they ought to be clear; and, wherever this is the caſe, Perſpicuity, in expreſſing them, is always attainable. The obſcurity which reigns ſo much among many metaphyſical writers, is, for the moſt part, owing to the indiſtinctneſs of their own conceptions. They ſee the object but in a confuſed light; and, of courſe, can never exhibit it in a clear one to others.

PERSPICUITY in writing, is not to be conſidered as only a ſort of negative virtue, or freedom from defect. It has higher merit: It is a degree of poſitive beauty. We are pleaſed with an author, we conſider him as deſerving praiſe, who frees us from all fatigue of ſearching for his meaning; who carries us through his ſubject without any embarraſſment or confuſion; whoſe ſtyle flows always like a limpid ſtream, where we ſee to the very bottom.

THE ſtudy of Perſpicuity requires attention, firſt, to ſingle words and phraſes, and then to the conſtruction of ſentences. I begin with treating of the firſt, and ſhall confine myſelf to it in this Lecture.

PERSPICUITY, conſidered with reſpect to words and phraſes, requires theſe three qualities in them; *Purity*, *Propriety*, and *Preciſion*.

PURITY

PURITY and Propriety of Language, are often ufed indif-
criminately for each other; and, indeed, they are very nearly
allied. A diftinction, however, obtains between them. Purity,
is the ufe of fuch words, and fuch conftructions, as belong to
the idiom of the Language which we fpeak; in oppofition to
words and phrafes that are imported from other Languages, or
that are obfolete, or new coined, or ufed without proper authority. Propriety, is the felection of fuch words in the Language, as the beft and moft eftablifhed ufage has appropriated
to thofe ideas which we intend to exprefs by them. It implies
the correct and happy application of them, according to that
ufage, in oppofition to vulgarifms, or low expreffions; and to
words and phrafes, which would be lefs fignificant of the ideas
that we mean to convey. Style may be pure, that is, it may
all be ftrictly Englifh, without Scotticifms or Gallicifms, or
ungrammatical irregular expreffions of any kind, and may,
neverthelefs, be deficient in Propriety. The words may be ill
chofen ; not adapted to the fubject, nor fully expreffive of the
author's fenfe. He has taken all his words and phrafes from the
general mafs of Englifh Language ; but he has made his felection among thefe words unhappily. Whereas, Style cannot be
proper without being alfo pure ; and where both Purity and
Propriety meet, befides making Style perfpicuous, they alfo
render it graceful. There is no ftandard, either of Purity or
of Propriety, but the practice of the beft writers and fpeakers
in the country.

WHEN I mentioned obfolete or new-coined words as incon-
gruous with Purity of Style, it will be eafily underftood, that
fome exceptions are to be made. On certain occafions, they
may

may have grace. Poetry admits of greater latitude than profe, with refpect to coining, or, at leaft, new-compounding words; yet, even here, this liberty fhould be ufed with a fparing hand. In profe, fuch innovations are more hazardous, and have a worfe effect. They are apt to give Style an affected and conceited air; and fhould never be ventured upon, except by fuch, whofe eftablifhed reputation gives them fome degree of dictatorial power over Language.

THE introduction of foreign and learned words, unlefs where neceffity requires them, fhould always be avoided. Barren Languages may need fuch affiftances; but ours is not one of thefe. Dean Swift, one of our moft correct writers, valued himfelf much on ufing no words but fuch as were of native growth: and his Language may, indeed, be confidered as a ftandard of the ftricteft Purity and Propriety in the choice of words. At prefent, we feem to be departing from this ftandard. A multitude of Latin words have, of late, been poured in upon us. On fome occafions, they give an appearance of elevation and dignity to Style. But often alfo, they render it ftiff and forced: And, in general, a plain native Style, as it is more intelligible to all readers, fo, by a proper management of words, it can be made equally ftrong and expreffive with this Latinifed Englifh.

LET us now confider the import of Precifion in Language, which, as it is the higheft part of the quality denoted by Perfpicuity, merits a full explication; and the more, becaufe diftinct ideas are, perhaps, not commonly formed about it.

2　　　　　　　　　　　　　　　　THE

THE exact import of Precifion may be drawn from the ety-
mology of the word. It comes from " precidere," to cut off:
It imports retrenching all fuperfluities, and pruning the expreffion fo, as to exhibit neither more nor lefs than an exact copy
of his idea who ufes it. I obferved before, that it is often
difficult to feparate the qualities of Style from the qualities of
Thought; and it is found fo in this inftance. For, in order to
write with Precifion, though this be properly a quality of Style,
one muft poffefs a very confiderable degree of diftinctnefs and
accuracy in his manner of thinking.

THE words, which a man ufes to exprefs his ideas, may be
faulty in three refpects: They may either not exprefs that idea
which the author intends, but fome other which only refembles,
or is akin to it; or, they may exprefs that idea, but not quite
fully and completely; or, they may exprefs it, together with
fomething more than he intends. Precifion ftands oppofed to
all thefe three faults; but chiefly to the laft. In an author's
writing with Propriety, his being free of the two former faults
feems implied. The words which he ufes are proper; that is,
they exprefs that idea which he intends, and they exprefs it
fully; but to be Precife, fignifies, that they exprefs that idea,
and no more. There is nothing in his words which introduces
any foreign idea, any fuperfluous unfeafonable acceffory, fo as
to mix it confufedly with the principal object, and thereby to
render our conception of that object loofe and indiftinct. This
requires a writer to have, himfelf, a very clear apprehenfion of
the object he means to prefent to us; to have laid faft hold of
it in his mind; and never to waver in any one view he takes of
it: a perfection to which, indeed, few writers attain.

THE

THE use and importance of Precision, may be deduced from the nature of the human mind. It never can view, clearly and diftinctly, above one object at a time. If it muft look at two or three together, especially objects among which there is refemblance cr connection, it finds itfelf confused and embarraffed. It cannot clearly perceive in what they agree, and in what they differ. Thus, were any object, fuppose fome animal, to be prefented to me, of whofe ftructure I wanted to form a diftinct notion, I would desire all its trappings to be taken off, I would require it to be brought before me by itfelf, and to ftand alone, that there might be nothing to diftract my attention. The fame is the cafe with words. If, when you would inform me of your meaning, you also tell me more than what conveys it; if you join foreign circumftances to the principal object; if, by unneceffarily varying the expreffion, you fhift the point of view, and make me fee fometimes the object itfelf, and fometimes another thing that is connected with it; you thereby oblige me to look on feveral objects at once, and I lofe fight of the principal. You load the animal, you are fhowing me, with fo many trappings and collars, and bring fo many of the fame fpecies before me, fomewhat refembling, and yet fomewhat differing, that I fee none of them clearly.

THIS forms what is called a Loofe Style; and is the proper oppofite to Precision. It generally arifes from ufing a fuperfluity of words. Feeble writers employ a multitude of words to make themfelves underftood, as they think, more diftinctly; and they only confound the reader. They are fenfible of not having caught the precife expreffion, to convey what they would fignify; they do not, indeed, conceive their own meaning

ing very precifely themfelves; and, therefore, help it out, as they can, by this and the other word, which may, as they fuppofe, fupply the defect, and bring you fomewhat nearer to their idea: They are always going about it, and about it, but never juft hit the thing. The image, as they fet it before you, is always feen double; and no double image is diftinct. When an author tells me of his hero's *courage* in the day of battle, the expreffion is precife, and I underftand it fully. But if, from the defire of multiplying words, he will needs praife his *courage* and *fortitude*; at the moment he joins thefe words together, my idea begins to waver. He means to exprefs one quality more ftrongly; but he is, in truth, expreffing two. *Courage* refifts danger; *fortitude* fupports pain. The occafion of exerting each of thefe qualities is different; and being led to think of both together, when only one of them fhould be in my view, my view is rendered unfteady, and my conception of the object indiftinct.

FROM what I have faid, it appears that an author may, in a qualified fenfe, be perfpicuous, while yet he is far from being precife. He ufes proper words, and proper arrangement; he gives you the idea as clear as he conceives it himfelf; and fo far he is perfpicuous: but the ideas are not very clear in his own mind; they are loofe and general; and, therefore, cannot be expreffed with Precifion. All fubjects do not equally require Precifion. It is fufficient, on many occafions, that we have a general view of the meaning. The fubject, perhaps, is of the known and familiar kind; and we are in no hazard of miftaking the fenfe of the author, though every word which he ufes be not precife and exact.

Few authors, for inftance, in the Englifh Language, are more clear and perfpicuous, on the whole, than Archbifhop Tillotfon, and Sir William Temple; yet neither of them are remarkable for Precifion. They are loofe and diffufe; and accuftomed to exprefs their meaning by feveral words, which fhew you fully whereabouts it lies, rather than to fingle out thofe expreffions, which would convey clearly the idea they have in view, and no more. Neither, indeed, is Precifion the prevailing character of Mr. Addifon's Style; although he is not fo deficient in this refpect as the other two authors.

Lord Shaftsbury's faults, in point of Precifion, are much greater than Mr. Addifon's; and the more unpardonable, becaufe he is a profeffed philofophical writer; who, as fuch, ought, above all things, to have ftudied Precifion. His Style has both great beauties, and great faults; and, on the whole, is by no means a fafe model for imitation. Lord Shaftfbury was well acquainted with the power of words; thofe which he employs are generally proper and well founding; he has great variety of them; and his arrangement, as fhall be afterwards fhown, is commonly beautiful. His defect, in Preeifion, is not owing fo much to indiftinct or confufed ideas, as to perpetual affectation. He is fond, to excefs, of the pomp and parade of Language; he is never fatisfied with expreffing any thing clearly and fimply; he muft always give it the drefs of ftate and majefty. Hence perpetual circumlocutions, and many words and phrafes employed to defcribe fomewhat, that would have been defcribed much better by one of them. If he has occafion to mention any perfon or author, he very rarely mentions him by his proper name. In the treatife, entitled, Advice to an

Author,

Author, he defcants for two or three pages together upon Ariftotle, without once naming him in any other way, than the Mafter Critic, the Mighty Genius and Judge of Art, the Prince of Critics, the Grand Mafter of Art, and Confummate Philologift. In the fame way, the Grand Poetic Sire, the Philofophical Patriarch, and his Difciple of Noble Birth, and lofty Genius, are the only names by which he condefcends to diftinguifh Homer, Socrates, and Plato, in another paffage of the fame treatife. This method of diftinguifhing perfons is extremely affected; but it is not fo contrary to Precifion, as the frequent circumlocutions he employs for all moral ideas; attentive, on every occafion, more to the pomp of Language, than to the clearnefs which he ought to have ftudied as a philofopher. The moral fenfe, for inftance, after he had once defined it, was a clear term; but, how vague becomes the idea, when, in the next page, he calls it, " That natural affection, and " anticipating fancy, which makes the fenfe of right and " wrong?" Self examination, or reflection on our own conduct, is an idea conceived with eafe; but when it is wrought into all the forms of, " A man's dividing himfelf into two " parties, becoming a felf-dialogift, entering into partnerfhip " with himfelf, forming the dual number practically within " himfelf;" we hardly know what to make of it. On fome occafions, he fo adorns, or rather loads with words, the plaineft and fimpleft propofitions, as, if not to obfcure, at leaft, to enfeeble them.

In the following paragraph, for example, of the Inquiry concerning Virtue, he means to fhow, that, by every ill action we hurt our mind, as much as one who fhould fwallow poifon, or give himself a wound, would hurt his body.　Obferve what a redundancy of words he pours forth : " Now, if the fabrick " of the mind or temper appeared to us, fuch as it really is; if " we faw it impoffible to remove hence any one good or " orderly affection, or to introduce any ill or diforderly one, " without drawing on, in fome degree, that diffolute ftate " which, at its height, is confeffed to be fo miferable; it would " then, undoubtedly, be confeffed, that fince no ill, immoral, " or unjuft action, can be committed, without either a new " inroad and breach on the temper and paffions, or a further " advancing of that execution already done; whoever did ill, " or acted in prejudice of his integrity, good-nature, or worth, " would, of neceffity, act with greater cruelty towards himfelf, " than he who fcrupled not to fwallow what was poifonous, " or who, with his own hands, fhould voluntarily mangle or " wound his outward form or conftitution, natural limbs or body *."　Here, to commit a bad action, is, firft, " To remove " a good and orderly affection, and to introduce an ill or " diforderly one;" next, it is, " To commit an action that is ill, " immoral, and unjuft;" and in the next line, it is, " To do " ill, or to act in prejudice of integrity, good-nature, and " worth;" nay, fo very fimple a thing as a man's wounding himfelf, is, " To mangle, or wound, his outward form and " conftitution, his natural limbs or body."　Such fuperfluity of words is difguftful to every reader of correct tafte ; and ferves no purpofe but to embarrafs and perplex the fenfe.　This fort of Style is elegantly defcribed by Quinctilian, " Eft in quibuf- " dam turba inanium verborum, qui dum communem lo-

---

* Characterift. Vol. II. p. 85.

" quendi

" quendi morem reformidant, ducti fpecie nitoris, circumeunt
" omnia copiofa loquacitate quæ dicere volunt *." Lib. vii.
cap. 2.

THE great fource of a loofe Style, in oppofition to Precifion, is the injudicious ufe of thofe words termed Synonymous.
They are called Synonymous, becaufe they agree in expreffing
one principal idea ; but, for the moft part, if not always, they
exprefs it with fome diverfity in the circumftances. They are
varied by fome acceffory idea which every word introduces,
and which forms the diftinction between them. Hardly, in
any Language, are there two words that convey precifely the
fame idea ; a perfon thoroughly converfant in the propriety of
the Language, will always be able to obferve fomething that
diftinguifhes them. As they are like different fhades of the
fame colour, an accurate writer can employ them to great advantage, by ufing them, fo as to heighten and to finifh the
picture which he gives us. He fupplies by one, what was
wanting in the other, to the force, or to the luftre of the image
which he means to exhibit. But, in order to this end, he muft
be extremely attentive to the choice which he makes of them.
For the bulk of writers are very apt to confound them with
each other ; and to employ them carelefsly, merely for the
fake of filling up a period, or of rounding and diverfifying
the Language, as if their fignification were exactly the fame,
while, in truth, it is not. Hence a certain mift, and indiftinctnefs, is unwarily thrown over Style.

* " A crowd of unmeaning words is brought together, by fome authors,
" who, afraid of expreffing themfelves after a common and ordinary manner,
" and allured by an appearance of fplendour, furround every thing which they
" mean to fay with a certain copious loquacity."

IN the Latin Language, there are no two words we would more readily take to be fynonymous, than *amare* and *diligere*. Cicero, however, has fhewn us, that there is a very clear diftinction betwixt them, " Quid ergo," fays he, in one of his epiftles, " tibi commendem eum quem tu ipfe diligis ? Sed " tamen ut fcires eum non a me *diligi* folum, verum etiam " *amari*, ob eam rem tibi hæc fcribo *." In the fame manner *tutus* and *fecurus*, are words which we would readily confound ; yet their meaning is different. *Tutus*, fignifies out of danger ; *fecurus*, free from the dread of it. Seneca has elegantly marked this diftinction ; " Tuta fcelera effe poffunt, " fecura non poffunt †." In our own Language, very many inftances might be given of a difference in meaning among words reputed Synonymous ; and, as the fubject is of importance, I fhall now point out fome of thefe. The inftances which I am to give, may themfelves be of ufe ; and they will ferve to fhew the neceffity of attending, with care and ftrictnefs, to the exact import of words, if ever we would write with Propriety or Precifion.

Aufterity, Severity, Rigour. Aufterity, relates to the manner of living ; Severity, of thinking ; Rigour, of punifhing. To Aufterity, is oppofed Effeminacy ; to Severity, Relaxation ; to Rigour, Clemency. A Hermit, is auftere in his life ; a Cafuift, fevere in his application of religion or law ; a Judge, rigorous in his fentences.

Cuftom, Habit. Cuftom, refpects the action ; Habit, the actor. By Cuftom, we mean the frequent repetition of the fame

---

* Ad Famil. l. 13. ep. 47.   † Epif. 97.

act ;

act; by Habit, the effect which that repetition produces on the
mind or body. By the Custom of walking often on the streets,
one acquires a Habit of idleness.

Surprised, astonished, amazed, confounded. I am surprised
with what is new or unexpected; I am astonished, at what is
vast or great; I am amazed, with what is incomprehensible; I
am confounded, by what is shocking or terrible.

Desist, renounce, quit, leave off. Each of these words imply
some pursuit or object relinquished; but from different motives.
We desist, from the difficulty of accomplishing. We renounce,
on account of the disagreeableness of the object, or pursuit.
We quit, for the sake of some other thing which interests us
more; and we leave off, because we are weary of the design.
A Politician desists from his designs, when he finds they are
impracticable; he renounces the court, because he has been
affronted by it; he quits ambition for study or retirement; and
leaves off his attendance on the great, as he becomes old and
weary of it.

Pride, Vanity. Pride, makes us esteem ourselves; Vanity,
makes us desire the esteem of others. It is just to say,
as Dean Swift has done, that a man is too proud to be
vain.

Haughtiness, Disdain. Haughtiness, is founded on the high
opinion we entertain of ourselves; Disdain, on the low opinion
we have of others.

9

To diſtinguiſh, to ſeparate. We diſtinguiſh, what we want not to confound with another thing; we ſeparate, what we want to remove from it. Objects are diſtinguiſhed from one another, by their qualities. They are ſeparated, by the diſtance of time or place.

To weary, to fatigue. The continuance of the ſame thing wearies us; labour fatigues us. I am weary with ſtanding; I am fatigued with walking. A ſuitor wearies us by his perſeverance; fatigues us by his importunity.

To abhor, to deteſt. To abhor, imports, ſimply, ſtrong diſlike; to deteſt, imports alſo ſtrong diſapprobation. One abhors being in debt; he deteſts treachery.

To invent, to diſcover. We invent things that are new; we diſcover what was before hidden. Galileo invented the teleſcope; Harvey diſcovered the circulation of the blood.

Only, alone. Only, imports that there is no other of the ſame kind; alone, imports being accompanied by no other. An only child, is one who has neither brother nor ſiſter; a child alone, is one who is left by itſelf. There is a difference, therefore, in preciſe Language, betwixt theſe two phraſes, " Virtue only makes us happy;" and, " Virtue alone makes " us happy." Virtue only makes us happy, imports, that nothing elſe can do it. Virtue alone makes us happy, imports, that virtue, by itſelf, or unaccompanied with other advantages, is ſufficient to do it.

Entire,

Entire, Complete. A thing is entire, by wanting none of its parts; complete, by wanting none of the appendages that belong to it. A man may have an entire houfe to himfelf; and yet not have one complete apartment.

Tranquillity, Peace, Calm. Tranquillity, refpects a fituation free from trouble, confidered in itfelf; Peace, the fame fituation with refpect to any caufes that might interrupt it; Calm, with regard to a difturbed fituation going before, or following it. A good man enjoys Tranquillity, in himfelf; Peace, with others; and Calm, after the ftorm.

A Difficulty, an Obftacle. A Difficulty, embarraffes; an Obftacle, ftops us. We remove the one; we furmount the other. Generally, the firft, expreffes fomewhat arifing from the nature and circumftances of the affair; the fecond, fomewhat arifing from a foreign caufe. Philip found Difficulty in managing the Athenians from the nature of their difpofitions; but the eloquence of Demofthenes was the greateft Obftacle to his defigns.

Wifdom, Prudence. Wifdom, leads us to fpeak and act what is moft proper. Prudence, prevents our fpeaking or acting improperly. A wife man, employs the moft proper means for fuccefs; a prudent man, the fafeft means for not being brought into danger.

Enough, Sufficient. Enough, relates to the quantity which one wifhes to have of any thing. Sufficient, relates to the ufe that is to be made of it. Hence, Enough, generally imports a

greater

greater quantity than Sufficient does. The covetous man never has enough; although he has what is fufficient for nature.

To avow, to acknowledge, to confefs. Each of thefe words imports the affirmation of a fact, but in very different circumftances. To avow, fuppofes the perfon to glory in it; to acknowledge, fuppofes a fmall degree of faultinefs, which the acknowledgment compenfates; to confefs, fuppofes a higher degree of crime. A patriot avows his oppofition to a bad minifter, and is applauded; a gentleman acknowledges his miftake, and is forgiven; a prifoner confeffes the crime he is accufed of, and is punifhed.

To remark, to obferve. We remark, in the way of attention, in order to remember; we obferve, in the way of examination, in order to judge. A traveller remarks the moft ftriking objects he fees; a general obferves all the motions of his enemy.

Equivocal, Ambiguous. An Equivocal Expreffion is, one which has one fenfe open, and defigned to be underftood; another fenfe concealed, and underftood only by the perfon who ufes it. An Ambiguous Expreffion is, one which has apparently two fenfes, and leaves us at a lofs which of them to give it. An equivocal expreffion is ufed with an intention to deceive; an ambiguous one, when it is ufed with defign, is, with an intention not to give full information. An honeft man will never employ an equivocal expreffion; a confufed man may often utter ambiguous ones, without any defign. I fhall give only one inftance more.

With,

With, *By*. Both thefe particles exprefs the connection between fome inftrument, or means of effecting an end, and the
agent who employs it : but *with*, expreffes a more clofe and
immediate connection ; *by*, a more remote one. We kill a
man *with* a fword ; he dies *by* violence. The criminal is bound
with ropes *by* the executioner. The proper diftinction in the
ufe of thefe particles, is elegantly marked in a paffage of Dr.
Robertfon's Hiftory of Scotland. When one of the old Scottifh
kings was making an enquiry into the tenure *by* which his
nobles held their lands, they ftarted up, and drew their fwords :
" *By* thefe," faid they, " we acquired our lands, and *with*
" thefe, we will defend them." " *By* thefe we acquired our
" lands;" fignifies the more remote means of acquifition by
force and martial deeds; and, " *with* thefe we will defend
" them ;" fignifies the immediate direct inftrument, the fword,
which they would employ in their defence.

THESE are inftances of words, in our Language, which, by
carelefs writers, are apt to be employed as perfectly fynonymous, and yet are not fo. Their fignifications approach, but
are not precifely the fame. The more the diftinction in the
meaning of fuch words is weighed, and attended to, the more
clearly and forcibly fhall we fpeak or write *.

FROM

* In French, there is a very ufeful treatife on this fubject, the Abbé
Girard's *Synonymes Françoifes*, in which he has made a large collection of fuch
apparent Synonymes in the Language, and fhown, with much accuracy, the
difference in their fignification. It were much to be wifhed, that fome fuch
work were undertaken for our tongue, and executed with equal tafte and
judgment. Nothing would contribute more to precife and elegant writing.
In the mean time, this French Treatife may be perufed with confiderable

FROM all that has been faid on this head, it will now appear, that, in order to write or fpeak with Precifion, two things are efpecially requifite ; one, that an author's own ideas be clear and diftinct ; and the other, that he have an exact and full comprehenfion of the force of thofe words which he employs. Natural genius is here required ; labour and attention ftill more. Dean Swift is one of the authors, in our Language, moft diftinguifhed for Precifion of Style. In his writings, we feldom or never find vague expreffions, and fynonymous words, careleffly thrown together. His meaning is always clear, and ftrongly marked.

I HAD occafion to obferve before, that though all fubjects of writing or difcourfe demand Perfpicuity, yet all do not require the fame degree of that exact Precifion, which I have endeavoured to explain. It is, indeed, in every fort of writing, a great beauty to have, at leaft, fome meafure of Precifion, in diftinction from that loofe profufion of words which imprints no clear idea on the reader's mind. But we muft, at the fame time, be on our guard, left too great a ftudy of Precifion, efpecially in fubjects where it is not ftrictly requifite, betray us into a dry and barren Style ; left, from the defire of pruning too clofely, we retrench all copioufnefs and ornament. Some degree of this failing may, perhaps, be remarked in Dean Swift's ferious works. Attentive only to exhibit his ideas clear

profit. It will accuftom perfons to weigh, with attention, the force of words; and will fuggeft feveral diftinctions betwixt fynonymous terms in our own language, analogous to thofe which he has pointed out in the French ; and, accordingly, feveral of the inftances above given were fuggefted by the work of this author.

and

and exact, refting wholly on his fenfe and diftinctnefs, he appears to reject, difdainfully, all embellifhment which, on fome
occafions, may be thought to render his manner fomewhat hard
and dry. To unite together Copioufnefs and Precifion, to be
flowing and graceful, and, at the fame time, correct and exact
in the choice of every word, is, no doubt, one of the higheft
and moft difficult attainments in writing. Some kinds of compofition may require more of Copioufnefs and Ornament;
others, more of Precifion and Accuracy; nay, in the fame
compofition, the different parts of it may demand a proper
variation of manner. But we muft ftudy never to facrifice,
totally, any one of thefe qualities to the other; and, by a
proper management, both of them may be made fully confiftent, if our own ideas be precife, and our knowledge and
ftock of words be, at the fame time, extenfive.

D d 2

LECTURE XI.

STRUCTURE OF SENTENCES.

HAVING begun to treat of Style, in the laſt Lecture I conſidered its fundamental quality, Perſpicuity. What I have ſaid of this, relates chiefly to the choice of Words. From words I proceed to Sentences; and as, in all writing and diſcourſe, the proper compoſition and ſtructure of Sentences is of the higheſt importance, I ſhall treat of this fully. Though Perſpicuity be the general head under which I, at preſent, conſider Language, I ſhall not confine myſelf to this quality alone, in Sentences, but ſhall enquire alſo, what is requiſite for their Grace and Beauty: that I may bring together, under one view, all that ſeems neceſſary to be attended to in the conſtruction and arrangement of words in a Sentence.

IT is not eaſy to give an exact definition of a Sentence, or Period, farther, than as it always implies ſome one complete propoſition or enunciation of thought. Ariſtotle's definition

is,

is, in the main, a good one: " Λεξις εχϭσα αϱχην και τελευτην "καθ᾽ αυτην, και μεγεθος ευσυνοπτον:" " A form of Speech which " hath a beginning and an end within itfelf, and is of fuch a " length as to be eafily comprehended at once." This, how- ever, admits of great latitude. For a Sentence, or Period, con- fifts always of component parts, which are called its members; and as thefe members may be either few or many, and may be connected in feveral different ways, the fame thought, or mental propofition, may often be either brought into one Sentence, or fplit into two or three, without the material breach of any rule.

THE firft variety that occurs in the confideration of Sen- tences, is, the diftinction of long and fhort ones. The precife length of Sentences, as to the number of words, or the num- ber of members, which may enter into them, cannot be afcer- tained by any definite meafure. Only, it is obvious, there may be an extreme on either fide. Sentences, immoderately long, and confifting of too many members, always tranfgrefs fome one or other of the rules which I fhall mention foon, as neceffary to be obferved in every good Sentence. In difcourfes that are to be fpoken, regard muft be had to the eafinefs of pronunciation, which is not confiftent with too long periods. In compofitions where pronunciation has no place, ftill, how- ever, by ufing long periods too frequently, an author over- loads the reader's ear, and fatigues his attention. For long Periods require, evidently, more attention than fhort ones, in order to perceive clearly the connexion of the feveral parts, and to take in the whole at one view. At the fame time, there may be an excefs in too many fhort Sentences alfo; by which

the

the fenfe is fplit and broken, the connexion of thought weakened, and the memory burdened, by prefenting to it a long fucceffion of minute objects.

WITH regard to the length and conftruction of Sentences, the French critics make a very juft diftinction of Style, into *Style Periodique*, and *Style Coupé*. The *Style Periodique* is, where the fentences are compofed of feveral members linked together, and hanging upon one another, fo that the fenfe of the whole is not brought out till the clofe. This is the moft pompous, mufical, and oratorical manner of compofing.; as in the following fentence of Sir William Temple: " If you " look about you, and confider the lives of others as well as " your own; if you think how few are born with honour, " and how many die without name or children; how little " beauty we fee, and how few friends we hear of; how " many difeafes, and how much poverty there is in the world; " you will fall down upon your knees, and, inftead of repin- " ing at one affliction, will admire fo many bleffings which you " have received from the hand of God." (Letter to Lady Effex.) Cicero abounds with Sentences conftructed after this manner.

THE *Style Coupé* is, where the fenfe is formed into fhort in- dependent propofitions, each complete within itfelf; as in the following of Mr. Pope: " I confefs, it was want of confider- " ation that made me an author. I writ, becaufe it amufed " me. I corrected, becaufe it was as pleafant to me to correct " as to write. I publifhed, becaufe, I was told, I might pleafe " fuch as it was a credit to pleafe." (Preface to his works.)

I

This

This is very much the French method of writing; and always suits gay and easy subjects. The *Style Periodique*, gives an air of gravity and dignity to composition. The *Style Coupé*, is more lively and striking. According to the nature of the composition, therefore, and the general character it ought to bear, the one or other may be predominant. But, in almost every kind of composition, the great rule is to intermix them. For the ear tires of either of them when too long continued : Whereas, by a proper mixture of long and short Periods, the ear is gratified, and a certain sprightliness is joined with majesty in our style. " Non semper," says Cicero (describing very expressively, these two different kinds of Styles, of which I have been speaking,) " non semper utendum est " perpetuitate, & quasi conversione verborum; sed sæpe car- " penda membris minutioribus oratio est *."

THIS variety is of so great consequence, that it must be studied, not only in the succession of long and short Sentences, but in the structure of our Sentences also. A train of Sentences, constructed in the same manner, and with the same number of members, whether long or short, should never be allowed to succeed one another. However musical each of them may be, it has a better effect to introduce even a discord, than to cloy the ear with the repetition of similar sounds : For, nothing is so tiresome as perpetual uniformity. In this article of the construction and distribution of his Sentences, Lord Shaftsbury has shown great art. In the last Lecture, I observed, that he is

* " It is not proper always to employ a continued train, and a sort of re-
" gular compass of phrases; but style ought to be often broken down into
" smaller members."

often

often guilty of facrificing precifion of ftyle to pomp of expreffion; and that there runs through his whole manner, a ftiffnefs and affectation, which render him very unfit to be confidered as a general model. But, as his ear was fine, and as he was extremely attentive to every thing that is elegant, he has ftudied the proper intermixture of long and fhort Sentences, with variety and harmony in their ftructure, more than any other Englifh author: and for this part of compofition he deferves attention.

FROM thefe general obfervations, let us now defcend to a more particular confideration of the qualities that are required to make a Sentence perfect. So much depends upon the proper conftruction of Sentences, that, in every fort of compofition, we cannot be too ftrict in our attentions to it. For, be the fubject what it will, if the Sentences be conftructed in a clumfy, perplexed, or feeble manner, it is impoffible that a work, compofed of fuch Sentences, can be read with pleafure, or even with profit. Whereas, by giving attention to the rules which relate to this part of ftyle, we acquire the habit of expreffing ourfelves with Perfpicuity and Elegance; and, if a diforder chance to arife in fome of our Sentences, we immediately fee where it lies, and are able to rectify it *.

THE

* On the Structure of Sentences, the Antients appear to have beftowed a a great deal of attention and care. The Treatife of Demetrius Phalereus, περι Εϱμηνειας, abounds with obfervations upon the choice and collocation of words carried to fuch a degree of nicety, as would frequently feem to us minute. The Treatife of Dyonyfius of Halicarnaffus, περι συνθεσεως ονοματων, is more mafterly; but is chiefly confined to the mufical ftructure of Periods; a fubject, for which the Greek Language afforded much more affiftance to their writers,

than

THE properties moſt eſſential to a perfect Sentence, ſeem to me, the four following: 1. Clearneſs and Preciſion. 2. Unity. 3. Strength. 4. Harmony. Each of theſe I ſhall illuſtrate ſeparately, and at ſome length.

THE firſt is, Clearneſs and Preciſion. The leaſt failure here, the leaſt degree of ambiguity, which leaves the mind in any ſort of ſuſpence as to the meaning, ought to be avoided with the greateſt care; nor is it ſo eaſy a matter to keep always clear of this, as one might, at firſt, imagine. Ambiguity ariſes from two cauſes: either from a wrong choice of words, or a wrong collocation of them. Of the choice of words, as far as regards Perſpicuity, I treated fully in the laſt Lecture. Of the collocation of them, I am now to treat. The firſt thing to be ſtudied here, is, to obſerve exactly the rules of grammar, as far as theſe can guide us. But as the grammar of our Language is not extenſive, there may often be an ambiguous collocation of words, where there is no tranſgreſſion of any grammatical rule. The relations which the words, or members of a period, bear to one another, cannot be pointed out in Engliſh, as in the Greek or Latin, by means of termination; it is aſcertained only by the poſition in which they ſtand. Hence a capital rule in the arrangement of Sentences is, that the words or members moſt nearly related, ſhould be placed in the Sentence, as near to each other as poſſible; ſo as to make their mutual relation clearly appear. This is a rule not always obſerved,

than our Tongue admits. On the arrangement of words, in Engliſh Sentences, the xviiith chapter of Lord Kaims's Elements of Criticiſm ought to be conſulted; and alſo, the 2d Volume of Dr. Campbell's Philoſophy of Rhetoric.

VOL. I.　　　　　　E e　　　　　　even

even by good writers, as ſtrictly as it ought to be. It will be neceſſary to produce ſome inſtances, which will both ſhow the importance of this rule, and make the application of it be underſtood.

FIRST, In the poſition of adverbs, which are uſed to qualify the ſignification of ſomething which either precedes or follows them, there is often a good deal of nicety. " By greatneſs," ſays Mr. Addiſon, in the Spectator, No. 412. " I do not only " mean the bulk of any ſingle object, but the largeneſs of a " whole view." Here the place of the adverb *only*, renders it a limitation of the following word, mean. " I do not only " mean." The queſtion may then be put, What does he more than mean ? Had he placed it after *bulk*, ſtill it would have been wrong. " I do not mean the *bulk only* of any ſingle ob- " ject." For we might then aſk, What does he mean more than the bulk ? Is it the colour ? Or any other property ? Its proper place, undoubtedly, is, after the word *object*. " By " greatneſs, I do not mean the bulk of any ſingle object only ;" for then, when we put the queſtion, What more does he mean than the bulk of a ſingle object ? The anſwer comes out exact- ly as the author intends, and gives it ; " The largeneſs of a " whole view."—" Theiſm," ſays Lord Shaftſbury, " can " only be oppoſed to polytheiſm, or atheiſm." Does he mean that theiſm is capable of nothing elſe, except being oppoſed to polytheiſm or atheiſm ? This is what his words literally import, through the wrong collocation of *only*. He ſhould have ſaid, " Theiſm can be oppoſed only to polytheiſm or atheiſm."—In like manner, Dean Swift (Project for the advancement of Religion), " The Romans underſtood liberty, at leaſt, as well

" as

" as we." Thefe words are capable of two different fenfes, according as the emphafis, in reading them, is laid upon *liberty*, or upon *at leaft*. In the firft cafe, they will fignify, that whatever other things we may underftand better than the Romans, *liberty*, at leaft, was one thing which they underftood as well as we. In the fecond cafe, they will import, that liberty was underftood, *at leaft* as well by them as by us; meaning, that by them it was better underftood. If this laft, as I make no doubt, was Dean Swift's own meaning, the ambiguity would have been avoided, and the fenfe rendered independent of the manner of pronouncing, by arranging the words thus: " The " Romans underftood liberty as well, at leaft, as we." The fact is, with refpect to fuch adverbs, as, *only, wholly, at leaft*, and the reft of that tribe, that in common difcourfe, the tone and emphafis we ufe in pronouncing them, generally ferves to fhow their reference, and to make the meaning clear; and hence, we acquire a habit of throwing them in loofely in the courfe of a period. But, in writing, where a man fpeaks to the eye, and not to the ear, he ought to be more accurate; and fo to connect thofe adverbs with the words which they qualify, as to put his meaning out of doubt upon the firft infpection.

SECONDLY, When a circumftance is interpofed in the middle of a Sentence, it fometimes requires attention how to place it, fo as to diveft it of all ambiguity. For inftance: " Are thefe " defigns" (fays Lord Bolingbroke, Differ. on Parties, Dedicat.) " Are thefe defigns which any man, who is born a Briton, in " any circumftances, in any fituation, ought to be afhamed " or afraid to avow?" Here we are left at a lofs, whether thefe words, " *in any circumftances, in any fituation*," are connected

E e 2   with,

with, " a man born in Britain, in any circumſtances, or ſitua
" tion," or with that man's " avowing his deſigns, in any
" circumſtances, or ſituation, into which he may be brought?"
If the latter, as ſeems moſt probable, was intended to be the
meaning, the arrangement ought to have been conducted thus:
" Are theſe deſigns, which any man who is born a Briton,
" ought to be aſhamed or afraid, in any circumſtances, in any
" ſituation, to avow?"　But,

THIRDLY, Still more attention is required to the proper
diſpoſition of the relative pronouns, *who, which, what, whoſe,*
and of all thoſe particles which expreſs the connection of the
parts of Speech with one another. As all reaſoning depends
upon this connection, we cannot be too accurate and preciſe
here. A ſmall error may overcloud the meaning of the whole
Sentence; and even, where the meaning is intelligible, yet
where theſe relative particles are out of their proper place, we
always find ſomething awkward and disjointed in the Structure
of the Sentence. Thus, in the Spectator (No. 54.) " This
" kind of wit," ſays Mr. Addiſon, " was very much in vogue
" among our countrymen, about an age or two ago, who did
" not practiſe it for any oblique reaſon, but purely for the ſake
" of being witty." We are at no loſs about the meaning here;
but the conſtruction would evidently be mended by diſpoſing
of the circumſtance, " about an age or two ago," in ſuch a
manner as not to ſeparate the relative *who,* from its antecedent
our countrymen; in this way: " About an age or two ago,
" this kind of wit was very much in vogue among our
" countrymen, who did not practiſe it for any oblique reaſon,
" but purely for the ſake of being witty." Spectator, No. 412.
" We

" We no where meet with a more glorious and pleafing fhow
" in nature, than what appears in the heavens at the rifing and
" fetting of the fun, *which* is wholly made up of thefe different
" ftains of light, that fhow themfelves in clouds of a different
" fituation." *Which* is here defigned to connect with the word
fhow, as its antecedent; but it ftands fo wide from it, that
without a careful attention to the fenfe, we would be naturally
led, by the rules of fyntax, to refer it to the rifing and fetting of
the fun, or to the fun itfelf; and, hence, an indiftinctnefs is
thrown over the whole Sentence. The following paffage in
Bifhop Sherlock's Sermons (Vol. II. Serm. 15.) is ftill more
cenfurable: " It is folly to pretend to arm ourfelves againft
" the accidents of life, by heaping up treafures, which nothing
" can protect us againft, but the good providence of our
" Heavenly Father." *Which*, always refers grammatically to
the immediately preceding fubftantive, which here is, " trea-
" fures;" and this would make nonfenfe of the whole Period.
Every one feels this impropriety. The Sentence ought to have
ftood thus: " It is folly to pretend, by heaping up treafures,
" to arm ourfelves againft the accidents of life, which nothing
" can protect us againft but the good providence of our
" Heavenly Father."

OF the like nature is the following inaccuracy of Dean
Swift's. He is recommending to young clergymen, to write
their fermons fully and diftinctly. " Many," fays he, " act
" fo directly contrary to this method, that, from a habit of
" faving time and paper, which they acquired at the univerfity,
" they write in fo diminutive a manner, that they can hardly
" read what they have written." He certainly does not mean,
that

that they had acquired time and paper at the univerſity, but that they had acquired this habit there; and therefore his words ought to have run thus: " from a habit which they " have acquired at the univerſity of ſaving time and paper, " they write in ſo diminutive a manner." In another paſſage, the ſame author has left his meaning altogether uncertain, by miſplacing a relative. It is in the concluſion of his letter to a member of parliament, concerning the Sacramental Teſt: " Thus I have fairly given you, Sir, my own opinion, as well " as that of a great majority of both houſes here, relating to " this weighty affair; upon which I am confident you may " ſecurely reckon." Now I aſk, what it is he would have his correſpondent to reckon upon, ſecurely? The natural con-ſtruction leads to theſe words, " this weighty affair." But, as it would be difficult to make any ſenſe of this, it is more pro-bable he meant that the majority of both houſes might be ſecurely reckoned upon; though certainly this meaning, as the words are arranged, is obſcurely expreſſed. The ſentence would be amended by arranging thus: " Thus, Sir, I have " given you my own opinion, relating to this weighty affair, " as well as that of a great majority of both houſes here; " upon which I am confident you may ſecurely reckon."

Several other inſtances might be given; but I reckon thoſe which I have produced ſufficient to make the rule underſtood; that, in the conſtruction of ſentences, one of the firſt things to be attended to, is, the marſhalling of the words in ſuch order as ſhall moſt clearly mark the relation of the ſeveral parts of the ſentence to one another; particularly, that adverbs ſhall always be made to adhere cloſely to the words which they are

intended

intended to qualify; that, where a circumſtance is thrown in, it ſhall never hang looſe in the midſt of a period, but be determined by its place to one or other member of it; and that every relative word which is uſed, ſhall inſtantly preſent its antecedent to the mind of the reader, without the leaſt obſcurity. I have mentioned theſe three caſes, becauſe I think they are the moſt frequent occaſions of ambiguity . creeping into ſentences.

With regard to Relatives, I muſt farther obſerve, that obſcurity often ariſes from the too frequent repetition of them, particularly of the pronouns *who*, and *they*, and *them*, and *theirs*, when we have occaſion to refer to different perſons; as, in the following ſentence of archbiſhop Tillotſon (vol. I. ſerm. 42.):
" Men look with an evil eye upon the good that is in others;
" and think that their reputation obſcures them, and their
" commendable qualities ſtand in their light; and therefore
" they do what they can to caſt a cloud over them, that
" the bright ſhining of their virtues may not obſcure
" them." This is altogether careleſs writing. It renders ſtyle often obſcure, always embarraſſed and inelegant. When we find theſe perſonal pronouns crowding too faſt upon us, we have often no method left, but to throw the whole ſentence into ſome other form, which may avoid thoſe frequent references to perſons who have before been mentioned.

All languages are liable to ambiguities. Quinctilian gives us ſome inſtances in the Latin, ariſing from faulty arrangement. A man, he tells us, ordered, by his will, to have erected for him, after his death, " Statuam auream haſtam tenentem;" upon
which

which arofe a difpute at law, whether the whole ftatue, or the
fpear only, was to be of gold? The fame author obferves, very
properly, that a fentence is always faulty, when the collocation
of the words is ambiguous, though the fenfe can be gathered.
If any one fhould fay, " Chremetem audivi percufliffe De-
" meam," this is ambiguous both in fenfe and ftructure,
whether Chremes or Demea gave the blow. But if this
expreffion were ufed, " Se vidiffe hominem librum fcribentem,"
although the meaning be clear, yet Quinctilian infifts that the
arrangement is wrong. " Nam," fays he, " etiamfi librum ab
" homine fcribi pateat, non certè hominem a libro, malè
" tamen compofuerat, feceratque ambiguum quantum in ipfo
" fuit." Indeed, to have the relation of every word and
member of a fentence marked in the moft proper and diftinct
manner, gives not clearnefs only, but grace and beauty to a
fentence, making the mind pafs fmoothly and agreeably along
all the parts of it.

I PROCEED now to the fecond quality of a well-arranged
fentence, which I termed its Unity. This is a capital property.
In every compofition, of whatever kind, fome degree of unity
is required, in order to render it beautiful. There muft be
always fome connecting principle among the parts. Some
one object muft reign and be predominant. This, as I fhall
hereafter fhew, holds in Hiftory, in Epic and Dramatic
Poetry, and in all orations. But moft of all, in a fingle fentence, is required the ftricteft unity. For the very nature of a
fentence implies one propofition to be expreffed. It may
confift of parts, indeed; but thefe parts muft be fo clofely
bound together, as to make the impreffion upon the mind, of

**

one

one object, not of many. Now, in order to preserve this unity of a sentence, the following rules must be observed :

IN the first place, during the course of the sentence, the scene should be changed as little as possible. We should not be hurried by sudden transitions from person to person, nor from subject to subject. There is commonly, in every sentence, some person or thing, which is the governing word. This should be continued so, if possible, from the beginning to the end of it. Should I express myself thus : " After we came to " anchor, they put me on shore, where I was welcomed by all " my friends, who received me with the greatest kindness." In this sentence, though the objects contained in it have a sufficient connection with each other, yet, by this manner of representing them, by shifting so often both the place and the person, *we*, and *they*, and *I*, and *who*, they appear in such a disunited view, that the sense of connection is almost lost. The sentence is restored to its proper unity, by turning it after the following manner : " Having come to an anchor, I was put " on shore, where I was welcomed by all my friends, and re- " ceived with the greatest kindness." Writers who transgress this rule, for the most part transgress, at the same time,

A SECOND rule; never to crowd into one sentence, things which have so little connection, that they could bear to be divided into two or three sentences. The violation of this rule never fails to hurt, and displease a reader. Its effect, indeed, is so bad, that, of the two, it is the safest extreme, to err rather by too many short sentences, than by one that is overloaded and embarraffed. Examples abound in authors. I fhall produce fome, to juftify what I now fay. " Archbifhop Tillotfon," fays an Author of the Hiftory of England, " died in this year. " He was exceedingly beloved both by King William and " Queen Mary, who nominated Dr. Tennifon, Bifhop of " Lincoln, to fucceed him." Who would expect the latter part of this fentence to follow, in confequence of the former ? " He was exceedingly beloved by both King and Queen," is the propofition of the fentence : we look for fome proof of this, or at leaft fomething related to it, to follow ; when we are on a fudden carried off to a new propofition, " who nominated " Dr. Tennifon to fucceed him." The following is from Middleton's Life of Cicero : " In this uneafy ftate, both of his " public and private life, Cicero was oppreffed by a new and " cruel affliction, the death of his beloved daughter Tullia ; " which happened foon after her divorce from Dolabella ; " whofe manners and humours were entirely difagreeable to " her." The principal object in this fentence is, the death of Tullia, which was the caufe of her father's affliction ; the date of it, as happening foon after her divorce from Dolabella, may enter into the fentence with propriety ; but the fubjunction of Dolabella's character is foreign to the main object ; and breaks the unity and compactnefs of the fentence totally, by fetting a new picture before the reader. The following fentence, from a tranflation of Plutarch, is ftill worfe : " Their march," fays the Author, fpeaking of the Greeks under Alexander, " their " march was through an uncultivated country, whofe favage " inhabitants fared hardly, having no other riches than a breed " of lean fheep, whofe flefh was rank and unfavoury, by rea- " fon of their continual feeding upon fea-fifh." Here the

scene

scene is changed upon us again and again. The march of the Greeks, the defcription of the inhabitants through whofe country they travelled, the account of their fheep, and the caufe of their fheep being ill-tafted food, form a jumble of objects, flightly related to each other, which the reader cannot, without much difficulty, comprehend under one view.

THESE examples have been taken from fentences of no great length, yet over-crowded. Authors who deal in long fentences, are very apt to be faulty in this article. One need only open Lord Clarendon's Hiftory, to find examples every where. The long, involved, and intricate fentences of that Author, are the greateft blemifh of his compofition; though, in other refpects, as a Hiftorian, he has confiderable merit. In later, and more correct writers than Lord Clarendon, we find a period fometimes running out fo far, and comprehending fo many particulars, as to be more properly a difcourfe than a fentence. Take, for an inftance, the following from Sir William Temple, in his Effay upon Poetry: " The ufual accepta-
" tion takes Profit and Pleafure for two different things; and not
" only calls the followers or votaries of them by the feveral names
" of Bufy and Idle Men; but diftinguifhes the faculties of the
" mind, that are converfant about them, calling the operations of
" the firft, Wifdom; and of the other, Wit; which is a Saxon
" word, ufed to exprefs what the Spaniards and Italians call *In-*
" *genio*, and the French, *Efprit*, both from the Latin; though I
" think Wit more particularly fignifies that of Poetry, as may
" occur in Remarks on the Runic Language." When one arrives at the end of fuch a puzzled fentence, he is furprifed to

find

find himſelf got to ſo great a diſtance from the object with which he at firſt ſet out.

LORD SHAFTSBURY, often betrayed into faults by his love of magnificence, ſhall afford us the next example. It is in his Rhapſody, where he is deſcribing the cold regions : " At " length," ſays he, " the Sun approaching, melts the ſnow, ſets " longing men at liberty, and affords them means and time to " make proviſion againſt the next return of Cold." This firſt ſentence is correct enough ; but he goes on : " It breaks the " icy fetters of the main, where vaſt ſea-monſters pierce " through floating iſlands, with arms which can withſtand the " cryſtal rock ; whilſt others, who of themſelves ſeem great " as iſlands, are by their bulk alone armed againſt all but Man, " whoſe ſuperiority over creatures of ſuch ſtupendous ſize and " force, ſhould make him mindful of his privilege of Reaſon, " and force him humbly to adore the great Compoſer of theſe " wondrous frames, and the Author of his own ſuperior " wiſdom." Nothing can be more unhappy or embarraſſed than this ſentence ; the worſe too, as it is intended to be deſcriptive, where every thing ſhould be clear. It forms no diſtinct image whatever. The *It*, at the beginning, is ambiguous, whether it mean the Sun or the Cold. The object is changed three times in the ſentence ; beginning with the Sun, which breaks the icy fetters of the main ; then the Sea-monſters become the principal perſonages ; and laſtly, by a very unexpected tranſition, Man is brought into view, and receives a long and ſerious admonition before the ſentence cloſes. I do not at preſent inſiſt on the impropriety of ſuch expreſſions as, *God's being the Compoſer of Frames* ; and the

Sea-

Sea-monſters having *arms that withſtand rocks.* Shaftſbury's
ſtrength lay in reaſoning and ſentiment, more than in deſcription; however much his deſcriptions have been ſometimes
admired.

I SHALL only give one inſtance more on this head, from
Dean Swift; in his propoſal, too, for correcting the Engliſh
Language: where, in place of a ſentence, he has given a looſe
diſſertation upon ſeveral ſubjects. Speaking of the progreſs of
our language, after the time of Cromwell: " To this ſuc-
" ceeded," ſays he, " that licentiouſneſs, which entered with
" the Reſtoration, and, from infecting our religion and mo-
" rals, fell to corrupt our language; which laſt was not like to
" be much improved by thoſe, who at that time made up the
" court of King Charles the Second; either ſuch as had fol-
" lowed him in his baniſhment, or who had been altogether
" converſant in the dialect of theſe fanatic times; or young
" men, who had been educated in the ſame country: ſo that
" the Court, which uſed to be the ſtandard of correctneſs and
" propriety of ſpeech, was then, and I think has ever ſince
" continued, the worſt ſchool in England for that accom-
" pliſhment; and ſo will remain, till better care be taken in the
" education of our nobility, that they may ſet out into the
" world with ſome foundation of literature, in order to
" qualify them for patterns of politeneſs." How many
different facts, reaſonings, and obſervations, are here preſented to the mind at once! and yet ſo linked together by
the Author, that they all make parts of a ſentence, which admits
of no greater diviſion in pointing, than a ſemicolon between any
of its members? Having mentioned pointing, I ſhall here take

notice,

notice, that it is in vain to propofe, by arbitrary punctuation, to amend the defects of a Sentence, to correct its ambiguity, or to prevent its confufion. For commas, colons, and points, do not make the proper divifions of thought ; but only ferve to mark thofe which arife from the tenor of the Author's expreffion : and, therefore, they are proper or not, juft according as they correfpond to the natural divifions of the fenfe. When they are inferted in wrong places, they deferve, and will meet with, no regard.

I PROCEED to a third rule, for preferving the Unity of Sentences; which is, to keep clear of all Parenthefes in the middle of them. On fome occafions, thefe may have a fpirited appearance ; as prompted by a certain vivacity of thought, which can glance happily afide, as it is going along. But, for the moft part, their effect is extremely bad; being a fort of wheels within wheels; fentences in the midft of fentences; the perplexed method of difpofing of fome thought, which a writer wants art to introduce in its proper place. It were needlefs to give many inftances, as they occur fo often among incorrect writers. I fhall produce one from Lord Bolingbroke, the rapidity of whofe genius, and manner of writing, betrays him frequently into inaccuracies of this fort. It is in the Introduction to his Idea of a Patriot King, where he writes thus : " It " feems to me, that, in order to maintain the fyftem of the " world, at a certain point, far below that of ideal perfection " (for we are made capable of conceiving what we are incapable " of attaining), but, however, fufficient, upon the whole, to " conftitute a ftate eafy and happy, or at the worft, tolerable ; " I fay, it feems to me, that the Author of Nature has thought
" fit

4

" fit to mingle, from time to time, among the focieties of men,
" a few, and but a few, of thofe on whom he is gracioufly
" pleafed to beftow a larger portion of the Ethereal Spirit,
" than is given, in the ordinary courfe of his government, to
" the fons of men." A very bad Sentence this; into which,
by the help of a Parenthefis, and other interjeĉted circumftances, his Lordfhip had contrived to thruft fo many things,
that he is forced to begin the conftruĉtion again with the phrafe
I fay; which, whenever it occurs, may be always affumed as a
fure mark of a clumfy ill-conftruĉted Sentence; excufable in
fpeaking, where the greateft accuracy is not expeĉted, but in
polifhed writing, unpardonable.

I SHALL add only one rule more for the Unity of a Sentence, which is, to bring it always to a full and perfeĉt clofe.
Every thing that is one, fhould have a beginning, a middle,
and an end. I need not take notice, that an unfinifhed Sentence is no Sentence at all, according to any grammatical rule.
But very often we meet with Sentences that are, fo to fpeak,
more than finifhed. When we have arrived at what we expeĉted was to be the conclufion, when we have come to the
word on which the mind is naturally led, by what went before,
to reft; unexpeĉtedly, fome circumftance pops out, which
ought to have been omitted, or to have been difpofed of elfewhere; but which is left lagging behind, like a tail adjeĉted to
the Sentence; fomewhat that, as Mr. Pope defcribes the Alex-
andrine line,

" Like a wounded fnake, drags its flow length along."

All

All thefe adjections to the proper clofe, disfigure a Sentence extremely. They give it a lame ungraceful air, and, in particular, they break its Unity. Dean Swift, for inftance, in his Letter to a Young Clergyman, fpeaking of Cicero's writings, expreffes himfelf thus : " With thefe writings, young divines " are more converfant, than with thofe of Demofthenes, who, " by many degrees, excelled the other; at leaft, as an orator." Here the natural clofe of the Sentence is at thefe words, " ex- " celled the other." Thefe words conclude the propofition ; we look for no more ; and the circumftance added, " at leaft, " as an orator," comes in with a very halting pace. How much more compact would the Sentence have been, if turned thus : " With thefe writings, young divines are more con- " verfant, than with thofe of Demofthenes, who, by many de- " grees, as an orator at leaft, excelled the other." In the following Sentence, from Sir William Temple, the adjection to the Sentence is altogether foreign to it. Speaking of Burnet's Theory of the Earth, and Fontenelle's Plurality of Worlds, " The firft," fays he, " could not end his learned treatife, " without a panegyric of modern learning, in comparifon of the " antient ; and the other, falls fo grofsly into the cenfure of " the old poetry, and preference of the new, that I could not " read either of thefe ftrains without fome indignation ; which " no quality among men is fo apt to raife in me as felf-fufficiency." The word " indignation," concluded the Sentence ; the laft member, " which no quality among men is fo apt to raife in " me as felf-fufficiency," is a propofition altogether new, added after the proper clofe.   8

LECTURE XII.

STRUCTURE OF SENTENCES.

HAVING treated of Perfpicuity and Unity, as neceffary to be ftudied in the Structure of Sentences, I proceed to the third quality of a correct Sentence, which I termed Strength. By this, I mean, fuch a difpofition of the feveral words and members, as fhall bring out the fenfe to the beft advantage; as fhall render the impreffion, which the Period is defigned to make, moft full and complete; and give every word, and every member, its due weight and force. The two former qualities of Perfpicuity and Unity, are, no doubt, abfolutely neceffary to the production of this effect; but more is ftill requifite. For a Sentence may be clear enough; it may alfo be compact enough, in all its parts, or have the requifite unity; and yet, by fome unfavourable circumftance in the ftructure, it may fail in that ftrength or livelinefs of impreffion, which a more happy arrangement would have produced.

THE firſt rule which I ſhall give, for promoting the Strength of a Sentence, is, to prune it of all redundant words. Theſe may, ſometimes, be conſiſtent with a conſiderable degree both of Clearneſs and Unity ; but they are always enfeebling. They make the Sentence move along tardy and encumbered ;

> Eſt brevitate opus, ut currat ſententia, neu ſe
> Impediat verbis, laſſas onerantibus aures *.

It is a general maxim, that any words, which do not add ſome importance to the meaning of a Sentence, always ſpoil it. They cannot be ſuperfluous, without being hurtful. " Obſtat," ſays Quinctilian, " quicquid non adjuvat." All that can be eaſily ſupplied in the mind, is better left out in the expreſſion. Thus: " Content with deſerving a triumph, he refuſed the " honour of it," is better Language than to ſay, " Being con- " tent with deſerving a triumph, he refuſed the honour of it." I conſider it, therefore, as one of the moſt uſeful exerciſes of correction, upon reviewing what we have written or compoſed, to contract that round-about method of expreſſion, and to lop off thoſe uſeleſs excreſcences which are commonly found in a firſt draught. Here a ſevere eye ſhould be employed ; and we ſhall always find our Sentences acquire more vigour and energy when thus retrenched ; provided always, that we run not into the extreme of pruning ſo very cloſe, as to give a hardneſs and dryneſs to ſtyle. For here, as in all other things, there is a due medium. Some regard, though not the principal, muſt be had to fullneſs and ſwelling of ſound. Some leaves muſt be left to ſhelter and ſurround the fruit.

* " Conciſe your diction, let your ſenſe be clear,
  " Nor, with a weight of words, fatigue the ear.   FRANCIS.

As

As Sentences fhould be cleared of redundant words, fo alfo of redundant members. As every word ought to prefent a new idea, fo every member ought to contain a new thought. Oppofed to this, ftands the fault we fometimes meet with, of the laft member of a period, being no other than the echo of the former, or the repetition of it in fomewhat a different form. For example; fpeaking of Beauty, " The very firft difcovery " of it," fays Mr. Addifon, " ftrikes the mind with inward " joy, and fpreads delight through all its faculties." (No. 412.) And elfewhere, " It is impoffible for us to behold the divine " works with coldnefs or indifference, or to furvey fo many " beauties, without a fecret fatisfaction and complacency." (No. 413.) In both thefe inftances, little or nothing is added by the fecond member of the Sentence to what was already expreffed in the firft : And though the free and flowing manner of fuch an author as Mr. Addifon, and the graceful harmony of his period, may palliate fuch negligences ; yet, in general, it holds, that ftyle, freed from this prolixity, appears both more ftrong, and more beautiful. The attention becomes remifs, the mind falls into inaction, when words are multiplied without a correfponding multiplication of ideas.

AFTER removing fuperfluities, the fecond direction I give, for promoting the Strength of a Sentence, is, to attend particularly to the ufe of copulatives, relatives, and all the particles employed for tranfition and connection. Thefe little words, *but, and, which, whofe, where,* &c. are frequently the moft important words of any; they are the joints or hinges upon which all Sentences turn, and, of courfe, much, both of their gracefulnefs and ftrength, muft depend upon fuch particles.

ticles.   The varieties in using them are, indeed, so infinite, that no particular system of rules, respecting them, can be given.   Attention to the practice of the most accurate writers, joined with frequent trials of the different effects, produced by a different usage of those particles, must here direct us*.   Some observations, I shall mention, which have occurred to me as useful, without pretending to exhaust the subject.

WHAT is called splitting of particles, or separating a preposition from the noun which it governs, is always to be avoided. As if I should say, " Though virtue borrows no assistance from, " yet it may often be accompanied by, the advantages of " fortune."   In such instances, we feel a sort of pain, from the revulsion, or violent separation of two things, which, by their nature, should be closely united.   We are put to a stand in thought ; being obliged to rest for a little on the preposition by itself, which, at the same time, carries no significancy, till it is joined to its proper substantive noun.

SOME writers needlessly multiply demonstrative and relative particles, by the frequent use of such phraseology as this : " There is nothing which disgusts us sooner than the empty " pomp of Language."   In introducing a subject, or laying down a proposition, to which we demand particular attention, this sort of style is very proper ; but, in the ordinary current of discourse, it is better to express ourselves more simply and

---

* On this head, Dr. Lowth's Short Introduction to English Grammar deserves to be consulted ; where several niceties of the Language are well pointed out.

shortly :

shortly: " Nothing difgufts us fooner than the empty pomp of
" Language."

OTHER writers make a practice of omitting the Relative, in a phrafe of a different kind from the former, where they think the meaning can be underftood without it. As, " The man " I love."—" The dominions we poffeffed, and the conquefts " we made." But though this elliptical ftyle be intelligible, and is allowable in converfation and epiftolary writing, yet, in all writings of a ferious or dignified kind, it is ungraceful. There, the Relative fhould always be inferted in its proper place, and the conftruction filled up: " The man whom I " love."—" The dominions which we poffeffed, and the con- " quefts which we made."

WITH regard to the Copulative particle, *and*, which occurs fo frequently in all kinds of compofition, feveral obfervations are to be made. Firft, It is evident, that the unneceffary repeti- tion of it enfeebles ftyle. It has the fame fort of effect, as the frequent ufe of the vulgar phrafe, *and fo*, when one is telling a ftory in common converfation. We fhall take a Sentence from Sir William Temple, for an inftance. He is fpeaking of the refinement of the French Language : " The academy fet up by " Cardinal Richelieu, to amufe the wits of that age and " country, and divert them from raking into his politics and " miniftry, brought this into vogue; and the French wits have, " for this laft age, been wholly turned to the refinement of " their Style and Language; and, indeed, with fuch fuccefs, " that it can hardly be equalled, and runs equally through their " verfe, and their profe." Here are no fewer than eight *ands*

**

in

in one fentence.   This agreeable writer too often makes his fentences drag in this manner, by a carelefs multiplication of Copulatives.   It is ftrange how a writer, fo accurate as Dean Swift, fhould have ftumbled on fo improper an application of this particle, as he has made in the following fentence; Effay on the Fates of Clergymen.   " There is no talent fo ufeful " towards rifing in the world, or which puts men more out of " the reach of fortune, than that quality generally poffeft by " the dulleft fort of people, and is, in common language, called " Difcretion; a fpecies of lower prudence, by the affiftance of " which, &c." By the infertion of, *and is*, in place of, *which is*, he has not only clogged the Sentence, but even made it ungrammatical.

BUT, in the next place, it is worthy of obfervation, that though the natural ufe of the conjunction, *and*, be to join objects together, and thereby, as one would think, to make their connexion more clofe; yet, in fact, by dropping the conjunction, we often mark a clofer connexion, a quicker fucceffion of objects, than when it is inferted between them.   Longinus makes this remark; which, from many inftances, appears to be juft: " Veni, vidi, vici *," expreffes, with more fpirit, the rapidity and quick fucceffion of conqueft, than if connecting particles had een ufed.   So, in the following defcription of a rout in Cæfar's Commentaries: " Noftri, emiffis pilis, " gladiis rem gerunt; repente poft tergum equitatus cernitur; " cohortes aliæ appropinquant.   Hoftes terga vertunt; fugien-

* " I came, I faw, I conquered."

" tibus

" tibus equites occurrunt; fit magna cædes." Bell. Gall.
l. 7 *.

HENCE, it follows, that when, on the other hand, we feek
to prevent a quick tranfition from one object to another, when
we are making fome enumeration, in which we wifh that the
objects fhould appear as diftinct from each other as poffible,
and that the mind fhould reft, for a moment, on each object by
itfelf; in this cafe, Copulatives may be multiplied with peculiar
advantage and grace. As when Lord Bolingbroke fays, " Such
" a man might fall a victim to power; but truth, and reafon,
" and liberty, would fall with him." In the fame manner,
Cæfar defcribes an engagement with the Nervii : " His equiti-
" bus facile pulfis ac proturbatis, incredibile celeritate ad flu-
" men decurrerunt; ut pene uno tempore, et ad filvas, et in
" flumine, et jam in manibus noftris, hoftes viderentur."
Bell. Gall. l. 2 †.   Here, although he is defcribing a quick fucceffion of events, yet, as it is his intention to fhow in how many
places the enemy feemed to be at one time, the Copulative is
very happily redoubled, in order to paint more ftrongly the
diftinction of thefe feveral places.

THIS attention to the feveral cafes, when it is proper to
omit, and when to redouble the Copulative, is of confiderable

" * Our men, after having difcharged their javelins, attack with fword in
" hand: of a fudden, the cavalry make their appearance behind ; other bodies
" of men are feen drawing near : the enemies turn their backs ; the horfe
" meet them in their flight ; a great flaughter enfues."
  † " The enemy, having eafily beat off, and fcattered this body of horfe,
" ran down with incredible celerity to the river ; fo that, almoft at one
" moment of time, they appeared to be in the woods, and in the river, and in
" the midft of our troops."

importance

importance to all who ftudy eloquence. For, it is a remarkable particularity in Language, that the omiffion of a connecting particle fhould fometimes ferve to make objects appear more clofely connected; and that the repetition of it fhould diftinguifh and feparate them, in fome meafure, from each other. Hence, the omiffion of it is ufed to denote rapidity; and the repetition of it is defigned to retard and to aggravate. The reafon feems to be, that, in the former cafe, the mind is fuppofed to be hurried fo faft through a quick fucceffion of objects, that it has not leifure to point out their connexion; it drops the Copulatives in its hurry; and crowds the whole feries together, as if it were but one object. Whereas, when we enumerate, with a view to aggravate, the mind is fuppofed to proceed with a more flow and folemn pace; it marks fully the relation of each object to that which fucceeds it; and, by joining them together with feveral Copulatives, makes you attend, that the objects, though connected, are yet, in themfelves, diftinct; that they are many, not one. Obferve, for inftance, in the following enumeration, made by the Apoftle Paul, what additional weight and diftinctnefs is given to each particular, by the repetition of a conjunction. " I am perfwaded, that neither death, nor life, nor " angels, nor principalities, nor powers, nor things prefent, " nor things to come, nor height, nor depth, nor any other " creature, fhall be able to feparate us from the love of God." Rom. viii. 38, 39. So much with regard to the ufe of Copulatives.

I PROCEED to a third rule, for promoting the ftrength of a Sentence, which is, to difpofe of the capital word, or words,

in

in that place of the Sentence, where they will make the fulleſt impreſſion. That ſuch capital words there are in every Sentence, on which the meaning principally reſts, every one muſt ſee; and that theſe words ſhould poſſeſs a conſpicuous and diſtinguiſhed place, is equally plain. Indeed, that place of the Sentence where they will make the beſt figure, whether the beginning, or the end, or, ſometimes, even the middle, cannot, as far as I know, be aſcertained by any preciſe rule. This muſt vary with the nature of the Sentence. Perſpicuity muſt ever be ſtudied in the firſt place; and the nature of our Language allows no great liberty in the choice of collocation. For the moſt part, with us, the important words are placed in the beginning of the Sentence. So Mr. Addiſon: " The pleaſures " of the imagination, taken in their full extent, are not ſo groſs " as thoſe of ſenſe, nor ſo refined as thoſe of the underſtand- " ing." And this, indeed, ſeems the moſt plain and natural order, to place that in the front which is the chief object of the propoſition we are laying down. Sometimes, however, when we intend to give weight to a Sentence, it is of advantage to ſuſpend the meaning for a little, and then bring it out full at the cloſe: " Thus," ſays Mr. Pope, " on whatever ſide we con- " template Homer, what principally ſtrikes us, is, his wonder- " ful invention." (Pref. to Homer.)

THE Greek and Latin writers had a conſiderable advantage above us, in this part of ſtyle. By the great liberty of inverſion, which their Languages permitted, they could chuſe the moſt advantageous ſituation for every word; and had it thereby in their power to give their Sentences more force. Milton, in his proſe works, and ſome other of our old Engliſh writers,

VOL. I.   H h   endeavoured

endeavoured to imitate them in this. But the forced conftructions, which they employed, produced obfcurity; and the
genius of our Language, as it is now written and fpoken, will
not admit fuch liberties. Mr. Gordon, who followed this inverted ftyle in his Tranflation of Tacitus, has, fometimes, done
fuch violence to the Language, as even to appear ridiculous; as
in this expreffion: " Into this hole, thruft themfelves three
" Roman fenators." He has tranflated fo fimple a phrafe as,
" Nullum eâ tempeftate bellum," by, " War at that time there
" was none." However, within certain bounds, and to a
limited degree, our Language does admit of inverfions; and
they are practifed with fuccefs by the beft writers. So Mr.
Pope, fpeaking of Homer, " The praife of judgment Virgil
" has juftly contefted with him, but his invention remains yet
" unrivalled." It is evident, that, in order to give the Sentence its due force, by contrafting properly the two capital words,
" judgment and invention," this is a happier arrangement
than if he had followed the natural order, which was, " Virgil
" has juftly contefted with him the praife of judgment, but his
" invention remains yet unrivalled."

SOME writers practife this degree of inverfion, which our
Language bears, much more than others; Lord Shaftfbury, for
inftance, much more than Mr. Addifon; and to this fort of
arrangement is owing, in a great meafure, that appearance of
ftrength, dignity, and varied harmony, which Lord Shaftfbury's ftyle poffeffes. This will appear from the following
Sentences of his Enquiry into Virtue; where all the words are
placed, not ftrictly in the natural order, but with that artificial
conftruction, which may give the period moft emphafis and
grace.

grace. He is fpeaking of the mifery of vice: " This, as to " the complete immoral ftate, is, what of their own accord, " men readily remark. Where there is this abfolute degeneracy, " this total apoftacy from all candor, truft, or equity, there " are few who do not fee and acknowledge the mifery which " is confequent. Seldom is the cafe mifconftrued, when at " worft. The misfortune is, that we look not on this de- " pravity, nor confider how it ftands, in lefs degrees. As if, " to be abfolutely immoral, were, indeed, the greateft mifery; " but, to be fo in a little degree, fhould be no mifery or harm " at all. Which, to allow, is juft as reafonable as to own, " that 'tis the greateft ill of a body to be in the utmoft manner " maimed or diftorted; but that, to lofe the ufe only of one " limb, or to be impaired in fome fingle organ or member, is " no ill worthy the leaft notice." (Vol. ii. p. 82.) Here is no violence done to the Language, though there are many inverfions. All is ftately, and arranged with art; which is the great characteriftic of this author's Style.

WE need only open any page of Mr. Addifon, to fee quite a different order in the conftruction of Sentences. " Our fight " is the moft perfect, and moft delightful of all our fenfes. It " fills the mind with the largeft variety of ideas, converfes " with its objects at the greateft diftance, and continues the " longeft in action, without being tired, or fatiated with its " proper enjoyments. The fenfe of feeling can, indeed, give " us a notion of extenfion, fhape, and all other ideas that enter " at the eye, except colours; but, at the fame time, it is very " much ftraitened and confined in its operations," &c. (Spectator, No. 411.) In this ftrain, he always procceeds,

following

following the moft natural and obvious order of the Language;
and if, by this means, he has lefs pomp and majefty than
Shaftfbury, he has, in return, more nature, more eafe and
fimplicity ; which are beauties of a higher order.

BUT whether we practife inverfion or not, and in whatever
part of the fentence we difpofe of the capital words, it is always
a point of great moment, that thefe capital words fhall ftand
clear and difentangled from any other words that would clog
them.   Thus, when there are any circumftances of time,
place, or other limitations, which the principal object of our
Sentence requires to have connected with it, we muft take
efpecial care to difpofe of them, fo as not to cloud that principal
object, nor to bury it under a load of circumftances.   This
will be made clearer by an example.   Obferve the arrangement of the following Sentence, in Lord Shaftfbury's Advice
to an Author.   He is fpeaking of modern poets, as compared
with the antient: " If, whilft they profefs only to pleafe, they
" fecretly advife, and give inftruction, they may now, per-
" haps, as well as formerly, be efteemed, with juftice, the beft
" and moft honourable among authors."   This is a well conftructed Sentence.   It contains a great many circumftances and
adverbs, neceffary to qualify the meaning ; *only, fecretly, as well,*
perhaps, now, with juftice, formerly; yet thefe are placed with
fo much art, as neither to embarrafs, nor weaken the Sentence; while that which is the capital object in it, viz. " Poets
" being juftly efteemed the beft and moft honourable among
" authors," comes out in the conclufion clear and detached,
and poffeffes its proper place.   See, now, what would have
been the effect of a different arrangement.   Suppofe him to
have

have placed the members of the Sentence thus : " If, whilſt " they profeſs to pleaſe only, they adviſe and give inſtruction " ſecretly, they may be eſteemed the beſt and moſt honour- " able among authors, with juſtice, perhaps, now, as well as " formerly." Here we have preciſely the ſame words, and the ſame ſenſe ; but, by means of the circumſtances being ſo intermingled as to clog the capital words, the whole becomes perplexed, without grace, and without ſtrength.

A FOURTH rule, for conſtructing Sentences with proper ſtrength, is, to make the members of them go on riſing and growing in their importance above one another. This ſort of arrangement is called a Climax, and is always conſidered as a beauty in compoſition. From what cauſe it pleaſes, is abun-- dantly evident. In all things, we naturally love to aſcend to what is more and more beautiful, rather than to follow the re-- trograde order. Having had once ſome conſiderable object ſet before us, it is, with pain, we are pulled back to attend to an inferior circumſtance. " Cavendum eſt," ſays Quinctilian, whoſe authority I always willingly quote, " ne decreſcat oratio, " & fortiori ſubjungatur aliquid infirmius ; ſicut, ſacrilego, " fur ; aut latroni petulans. Augeri enim debent ſententiæ & " inſurgere *. Of this beauty, in the conſtruction of Sen- tences, the orations of Cicero furniſh many examples. His pompous manner naturally led him to ſtudy it ; and, generally, in order to render the climax perfect, he makes both the ſenſe

---

* " Care muſt be taken, that our compoſition ſhall not fall off, and that a " weaker expreſſion ſhall not follow one of more ſtrength ; as if, after ſacri- " lege, we ſhould bring in theft ; or, having mentioned a robbery, we ſhould " ſubjoin petulance. Sentences ought always to riſe and grow."

and the found rife together, with a very magnificent fwell. So in his oration for Milo, fpeaking of a defign of Clodius's for affaffinating Pompey : " Atqui fi res, fi vir, fi tempus ullum " dignum fuit, certè hæc in illâ causâ fumma omnia fue- " runt. Infidiator erat in Foro collocatus, atque in Veftibulo " ipfo Senatûs ; ei viro autem mors parabatur, cujus in vitâ " nitebatur falus civitatis ; eo porrò reipublicæ tempore, quo fi " unus ille occidiffet, non hæc folùm civitas, fed gentes omnes " concidiffent." The following inftance, from Lord Boling- broke, is alfo beautiful : " This decency, this grace, this pro- " priety of manners to character, is fo effential to princes in " particular, that, whenever it is neglected, their virtues lofe a " great degree of luftre, and their defects acquire much aggra- " vation. Nay more ; by neglecting this decency and this " grace, and for want of a fufficient regard to appearances, " even their virtues may betray them into failings, their fail- " ings into vices, and their vices into habits unworthy of " princes, and unworthy of men." (Idea of a Patriot King.)

I MUST obferve, however, that this fort of full and oratorial climax, can neither be always obtained, nor ought to be always fought after. Only fome kinds of writing admit fuch fentences ; and, to ftudy them too frequently, efpecially if the fubject require not fo much pomp, is affected and difagreeable. But there is fomething approaching to a climax, which it is a general rule to ftudy, " ne decrefcat oratio," as Quinctilian fpeaks, " et ne fortiori fubjungatur aliquid infirmius." A weaker affertion or propofition fhould never come after a ftronger one ; and when our fentence confifts of two mem- bers, the longeft fhould, generally, be the concluding one.

There

There is a twofold reason for this last direction. Periods, thus divided, are pronounced more easily; and the shortest member being placed first, we carry it more readily in our memory as we proceed to the second, and see the connection of the two more clearly. Thus, to say, " when our passions have forsaken us, " we flatter ourselves with the belief that we have forsaken " them," is both more graceful and more clear, than to begin with the longest part of the proposition : " We flatter our- " selves with the belief that we have forsaken our passions, " when they have forsaken us." In general, it is always agreeable to find a sentence rising upon us, and growing in its importance to the very last word, when this construction can be managed without affectation, or unseasonable pomp. " If " we rise yet higher," says Mr. Addison, very beautifully, " and consider the fixed stars as so many oceans of flame, " that are each of them attended with a different set of planets; " and still discover new firmaments and new lights, that are " sunk farther in those unfathomable depths of æther; we are " lost in such a labyrinth of suns and worlds, and con- " founded with the magnificence and immensity of Nature" (Spect. No. 420.). Hence follows clearly,

A FIFTH rule for the strength of sentences ; which is, to avoid concluding them with an adverb, a preposition, or any inconsiderable word. Such conclusions are always enfeebling and degrading. There are sentences, indeed, where the stress and significancy rest chiefly upon some words of this kind. In this case, they are not to be considered as circumstances, but as the capital figures; and ought, in propriety, to have the principal place allotted them. No fault, for instance, can be

found

found with this fentence of Bolingbroke's : " In their profpe-
" rity, my friends fhall never hear of me; in their adverfity,
" always." Where *never*, and *always*, being emphatical
words, were to be fo placed, as to make a ftrong impreffion.
But I fpeak now of thofe inferior parts of fpeech, when introduced as circumftances, or as qualifications of more important
words. In fuch cafe, they fhould always be difpofed of in the
leaft confpicuous parts of the period ; and fo claffed with other
words of greater dignity, as to be kept in their proper fecondary ftation.

AGREEABLY to this rule, we fhould always avoid concluding with any of thofe particles, which mark the cafes of
nouns,—*of, to, from, with, by*. For inftance, it is a great deal
better to fay, " Avarice is a crime of which wife men are often
" guilty," than to fay, " Avarice is a crime which wife men are
" often guilty of." This is a phrafeology which all correct writers
fhun ; and with reafon. For, befides the want of dignity
which arifes from thofe monofyllables at the end, the imagination cannot avoid refting, for a little, on the import of the word
which clofes the fentence. And, as thofe prepofitions have no
import of their own, but only ferve to point out the relations
of other words, it is difagreeable for the mind to be left paufing
on a word, which does not, by itfelf, produce any idea, nor
form any picture in the fancy.

FOR the fame reafon, verbs which are ufed in a compound
fenfe, with fome of thefe prepofitions, are, though not fo bad,
yet ftill not fo beautiful conclufions of a period ; fuch as, *bring
about, lay hold of, come over to, clear up*, and many other of
                                                        this

this kind: inftead of which, if we can employ a fimple verb, it always terminates the fentence with more ftrength. Even the pronoun, *It*, though it has the import of a fubftantive noun, and indeed often forces itfelf upon us unavoidably, yet, when we want to give dignity to a fentence, fhould, if poffible, be avoided in the conclufion; more efpecially, when it is joined with fome of the prepofitions, as, *with it, in it, to it*. In the following fentence of the Spectator, which otherwife is abundantly noble, the bad effect of this clofe is fenfible: " There is not, in my opinion, a more pleafing and triumph-" ant confideration in religion, than this, of the perpetual pro-" grefs which the foul makes towards the perfection of its " nature, without ever arriving at a period in it." (No. 111.) How much more graceful the fentence, if it had been fo con-ftructed as to clofe with the word, *period!*

BESIDES particles and pronouns, any phrafe, which expreffes a circumftance only, always brings up the rear of a fentence with a bad grace. We may judge of this, by the following fentence from Lord Bolingbroke (Letter on the State of Parties at the Acceffion of King George I.): " Let me therefore " conclude by repeating, that divifion has caufed all the mif-" chief we lament; that union alone can retrieve it; and that " a great advance towards this union, was the coalition of " parties, fo happily begun, fo fuccefsfully carried on, and of " late fo unaccountably neglected; to fay no worfe." This laft phrafe, *to fay no worfe*, occafions a fad falling off at the end; fo much the more unhappy, as the reft of the period is con-ducted after the manner of a climax, which we expect to find growing to the laft.

THE proper difpofition of fuch circumftances in a fentence, is often attended with confiderable trouble, in order to adjuft them fo, as fhall confift equally with the perfpicuity and the grace of the period. Though neceffary parts, they are, however, like unfhapely ftones in a building, which try the fkill of an artift, where to place them with the leaft offence. " Jun-
" gantur," fays Quinctilian, " quo congruunt maximè ; ficut
" in ftructurâ faxorum rudium, etiam ipfa enormitas invenit
" cui applicari, et in quo poffit infiftere *."

THE clofe is always an unfuitable place for them. When the fenfe admits it, the fooner they are difpatched, generally fpeaking, the better; that the more important and.fignificant words may poffefs the laft place, quite difencumbered. It is a rule, too, never to crowd too many circumftances together, but rather to interfperfe them in different parts of the fentence, joined with the capital words on which they depend ; provided that care be taken, as I before directed, not to clog thofe capital. words with them. For inftance, when Dean Swift fays, " What I had the honour of mentioning to your Lordfhip, " fome time ago, in converfation, was not a new thought." (Letter to the Earl of Oxford.) Thefe two circumftances, *fometime ago*, and *in converfation*, which are here put together, would have had a better effect difjoined,, thus : " What I had " the honour, fometime ago, of mentioning to your Lordfhip " in converfation." And in the following fentence of Lord.

---

* " Let them be inferted wherever the happieft place for them can be
" found.; as, in a ftructure compofed of rough ftones, there are always places
" where the moft irregular and unfhapely may find fome adjacent one to
" which it can be joined, and fome bafis on which it may reft."

Boling-

Bolingbroke's (Remarks on the History of England): " A
" monarchy, limited like ours, may be placed, for aught I
" know, as it has been often reprefented, juft in the middle
" point, from whence a deviation leads, on the one hand, to
" tyranny, and on the other, to anarchy." The arrangement
would have been happier thus: " A monarchy, limited like
" ours, may, for aught I know, be placed, as it has often been
" reprefented, juft in the middle point, &c."

I SHALL give only one rule more, relating to the ftrength of
a fentence, which is, that in the members of a fentence, where
two things are compared or contrafted to one another; where
either a refemblance or an oppofition is intended to be expreffed; fome refemblance, in the language and conftruction,
fhould be preferved. For when the things themfelves correfpond to each other, we naturally expect to find the words
correfponding too. We are difappointed when it is otherwife; and
the comparifon, or contraft, appears more imperfect. Thus, when
Lord Bolingbroke fays, " The laughers will be for thofe who
" have moft wit; the ferious part of mankind, for thofe who
" have moft reafon on their fide;" (Differt. on Parties, Pref.)
the oppofition would have been more complete, if he had faid,
" The laughers will be for thofe who have moft wit; the
" ferious, for thofe who have moft reafon on their fide." The
following paffage from Mr. Pope's Preface to his Homer, fully
exemplifies the rule I am now giving: " Homer was the
" greater genius; Virgil, the better artift: in the one, we moft
" admire the man; in the other, the work. Homer hurries
" us with a commanding impetuofity; Virgil leads us with an
" attractive majefty. Homer fcatters with a generous pro-

" fufion;

" fufion; Virgil beftows with a careful magnificence. Homer,
" like the Nile, pours out his riches with a fudden overflow;
" Virgil, like a river in its banks, with a conftant ftream.——
" And when we look upon their machines, Homer feems like
" his own Jupiter in his terrors, fhaking Olympus, fcattering
" the lightnings, and firing the heavens; Virgil, like the fame
" Power, in his benevolence, counfelling with the gods, laying
" plans for empires, and ordering his whole creation."—Periods
thus conftructed, when introduced with propriety, and not returning too often, have a fenfible beauty. But we muft beware of
carrying our attention to this beauty too far. It ought only to
be occafionally ftudied, when comparifon or oppofition of objects naturally leads to it. If fuch a conftruction as this be
aimed at in all our fentences, it betrays into a difagreeable uniformity; produces a regularly returning clink in the period,
which tires the ear; and plainly difcovers affectation. Among
the ancients, the ftyle of Ifocrates is faulty in this refpect; and,
on that account, by fome of their beft critics, particularly by
Dionyfius of Halicarnaffus, he is feverely cenfured.

THIS finifhes what I had to fay concerning Sentences, confidered, with refpect to their meaning, under the three heads
of Perfpicuity, Unity, and Strength. It is a fubject on which
I have infifted fully, for two reafons: Firft, becaufe it is a
fubject, which, by its nature, can be rendered more didactic,
and fubjected more to precife rule, than many other fubjects of
criticifm; and next, becaufe it appears to me of confiderable
importance and ufe.

**

For though many of thofe attentions, which I have been recommending, may appear minute, yet their effect, upon writing and ftyle, is much greater than might, at firft, be imagined. A fentiment which is expreffed in a period, clearly, neatly, and happily arranged, makes always a ftronger impreffion on the mind, than one that is any how feeble or embarraffed. Every one feels this upon a comparifon: and if the effect be fenfible in one fentence, how much more in a whole difcourfe, or compofition, that is made up of fuch Sentences?

The fundamental rule of the conftruction of Sentences, and into which all others might be refolved, undoubtedly is, to communicate, in the cleareft and moft natural order, the ideas which we mean to transfufe into the minds of others. Every arrangement that does moft juftice to the fenfe, and expreffes it to moft advantage, ftrikes us as beautiful. To this point have tended all the rules I have given. And, indeed, did men always think clearly, and were they, at the fame time, fully mafters of the Language in which they write, there would be occafion for few rules. Their Sentences would then, of courfe, acquire all thofe properties of Precifion, Unity, and Strength, which I have recommended. For we may reft affured, that, whenever we exprefs ourfelves ill, there is, befides the mifmanagement of Language, for the moft part, fome miftake in our manner of conceiving the fubject. Embarraffed, obfcure, and feeble Sentences, are generally, if not always, the refult of embarraffed, obfcure, and feeble thought. Thought and Language act and re-act upon each

other

other mutually. Logic and Rhetoric have here, as in many other cafes, a ftrict connection; and he that is learning to arrange his fentences with accuracy and order, is learning, at the fame time, to think with accuracy and order; an obfervation which alone will juftify all the care and attention we have beftowed on this fubject.

LECTURE XIII.

STRUCTURE OF SENTENCES.—HARMONY.

HITHERTO we have confidered Sentences, with refpect to their meaning, under the heads of Perfpicuity,
Unity, and Strength. We are now to confider them, with
refpect to their found, their harmony, or agreeablenefs to the
ear.; which was the laft quality belonging to them that I pro-
pofed to treat of.

SOUND is a quality much inferior to fenfe; yet fuch as muft
not be difregarded. For, as long as founds are the vehicle of
conveyance for our ideas, there will be always a very confiderable connection between the idea which is conveyed, and the
nature of the found which conveys it. Pleafing ideas can
hardly be tranfmitted to the mind, by means of harfh and
difagreeable founds. The imagination revolts as foon as it
hears them uttered. " Nihil," fays Quinctilian, " poteft in-
" trare in affectum quod in aure, velut quodam veftibulo

4   " ftatim

" ſtatim offendit *."   Muſic has naturally a great power over all men to prompt and facilitate certain emotions: infomuch, that there are hardly any diſpoſitions which we wiſh to raiſe in others, but certain ſounds may be found concordant to thoſe diſpoſitions, and tending to promote them.   Now, Language can, in ſome degree, be rendered capable of this power of muſic; a circumſtance which muſt needs heighten our idea of Language as a wonderful invention.   Not content with ſimply interpreting our ideas to others, it can give them thoſe ideas enforced by correſponding ſounds; and to the pleaſure of communicated thought, can add the new and ſeparate pleaſure of melody.

IN the Harmony of Periods, two things may be conſidered. Firſt, Agreeable ſound, or modulation in general, without any particular expreſſion: Next, The ſound ſo ordered, as to become expreſſive of the ſenſe.   The firſt is the more common; the ſecond, the higher beauty.

FIRST, Let us conſider agreeable ſound, in general, as the property of a well-conſtructed Sentence: and, as it was of proſe Sentences we have hitherto treated, we ſhall confine ourſelves to them under this head.   This beauty of muſical conſtruction in proſe, it is plain, will depend. upon two things, the choice of words, and the arrangement of them.

I BEGIN with the choice of words; on which head, there is not much to be ſaid, unleſs I were to deſcend into a

---

* " Nothing can enter into the affections which ſtumbles at the threſhold, by offending the ear."

tedious

tedious and frivolous detail concerning the powers of the
feveral letters, or fimple founds, of which fpeech is compofed.
It is evident, that words are moft agreeable to the ear which are
compofed of fmooth and liquid founds, where there is a proper
intermixture of vowels and confonants; without too many
harfh confonants rubbing againft each other; or too many open
vowels in fucceffion, to caufe a hiatus, or difagreeable aperture
of the mouth. It may always be affumed as a principle, that,
whatever founds are difficult in pronunciation, are, in the fame
proportion, harfh and painful to the ear. Vowels give foft-
nefs; confonants, ftrength to the found of words. The mufic
of Language requires a juft proportion of both; and will be
hurt, will be rendered either grating or effeminate, by an excefs
of either. Long words are commonly more agreeable to the
ear than monofyllables. They pleafe it by the compofition,
or fucceffion of founds which they prefent to it; and, accordingly, the moft mufical Languages abound moft in them.
Among words of any length, thofe are the moft mufical, which
do not run wholly either upon long or fhort fyllables, but are
compofed of an intermixture of them; fuch as, *repent, produce,*
velocity, celerity, independent, impetuofity.

THE next head, refpecting the Harmony which refults from
a proper arrangement of the words and members of a period, is
more complex, and of greater nicety. For, let the words
themfelves be ever fo well chofen, and well founding, yet, if
they be ill difpofed, the mufic of the Sentence is utterly loft.
In the harmonious ftructure and difpofition of periods, no
writer whatever, antient or modern, equals Cicero. He had
ftudied this with care; and was fond, perhaps to excefs, of

what he calls, the " Plena ac numerofa oratio." We need only open his writings, to find inftances that will render the effect of mufical Language fenfible to every ear. What, for example, can be more full, round, and fwelling, than the following fentence of the 4th Oration againft Catiline? " Co-" gitate quantis laboribus fundatum imperium, quantâ virtute " ftabilitam libertatem, quantâ Deorum benignitate auctas ex-" aggeratafque fortunas, una nox pene delerit." In Englifh, we may take, for an inftance of a mufical Sentence, the following from Milton, in his Treatife on Education: " We fhall " conduct you to a hill-fide, laborious, indeed, at the firft " afcent; but elfe, fo fmooth, fo green, fo full of goodly " profpects, and melodious founds on every fide, that the harp " of Orpheus was not more charming." Every thing in this fentence confpires to promote the harmony. The words are happily chofen; full of liquids and foft founds; *laborious*, *fmooth*, *green*, *goodly*, *melodious*, *charming*: and thefe words fo artfully arranged, that, were we to alter the collocation of any one of them, we fhould, prefently, be fenfible of the melody fuffering. For, let us obferve, how finely the members of the period fwell one above another. " So fmooth, fo green,"—" fo full of goodly profpects,—and melodious founds on every " fide;"—till the ear, prepared by this gradual rife, is conducted to that full clofe on which it refts with pleafure;—" that the harp of Orpheus was not more charming."

THE ftructure of periods, then, being fufceptible of a melody very fenfible to the ear, our next enquiry fhould be, How this melodious ftructure is formed, what are the principles of it, and by what laws is it regulated? And, upon this fubject, were

I to

I to follow the antient rhetoricians, it would be eafy to give a great variety of rules. For here they have entered into a very minute and particular detail; more particular, indeed, than on any other head that regards Language. They hold, that to profe as well as to verfe, there belong certain numbers, lefs ftrict, indeed, yet fuch as can be afcertained by rule. They go fo far as to fpecify the feet, as they are called, that is, the fucceffion of long and fhort fyllables, which fhould enter into the different members of a Sentence, and to fhow what the effect of each of thefe will be. Wherever they treat of the Structure of Sentences, it is always the mufic of them that makes the principal object. Cicero and Quinctilian are full of this. The other qualities of Precifion, Unity, and Strength, which we confider as of chief importance, they handle flightly; but when they come to the " *junctura et numerus*," the modulation and harmony, there they are copious. Dyonyfius of Halicarnaffus, one of the moft judicious critics of antiquity, has written a treatife on the *Compofition of Words in a Sentence*, which is altogether confined to their mufical effect. He makes the excellency of a Sentence to confift in four things; firft, in the fweetnefs of fingle founds; fecondly, in the compofition of founds, that is, the numbers or feet; thirdly, in change or variety of found; and, fourthly, in found fuited to the fenfe. On all thefe points he writes with great accuracy and refinement; and is very worthy of being confulted; though, were one now to write a book on the Structure of Sentences, we fhould expect to find the fubject treated of in a more extenfive manner.

K k 2

In modern times, this whole fubject of the mufical ftructure of difcourfe, it is plain, has been much lefs ftudied; and, indeed, for feveral reafons, can be much lefs fubjected to rule. The reafons, it will be neceffary to give, both to juftify my not following the tract of the antient rhetoricians on this fubject, and to fhow how it has come to pafs, that a part of compofition, which once made fo confpicuous a figure, now draws much lefs attention.

In the firft place, the antient Languages, I mean the Greek and the Roman, were much more fufceptible than ours, of the graces and the powers of melody. The quantities of their fyllables were more fixed and determined; their words were longer, and more fonorous; their method of varying the terminations of nouns and verbs, both introduced a greater variety of liquid founds, and freed them from that multiplicity of little auxiliary words which we are obliged to employ; and, what is of the greateft confequence, the inverfions which their Languages allowed, gave them the power of placing their words in whatever order was moft fuited to a mufical arrangement. All thefe were great advantages which they enjoyed above us, for Harmony of Period.

In the next place, the Greeks and Romans, the former efpecially, were, in truth, much more mufical nations than we; their genius was more turned to delight in the melody of fpeech. Mufic is known to have been a more extenfive art among them than it is with us; more univerfally ftudied, and applied to a greater variety of objects. Several learned men, particularly the Abbé du Bos, in his Reflections on Poetry and

Painting,

Painting, have clearly proved, that the theatrical compofitions of the antients, both their tragedies and comedies, were fet to a kind of mufic. Whence, the *modos fecit*, and the *Tibiis dextris et finiftris*, prefixed to the editions of Terence's Plays. All fort of declamation and public fpeaking, was carried on by them in a much more mufical tone than it is among us. It approached to a kind of chanting or recitative. Among the Athenians, there was what was called the Nomic Melody; or a particular meafure prefcribed to the public officers, in which they were to promulgate the laws to the people; left, by reading them with improper tones, the laws might be expofed to contempt. Among the Romans, there is a noted ftory of C. Gracchus, when he was declaiming in public, having a mufician ftanding at his back, in order to give him the proper tones with a pipe or flute. Even when pronouncing thofe terrible tribunitial harangues, by whieh he inflamed the one half of the citizens of Rome againft the other, this attention to the mufic of Speech was, in thofe times, it feems, thought neceffary to fuccefs. Quinctilian, though he eondemns the excefs of this fort of pronunciation, yet allows a " cantus obfcurior" to be a beauty in a public fpeaker. Hence, that variety of accents, acute, grave, and circumflex, which we find marked upon the Greek fyllables, to exprefs, not the quantity of them, but the tone in which they were to be fpoken: the application of which is now wholly unknown to us. And though the Romans did not mark thofe accents in their writing, yet it appears, from Quinctilian, that they ufed them in pronunciation: " *Quantum, quale,*" fays he, " comparantes " gravi, interrogantes acuto tenore concludunt." As mufic then, was an object much more attended to in Speech, among the

the Greeks and Romans, than it is with us ; as, in all kinds of public ſpeaking, they employed a much greater variety of notes, of tones, or inflexions of voice, than we uſe; this is one clear reaſon of their paying a greater attention to that conſtruction of Sentences, which might beſt ſuit this muſical pronunciation.

It is farther known, that, in conſequence of the genius of their Languages, and of their manner of pronouncing them, the muſical arrangement of Sentences, did, in fact, produce a greater effect in publick ſpeaking among them, than it could poſſibly do in any modern oration ; another reaſon why it deſerved to be more ſtudied.   Cicero, in his treatiſe, intitled, *Orator*, tells us, " Conciones ſæpe exclamare vidi, cum verba aptè cecidiſſent. " Id enim expectant aures*."   And he gives a remarkable inſtance of the effect of a harmonious period upon a whole aſſembly, from a Sentence of one of Carbo's Orations, ſpoken in his hearing.   The Sentence was, " Patris dictum ſapiens temeritas " filii comprobavit."   By means of the ſound of which, alone, he tells us, " Tantus clamor concionis excitatus eſt, ut prorſus " admirabile eſſet."   He makes us remark the feet of which theſe words conſiſt, to which he aſcribes the power of the melody ; and ſhows how, by altering the collocation, the whole effect would be loſt; as thus: " Patris dictum ſapiens compro- " bravit temeritas filii."   Now, though it be true that Carbo's Sentence is extremely muſical, and would be agreeable, at this day, to any audience, yet I cannot believe that an Engliſh

---

* " I have often been witneſs to burſts of exclamation in the public aſſem-
" blies, when Sentences cloſed muſically ; for that is a pleaſure which the ear
" expects."

6   Sentence,

Sentence, equally harmonious, would, by its harmony alone, produce any fuch effect on a Britifh audience, or excite any fuch wonderful applaufe and admiration, as Cicero informs us this of Carbo produced. Our northern ears are too coarfe and obtufe. The melody of Speech has lefs power over us; and by our fimpler and plainer method of uttering words, Speech is, in truth, accompanied with lefs melody than it was among the Greeks and Romans *.

For thefe reafons, I am of opinion, that it is in vain to think of beftowing the fame attention upon the harmonious ftructure of our Sentences, that was beftowed by thefe antient nations. The doctrine of the Greek and Roman critics, on this head, has mifled fome to imagine, that it might be equally applied to our Tongue; and that our profe writing might be regulated by Spondees and Trochees, and Iambus's and Pœons, and other metrical feet. But, firft, our words cannot be meafured, or, at leaft, can be meafured very imperfectly by any feet of this kind. For, the quantity, the length and fhort-nefs of our fyllables, is not, by any means, fo fixed and fub-jected to rule, as in the Greek and Roman Tongues; but very often left arbitrary, and determined by the emphafis, and the fenfe. Next, though our profe could admit of fuch metrical regulation, yet, from our plainer method of pronouncing all

---

* " In verfu quidem, theatra tota exclamant fi fuit una fyllaba aut brevior
" aut longior. Nec verò multitudo pedes novit, nec ullos numeros tenet; nec
" illud quod offendit, aut cur, aut in quo offendat, intelligit; et tamen om-
" nium longitudinum et brevitatum in fonis, ficut acutarum, graviumque
" vocum, judicium ipfa natura in auribus noftris collocavit."
Cicero, Orator. c. 51.

fort

fort of difcourfe, the effect would not be at all fo fenfible to the ear, nor be relifhed with fo much pleafure, as among the Greeks and Romans: And, laftly, This whole doctrine about the meafures and numbers of profe, even as it is delivered by the antient rhetoricians themfelves, is, in truth, in a great meafure loofe and uncertain. It appears, indeed, that the melody of difcourfe was a matter of infinitely more attention to them, than ever it has been to the moderns. But, though they write a great deal about it, they have never been able to reduce it to any rules which could be of real ufe in practice. If we confult Cicero's *Orator*, where this point is difcuffed with the moft minutenefs, we will fee how much thefe antient critics differed from one another, about the feet proper for the conclufion, and other parts of a Sentence; and how much, after all, was left to the judgment of the ear. Nor, indeed, is it poffible to give precife rules concerning this matter, in any Language; as all profe compofition muft be allowed to run loofe in its numbers; and, according as the tenor of a difcourfe varies, the modulation of Sentences muft vary infinitely.

BUT, although I apprehend, that this mufical arrangement cannot be reduced into a fyftem, I am far from thinking, that it is a quality to be neglected in compofition. On the contrary, I hold its effect to be very confiderable; and that every one who ftudies to write with grace, much more, who feeks to pronounce in public, with fuccefs, will be obliged to attend to it not a little. But it is his ear, cultivated by attention and practice, that muft chiefly direct him. For any rules that can be given, on this fubject, are very general. Some

rules,

rules, however, there are, which may be of ufe to form the ear to the proper harmony of difcourfe. I proceed to mention fuch as appear to me moft material.

THERE are two things on which the mufic of a Sentence chiefly depends. Thefe are, the proper diftribution of the feveral members of it; and, the clofe or cadence of the whole.

FIRST, I fay, the diftribution of the feveral members is to be carefully attended to. It is of importance to obferve, that, whatever is eafy and agreeable to the organs of Speech, always founds grateful to the ear. While a period is going on, the termination of each of its members forms a paufe, or reft, in pronouncing: and thefe refts fhould be fo diftributed, as to make the courfe of the breathing eafy, and, at the fame time, fhould fall at fuch diftances, as to bear a certain mufical proportion to each other. This will be beft illuftrated by examples. The following Sentence is from Archbifhop Tillotfon: " This difcourfe concerning the eafinefs of God's commands " does, all along, fuppofe and acknowledge the difficulties of " the firft entrance upon a religious courfe; except, only in " thofe perfons who have had the happinefs to be trained up " to religion by the eafy and infenfible degrees of a pious and " virtuous education." Here there is no harmony; nay, there is fome degree of harfhnefs and unpleafantnefs; owing principally to this, that there is, properly, no more than one paufe or reft in the Sentence, falling betwixt the two members into which it is divided; each of which is fo long as to occafion a confiderable ftretch of the breath in pronouncing it.

OBSERVE, now, on the other hand, the eafe with which the
following Sentence, from Sir William Temple, glides along,
and the graceful intervals at which the paufes are placed.   He
is fpeaking farcaftically of man : " But God be thanked, his
" pride is greater than his ignorance, and what he wants in
" knowledge, he fupplies by fufficiency.   When he has looked
" about him, as far as he can, he concludes, there is no more
" to be feen ; when he is at the end of his line, he is at the
" bottom of the ocean ; when he has fhot his beft, he is fure
" none ever did, or ever can, fhoot better, or beyond it.   His
" own reafon he holds to be the certain meafure of truth ; and
" his own knowledge, of what is poffible in nature *."   Here
every thing is, at once, eafy to the breath, and grateful to the
ear ; and, it is this fort of flowing meafure, this regular and
proportional divifion of the members of his Sentences, which
renders Sir William Temple's ftyle always agreeable.   I muft
obferve, at the fame time, that a Sentence, with too many
refts, and thefe placed at intervals too apparently meafured and
regular, is apt to favour of affectation.

---

* On this inftance.—He is addreffing himfelf to Lady Effex, upon the death
of her child : " I was once in hope, that what was fo violent could not be
" long : But, when I obferved your grief to grow ftronger with age, and to
" increafe, like a ftream, the farther it ran ; when I faw it draw out to fuch
" unhappy confequences, and to threaten, no lefs than your child, your health,
" and your life, I could no longer forbear this endeavour, nor end it, without
" begging of you, for God's fake, and for your own, for your children, and
" your friends, your country, and your family, that you would no longer
" abandon yourfelf to a difconfolate paffion ; but that you would, at length,
" awaken your piety, give way to your prudence, or, at leaft, rouze the in
" vincible fpirit of the Percys, that never yet fhrunk at any difafter."

✱✱

THE

THE next thing to be attended to, is, the clofe or cadence of the whole Sentence, which, as it is always the part moft fenfible to the ear, demands the greateft care. So Quinctilian: " Non " igitur durum fit, neque abruptum, quo animi, velut refpirant " ac reficiuntur. Hæc eft fedes orationis; hoc auditor ex- " pectat; hic laus omnis declamat *." The only important rule that can be given here, is, that when we aim at dignity or elevation, the found fhould be made to grow to the laft; the longeft members of the period, and the fulleft and moft fono-rous words, fhould be referved to the conclufion. As an example of this, the following fentence of Mr. Addifon's may be given: " It fills the mind (fpeaking of fight) with the " largeft variety of ideas; converfes with its objects at the " greateft diftance; and continues the longeft in action, with- " out being tired or fatiated with its proper enjoyments." Every reader muft be fenfible of a beauty here, both in the proper divifion of the members and paufes, and the manner in which the Sentence is rounded, and conducted to a full and harmonious clofe.

THE fame holds in melody, that I obferved to take place with refpect to fignificancy; that a falling off at the end, always hurts greatly. For this reafon, particles, pronouns, and little words, are as ungracious to the ear, at the conclufion, as I formerly fhewed they were inconfiftent with ftrength of expreffion. It is more than probable, that the fenfe and the

* " Let there be nothing harfh or abrupt in the conclufion of the fen-
" tence, on which the mind paufes and refts. This is the moft material part
" in the ftructure of Difçourfe. Here every hearer expects to be gratified;
" here his applaufe breaks forth."

L l 2

found

found have here a mutual influence on each other. That
which hurts the ear, feems to mar the ftrength of the meaning ; and that which really degrades the fenfe, in confequence
of this primary effect, appears alfo to have a bad found.   How
difagreeable is the following fentence of an Author, fpeaking of
the Trinity !   " It is a myftery which we firmly believe the
" truth of, and humbly adore the depth of."   And how eafily
could it have been mended by this tranfpofition !   " It is a
" myftery, the truth of which we firmly believe, and the
" depth of which we humbly adore."   In general it feems to
hold, that a mufical clofe, in our language, requires either the
laft fyllable, or the penult, that is, the laft but one, to be a long
fyllable.   Words which confift moftly of fhort fyllables, as,
contrary, particular, retrofpect, feldom conclude a fentence har-
monioufly, unlefs a run of long fyllables, before, has rendered
them agreeable to the ear.

It is neceffary, however, to obferve, that Sentences, fo conftructed as to make the found always fwell and grow towards
the end, and to reft either on a long or a penult long fyllable,
give a difcourfe the tone of declamation.   The ear foon becomes acquainted with the melody, and is apt to be cloyed with
it. If we would keep up the attention of the reader or hearer, if
we would preferve vivacity and ftrength in our compofition,
we muft be very attentive to vary our meafures.   This regards
the diftribution of the members, as well as the cadence of the
period.   Sentences conftructed in a fimilar manner, with the
paufes falling at equal intervals, fhould never follow one another.   Short Sentences fhould be intermixed with long and
fwelling ones, to render difcourfe fprightly, as well as magnificent.

ficent. Even difcords, properly introduced, abrupt founds, departures from regular cadence, have fometimes a good effect. Monotony is the great fault into which writers are apt to fall, who are fond of harmonious arrangement: and to have only one tune, or meafure, is not much better than having none at all. A very vulgar ear will enable a writer to catch fome one melody, and to form the run of his Sentences according to it; which foon proves difgufting. But a juft and correct ear is requifite for varying and diverfifying the melody: and hence we fo feldom meet with authors, who are remarkably happy in this refpect.

Though attention to the mufic of Sentences muft not be neglected, yet it muft alfo be kept within proper bounds: for all appearances of an author's affecting harmony, are difagreeable; efpecially when the love of it betrays him fo far, as to facrifice, in any inftance, perfpicuity, precifion, or ftrength of fentiment, to found. All unmeaning words, introduced merely to round the period, or fill up the melody, *complementa numerorum*, as Cicero calls them, are great blemifhes in writing. They are childifh and puerile ornaments, by which a Sentence always lofes more in point of weight, than it can gain by fuch additions to the beauty of its found. Senfe has its own harmony, as well as found; and, where the fenfe of a period is expreffed with clearnefs, force, and dignity, it will feldom happen but the words will ftrike the ear agreeably; at leaft, a very moderate attention is all that is requifite for making the cadence of fuch a period pleafing: and the effect of greater attention is often no other, than to render compofition languid and enervated. After all the labour which Quinctilian.

lian beſtows on regulating the meaſures of proſe, he comes at laſt, with his uſual good ſenſe, to this concluſion : " In uni-
" verſum, ſi ſit neceſſe, duram potiùs atque aſperam compoſi-
" tionem malim eſſe, quam effeminatam ac enervem, qualis
" apud multos. Ideòque, vincta quædam de induſtria ſunt
" ſolvenda, ne laborata videantur ; neque ullum idoneum aut
" aptum verbum prætermittamus, gratiâ lenitatis *." (Lib. ix.
c. 4.)

CICERO, as I before obſerved, is one of the moſt remarkable patterns of a harmonious ſtyle. His love of it, however, is too viſible ; and the pomp of his numbers ſometimes detracts from his ſtrength. That noted cloſe of his, *eſſe videatur*, which, in the Oration Pro Lege Manilia, occurs eleven times, expoſed him to cenſure among his cotemporaries. We muſt obſerve, however, in defence of this great Orator, that there is a re-markable union in his ſtyle, of harmony with eaſe, which is always a great beauty ; and if his harmony be ſometimes thought ſtudied, that ſtudy appears to have coſt him little trouble.

AMONG our Engliſh claſſics, not many are diſtinguiſhcd for muſical arrangement. Milton, in ſome of his proſe works, has very finely turned periods ; but the writers of his age in-

_____

* " Upon the whole, I would rather chuſe, that compoſition ſhould appear
" rough and harſh, if that be neceſſary, than that it ſhould be enervated and
" effeminate, ſuch as we find the ſtyle of too many. Some ſentences, there-
" fore, which we have ſtudiouſly formed into melody, ſhould be thrown
" looſe, that they may not ſeem too much laboured ; nor ought we ever to
" omit any proper or expreſſive word, for the ſake of ſmoothing a period."

dulged

duiged a liberty of inverfion, which now would be reckoned contrary to purity of ftyle : and though this allowed their Sentences to be more ftately and fonorous, yet it gave them too much of a Latinized conftruction and order. Of later writers, Shaftfbury is, upon the whole, the moft correct in his numbers. As his ear was delicate, he has attended to mufic in all his Sentences ; and he is peculiarly happy in this refpect, that he has avoided the monotony into which writers, who ftudy the grace of found, are very apt to fall : having diverfified his periods with great variety. Mr. Addifon has alfo much harmony in his ftyle ; more eafy and fmooth, but lefs varied, than Lord Shaftfbury. Sir William Temple is, in general, very flowing and agreeable. Archbifhop Tillotfon is too often carelefs and languid ; and is much outdone by Bifhop Atterbury in the mufic of his periods. Dean Swift defpifed mufical arrangement altogether.

HITHERTO I have difcourfed of agreeable found, or modulation, in general. It yet remains to treat of a higher beauty of this kind ; the found adapted to the fenfe. The former was no more than a fimple accompaniment, to pleafe the ear ; the latter fuppofes a peculiar expreffion given to the mufic. We may remark two degrees of it : Firft, the current of found, adapted to the tenor of a difcourfe ; next, a particular refemblance effected between fome object, and the founds that are employed in defcribing it.

FIRST, I fay, the current of found may be adapted to the tenor of a difcourfe. Sounds have, in many refpects, a correfpondence with our ideas ; partly natural, partly the effect

of

of artificial affociations.　Hence it happens, that any one modulation of found continued, imprints on our Style a certain character and expreffion.　Sentences conftructed with the Ciceronian fulnefs and fwell, produce the impreffion of what is important, magnificent, fedate.　For this is the natural tone which fuch a courfe of fentiment affumes.　But they fuit no violent paffion, no eager reafoning, no familiar addrefs. Thefe always require meafures brifker, eafier, and often more abrupt.　And, therefore, to fwell, or to let down the periods, as the fubject demands, is a very important rule in oratory. No one tenor whatever, fuppofing it to produce no bad effect from fatiety, will anfwer to all different compofitions; nor even to all the parts of the fame compofition.　It were as abfurd to write a panegyric, and an invective, in a Style of the fame cadence, as to fet the words of a tender love-fong to the air of a warlike march.

OBSERVE how finely the following fentence of Cicero is adapted, to reprefent the tranquillity and eafe of a fatisfied ftate: " Etfi homini nihil eft magis optandum quam profpera, " æquabilis, perpetuaque fortuna, fecundo vitæ fine ulla offen- " fione curfu; tamen, fi mihi tranquilla et placata omnia " fuiffent, incredibili quâdam et pene divinâ, quâ nunc veftro " beneficio fruor, lætitiæ voluptate caruiffem *.　Nothing was ever more perfect in its kind : it paints, if we may fo fpeak, to the ear.　But, who would not have laughed, if Cicero had employed fuch periods, or fuch a cadence as this, in inveighing againft Mark Antony, or Catiline?　What is requifite, there- fore, is, that we previoufly fix, in our mind, a juft idea of the

---

* Orat. ad Quirites, poft Reditum.

general

general tone of found which fuits our fubject; that is, which the fentiments we are to exprefs, moft naturally affume, and in which they moft commonly vent themfelves; whether round and fmooth, or ftately and folemn, or brifk and quick, or interrupted and abrupt. This general idea muft direct the run of our compofition; to fpeak in the ftyle of mufic, muft give us the key note, muft form the ground of the melody; varied and diverfified in parts, according as either our fentiments are diverfified, or as is requifite for producing a fuitable variety to gratify the ear.

IT may be proper to remark, that our tranflators of the Bible have often been happy in fuiting their numbers to the fubject. Grave, folemn, and majeftic fubjects undoubtedly require fuch an arrangement of words as runs much on long fyllables; and, particularly, they require the clofe to reft upon fuch. The very firft verfes of the Bible, are remarkable for this melody: " In the beginning, God created the heavens and " the earth; and the earth was without form, and void; and " darknefs was upon the face of the deep; and the Spirit of " God moved on the face of the waters." Several other paffages, particularly fome of the Pfalms, afford ftriking examples of this fort of grave, melodious conftruction. Any compofition that rifes confiderably above the ordinary tone of profe, fuch as monumental infcriptions, and panegyrical characters, naturally runs into numbers of this kind.

BUT, in the next place, befides the general correfpondence of the current of found with the current of thought, there

may be a more particular expreſſion attempted, of certain objeĉts, by means of reſembling ſounds. This can be, ſometimes, accompliſhed in proſe compoſition; but there only in a
more faint degree; nor is it ſo much expeĉted there. In
poetry, chiefly, it is looked for; where attention to ſound is
more demanded, and where the inverſions and liberties of
poetical ſtyle give us a greater command of ſound; aſſiſted, too,
by the verſification, and that *cantus obſcurior*, to which we are
naturally led in reading poetry. This requires a little more
illuſtration.

THE ſounds of words may be employed for repreſenting,
chiefly, three claſſes of objeĉts; firſt, other ſounds; ſecondly,
motion; and, thirdly, the emotions and paſſions of the
mind.

FIRST, I ſay, by a proper choice of words, we may produce
a reſemblance of other ſounds which we mean to deſcribe, ſuch
as, the noiſe of waters, the roaring of winds, or the murmur-
ing of ſtreams. This is the ſimpleſt inſtance of this ſort of
beauty. For the medium through which we imitate, here, is
a natural one; ſounds repreſented by other ſounds; and between ideas of the ſame ſenſe, it is eaſy to form a conneĉtion.
No very great art is required in a poet, when he is deſcribing
ſweet and ſoft ſounds, to make uſe of ſuch words as have moſt
liquids and vowels, and glide the ſofteſt; or, when he is
deſcribing harſh ſounds, to throw together a number of harſh
ſyllables which are of difficult pronunciation. Here the common ſtruĉture of Language aſſiſts him; for, it will be found,
that, in moſt Languages, the names of many particular ſounds

are

are fo formed, as to carry fome affinity to the found which they
fignify; as with us, the *whiftling* of winds, the *buz* and *hum*
of infects, the *hifs* of ferpents, the *crafh* of falling timber; and
many other inftances, where the word has been plainly framed
upon the found it reprefents. I fhall produce a remarkable
example of this beauty from Milton, taken from two paffages
in Paradife Loft, defcribing the found made, in the one, by
the opening of the gates of Hell; in the other, by the opening
of thofe of Heaven. The contraft between the two, difplays,
to great advantage, the poet's art. The firft is the opening of
Hell's gates:

———————————On a fudden, open fly,
With impetuous recoil, and jarring found,
Th' infernal doors; and on their hinges grate
Harfh thunder.——————— B. I.

Obferve, now, the fmoothnefs of the other:

——————————Heaven opened wide
Her ever-during gates, harmonious found,
On golden hinges turning.——————— B. II.

The following beautiful paffage from Taffo's Gierufalemme,
has been often admired, on account of the imitation effected by
found of the thing reprefented:

Chiama gli habitator de l'ombre eterne
Il rauco fuon de la Tartarea tromba:
Treman le fpaciofe atre caverne,
Et l'aer cieco a quel rumor rimbomba;

Ni ftridendo cofi da le fuperne
Regioni dele cielo, il folgor piomba;
Ne fi fcoffa giammai la terra,
Quand i vapori in fen gravida ferra.   Cant. IV. Stanz. 4.

The fecond clafs of objects, which the found of words is often employed to imitate, is, Motion; as it is fwift or flow, violent or gentle, equable or interrupted, eafy or accompanied with effort. Though there be no natural affinity between found, of any kind, and motion, yet, in the imagination, there is a ftrong one; as appears from the connection between mufic and dancing. And, therefore, here it is in the poet's power to give us a lively idea of the kind of motion he would defcribe, by means of founds which correfpond, in our imagination, with that motion. Long fyllables naturally give the impreffion of flow motion; as in this line of Virgil:

Olli inter fefe magna vi brachia tollunt.

A fucceffion of fhort fyllables prefents quick motion to the mind; as,

Quadrupedante putrem fonitu quatit ungula campum.

Both Homer and Virgil are great mafters of this beauty; and their works abound with inftances of it; moft of them, indeed, fo often quoted, and fo well known, that it is needlefs to produce them. I fhall give one inftance, in Englifh, which feems happy. It is the defcription of a fudden calm on the feas, in a Poem, entitled, *The Fleece.*

With

———————— With eafy courfe
The veffels glide; unlefs their fpeed be ftopp'd
By dead calms, that oft lie on thefe fmooth feas
When ev'ry zephyr fleeps; then the fhrouds drop;
The downy feather, on the cordage hung,
Moves not; the flat fea fhines like yellow gold
Fus'd in the fire, or like the marble floor
Of fome old temple wide.————————————

THE third fet of objects, which I mentioned the found of words as capable of reprefenting, confifts of the paffions and emotions of the mind. Sound may, at firft view, appear foreign to thefe; but, that here, alfo, there is fome fort of connection, is fufficiently proved by the power which mufic has to awaken, or to affift certain paffions, and, according as its ftrain is varied, to introduce one train of ideas, rather than another. This, indeed, logically fpeaking, cannot be called a refemblance between the fenfe and the found, feeing long or fhort fyllables have no natural refemblance to any thought or paffion. But if the arrangement of fyllables, by their found alone, recal one fet of ideas more readily than another, and difpofe the mind for entering into that affection which the poet means to raife, fuch arrangement may, juftly enough, be faid to refemble the fenfe, or be fimilar and correfpondent to it. I admit, that, in many inftances, which are fuppofed to difplay this beauty of accommodation of found to the fenfe, there is much room for imagination to work; and, according as a reader is ftruck by a paffage, he will often fancy a refemblance between the found and the fenfe, which others cannot difcover. He modulates the numbers to his own difpofition of mind; and, in effect, makes the mufic which he imagines himfelf to hear.

hear.   However, that there are real inftances of this kind, and
that poetry is capable of fome fuch expreffion, cannot be
doubted.   Dryden's Ode on St. Cecilia's Day, affords a very
beautiful exemplification of it, in the Englifh Language.
Without much ftudy or reflection, a poet defcribing pleafure, joy, and agreeable objects, from the feeling of his
fubject, naturally runs into fmooth, liquid, and flowing
numbers.

> ———————Namque ipfa decoram
> Cæfariem nato genetrix, lumenque juventæ
> Purpureum, et lætos oculis afflarat honores.   Æn. I.

Or,

> Devenêre locos lætos & amæna vireta,
> Fortunatorum nemorum, fedefque beatas;
> Largior hic campos æther, & lumine veftit
> Purpureo, folemque fuum, fua fidera norant.   Æn. VI.

Brifk and lively fenfations, exact quicker and more animated
numbers.

> ————————Juvenum manus emicat ardens
> Littus in Hefperium.   Æn. VII.

Melancholy and gloomy fubjects, naturally exprefs themfelves
in flow meafures, and long words:

> In thofe deep folitudes and awful cells,
> Where heavenly penfive contemplation dwells.

> Et caligantem nigrâ formidine lucum.

I HAVE

I HAVE now given fufficient openings into this fubject: a
moderate acquaintance with the good poets, either antient or
modern, will fuggeft many inftances of the fame kind. And
with this, I finifh the difcuffion of the Structure of Sentences; having fully confidered them under all the heads
I mentioned; of Perfpicuity, Unity, Strength, and Mufical
Arrangement.

L E C T.
XIII.

LECTURE XIV.

ORIGIN AND NATURE OF FIGURATIVE LANGUAGE.

HAVING now finished what related to the construction of Sentences, I proceed to other rules concerning Style. My general division of the qualities of Style, was into Perspicuity and Ornament. Perspicuity, both in single words and in sentences, I have considered. Ornament, as far as it arises from a graceful, strong, or melodious construction of words, has also been treated of. Another, and a great branch of the ornament of Style, is, Figurative Language; which is now to be the subject of our consideration, and will require a full discussion.

Our first enquiry must be, What is meant by Figures of Speech * ?

IN

* On the subject of Figures of Speech, all the writers who treat of rhetoric or composition, have insisted largely. To make references, therefore, on this
subject,

In general, they always imply some departure from simplicity of expreſſion; the idea which we intend to convey, not only enunciated to others, but enunciated, in a particular manner, and with ſome circumſtance, added, which is deſigned to render the impreſſion more ſtrong and vivid. When I ſay, for inſtance, " That a good man enjoys comfort in the midſt " of adverſity ;" I juſt expreſs my thought in the ſimpleſt manner poſſible. But when I ſay, " To the upright there " ariſeth light in darkneſs ;" the ſame ſentiment is expreſſed in a figurative Style; a new circumſtance is introduced; light is put in the place of comfort, and darkneſs is uſed to ſuggeſt the idea of adverſity. In the ſame manner, to ſay, " It is im- " poſſible, by any ſearch we can make, to explore the divine " nature fully," is, to make a ſimple propoſition. But when we ſay, " Canſt thou, by ſearching, find out God ? Canſt thou " find out the Almighty to perfection ? It is high as Heaven, " what canſt thou do ? deeper than Hell, what canſt thou " know ?" This introduces a figure into Style ; the propoſition being not only expreſſed, but admiration and aſtoniſhment being expreſſed together with it.

BUT, though Figures imply a deviation from what may be reckoned the moſt ſimple form of Speech, we are not thence to conclude, that they imply any thing uncommon, or unnatural.

ſubject were endleſs. On the foundations of Figurative Language, in general, one of the moſt ſenſible and inſtructive writers, appears to me, to be M. Marſais, in his *Traité des Tropes pour ſervir d'Introduction à la Rhetorique, & à la Logique.* For obſervations on particular Figures, the *Elements of Criticiſm* may be conſulted, where the ſubject is fully handled, and illuſtrated by a great variety of examples.

This is fo far from being the cafe, that, on very many occafions, they are both the moſt natural, and the moſt common
method of uttering our ſentiments.   It is impoſſible to compoſe
any diſcourſe without uſing them often ; nay, there are few
Sentences of any length, in which ſome expreſſion or other,
that may be termed a Figure, does not occur.   From what
cauſes this happens, ſhall be afterwards explained.   The faƐt,
in the mean time, ſhows, that they are to be accounted part of
that Language which nature diƐtates to men.   They are not
the invention of the ſchools, nor the mere produƐt of ſtudy :
on the contrary, the moſt illiterate ſpeak in figures, as often as
the moſt learned.   Whenever the imaginations of the vulgar
are   much   awakened,   or   their   paſſions   inflamed   againſt   one
another, they will pour forth a torrent of Figurative Lan-
guage,   as   forcible   as   could   be   employed   by   the   moſt   artificial
declaimer.

WHAT then is it, which has drawn the attention of critics
and rhetoricians ſo much to theſe forms of Speech ? It is this :
They remarked, that in them conſiſts much of the beauty and
the force of Language ; and found them always to bear ſome
charaƐters, or diſtinguiſhing marks, by the help of which they
could reduce them under ſeparate claſſes and heads.   To this,
perhaps, they owe their name of Figures.   As the figure, or
ſhape of one body, diſtinguiſhes it from another, ſo theſe forms
of Speech have, each of them, a caſt or turn peculiar to itſelf,
which both diſtinguiſhes it from the reſt, and diſtinguiſhes it
from Simple Expreſſion.   Simple Expreſſion juſt makes our
idea known to others; but Figurative Language, over and
above, beſtows   a   particular   dreſs   upon   that   idea ;   a   dreſs,
which

which both makes it be remarked, and adorns it. Hence, this fort of Language became early a capital object of attention to thofe who ftudied the powers of Speech.

FIGURES, in general, may be defcribed to be that Language, which is prompted either by the imagination, or by the paffions. The juftnefs of this defcription will appear, from the more particular account I am afterwards to give of them. Rhetoricians commonly divide them into two great claffes; Figures of Words, and Figures of Thought. The former, Figures of Words, are commonly called Tropes, and confift in a word's being employed to fignify fomething that is different from its original and primitive meaning; fo that if you alter the word, you deftroy the Figure. Thus, in the inftance I gave before; " Light arifeth to the upright, in darknefs." The Trope confifts, in " light and darknefs" being not meant literally, but fubftituted for comfort and adverfity, on account of fome refemblance or analogy, which they are fuppofed to bear to thefe conditions of life. The other clafs, termed Figures of Thought, fuppofes the words to be ufed in their proper and literal meaning, and the figure to confift in the turn of the thought; as is the cafe in exclamations, interrogations, apoftrophes, and comparifons; where, though you vary the words that are ufed, or tranflate them from one Language into another, you may, neverthelefs, ftill preferve the fame Figure in the thought. This diftinction, however, is of no great ufe; as nothing can be built upon it in practice; neither is it always very clear. It is of little importance, whether we give to fome particular mode of expreffion the name of a Trope, or of a Figure; provided we remember, that Figurative Language always imports fome

colouring

colouring of the imagination, or fome emotion of paffion, expreffed in our Style : And, perhaps, figures of imagination, and
figures of paffion, might be a more ufeful diftribution of the
fubject. But without infifting on any artificial divifions, it will
be more ufeful, that I enquire into the Origin and the Nature
of Figures. Only, before proceeding to this, there are two
general obfervations which it may be proper to premife.

THE firft is, concerning the ufe of rules with refpect to Figurative Language. I admit, that perfons may both fpeak and
write with propriety, who know not the names of any of the
Figures of Speech, nor ever ftudied any rules relating to them.
Nature, as was before obferved, dictates the ufe of Figures;
and, like Monf. Jourdain, in Moliere, who had fpoken for forty
years in profe, without ever knowing it, many a one ufes
metaphorical expreffions to good purpofe, without any idea of
what a metaphor is. It will not, however, follow thence, that
rules are of no fervice. All fcience arifes from obfervations on
practice. Practice has always gone before method and rule;
but method and rule have afterwards improved and perfected
practice, in every art. We, every day, meet with perfons
who fing agreeably, without knowing one note of the gamut.
Yet, it has been found of importance to reduce thefe notes to a
fcale, and to form an art of mufic ; and it would be ridiculous
to pretend, that the art is of no advantage, becaufe the
practice is founded in nature. Propriety and beauty of Speech,
are certainly as improveable as the ear or the voice ; and to
know the principles of this beauty, or the reafons which render
one Figure, or one manner of Speech preferable to another,
cannot fail to affift and direct a proper choice.

BUT

But I muſt obſerve, in the next place, that, although this part of ſtyle merit attention, and be a very proper object of ſcience and rule; although much of the beauty of compoſition depends on figurative language; yet we muſt beware of imagining that it depends ſolely, or even chiefly, upon ſuch language. It is not ſo. The great place which the doctrine of tropes and figures has occupied in ſyſtems of rhetoric; the over-anxious care which has been ſhewn in giving names to a vaſt variety of them, and in ranging them under different claſſes, has often led perſons to imagine, that, if their compoſition was well beſpangled with a number of theſe ornaments of ſpeech, it wanted no other beauty; whence has ariſen much ſtiffneſs and affectation. For it is, in truth, the ſentiment or paſſion, which lies under the figured expreſſion, that gives it any merit. The figure is only the dreſs; the ſentiment is the body and the ſubſtance. No figures will render a cold or an empty compoſition intereſting; whereas, if a ſentiment be ſublime or pathetic, it can ſupport itſelf perfectly well, without any borrowed aſſiſtance. Hence ſeveral of the moſt affecting and admired paſſages of the beſt authors, are expreſſed in the ſimpleſt language. The following ſentiment from Virgil, for inſtance, makes its way at once to the heart, without the help of any figure whatever. He is deſcribing an Argive, who falls in battle, in Italy, at a great diſtance from his native country:

Sternitur, infelix, alieno vulnere, cœlumque
Aſpicit, et dulces moriens reminiſcitur Argos *. Æn. x. 781.

A ſin-

---

* " Anthares had from Argos travell'd·far,
  " Alcides' friend, and brother of the war;

" Now

LECT.
XIV.

A single stroke of this kind, drawn as by the very pencil of Nature, is worth a thousand figures. In the same manner, the simple style of Scripture: " He spoke, and it was done ; he " commanded, and it stood fast."——" God said, let there be " light ; and there was light," imparts a lofty conception to much greater advantage, than if it had been decorated by the most pompous metaphors. The fact is, that the strong pathetic, and the pure sublime, not only have little dependance on

> " Now falling, by another's wound, his eyes
> " He casts to Heaven, on Argos thinks, and dies."

In this translation, much of the beauty of the original is lost. " On Argos " thinks and dies," is by no means equal to " dulces moriens reminiscitur " Argos :" " As he dies, he remembers his beloved Argos."——It is indeed observable, that in most of those tender and pathetic passages, which do so much honour to Virgil, that great poet expresses himself with the utmost simplicity ; as,

> Te, dulcis Conjux, te solo in littore secum,
> Te veniente die, te decedente canebat.   GEORG. IV.

And so in that moving prayer of Evander, upon his parting with his son Pallas :

> At vos, O Superi ! et Divûm tu maxime rector
> Jupiter, Arcadii quæso miserescite regis,
> Et patrias audite preces.   Si numina vestra
> Incolumem Pallanta mihi, si fata reservant,
> Si visurus eum vivo, et venturus in unum,
> Vitam oro ; patiar quemvis durare laborem !
> Sin aliquem infandum casum, Fortuna, minaris,
> Nunc, O nunc liceat crudelem abrumpere vitam !
> Dum curæ ambiguæ, dum spes incerta futuri ;
> Dum te, chare Puer ! mea sera et sola voluptas !
> Amplexu teneo ; gravior ne nuncius aures
> Vulneret——   ÆN. VIII. 572.

figures

figures of fpeech, but, generally, reject them. The proper region of thefe ornaments is, where a moderate degree of elevation and paffion is predominant; and there they contribute to the embellifhment of difcourfe, only, when there is a bafis of folid thought and natural fentiment; when they are inferted in their proper place; and when they rife, of themfelves, from the fubject, without being fought after.

HAVING premifed thefe obfervations, I proceed to give an account of the origin and nature of Figures; principally of fuch as have their dependance on language; including that numerous tribe, which the rhetoricians call Tropes.

AT the firft rife of language, men would begin with giving names to the different objects which they difcerned, or thought of. This nomenclature would, at the beginning, be very narrow. According as men's ideas multiplied, and their acquaintance with objects increafed, their ftock of names and words would increafe alfo. But to the infinite variety of objects and ideas, no language is adequate. No language is fo copious, as to have a feparate word for every feparate idea. Men naturally fought to abridge this labour of multiplying words *in infinitum;* and, in order to lay lefs burden on their memories, made one word, which they had already appropriated to a certain idea or object, ftand alfo for fome other idea or object; between which and the primary one, they found, or fancied, fome relation. Thus, the prepofition, *in,* was originally invented to exprefs the circumftance of place: " The man was killed *in* the wood." In progrefs of time, words were wanted to exprefs men's being connected with certain conditions of fortune, or certain fitua-

8

tions

tions of mind ; and some resemblance, or analogy, being fancied between these, and the place of bodies, the word, *in*, was employed to express men's being so circumstanced ; as, one's being *in* health or *in* sickness, *in* prosperity or *in* adversity, *in* joy or *in* grief, *in* doubt, or *in* danger, or *in* safety. Here we see this preposition, *in*, plainly assuming a tropical signification, or carried off from its original meaning, to signify something else, which relates to, or resembles it.

TROPES of this kind abound in all languages ; and are plainly owing to the want of proper words. The operations of the mind and affections, in particular, are, in most languages, described by words taken from sensible objects. The reason is plain. The names of sensible objects, were, in all languages, the words most early introduced ; and were, by degrees, extended to those mental objects, of which men had more obscure conceptions, and to which they found it more difficult to assign distinct names. They borrowed, therefore, the name of some sensible idea, where their imagination found some affinity. Thus, we speak of, a *piercing* judgment, and a *clear* head ; a *soft* or a *hard* heart ; a *rough* or a *smooth* behaviour. We say, *inflamed* by anger, *warmed* by love, *swelled* with pride, *melted* into grief ; and these are almost the only significant words which we have for such ideas.

BUT, although the barrenness of language, and the want of words, be doubtless one cause of the invention of tropes ; yet it is not the only, nor, perhaps, even the principal source of this form of speech. Tropes have arisen more frequently, and spread themselves wider, from the influence which Imagination

I

possesses

poſſeſſes over all language. The train on which this has proceeded among all nations, I ſhall endeavour to explain.

EVERY object which makes any impreſſion on the human
mind, is conſtantly accompanied with certain circumſtances and
relations, that ſtrike us at the ſame time. It never preſents itſelf to
our view, *iſolé*, as the French expreſs it; that is, independent on,
and ſeparated from, every other thing; but always occurs as ſome-
how related to other objects; going before them, or following
after them; their effect or their cauſe; reſembling them, or
oppoſed to them; diſtinguiſhed by certain qualities, or ſur-
rounded with certain circumſtances. By this means, every idea
or object carries in its train ſome other ideas, which may be
conſidered as its acceſſories. Theſe acceſſories often ſtrike the
imagination more than the principal idea itſelf. They are,
perhaps, more agreeable ideas; or they are more familiar to our
conceptions; or they recal to our memory a greater variety of
important circumſtances. The imagination is more diſpoſed to
reſt upon ſome of them; and therefore, inſtead of uſing the
proper name of the principal idea which it means to expreſs,
it employs, in its place, the name of the acceſſory or
correſpondent idea; although the principal have a proper and
well-known name of its own. Hence a vaſt variety of tropical
or figurative words obtain currency in all languages, through
choice, not neceſſity; and men of lively imaginations are every
day adding to their number.

THUS, when we deſign to intimate the period, at which a
ſtate enjoyed moſt reputation or glory, it were eaſy to employ
the proper words for expreſſing this; but as this readily con-

nects, in our imagination, with the flourishing period of a plant or a tree, we lay hold of this correspondent idea, and say, " The Roman empire flourished most under Augustus." The leader of a faction, is plain language; but, because the head is the principal part of the human body, and is supposed to direct all the animal operations, resting upon this resemblance, we say, " Catiline was the head of the party." The word, *Voice*, was originally invented to signify the articulate found, formed by the organs of the mouth; but, as by means of it men signify their ideas and their intentions to each other, *Voice* soon assumed a great many other meanings, all derived from this primary effect. " To give our Voice" for any thing, signified, to give our sentiment in favour of it. . Not only so; but *Voice* was transferred to signify any intimation of will or judgment, though given without the least interposition of Voice in its literal sense, or any found uttered at all. Thus we speak of listening to the *Voice* of Conscience, the *Voice* of Nature, the *Voice* of God. This usage takes place, not so much from barrenness of language, or want of a proper word, as from an allusion which we choose to make to *Voice*, in its primary sense, in order to convey our idea, connected with a circumstance which appears to the fancy to give it more sprightliness and force.

THE account which I have now given, and which seems to be a full and fair one, of the introduction of Tropes into all Languages, coincides with what Cicero shortly hints, in his third book De Oratore. " Modus transferendi verba late " patet; quam necessitas primum genuit, coacta inopia et an- " gustias; post autem delectatio, jucunditasque celebravit. Nam

"· ut

" ut veſtis, frigoris depellendi cauſâ reperta primo, poſt adhi-
" beri cæpta eſt ad ornatum etiam corporis et dignitatem, ſic
" verbi tranſlatio inſtituta eſt inopiæ cauſâ, frequentata, de-
" lectationis *."

FROM what has been ſaid, it clearly appears, how that muſt
come to paſs, which I had occaſion to mention in a former
Lecture, that all Languages are moſt figurative in their early
ſtate. Both the cauſes to which I aſcribed the origin of
Figures, concur in producing this effect at the beginnings of
ſociety. Language is then moſt barren; the ſtock of proper
names, which have been invented for things, is ſmall; and, at
the ſame time, imagination exerts great influence over the conceptions of men, and their method of uttering them; ſo that,
both from neceſſity and from choice, their Speech will, at that
period, abound in Tropes. For the ſavage tribes of men are
always much given to wonder and aſtoniſhment. Every new
object ſurpriſes, terrifies, and makes a ſtrong impreſſion on
their mind; they are governed by imagination and paſſion,
more than by reaſon; and, of courſe, their ſpeech muſt be
deeply tinctured by their genius. In fact, we find, that this is
the character of the American and Indian Languages; bold,
picturesque, and metaphorical; full of ſtrong alluſions to ſen-

---

* " The figurative uſage of words is very extenſive; an uſage to which ne-
" ceſſity firſt gave riſe, on account of the paucity of words, and barrenneſs
" of Language; but which the pleaſure that was found in it afterwards
" rendered frequent. For, as garments were firſt contrived to defend our
" bodies from the cold, and afterwards were employed for the purpoſe of
" ornament and dignity, ſo Figures of Speech, introduced by want, were
" cultivated for the ſake of entertainment."

ſible

fible qualities, and to fuch objects as ftruck them moft in their wild and folitary life. An Indian chief makes a harangue to his tribe, in a ftyle full of ftronger metaphors than a European would ufe in an epic poem.

As Language makes gradual progrefs towards refinement, almoft every object comes to have a proper name given to it, and Perfpicuity and Precifion are more ftudied. But ftill, for the reafons before given, borrowed words, or as rhetoricians call them, Tropes, muft continue to occupy a confiderable place. In every Language, too, there are a multitude of words, which, though they were Figurative in their firft application to certain objects, yet, by long ufe, lofe that figurative power wholly, and come to be confidered as fimple and literal expreffions. In this cafe, are the terms which I remarked before, as transferred from fenfible qualities to the operations or qualities of the mind, a *piercing* judgment, a *clear* head, a *hard* heart, and the like. There are other words which remain in a fort of middle ftate; which have neither loft wholly their figurative application, nor yet retain fo much of it, as to imprint any remarkable character of figured Language on our ftyle; fuch as thefe phrafes, " apprehend one's meaning;" " enter on a fubject;" " follow out an argument;" " ftir up " ftrife;" and a great many more, of which our Language is full. In the ufe of fuch phrafes, correct writers will always preferve a regard to the figure or allufion on which they are founded, and will be careful not to apply them in any way that is inconfiftent with it. One may be " fheltered under the " patronage of a great man;" but it were wrong to fay, " fheltered under the mafque of diffimulation," as a mafque
conceals,

conceals, but does not fhelter. An object, in defcription, may be " clothed," if you will, " with epithets ;" but it is not fo proper to fpeak of its being " clothed with circumftances ;" as the word " circumftances," alludes to ftanding round, not to clothing. Such attentions as thefe are requifite in the common run of Style.

What has been faid on this fubject, tends to throw light on the nature of Language in general; and will lead to the reafons, Why Tropes or Figures contribute to the beauty and grace of Style.

First, They enrich Language, and render it more copious. By their means, words and phrafes are multiplied for expreffing all forts of ideas ; for defcribing even the minuteft differences ; the niceft fhades and colours of thought ; which no Language could poffibly do by proper words alone, without affiftance from Tropes.

Secondly, They beftow dignity upon Style. The familiarity of common words, to which our ears are much accuftomed, tends to degrade Style. When we want to adapt our Language to the tone of an elevated fubject, we would be greatly at a lofs, if we could not borrow affiftance from Figures; which, properly employed, have a fimilar effect on Language, with what is produced by the rich and fplendid drefs of a perfon of rank ; to create refpect, and to give an air of magnificence to him who wears it. Affiftance of this kind, is often needed in profe compofitions ; but poetry could not fubfift without it. Hence Figures form the conftant Language of poetry.

poetry. To fay, that " the fun rifes," is trite and common; but it becomes a magnificent image when expreffed, as Mr. Thomfon has done :

> But yonder comes the powerful king of day
> Rejoicing in the eaft.——

To fay, that " all men are fubject alike to death," prefents only a vulgar idea; but it rifes and fills the imagination, when painted thus by Horace :

> Pallida mors æquo pulfat pede, pauperum tabernas
> Regumque turres.

Or,

> Omnes eodem cogimur; omnium,
> Verfatur urna, ferius, ocyus,
> Sors exitura, & nos in eternum
> Exilium impofitura cymbæ*

In the third place, Figures give us the pleafure of enjoying two objects prefented together to our view, without confufion; the principal idea, which is the fubject of the difcourfe, along with its acceffory, which gives it the figurative drefs. We fee one

---

* With equal pace, impartial fate,
  Knocks at the palace, as the cottage gate.

Or,

> We all muft tread the paths of fate;
> And ever fhakes the mortal urn;
> Whofe lot embarks us, foon or late,
> On Charon's boat; ah! never to return.

FRANCIS.

thing

thing in another, as Ariftotle expreffes it; which is always agreeable to the mind. For there is nothing with which the fancy is more delighted, than with comparifons, and refemblances of objects; and all Tropes are founded upon fome relation or analogy between one thing and another. When, for inftance, in place of " youth," I fay, the " morning of " life ;" the fancy is immediately entertained with all the refembling circumftances which prefently occur between thefe two objects. At one moment, I have in my eye a certain period of human life, and a certain time of the day, fo related to each other, that the imagination plays between them with pleafure, and contemplates two fimilar objects, in one view, without embarraffment or confufion. Not only fo, but,

In the fourth place, Figures are attended with this farther advantage, of giving us frequently a much clearer and more ftriking view of the principal object, than we could have if it were expreffed in fimple terms, and divefted of its acceffory idea. This is, indeed, their principal advantage, in virtue of which, they are very properly faid to illuftrate a fubject, or to throw light upon it. For they exhibit the object, on which they are employed, in a picturefque form; they can render an abftract conception, in fome degree, an object of fenfe; they furround it with fuch circumftances, as enable the mind to lay hold of it fteadily, and to contemplate it fully. " Thofe perfons," fays one, " who gain the hearts of moft people, who are chofen as " the companions of their fofter hours, and their reliefs from " anxiety and care, are feldom perfons of fhining qualities, or " ftrong virtues: it is rather the foft green of the foul, on " which we reft our eyes, that are fatigued with beholding

4:

" more

" more glaring objects." Here, by a happy allusion to a colour, the whole conception is conveyed clear and strong to the mind in one word. By a well chosen Figure, even conviction is assisted, and the impression of a truth upon the mind, made more lively and forcible than it would otherwise be. As in the following illustration of Dr. Young's : " When we dip too deep " in pleasure, we always stir a sediment that renders it impure " and noxious;" or in this, " A heart boiling with violent " passions, will always send up infatuating fumes to the head." An image that presents so much congruity between a moral and a sensible idea, serves like an argument from analogy, to enforce what the author asserts, and to induce belief.

BESIDES, whether we are endeavouring to raise sentiments of pleasure or aversion, we can always heighten the emotion by the figures which we introduce ; leading the imagination to a train, either of agreeable or disagreeable, of exalting or deba-sing ideas, correspondent to the impression which we seek to make. When we want to render an object beautiful, or mag-nificent, we borrow images from all the most beautiful or splendid scenes of nature; we thereby, naturally, throw a lustre over our object ; we enliven the reader's mind ; and dispose him to go along with us, in the gay and pleasing impressions which we give him of the subject. This effect of Figures is happily touched in the following lines of Dr. Akenside, and illustrated by a very sublime figure :

———————Then the inexpressive strain,
Diffuses its enchantment. Fancy dreams
Of sacred fountains and Elysian groves,

And

And vales of blifs.   The intellectual power
Bends from his awful throne a wond'ring ear,
And fmiles.———————   Pleaf. of Imaginat. I. 124.

WHAT I have now explained, concerning the ufe and effects
of Figures, naturally leads us to reflect on the wonderful
power of Language; and, indeed, we cannot reflect on it
without the higheft admiration.   What a fine vehicle is it now
become for all the conceptions of the human mind; even for
the moft fubtile and delicate workings of the imagination!
What a pliant and flexible inftrument in the hand of one who
can employ it fkilfully; prepared to take every form which
he chufes to give it! Not content with a fimple communication
of ideas and thoughts, it paints thofe ideas to the eye; it gives
colouring and relievo, even to the moft abftract conceptions.   In
the figures which it ufes, it fets mirrors before us, where we
may behold objects, a fecond time, in their likenefs.   It enter-
tains us, as with a fucceffion of the moft fplendid pictures;
difpofes, in the moft artificial manner, of the light and fhade,
for viewing every thing to the beft advantage; in fine, from
being a rude and imperfect interpreter of men's wants and neceffities, it has now paffed into an inftrument of the moft delicate and refined luxury.

To make thefe effects of Figurative Language fenfible,
there are few authors in the Englifh Language, whom
I can refer to with more advantage than Mr. Addifon,
whofe imagination is, at once, remarkably rich, and remarkably correct and chafte.   When he is treating, for
inftance, of the effect which light and colours have to entertain

VOL. I.   P p   the

the fancy, confidered in Mr. Locke's view of them as
fecondary qualities, which have no real exiftence in matter,
but are only ideas in the mind, with what beautiful painting
has he adorned this philofophic fpeculation? " Things," fays
he, " would make but a poor appearance to the eye, if we
" faw them only in their proper figures and motions. Now,
" we are every where entertained with pleafing fhows and ap-
" paritions; we difcover imaginary glories in the heavens, and
" in the earth, and fee fome of this vifionary beauty poured
" out upon the whole creation. But what a rough unfightly
" fketch of nature fhould we be entertained with, did all her
" colouring difappear, and the feveral diftinctions of light and
" fhade vanifh ? In fhort, our fouls are, at prefent, delightfully
" loft, and bewildered in a pleafing delufion; and we walk
" about, like the enchanted hero of a romance, who fees
" beautiful caftles, woods, and meadows; and, at the fame
" time, hears the warbling of birds, and the purling of
" ftreams ; but, upon the finifhing of fome fecret fpell, the
" fantaftic fcene breaks up, and the difconfolate knight finds
" himfelf on a barren heath, or in a folitary defert. It is not
" improbable, that fomething like this may be the ftate of the
" foul after its firft feparation, in refpect of the images it will
" receive from matter." No. 413. Spec.

HAVING thus explained, at fufficient length, the Origin,
the Nature, and the Effects of Tropes, I fhould proceed next to
the feveral kinds and divifions of them. But, in treating of
thefe, were I to follow the common tract of the fcholaftic
writers on Rhetoric, I fhould foon become tedious, and, I apprehend, ufelefs, at the fame time. Their great bufinefs has
9
been,

been, with a moſt patient and frivolous induſtry, to branch
them out under a vaſt number of diviſions, according to all
the ſeveral modes in which a word may be carried from its
literal meaning, into one that is Figurative, without doing any
more ; as if the mere knowledge of the names and claſſes of all
the Tropes that can be formed, could be of any advantage towards the proper, or graceful uſe of Language. All that I
purpoſe is, to give, in a few words, before finiſhing this Lecture, a general view of the ſeveral ſources whence the tropical
meaning of words is derived: after which I ſhall, in ſubſequent Lectures, deſcend to a more particular conſideration
of ſome of the moſt conſiderable Figures of Speech, and ſuch
as are in moſt frequent uſe ; by treating of which, I ſhall give
all the inſtruction I can, concerning the proper employment of
Figurative Language, and point out the errors and abuſes which
are apt to be committed in this part of ſtyle.

ALL Tropes, as I before obſerved, are founded on the relation which one object bears to another; in virtue of which,
the name of the one can be ſubſtituted inſtead of the name
of the other ; and by ſuch a ſubſtitution, the vivacity of
the idea is commonly meant to be increaſed. Theſe relations,
ſome more, ſome leſs intimate, may all give riſe to Tropes. One
of the firſt and moſt obvious relations is, that between a cauſe
and its effect. Hence, in Figurative Language, the cauſe is,
ſometimes, put for the effect. Thus, Mr. Addiſon, writing of
Italy :

Bloſſoms, and fruits, and flowers, together riſe,
And the whole year in gay confuſion lies.

P p 2 Where

Where the " whole year" is plainly intended, to fignify the effects or productions of all the feafons of the year. At other times, again, the effect is put for the caufe; as, " grey hairs" frequently for old age, which caufes grey hairs; and " fhade," for trees that produce the fhade. The relation between the container and the thing contained, is alfo fo intimate and obvious, as naturally to give rife to Tropes:

> ————————Ille impiger haufit
> Spumantem pateram & pleno fe proluit auro.

Where every one fees, that the cup and the gold are put for the liquor that was contained in the golden cup. In the fame manner, the name of any country, is often ufed to denote the inhabitants of that country; and Heaven, very commonly employed to fignify God, becaufe he is conceived as dwelling in Heaven. To implore the affiftance of Heaven, is the fame as to implore the affiftance of God. The relation betwixt any eftablifhed fign and the thing fignified, is a further fource of Tropes. Hence,

> Cedant arma togæ; concedat laurea linguæ.

The " toga," being the badge of the civil profeffions, and the " laurel," of military honours, the badge of each is put for the civil and military characters themfelves. To " affume the " fceptre," is a common phrafe for entering on royal authority. To Tropes, founded on thefe feveral relations, of caufe and effect, container and contained, fign and thing fignified, is given the name of Metonymy.

When the Trope is founded on the relation between an antecedent and a confequent, or what goes before, and immediately

mediately follows after, it is then called a Metalepfis; as in the Roman phrafe of " Fuit," or " Vixit," to exprefs that one was dead. " Fuit Ilium et ingens gloria Dardanidum," fignifies, that the glory of Troy is now no more.

WHEN the whole is put for a part, or a part for the whole; a genus for a fpecies, or a fpecies for a genus ; the fingular for the plural, or the plural for the fingular number ; in general, when any thing lefs, or any thing more, is put for the precife objeƈt meant; the figure is then called a Synecdoche. It is very common, for inftance, to defcribe a whole objeƈt by fome remarkable part of it; as when we fay, " A fleet of fo many " fail," in the place of " fhips;" when we ufe the " head" for the " perfon," the " pole" for the " earth," the " waves" for the " fea." In like manner, an attribute may be put for a fubjeƈt; as, " Youth and Beauty," for " the young and beau-" tiful;" and fometimes a fubjeƈt for its attribute. But it is needlefs to infift longer on this enumeration, which ferves little purpofe. I have faid enough, to give an opening into that great variety of relations between objeƈts, by means of which, the mind is affifted to pafs eafily from one to another ; and, by the name of the one, underftands the other to be meant. It is always fome acceffory idea, which recals the principal to the imagination ; and commonly recals it with more force, than if the principal idea had been expreffed.

THE relation which, of all others, is by far the moft fruitful of Tropes, I have not yet mentioned; that is, the relation of Similitude and Refemblance. On this is founded what is called the Metaphor: when, in place of ufing the proper name of any object,

3

object, we employ, in its place, the name of some other which is like it; which is a fort of picture of it, and which thereby awakens the conception of it with more force or grace. This figure is more frequent than all the rest put together; and the language, both of profe and verfe, owes to it much of its elegance and grace. This, therefore, deferves very full and particular confideration; and fhall be the fubject of the next Lecture.

LECTURE XV.

METAPHOR.

AFTER the preliminary obfervations I have made, re- lating to Figurative Language in general, I come now to treat feparately of fuch Figures of Speech, as occur moft fre- quently, and require particular attention : and I begin with Metaphor. This is a figure founded entirely on the refem- blance which one object bears to another. Hence, it is much allied to Simile, or Comparifon ; and is indeed no other than a comparifon, expreffed in an abridged form. When I fay of fome great minifter, " that he upholds the ftate, like a pillar " which fupports the weight of a whole edifice," I fairly make a comparifon ; but when I fay of fuch a minifter, " that he is " the Pillar of the ftate," it is now become a Metaphor. The comparifon betwixt the Minifter and a Pillar, is made in the mind ; but is expreffed without any of the words that denote comparifon. The comparifon is only infinuated, not ex- preffed : the one object is fuppofed to be fo like the other, that, without formally drawing the comparifon, the name of

the

the one may be put in the place of the name of the other.
" The minifter is the Pillar of the ftate." This, therefore, is
a more lively and animated manner of expreffing the refemblances which imagination traces among objects. There is
nothing which delights the fancy more, than this act of
comparing things together, difcovering refemblances between
them, and defcribing them by their likenefs. The mind thus
employed, is exercifed without being fatigued; and is gratified
with the confcioufnefs of its own ingenuity. We need not be
furprifed, therefore, at finding all Language tinctured ftrongly
with Metaphor. It infinuates itfelf even into familiar converfation; and, unfought, rifes up of its own accord in the mind.
The very words which I have cafually employed in defcribing
this, are a proof of what I fay; *tinctured, infinuates, rifes up,*
are all of them metaphorical expreffions, borrowed from fome
refemblance which fancy forms between fenfible objects, and
the internal operations of the mind; and yet the terms are no
lefs clear, and, perhaps, more expreffive, than if words had
been ufed, which were to be taken in the ftrict and literal
fenfe.

Though all Metaphor imports comparifon, and, therefore,
is, in that refpect, a figure of thought; yet, as the words in a
Metaphor are not taken literally, but changed from their
proper to a Figurative fenfe, the Metaphor is commonly ranked
among Tropes or Figures of words. But, provided the nature
of it be well underftood, it fignifies very little whether we call
it a Figure or a Trope. I have confined it to the expreffion of
refemblance between two objects. I muft remark, however,
that the word Metaphor is fometimes ufed in a loofer and more

extended

extended fenfe; for the application of a term in any figurative fignification, whether the figure be founded on refemblance, or on fome other relation, which two objects bear to
one another. For inftance; when grey hairs are put for old
age, as, " to bring one's grey hairs with forrow to the grave ;"
fome writers would call this a Metaphor, though it is not
properly one, but what rhetoricians call a Metonymy; that is,
the effect put for the caufe; " grey hairs" being the effect of
old age, but not bearing any fort of refemblance to it. Ariftotle,
in his Poetics, ufes Metaphor in this extended fenfe, for any
figurative meaning impofed upon a word; as a whole put for
the part, or a part for the whole ; a fpecies for the genus, or
a genus for the fpecies. But it would be unjuft to tax this
moft acute writer with any inaccuracy on this account ; the
minute fubdivifions, and various names of Tropes, being unknown in his days, and the invention of later rhetoricians.
Now, however, when thefe divifions are eftablifhed, it is inaccurate to call every figurative ufe of terms, promifcuoufly, a
Metaphor.

Of all the figures of Speech, none comes fo near to painting
as Metaphor. Its peculiar effect is to give light and ftrength
to defcription ; to make intellectual ideas, in fome fort, vifible
to the eye, by giving them colour, and fubftance, and fenfible
qualities. In order to produce this effect, however, a delicate
hand is required ; for, by a very little inaccuracy, we are in
hazard of introducing confufion, in place of promoting Perfpicuity. Several rules, therefore, are neceffary to be given for
the proper management of Metaphors. But, before entering
on thefe, I fhall give one inftance of a very beautiful Metaphor,

phor, that I may fhow the figure to full advantage. I fhall. take my inftance from Lord Bolingbroke's Remarks on the Hiftory of England. Juft at the conclufion of his work, he is fpeaking of the behaviour of Charles I. to his laft parliament : " In " a word," fays he, " about a month after their meeting, he " diffolved them; and, as foon as he had diffolved them, he " repented ; but he repented too late of his rafhnefs. Well " might he repent ; for the veffel was now full, and this laft " drop made the waters of bitternefs overflow." " Here," he adds, " we draw the curtain, and put an end to our remarks." Nothing could be more happily thrown off. The Metaphor, we fee, is continued through feveral expreffions. The *veffel* is put for the ftate, or temper of the nation already *full*, that is, provoked to the higheft by former oppreffions and wrongs ; this *laft drop*, ftands for the provocation recently received by the abrupt diffolution of the parliament ; and the *overflowing of the waters of bitternefs*, beautifully expreffes all the effects of refentment let loofe by an exafperated people.

On this paffage, we may make two remarks in paffing. The one, that nothing forms a more fpirited and dignified conclufion of a fubject, than a figure of this kind happily placed at the clofe. We fee the effect of it, in this inftance. The author goes off with a good grace ; and leaves a ftrong and full impreffion of his fubject on the reader's mind. My other remark is, the advantage which a Metaphor frequently has above a formal comparifon. How much would the fentiment here have been enfeebled, if it had been expreffed in the ftyle of a regular fimile, thus : " Well might he repent ; for " the ftate of the nation, loaded with grievances and provoca-

" tions,

" tions, refembled a veffel that was now full, and this fuper-
" added provocation, like the laft drop infufed, made their
" rage and refentment, as waters of bitternefs, overflow."
It has infinitely more fpirit and force as it now ftands, in the
form of a Metaphor. " Well might he repent; for the veffel
" was now full; and this laft drop made the waters of bitternefs
" overflow."

HAVING mentioned, with applaufe, this inftance from
Lord Bolingbroke, I think it incumbent on me here to take
notice, that, though I may have recourfe to this author, fometimes, for examples of ftyle, it is his ftyle only, and not his fentiments, that deferve praife. It is, indeed, my opinion, that there
are few writings in the Englifh Language, which, for the matter
contained in them, can be read with lefs profit or fruit, than Lord
Bolingbroke's works. His political writings have the merit of
a very lively and eloquent ftyle ; but they have no other ;
being, as to the fubftance, the mere temporary productions of
faction and party; no better, indeed, than pamphlets written
for the day. His Pofthumous, or, as they are called, his
Philofophical Works, wherein he attacks religion, have ftill
lefs merit ; for they are as loofe in the ftyle as they are flimfy
in the reafoning. An unhappy inftance, this author is, of
parts and genius fo miferably perverted by faction and paffion,
that, as his memory will defcend to pofterity with little honour,
fo his productions will foon pafs, and are, indeed, already
paffing into neglect and oblivion.

Q q 2

RETURNING

RETURNING from this digreffion to the fubject before us, I proceed to lay down the rules to be obferved in the conduct of Metaphors ; and which are much the fame for Tropes of every kind.

THE firft which I fhall mention, is, that they be fuited to the nature of the fubject of which we treat ; neither too many, nor too gay, nor too elevated for it ; that we neither attempt to force the fubject, by means of them, into a degree of eleva-tion which is not congruous to it ; nor, on the other hand, allow it to fink below its proper dignity.   This is a direction which belongs to all Figurative Language, and fhould be ever kept in view. Some Metaphors are allowable, nay beautiful, in poetry, which it would be abfurd and unnatural to employ in profe ; fome may be graceful in orations, which would be very improper in hiftorical, or philofophical compofition.   We muft remember, that figures are the drefs of our fentiments.   As there is a natural congruity between drefs, and the character or rank of the perfon who wears it, a violation of which con-gruity never fails to hurt ; the fame holds precifely as to the application of figures to fentiment. The exceffive, or unfeafon-able employment of them, is mere foppery in writing. It gives a boyifh air to compofition ; and, inftead of raifing a fubject, in fact, diminifhes its dignity.   For, as in life, true dignity muft be founded on character, not on drefs and appearance, fo the dignity of compofition muft arife from fentiment and thought, not from ornament. The affectation and parade of ornament, detract as much from an author, as they do from a man. Figures and Metaphors, therefore, fhould, on no occafion, be ftuck on too profufely ; and never fhould be fuch as refufe

†

to

to accord with the ſtrain of our ſentiment. Nothing can be
more unnatural, than for a writer to carry on a train of reaſoning, in the ſame ſort of Figurative Language, which he
would uſe in deſcription. When he reaſons, we look only for
perſpicuity; when he deſcribes, we expect embelliſhment;
when he divides, or relates, we deſire plainneſs and ſimplicity.
One of the greateſt ſecrets in compoſition is, to know when to
be ſimple. This always gives a heightening to ornament, in
its proper place. The right diſpoſition of the ſhade, makes the
light and colouring ſtrike the more: " Is enim eſt eloquens,"
ſays Cicero," " qui et humilia ſubtiliter, et magna graviter, et
" mediocria temperatè poteſt dicere.—Nam qui nihil poteſt
" tranquillè, nihil leniter, nihil definitè, diſtinctè, poteſt dicere,
" is, cum non præparatis auribus inflammare rem cæpit, furere
" apud ſanos, et quaſi inter ſobrios bacchari temulentus vide-
" tur *." This admonition ſhould be particularly attended to by
young practitioners in the art of writing, who are apt to be
carried away by an undiſtinguiſhing admiration of what is
ſhowy and florid, whether in its place or not †.

THE

---

* " He is truly eloquent, who can diſcourſe of humble ſubjects in a plain
" ſtyle, who can treat important ones with dignity, and ſpeak of things,
" which are of a middle nature, in a temperate ſtrain. For one who, upon
" no occaſion, can expreſs himſelf in a calm, orderly, diſtinct manner, when
" he begins to be on fire before his readers are prepared to kindle along with
" him, has the appearance of raving like a madman among perſons who are
" in their ſenſes, or of reeling like a drunkard in the midſt of ſober company."

† What perſon, of the leaſt taſte, can bear the following paſſage, in a late
hiſtorian. He is giving an account of the famous act of parliament againſt
irregular Marriages in England: " The bill," ſays he, " underwent a great
" number of alterations and amendments, which were not effected without
" violent conteſt." This is plain Language, ſuited to the ſubject; and we

naturally

THE fecond rule, which I give, refpects the choice of objects, from whence Metaphors, and other Figures, are to be
drawn. The field for Figurative Language is very wide. All
nature, to fpeak in the ftyle of figures, opens its ftores to us,
and admits us to gather, from all fenfible objects, whatever can
illuftrate intellectual or moral ideas. Not only the gay and
fplendid objects of fenfe, but the grave, the terrifying, and
even the gloomy and difmal, can, on different occafions, be
introduced into figures with propriety. But we muft beware
of ever ufing fuch allufions as raife in the mind difagreeable,
mean, vulgar, or dirty ideas. Even, when Metaphors are
chofen in order to vilify and degrade any object, an author
fhould ftudy never to be naufeous in his allufions. Cicero
blames an orator of his time, for terming his enemy " Stercus
" Curiæ;" " quamvis fit fimile," fays he, " tamen eft de-
" formis cogitatio fimilitudinis." But, in fubjects of dignity,
it is an unpardonable fault to introduce mean and vulgar Metaphors. In the treatife on the Art of Sinking, in Dean Swift's
works, there is a full and humourous collection of inftances
of this kind, wherein authors, inftead of exalting, have contrived to degrade, their fubjects by the figures they employed.
Authors of greater note than thofe which are there quoted,
have, at times, fallen into this error. Archbifhop Tillotfon,
for inftance, is. fometimes negligent in his choice of Meta-

---

naturally expect, that he fhould go on in the fame ftrain, to tell us, that, after
thefe contefts, it was carried by a great majority of voices, and obtained the
royal affent. But how does he exprefs himfelf in finifhing the period?
" At length, however, it was floated through both houfes, on the tide of
" a great majority, and fteered into the fafe harbour of royal approbation."
Nothing can be more puerile than fuch Language. Smollet's Hiftory of England, as quoted in Critical Review for Oct. 1761, p. 251.

phors ;

phors; as, when fpeaking of the day of judgment, he defcribes
the world, as " cracking about the finners ears." Shakefpeare,
whofe imagination was rich and bold, in a much greater degree
than it was delicate, often fails here. The following, for
example, is a grofs tranfgreffion; in his Henry V. having
mentioned a dunghill, he prefently raifes a Metaphor from the
fteam of it; and on a fubject too, that naturally led to much
nobler ideas :

> And thofe that leave their valiant bones in France,
> Dying like men, though buried in your dunghills
> They fhall be fam'd; for there the fun fhall greet them,
> And draw their honours reeking up to heaven.
>
> Act. IV. Sc. 8.

In the third place, as Metaphors fhould be drawn from objects of fome dignity, fo particular care fhould be taken that the
refemblance, which is the foundation of the Metaphor, be clear
and perfpicuous, not far-fetched, nor difficult to difcover. The
tranfgreffion of this rule makes, what are called harfh or forced
Metaphors, which are always difpleafing, becaufe they puzzle
the reader, and, inftead of illuftrating the thought, render it
perplexed and intricate. With Metaphors of this kind, Cowley
abounds. He, and fome of the writers of his age, feem to
have confidered it as the perfection of wit, to hit upon likeneffes between objects which no other perfon could have difcovered; and, at the fame time, to purfue thofe Metaphors fo
far, that it requires fome ingenuity to follow them out, and
comprehend them. This makes a Metaphor refemble an
ænigma; and is the very reverfe of Cicero's rule on this head:

" Vere-

LECT.　" Verecunda debet effe tranflatio ; ut deducta effe in alienum
XV.　　" locum non irruiffe, atque ut voluntario non vi veniffe vi-
　　　" deatur *." How forced and obfcure, for inftance, are the
following verfes of Cowley, fpeaking of his miftrefs :

> Wo to her ftubborn heart, if once mine come
> 　　　Into the felf-fame room,
> 　　'Twill tear and blow up all within,
> Like a Granada, fhot into a magazine.
> Then fhall love keep the afhes and torn parts,
> 　　　Of both our broken hearts ;
> 　　Shall out of both one new one make ;
> From her's th' alloy, from mine the metal take ;
> For of her heart, he from the flames will find
> 　　　But little left behind ;
> 　　Mine only will remain entire,
> No drofs was there to perifh in the fire.

In this manner he addreffes fleep :

> In vain, thou drowfy God, I thee invoke,
> For thou who doft from fumes arife,
> Thou who man's foul doft overfhade,
> With a thick cloud by vapours made ;
> Canft have no power to fhut his eyes,
> Whofe flame's fo pure, that it fends up no fmoke.
> Yet how do tears but from fome vapours rife ?

---

* " Every Metaphor fhould be modeft, fo that it may carry the appearance
" of having been led, not of having forced itfelf into the place of that word
" whofe room it occupies ; that it may feem to have come thither of its own
" accord, and not by conftraint." De Oratore, L. III. c. 53.

Tears

Tears that bewinter all my year;
  The fate of Egypt I fuſtain,
  And never feel the dew of rain,
From clouds which in the head appear:
But all my too much moiſture owe
To overflowings of the heart below *.

Trite and common refemblances ſhould indeed be avoided in our Metaphors. To be new, and not vulgar, is a beauty. But when they are fetched from ſome likeneſs too remote, and lying too far out-of the road of ordinary thought, then, beſides their obſcurity, they have alſo the diſadvantage of appearing laboured, and, as the French call it, " recherché :" whereas Metaphor, like every other ornament, loſes its whole grace, when it does not ſeem natural and eaſy.

It is but a bad and ungraceful ſoftening, which writers ſometimes uſe for a harſh metaphor, when they palliate it with the expreſſion, *as it were.* This is but an awkward paren-theſis ; and Metaphors, which need this apology of an *as it were*, had, generally, be better omitted. Metaphors, too, borrowed from any of the ſciences, eſpecially ſuch of them as belong to particular profeſſions, are almoſt always faulty by their obſcurity.

In the fourth place, it muſt be carefully attended to, in the conduct of Metaphors, never to jumble metaphorical and plain language together ; never to conſtruct a period ſo, that part of

* See an excellent criticiſm on this ſort of metaphyſical poetry, in Dr. Johnſon's Life of Cowley.

it muſt be underſtood metaphorically, part literally : which always produces a moſt diſagreeable confuſion.　Inſtances, which are but too frequent, even in good authors, will make this rule, and the reaſon of it, be clearly underſtood.　In Mr. Pope's tranſlation of the Odyſſey, Penelope, bewailing the abrupt departure of her ſon Telemachus, is made to ſpeak thus:.

> Long to my joys my deareſt Lord is loſt,
> His country's buckler, and the Grecian boaſt;
> Now from my fond embrace by tempeſts torn,
> Our other column of the ſtate is borne,
> Nor took a kind adieu, nor ſought conſent *.　　　IV. 962.

Here, in one line, her ſon is figured as a column; and in the next, he returns to be a perſon, to whom it belongs to take adieu, and to aſk conſent.　This is inconſiſtent.　The Poet ſhould either have kept himſelf to the idea of a Man, in the literal ſenſe; or, if he figured him by a Column, he ſhould have aſcribed nothing to him but what belonged to it.　He was not at liberty to aſcribe to that Column the actions and properties of a Man.　Such unnatural mixtures render the image indiſtinct; leaving it to waver, in our conception, between the figurative and the literal ſenſe.　Horace's rule, which he

---

* In the original, there is no alluſion to a Column, and the metaphor is regularly ſupported :

Ἡ πριν μεν ποσιν ἐθλον απώλεσα θυμολεοντα
Παντοιης ἀρετῆσι κεκασμενον ἐν Δαναοισι
Εθλον, τȣ κλεος ἑυρυ καθ᾽ Ἑλλαδα και μεσον Ἀργος·
Νυν δ᾽αυ παιδ᾽ ἀγαπηΐον ανηρειψανΊο θυελλαι
Ἀκλεα ἐκ μεγαρων, ȣδ᾽ ὁρμηθενΊος ακȣσα.　　　Δ. 724.

applies

7

applies to Characters, should be observed by all writers who deal in Figures:

——Servetur ad imum,
Qualis ab incepto procefferit, et fibi conftet.

Mr. Pope, elfewhere, addreffing himfelf to the King, fays,

To thee the World its prefent homage pays,
The harveft early, but mature the praife.

This, though not fo grofs, is a fault, however, of the fame kind. It is plain, that, had not the rhyme mifled him to the choice of an improper phrafe, he would have faid,

The Harveft early, but mature the crop:

And fo would have continued the figure which he had begun. Whereas, by dropping it unfinifhed, and by employing the literal word, *praife*, when we were expecting fomething that related to the Harveft, the figure is broken, and the two members of the fentence have no proper correfpondence with each other:

The *Harveft* early, but mature the *Praife*.

The Works of Offian abound with beautiful and correct Metaphors; fuch as that on a Hero: " In peace, thou art the " Gate of Spring; in war, the Mountain Storm." Or this, on a Woman: " She was covered with the Light of Beauty; but " her heart was the Houfe of Pride." They afford, however, one inftance of the fault we are now cenfuring: " Trothal " went forth with the Stream of his people, but they met a

R r 2 " Rock:

" Rock: for Fingal ftood unmoved; broken they rolled back " from his fide. Nor did they roll in fafety; the fpear of the " King purfued their flight." At the beginning, the Metaphor is very beautiful.. The Stream, the unmoved Rock, the Waves rolling back broken, are expreffions employed in the proper and confiftent language of Figure; but, in the end, when we are told, " they did not roll in fafety, becaufe the fpear of the King " purfued their flight," the literal meaning is improperly mixed with the Metaphor: they are, at one and the fame time, prefented to us as *waves* that *roll*, and men that may be *purfued* and *wounded with a fpear*. If it be faulty to jumble together, in this manner, metaphorical and plain language, it is ftill more fo,

In the fifth place, to make two different Metaphors meet on one objeƈt. This is what is called mixed Metaphor, and is indeed one of the groffeft abufes of this figure; fuch as Shakepeare's expreffion, " to take arms againft a fea of troubles." This makes a moft unnatural medley, and confounds the imagination entirely. Quinƈtilian has fufficiently guarded us againft it. " Id imprimis eft cuftodiendum, ut quo genere " cœperis tranflationis, hoc finias. Multi autem cùm initium a " tempeftate fumferunt, incendio aut ruina finiunt; quæ eft in- " confequentia rerum fœdiffima *." Obferve, for inftance, what an inconfiftent groupe of objeƈts is brought together by Shakefpeare, in the following paffage of the Tempeft; fpeaking

* " We muft be particularly attentive to end with the fame kind of Meta- " phor with which we have begun. Some, when they begin the figure with " a Tempeft, conclude it with a conflagration; which forms a fhameful in- " confiftency." 8

of

of perfons recovering their judgment after the enchantment, which held them, was diffolved :

> ———— The charm diffolves apace,
> And as the morning fteals upon the night
> Melting the darknefs, fo their rifing fenfes
> Begin to chafe the ignorant fumes that mantle
> Their clearer reafon.————

So many ill-forted things are here joined, that the mind can fee nothing clearly ; the morning *ftealing* upon the darknefs, and at the fame time *melting* it ; the fenfes of men *chafing fumes*, *ignorant fumes*, and *fumes* that *mantle*. So again in Romeo and Juliet :

> ——— ——— ———as glorious,
> As is a winged meffenger from heaven,
> Unto the white upturned wondering eyes
> Of mortals, that fall back to gaze on him,
> When he beftrides the lazy pacing clouds,
> And fails upon the bofom of the air.

Here, the Angel is reprefented, as, at one moment, *beftriding* the clouds, and *failing* upon the air; and upon the *bofom* of the air too ; which forms fuch a confufed picture, that it is impoffible for any imagination to comprehend it.

MORE correct writers than Shakefpeare, fometimes fall into this error of mixing Metaphors. It is furprifing how the following inaccuracy fhould have efcaped Mr. Addifon, in his Letter from Italy :

I bridle

I bridle in my ſtruggling muſe with pain,
That longs to launch into a bolder ſtrain *.

The muſe, figured as a horſe, may be *bridled*; but when we ſpeak of *launching*, we make it a ſhip; and, by no force of imagination, can it be ſuppoſed both a horſe and a ſhip at one moment; *bridled*, to hinder it from *launching*. The ſame Author, in one of his numbers in the Spectator, ſays, " There " is not a ſingle view of human nature, which is not ſufficient " to extinguiſh the ſeeds of pride." Obſerve the incoherence of the things here joined together, making " a view extin- " guiſh, and extinguiſh ſeeds."

HORACE alſo, is incorrect, in the following paſſage:

Urit enim fulgore ſuo qui pregravat artes
Infra ſe poſitas.———— ——

Urit qui *pregravat*.—He dazzles who bears down with his weight; makes plainly an inconſiſtent mixture of metaphorical ideas. Neither can this other paſſage be altogether vindicated:

Ah! quantâ laboras in Charybdi,
Digne puer, meliore flammâ!

Where a whirlpool of water, Charybdis, is ſaid to be a flame, not good enough for this young man; meaning, that he was unfortunate in the object of his paſſion. Flame is, indeed,

* In my obſervation on this paſſage, I find, that I had coincided with Dr. Johnſon, who paſſes a ſimilar cenſure upon it, in his life of Addiſon.

become

become almoſt a literal word for the paſſion of love; but as it ſtill retains, in ſome degree, its figurative power, it ſhould never have been uſed as ſynonymous with water, and mixed with it in the ſame Metaphor. When Mr. Pope (Eloiſa to Abelard) ſays,

> All then is full, poſſeſſing and poſſeſt,
> No craving void left aking in the breaſt;

A *void* may, metaphorically, be ſaid to *crave*; but can a void be ſaid to *ake* ?

A GOOD rule has been given for examining the propriety of Metaphors, when we doubt whether or not they be of the mixed kind; namely, that we ſhould try to form a picture upon them, and conſider how the parts would agree, and what ſort of figure the whole would preſent, when delineated with a pencil. By this means, we ſhould become ſenſible, whether inconſiſtent circumſtances were mixed, and a monſtrous image thereby produced, as in all thoſe faulty inſtances, I have now been giving; or whether the object was, all along, preſented in one natural and conſiſtent point of view.

As Metaphors ought never to be mixed, ſo, in the ſixth place, we ſhould avoid crowding them together on the ſame object. Suppoſing each of the Metaphors to be preſerved diſtinct, yet, if they be heaped on one another, they produce a confuſion ſomewhat of the ſame kind with the mixed Metaphor. We may judge of this by the following paſſage from Horace :

Motum

Motum ex Metello confule civicum,
Bellique caufas, et vitia, et modos,
Ludumque fortunæ, gravefque
Principum amicitias, & arma
Nondum expiatis uncta cruoribus,
Periculofæ plenum opus aleæ,
Tractas, et incedis per ignes
Suppofitos cineri dolofo *.　　　　　Lib. 2. I.

This paffage, though very poetical, is, however, harfh and obfcure; owing to no other caufe but this, that three diftinct Metaphors are crowded together, to defcribe the difficulty of Pollio's writing a hiftory of the civil wars. Firft, " Tractas " arma uncta cruoribus nondum expiatis;" next, " Opus " plenum periculofæ aleæ;" and then; " Incedis per ignes " fuppofitos dolofo cineri." The mind has difficulty in paffing readily through fo many different views given it, in quick fucceffion, of the fame object.

THE only other rule concerning Metaphors which I fhall add, in the feventh place, is, that they be not too far purfued.

* Of warm commotions, wrathful jars,
　The growing feeds of civil wars;
　Of double fortune's cruel games,
　The fpecious means, the private aims,
And fatal friendfhips of the guilty great,
Alas! how fatal to the Roman ftate!
　Of mighty legions late fubdued,
　And arms with Latian blood embru'd;
　Yet unatoned (a labour vaft!
　Doubtful the die, and dire the caft!)
　You treat adventurous, and incautious tread,
On fires with faithlefs embers overfpread.
　　　　　　　　　　　　　　　　FRANCIS.

If

If the refemblance, on which the figure is founded, be long dwelt upon, and carried into all its minute circumftances, we make an allegory inftead of a metaphor; we tire the reader, who foon wearies of this play of fancy; and we render our difcourfe obfcure. This is called, ftraining a Metaphor. Cowley deals in this to excefs; and to this error is owing, in a great meafure, that intricacy and harfhnefs, in his figurative Language, which I before remarked. Lord Shaftfbury, is fometimes guilty of purfuing his Metaphors too far. Fond, to a high degree, of every decoration of ftyle, when once he had hit upon a figure that pleafed him, he was extremely loth to part with it. Thus, in his advice to an author, having taken up foliloquy, or meditation, under the Metaphor of a proper method of evacuation for an author, he purfues this Metaphor through feveral pages, under all the forms " of difcharging " crudities, throwing off froth and fcum, bodily operation, " taking phyfic, curing-indigeftion, giving vent to choler, bile, " flatulencies, and tumours;" till at laft, the idea becomes naufeous. Dr. Young alfo often trefpaffes in the fame way. The merit, however, of this writer, in figurative Language, is great, and deferves to be remarked. No writer, antient or modern, had a ftronger imagination than Dr. Young, or one more fertile in figures of every kind. His Metaphors are often new, and often natural and beautiful. But, as his imagination was ftrong and rich, rather than delicate and correct, he fometimes gives it too loofe reins. Hence, in his Night Thoughts, there prevails an obfcurity, and a hardnefs in his ftyle. The Metaphors are frequently too bold, and frequently too far purfued; the reader is dazzled rather than enlightened; and kept conftantly on the ftretch to comprehend, and keep pace with,

L E C T. the author.   We may obferve, for inftance, how the following
  XV.   Metaphor is fpun out:

> Thy thoughts are vagabonds; all outward bound,
> Midft fands and rocks, and ftorms, to cruife for pleafure,
> If gained, dear bought; and better mifs'd than gain'd.
> Fancy and fenfe, from an infeded fhore,
> Thy cargo brings; and peftilence the prize;
> Then fuch the thirft, infatiable thirft,
> By fond indulgence but inflam'd the more,
> Fancy ftill cruizes, when poor fenfe is tired.

Speaking of old age, he fays, it fhould

> Walk thoughtful on the filent folomn fhore
> Of that vaft ocean, it muft fail fo foon;
> And put good works on board; and wait the wind
> That fhortly blows us into worlds unknown.

THE two firft lines are uncommonly beautiful; " walk
" thoughtful on the filent, &c." but when he continues the
Metaphor, " to putting good works on board, and waiting the
" wind," it plainly becomes ftrained, and finks in dignity.
Of all the Englifh authors, I know none fo happy in his Metaphors as Mr. Addifon.   His imagination was neither fo rich
nor fo ftrong as Dr. Young's; but far more chafte and delicate.
Perfpicuity, natural grace and eafe, always diftinguifh his figures.
They are neither harfh nor ftrained; they never appear to have
been ftudied or fought after; but feem to rife of their own accord from the fubjed, and conftantly embellifh it.

I HAVE

I HAVE now treated fully of the Metaphor, and the rules that fhould govern it, a part of the doctrine of ftyle fo important, that it required particular illuftration. I have only to add a few words concerning Allegory.

AN Allegory may be regarded as a continued Metaphor; as it is the reprefentation of fome one thing by another that refembles it, and that is made to ftand for it. Thus, in Prior's Henry and Emma, Emma in the following allegorical manner defcribes her conftancy to Henry :

> Did I but purpofe to embark with thee
> On the fmooth furface of a fummer's fea,
> While gentle zephyrs play with profperous gales,
> And fortune's favour fills the fwelling fails ;
> But would forfake the fhip, and make the fhore,
> When the winds whiftle, and the tempefts roar ?

WE may take alfo from the Scriptures a very fine example of an Allegory, in the 80th Pfalm ; where the people of Ifrael are reprefented under the image of a vine, and the figure is fupported throughout with great correctnefs and beauty : " Thou " haft brought a vine out of Egypt, thou haft caft out the " heathen, and planted it. Thou preparedft room before it, " and didft caufe it to take deep root, and it filled the land. " The hills were covered with the fhadow of it ; and the " boughs thereof were like the goodly cedars. She fent out " her boughs into the fea, and her branches into the river. " Why haft thou broken down her hedges, fo that all they " which pafs by the way do pluck her ? The boar out of the " wood doth wafte it ; and the wild beaft of the field doth

" devour

" devour it.   Return, we befeech thee, O God of Hofts, look
" down from Heaven, and behold, and vifit this vine !"   Here
there is no circumftance (except perhaps one phrafe at the beginning, " thou haft caft out the heathen,") that does not
ftrictly agree to a vine, whilft, at the fame time, the whole
quadrates happily with the Jewifh ftate reprefented by
this figure. This is the firft and principal requifite in the
conduct of an Allegory, that the figurative and the literal
meaning be not mixed inconfiftently together.   For inftance,
inftead of defcribing the vine, as wafted by the boar from
the wood, and devoured by the wild beaft of the field, had
the Pfalmift faid, it was afflicted by heathens, or overcome
by enemies (which is the real meaning), this would have
ruined the Allegory, and produced the fame confufion, of which
I gave examples in Metaphors, when the figurative and literal
fenfe are mixed and jumbled together.   Indeed, the fame rules
that were given for Metaphors, may alfo be applied to Allegories, on account of the affinity they bear to each other.   The
only material difference between them, befides the one being
fhort, and the other being prolonged, is, that a Metaphor always explains itfelf by the words that are connected with it in
their proper and natural meaning; as when I fay, " Achilles
" was a Lion;" an " able Minifter is the Pillar of the State."
My Lion and my Pillar are fufficiently interpreted by the mention of Achilles and the Minifter, which I join to them; but
an Allegory is, or may be, allowed to ftand more difconnected
with the literal meaning; the interpretation not fo directly
pointed out, but left to our own reflection.

ALLE-

ALLEGORIES were a favourite method of delivering inftruc-
tions in ancient times ; for what we call Fables or Parables are
no other than Allegories ; where, by words and actions attributed to beafts or inanimate objects, the difpofitions of men are
figured ; and what we call the moral, is the unfigured fenfe or
meaning of the Allegory. An Ænigma or Riddle is alfo a
fpecies of Allegory ; one thing reprefented or imaged by
another ; but purpofely wrapt up under fo many circumftances,
as to be rendered obfcure. Where a riddle is not intended,
it is always a fault in Allegory to be too dark. The meaning
fhould be eafily feen through the figure employed to fhadow it.
However the proper mixture of light and fhade in fuch compofitions, the exact adjuftment of all the figurative circum-
ftances-with the literal fenfe, fo as neither to lay the meaning
too bare and open, nor to cover and wrap it up too much, has
ever been found an affair of great nicety ; and there are few
fpecies of compofition in which it is more difficult to write
fo as to pleafe and command attention, than in Allegories. In
fome of the vifions of the Spectator, we have examples of Allegories very happily executed.

LECTURE XVI.

HYPERBOLE——PERSONIFICATION——APOSTROPHE.

THE next figure concerning which I am to treat, is called Hyperbole, or Exaggeration. It confifts in magnifying an object beyond its natural bounds. It may be confidered fometimes as a trope, and fometimes as a figure of thought: and here indeed the diftinction between thefe two claffes begins not to be clear, nor is it of any importance that we fhould have recourfe to metaphyfical fubtilties, in order to keep them diftinct. Whether we call it trope or figure, it is plain that it is a mode of fpeech which hath fome foundation in nature. For in all languages, even in common converfation, hyperbolical expreffions very frequently occur; as fwift as the wind; as white as the fnow, and the like; and our common forms of compliment are almoft all of them extravagant Hyperboles. If any thing be remarkably good or great in its kind, we are inftantly ready to add to it fome exaggerating epithet; and to make it the greateft or beft we ever faw. The imagination has always a

4

tendency

tendency to gratify itfelf, by magnifying its prefent object, and L E C T.
XVI. carrying it to excefs. More or lefs of this hyperbolical turn will prevail in language, according to the livelinefs of imagination among the people who fpeak it. Hence young people deal always much in Hyperboles. Hence the language of the Orientals was far more hyperbolical than that of the Europeans, who are of more phlegmatic, or, if you pleafe, of more correct imagination. Hence, among all writers in early times, and in the rude periods of fociety, we may expect this figure to abound. Greater experience, and more cultivated fociety, abate the warmth of imagination, and chaften the manner of expreffion.

THE exaggerated expreffions to which our ears are accuftomed in converfation, fcarcely ftrike us as Hyperboles. In an inftant we make the proper abatement, and underftand them according to their juft value. But when there is fomething ftriking and unufual in the form of a hyperbolical expreffion, it then rifes into a figure of fpeech which draws our attention : and here it is neceffary to obferve, that unlefs the reader's imagination be in fuch a ftate as difpofes it to rife and fwell along with the hyperbolical expreffion, he is always hurt and offended by it. For a fort of difagreeable force is put upon him ; he is required to ftrain and exert his fancy, when he feels no inclination to make any fuch effort. Hence the Hyperbole is a figure of difficult management ; and ought neither to be frequently ufed, nor long dwelt upon. On fome occafions, it is undoubtedly proper; being, as was before obferved, the natural ftyle of a fprightly and heated imagination, but when Hyperboles are unfeafonable, or too frequent, they render a compofi-

tion

tion frigid and unaffecting. They are the refource of an author of feeble imagination; of one, defcribing objects which either want native dignity in themfelves; or whofe dignity he cannot fhow by defcribing them fimply, and in their juft proportions, and is therefore obliged to reft upon tumid and exaggerated expreffions.

HYPERBOLES are of two kinds; either fuch as are employed in defcription, or fuch as are fuggefted by the warmth of paffion. The beft by far, are thofe which are the effect of paffion: for if the imagination has a tendency to magnify its objects beyond their natural proportion, paffion poffeffes this tendency in a vaftly ftronger degree; and therefore not only excufes the moft daring figures, but very often renders them natural and juft. All paffions, without exception, love, terror, amazement, indignation, anger, and even grief, throw the mind into confufion, aggravate their objects, and of courfe prompt a hyperbolical ftyle. Hence the following fentiments of Satan in Milton, as ftrongly as they are defcribed, contain nothing but what is natural and proper; exhibiting the picture of a mind agitated with rage and defpair:

> Me miferable! which way fhall I flie
> Infinite wrath, and infinite defpair?
> Which way 1 flie is Hell, myfelf am Hell;
> And in the loweft depth, a lower deep
> Still threat'ning to devour me, opens wide,
> To which the Hell I fuffer feems a Heaven.

B. iv. l. 73.

IN fimple defcription, though Hyperboles are not excluded, yet they muft be ufed with more caution, and require more

I　　　　　　　　　　　　　　　　preparation,

preparation, in order to make the mind relifh them. Either the object defcribed muft be of that kind, which of itfelf feizes the fancy ftrongly, and difpofes it to run beyond bounds; fomething vaft, furprifing, and new; or the writer's art muft be exerted in heating the fancy gradually, and preparing it to think highly of the object which he intends to exaggerate. When a Poet is defcribing an earthquake or a ftorm, or when he has brought us into the midft of a battle, we can bear ftrong Hyperboles without difpleafure. But when he is defcribing only a woman in grief, it is impoffible not to be difgufted with fuch wild exaggeration as the following, in one of our dramatic Poets:

————— I found her on the floor
In all the ftorm of grief, yet beautiful;
Pouring forth tears at fuch a lavifh rate,
That were the world on fire, they might have drown'd
The wrath of Heaven, and quench'd the mighty ruin.

LEE.

THIS is mere bombaft. The perfon herfelf who was under the diftracting agitations of grief, might be permitted to hyperbolize ftrongly; but the fpectator defcribing her, cannot be allowed an equal liberty: for this plain reafon, that the one is fuppofed to utter the fentiments of paffion, the other fpeaks only the language of defcription, which is always, according to the dictates of nature, on a lower tone: a diftinction, which however obvious, has not been attended to by many writers.

How far a Hyperbole, fuppofing it properly introduced, may be fafely carried without overftretching it; what is the

proper meafure and boundary of this figure, cannot, as far as I
know, be afcertained by any precife rule.   Good fenfe and juft
tafte muft determine the point, beyond which, if we pafs, we
become extravagant.   Lucan may be pointed out as an author
apt to be exceffive in his Hyperboles.   Among the compliments paid by the Roman Poets to their Emperors, it had become fafhionable to afk them, what part of the heavens they
would chufe for their habitation, after they fhould have become
Gods ? Virgil had already carried this fufficiently far in his
addrefs to Auguftus :

———— Tibi brachia contrahit ingens
Scorpius, & Cœli jufta plus parte relinquit *."   GEOR. I.

But this did not fuffice Lucan.   Refolved to outdo all his pre-
deceffors, in a like addrefs to Nero, he very gravely befeeches
him not to choofe his place near either of the poles, but to be
fure to occupy juft the middle of the heavens, left, by going
either to one fide or other, his weight fhould overfet the univerfe :

Sed neque in Arctoo fedem tibi legeris orbe
Nec polus adverfi calidus qua mergitur auftri ;
Ætheris immenfi partem fi prefferis unam
Sentiet axis onus.   Librati pondera Cœli
Orbe tene medio † .————   PHARS. I. 53.

Such

---

* " The Scorpion ready to receive thy laws,
  " Yields half his region, and contracts his paws."   DRYDEN.

† But, oh ! whatever be thy Godhead great,
  Fix not in regions too remote thy feat ;

Nor

Such thoughts as these, are what the French call *outrés*, and always proceed from a false fire of genius. The Spanish and African writers, as Tertullian, Cyprian, Augustin, are remarked for being fond of them. As in that epitaph on Charles V. by a Spanish writer :

> Pro tumulo ponas orbem, pro tegmine cœlum,
> Sidera pro facibus, pro lacrymis maria.

Sometimes they dazzle and impose by their boldness; but wherever reason and good sense are so much violated, there can be no true beauty. Epigrammatic writers are frequently guilty in this respect; resting the whole merit of their epigrams on some extravagant hyperbolical turn; such as the following of Dr. Pitcairn's, upon Holland's being gained from the ocean :

> Tellurem fecere Dii; sua littora Belgæ;
>   Immensæque molis opus utrumque fuit;
> Dii vacuo sparsas glomerarunt æthere terras,
>   Nil ibi quod operi possit obesse fuit.
> At Belgis, maria & cœli naturaque rerum
>   Obstitit; obstantes hi domuêre Deos.

> Nor deign thou near the frozen Bear to shine,
> Nor where the sultry southern stars decline.
> Press not too much on any part the sphere,
> Hard were the task thy weight divine to bear ;
> Soon would the axis feel the unusual load,
> And, groaning, bend beneath th' incumbent God ;
> O'er the mid orb more equal shalt thou rise,
> And with a juster balance fix the skies.   Rowe.

L E C T.   So much for the Hyperbole.   We proceed now to thofe figures
   XVI.   which lie altogether in the thought; where the words are taken
            in their common and literal fenfe.

AMONG thefe, the firft place is unqueftionably due to Perfonification, or that figure by which we attribute life and action
to inanimate objects. The technical term for this is Profopopoia;
but as Perfonification is of the fame import, and more allied to
our own language, it will be better to ufe this word.

IT is a figure, the ufe of which is very extenfive, and its
foundation laid deep in human nature. At firft view, and
when confidered abftractly, it would appear to be a figure of
the utmoft boldnefs, and to border on the extravagant and ridiculous.   For what can feem more remote from the tract of
reafonable thought, than to fpeak of ftones and trees, and fields
and rivers, as if they were living creatures, and to attribute to
them thought and fenfation, affections and actions ? One might
imagine this to be no more than childifh conceit, which no
perfon of tafte could relifh.   In fact, however, the cafe is very
different.   No fuch ridiculous effect is produced by Perfonification, when properly employed ; on the contrary, it is found to
be natural and agreeable ; nor is any very uncommon degree of
paffion required, in order to make us relifh it.   All poetry,
even in its moft gentle and humble forms, abounds with it.
From profe, it is far from being excluded ; nay, in common
converfation, very frequent approaches are made to it.   When
we fay, the ground *thirfts* for rain, or the earth *fmiles* with
plenty ; when we fpeak of ambitions being *reftlefs*, or a difeafe
being *deceitful*, fuch expreffions fhow the facility with which
                                                              the

the mind can accommodate the properties of living creatures to things that are inanimate, or to abſtract conceptions of its own forming.

INDEED, it is very remarkable, that there is a wonderful proneneſs in human nature to animate all objects. Whether this ariſes from a ſort of aſſimilating principle, from a pro-penſion to ſpread a reſemblance of ourſelves over all other things, or from whatever other cauſe it ariſes, ſo it is, that almoſt every emotion, which in the leaſt agitates the mind, beſtows upon its object a momentary idea of life. Let a man, by an unwary ſtep, ſprain his ankle, or hurt his foot upon a ſtone, and, in the ruffled diſcompoſed moment, he will, ſome-times, feel himſelf diſpoſed to break the ſtone in pieces, or to utter paſſionate expreſſions againſt it, as if it had done him an injury. If one has been long accuſtomed to a certain ſet of objects, which have made a ſtrong impreſſion on his imagina-tion ; as to a houſe, where he has paſſed many agreeable years ; or to fields, and trees, and mountains, among which he has often walked with the greateſt delight ; when he is obliged to part with them, eſpecially if he has no proſpect of ever ſeeing them again, he can ſcarce avoid having ſomewhat of the ſame feeling as when he is leaving old friends. They ſeem endowed with life. They become objects of his affection ; and, in the moment of his parting, it ſcarce ſeems abſurd to him, to give vent to his feeling in words, and to take a formal adieu.

So ſtrong is that impreſſion of life which is made upon us, by the more magnificent and ſtriking objects of nature eſpe-cially, that I doubt not, in the leaſt, of this having been one

cauſe

caufe of the multiplication of divinities in the Heathen world. Dryads and Naiads, the Genius of the wood, and the God of the river, were, in men of lively imaginations, in the early ages of the world, eafily grafted upon this turn of mind. When their favourite rural objects had often been animated in their fancy, it was an eafy tranfition to attribute to them fome real divinity, fome unfeen power or genius which inhabited them, or in fome peculiar manner belonged to them. Imagination was highly gratified, by thus gaining fomewhat to reft upon with more ftability; and when belief coincided fo much with imagination, very flight caufes would be fufficient to eftablifh it.

FROM this deduction, may be eafily feen how it comes to pafs, that perfonification makes fo great a figure in all compofitions, where imagination or paffion have any concern. On innumerable occafions, it is the very Language of imagination and paffion, and, therefore, deferves to be attended to, and examined with peculiar care. There are three different degrees of this figure; which it is neceffary to remark and diftinguifh, in order to determine the propriety of its ufe. The firft is, when fome of the properties or qualities of living creatures are afcribed to inanimate objects; the fecond, when thofe inanimate objects are introduced as acting like fuch as have life; and the third, when they are reprefented, either as fpeaking to us, or as liftening to what we fay to them.

THE firft, and loweft degree of this figure, confifts in afcribing to inanimate objects fome of the qualities of living creatures. Where this is done, as is moft commonly the cafe, in a

word,

word, or two, and by way of an epithet added to the object, as, " a raging ftorm, a deceitful difeafe, a cruel difafter," &c. it raifes the ftyle fo little, that the humbleft difcourfe will admit it without any force. This, indeed, is fuch an obfcure degree of Perfonification; that one may doubt whether it deferves the name, and might not be claffed with fimple Metaphors, which efcape in a manner unnoticed. Happily employed, however, it fometimes adds beauty and fprightlinefs to an expreffion; as in this line of Virgil:

Aut conjurato defcendens Dacus ab Iftro. Geor. II. 474.

Where the perfonal epithet, *conjurato*, applied to the river *Iftro*, is infinitely more poetical than if it had been applied to the perfon, thus:

Aut conjuratus defcendens Dacus ab Iftro.

A very little tafte will make any one feel the difference between thefe two lines.

THE next degree of this figure is, when we introduce in-animate objects acting like thofe that have life. Here we rife a ftep higher, and the Perfonification becomes fenfible. Ac-cording to the nature of the action, which we attribute to thofe inanimate objects, and the particularity with which we defcribe it, fuch is the ftrength of the figure. When purfued to any length, it belongs only to ftudied harangues, to highly figured and elo-quent difcourfe; when flightly touched, it may be admitted into fubjects of lefs elevation. Cicero, for inftance, fpeaking of the cafes where killing another is lawful in felf-defence,

I

ufes the following words : " Aliquando nobis gladius ad occi-
" dendum hominem ab ipfis porrigitur legibus." (Orat. pro
Milone.) The expreffion is happy. The laws are perfonified,
as reaching forth their hand to give us a fword for putting one
to death. Such fhort perfonifications as thefe may be admitted,
even into moral treatifes, or works of cool reafoning; and,
provided they be eafy and not ftrained, and that we be not cloyed
with too frequent returns of them, they have a good effect on
ftyle, and render it both ftrong and lively.

THE genius of our Language gives us an advantage in the
ufe of this figure. As, with us, no fubftantive nouns have
gender, or are mafculine and feminine, except the proper
names of male and female creatures; by giving a gender to any
inanimate object, or abftract idea, that is, in place of the pronoun *it*, ufing the perfonal pronouns, *he* or *fhe*, we prefently
raife the ftyle, and begin perfonification. In folemn difcourfe,
this can often be done to good purpofe, when fpeaking of religion, or virtue, or our country, or any fuch object of dignity.
I fhall give a remarkably fine example, from a fermon of
Bifhop Sherlock's, where we fhall fee natural religion beautifully
perfonified, and be able to judge from it, of the fpirit and
grace which this figure, when well conducted, beftows on a
difcourfe. I muft take notice, at the fame time, that it is an
inftance of this figure, carried as far as profe, even in its higheft
elevation, will admit, and, therefore, fuited only to compofitions where the great efforts of eloquence are allowed. The
Author is comparing together our Saviour and Mahomet :
" Go," fays he, " to your natural Religion; lay before her
" Mahomet, and his difciples, arrayed in armour and blood,
" riding

" riding in triumph over the spoils of thousands who fell by
" his victorious sword. Shew her the cities which he set in
" flames, the countries which he ravaged and destroyed, and
" the miserable distress of all the inhabitants of the earth.
" When she has viewed him in this scene, carry her into his
" retirement ; shew her the Prophet's chamber ; his concubines
" and his wives ; and let her hear him allege revelation, and
" a divine commission, to justify his adultery and lust. When
" she is tired with this prospect, then shew her the blessed
" Jesus, humble and meek, doing good to all the sons of men.
" Let her see him in his most retired privacies ; let her follow
" him to the mount, and hear his devotions and supplica-
" tions to God. Carry her to his table, to view his poor
" fare ; and hear his heavenly discourse. Let her attend him
" to the tribunal, and consider the patience with which he
" endured the scoffs and reproaches of his enemies. Lead her
" to his cross ; let her view him in the agony of death, and
" hear his last prayer for his persecutors ; *Father, forgive*
" *them, for they know not what they do!*—When Na-
" tural Religion has thus viewed both, ask her, Which is the
" Prophet of God ? But her answer we have already had,
" when she saw part of this scene, through the eyes of the
" Centurion, who attended at the cross. By him she spoke,
" and said, *Truly, this Man was the Son of God**." This is
more than elegant ; it is truly sublime. The whole passage is
animated ; and the figure rises at the conclusion, when Natural
Religion, who, before, was only a spectator, is introduced as
speaking by the Centurion's voice. It has the better effect too,

---

* Bishop Sherlock's Sermons, Vol. I. Disc. ix.

that it occurs at the conclusion of a discourse, where we naturally look for most warmth and dignity. Did Bishop Sherlock's
sermons, or, indeed, any English sermons whatever, afford us
many passages equal to this, we should oftner have recourse to
them for instances of the beauty of Composition.

HITHERTO we have spoken of prose; in poetry, Personifications of this kind are extremely frequent, and are, indeed, the
life and soul of it. We expect to find every thing animated
in the descriptions of a poet who has a lively fancy. Accordingly Homer, the father and prince of poets, is remarkable
for the use of this figure. War, peace, darts, spears, towns,
rivers, every thing, in short, is alive in his writings. The
same is the case with Milton and Shakespeare. No Personification, in any author, is more striking, or introduced on a
more proper occasion, than the following of Milton's, on occasion of Eve's eating the forbidden fruit:

> So saying, her rash hand, in evil hour
> Forth reaching to the fruit, she pluck'd, she eat;
> Earth felt the wound; and nature, from her seat
> Sighing, through all her works, gave signs of woe,
> That all was lost.————　　　　　　　ix. 780.

All the circumstances and ages of men, poverty, riches, youth,
old age, all the dispositions and passions, melancholy, love,
grief, contentment, are capable of being personified in poetry,
with great propriety. Of this, we meet with frequent examples
in Milton's Allegro and Penserofo, Parnell's Hymn to Contentment, Thomson's Seasons, and all the good poets: nor,
indeed, is it easy to set any bounds to Personifications of this
kind, in poetry.

ONE

ONE of the greateſt pleaſures we receive from poetry, is, to find ourſelves always in the midſt of our fellows ; and to ſee every thing thinking, feeling, and acting, as we ourſelves do. This is, perhaps, the principal charm of this ſort of figured ſtyle, that it introduces us into ſociety with all nature, and intereſts us, even in inanimate objects, by forming a connection between them and us, through that ſenſibility which it aſcribes to them.   This is exemplified in the following beautiful paſſage of Thomſon's Summer, wherein the life which he beſtows upon all nature, when deſcribing the effects of the riſing ſun, renders the ſcenery uncommonly gay and intereſting :

> But yonder comes the powerful king of day
> Rejoicing in the eaſt.   The leſſening cloud,
> The kindling azure, and the mountain's brim
> Tipt with æthereal gold, his near approach
> Betoken glad. ——— ———
> ——————By thee refined,
> In briſker meaſures, the relucent ſtream
> Friſks o'er the mead.   The precipice abrupt,
> Projecting horror on the blacken'd flood,
> Softens at thy return.   The deſart joys,
> Wildly, through all his melancholy bounds.
> Rude ruins glitter ; and the briny deep,
> Seen from ſome pointed promontory's top,
> Reflects from every fluctuating wave,
> A glance extenſive as the day.——

The ſame effect is remarkable in that fine paſſage of Milton :

> —————To the nuptial bower,
> I led her bluſhing like the morn.   All heaven

And

And happy conftellations, on that hour,
Shed their felecteft influence.   The earth
Gave figns of gratulation, and each hill.
Joyous the birds; frefh gales, and gentle airs
Whifpered it to the woods, and from their wings
Flung rofe, flung odour from the fpicy fhrub,
Difporting.————

THE third and higheft degree of this figure remains to be
mentioned, when inanimate objects are introduced, not only as
feeling and acting, but as fpeaking to us, or hearing and liftening when we addrefs ourfelves to them.   This, though on
feveral occafions far from being unnatural, is, however, more
difficult in the execution, than the other kinds of Perfonification.   For this is plainly the boldeft of all rhetorical figures;
it is the ftyle of ftrong paffion only; and, therefore, never to be
attempted, unlefs when the mind is confiderably heated and
agitated.   A flight Perfonification of fome inanimate thing,
acting as if it had life, can be relifhed by the mind, in the midft
of cool defcription, and when its ideas are going on in the
ordinary train.   But it muft be in a ftate of violent emotion,
and have departed confiderably from its common tract of
thought, before it can fo far realife the Perfonification of an infenfible object, as to conceive it liftening to what we fay, or
making any return to us.   All ftrong paffions, however, have
a tendency to ufe this figure; not only love, anger, and indignation, but even thofe which are feemingly more difpiriting,
fuch as, grief, remorfe, and melancholy.   For all paffions
ftruggle for vent, and if they can find no other object, will,
rather than be filent, pour themfelves forth to woods, and
rocks, and the moft infenfible things; efpecially, if thefe be

any

any how connected with the caufes and objects that have thrown the mind into this agitation. Hence, in poetry, where the greateft liberty is allowed to the Language of paffion, it is eafy to produce many beautiful examples of this figure. Milton affords us an extremely fine one, in that moving and tender addrefs which Eve makes to Paradife, juft before fhe is compelled to leave it.

> Oh! unexpected ftroke, worfe than of death!
> Muft I thus leave thee, Paradife! thus leave
> Thee, native foil, thefe happy walks, and fhades,
> Fit haunt of Gods! where I had hope to fpend
> Quiet, though fad, the refpite of that day,
> Which muft be mortal to us both. O flowers!
> That never will in other climate grow,
> My early vifitation, and my laft
> At ev'n, which I bred up with tender hand,
> From your firft op'ning buds, and gave you names!
> Who now fhall rear you to the fun, or rank
> Your tribes, and water from th' ambrofial fount?
>
> Book II. l. 268.

This is altogether the language of nature, and of female paffion. It is obfervable, that all plaintive paffions are peculiarly prone to the ufe of this figure. The complaints which Philoctetes, in Sophocles, pours out to the rocks and caves of Lemnos, amidft the excefs of his grief and defpair, are remarkably fine examples of it *. And there are frequent examples, not in

poetry

---

* Ὦ λιμενες, ἀ προϐλητες, ω᾿ ξυνουσιαι
Θηρων ορειων, ω᾿ καταρῥωγες πετραι
Ὑμιν ταδ᾿· ἒ γαρ αλλον ὃιδ᾿ ὁτω λεγω·
Ἀνακλαιομαι παρασι τοις ειωθεσιν, &c.

O mountains,

poetry only, but in real life, of perfons, when juft about to fuffer death, taking a paffionate farewel of the fun, moon, and ftars, or other fenfible objects around them.

THERE are two great rules for the management of this fort of Perfonification. The firft rule is, never to attempt it, unlefs when prompted by ftrong paffion, and never to continue it when the paffion begins to flag. It is one of thofe high ornaments, which can only find place in the moft warm and fpirited parts of compofition; and there, too, muft be employed with moderation.

THE fecond rule is, never to perfonify any object in this way, but fuch as has fome dignity in itfelf, and can make a proper figure in this elevation to which we raife it. The obfervance of this rule is required, even in the lower degrees of Perfonification; but ftill more, when an addrefs is made to the perfonified object. To addrefs the corpfe of a deceafed friend, is natural; but to addrefs the clothes which he wore, introduces mean and degrading ideas. So alfo, addreffing the feveral parts of one's body, as if they were animated, is not congruous to the dignity of paffion. For this reafon, I muft condemn the following paffage, in a very beautiful Poem of Mr. Pope's, Eloifa to Abelard.

" O mountains, rivers, rocks, and favage herds,
" To you I fpeak! to you alone, I now
" Muft breathe my forrows! you are wont to hear
" My fad complaints, and I will tell you all
" That I have fuffered from Achilles' fon!"

FRANKLIN.

Dear

Dear fatal name ! reſt ever unreveal'd,
Nor paſs theſe lips in holy ſilence ſealed.
Hide it, my heart, within that cloſe diſguiſe,
Where, mixed with Gods, his lov'd idea lies :
Oh ! write it not, my hand !—his name appears
Already written—Blot it out, my tears !

Here are ſeveral different objects and parts of the body perſonified ; and each of them are addreſſed or ſpoken to ; let us
conſider with what propriety. The firſt is, the name of Abelard : " Dear fatal name ! reſt ever," &c. To this, no reaſon-
able objection can be made. For, as the name of a perſon
often ſtands for the perſon himſelf, and ſuggeſts the ſame ideas,
it can bear this Perſonification with ſufficient dignity. Next,
Eloiſa ſpeaks to herſelf ; and perſonifies her heart for this purpoſe : " Hide it, my heart, within that cloſe," &c. As the
heart is a dignified part of the human frame, and is often put
for the mind, or affections, this alſo may paſs without blame.
But, when from her heart ſhe paſſes to her hand, and tells her
hand not to write his name, this is forced and unnatural ; a
perſonified hand is low, and not in the ſtyle of true paſſion :
and the figure becomes ſtill worſe, when, in the laſt place, ſhe
exhorts her tears to blot out what her hand had written :
" Oh ! write it not," &c. There is, in theſe two lines, an air
of epigrammatic conceit, which native paſſion never ſuggeſts ;
and which is altogether unſuitable to the tenderneſs which
breathes through the reſt of that excellent Poem.

In proſe compoſitions, this figure requires to be uſed with
ſtill greater moderation and delicacy. The ſame liberty is not

7   allowed

allowed to the imagination there, as in poetry. The fame affiftances cannot be obtained for raifing paffion to its proper height
by the force of numbers, and the glow of ftyle.   However,
addreffes to inanimate objects are not excluded from profe; but
have their place only in the higher fpecies of oratory.   A public Speaker may on fome occafions very properly addrefs religion
      virtue; or his native country, or fome city or province,
which has fuffered perhaps great calamities, or been the fcene of
fome memorable action.   But we muft remember, that as fuch
addreffes are among the higheft efforts of eloquence, they fhould
never be attempted, unlefs by perfons of more than ordinary
genius.   For if the orator fails in his defign of moving our paffions by them, he is fure of being laughed at. Of all frigid things,
the moft frigid, are the awkward and unfeafonable attempts
fometimes made towards fuch kinds of Perfonification, efpecially
if they be long continued.   We fee the writer or fpeaker toil-
ing, and labouring, to exprefs the language of fome paffion,
which he neither feels himfelf, nor can make us feel.   We remain not only cold, but frozen; and are at full leifure to criticife on the ridiculous figure which the perfonified object makes,
when we ought to have been tranfported with a glow of enthufiafm.   Some of the French writers, particularly Boffuet and
Flechier, in their fermons and funeral orations, have attempted
and executed this figure, not without warmth and dignity.
Their works are exceedingly worthy of being confulted, for
inftances of this, and of feveral other ornaments of ftyle.   Indeed the vivacity and ardour of the French genius is more fuited
to this animated kind of oratory, than the more correct but
more phlegmatic genius of the Britifh, who in their profe works

I   very

very rarely attempt any of the high figures of eloquence *. So much for Perfonifications or Profopopœia, in all its different forms.

* In the " Oraifons Funebres de M. Boffuet," which I confider as one of the mafter-pieces of modern eloquence, Apoftrophes and addreffes, to perfonified objects, frequently occur, and are fupported with much fpirit. Thus, for in-ftance, in the funeral oration of Mary of Auftria, Queen of France, the author addreffes Algiers, in the profpect of the advantage which the arms of Louis XIV. were to gain over it : " Avant lui la France, prefque fans vaiffeaux, tenoit en " vain aux deux mers. Maintenant, on les voit couvertes depuis le Levant " jufqu'au couchant de nos flottes victorieufes; & la hardieffe Françoife port " par tout la terreur avec le nom de Louis. Tu cederas, tu tomberas fous ce " vainqueur, Alger! riche des depouilles de la Chretienté. Tu difois en ton " cœur avare, je tiens le mer fous ma loix, et les nations font ma proie. La " legereté de tes vaiffeaux te donnoit de la confiance. Mais tu te verras at- " taqué dans tes murailles, comme un oiffeau raviffant qu'on iroit chercher " parmi fes rochers, & dans fon nid, où il partage fon butin à fes petits. Tu " rends dejà tes efclaves. Louis a brifé les fers, dont tu acablois fes fujets, " &c." In another paffage of the fame oration, he thus apoftrophizes the Ifle of Pheafants, which had been rendered famous by being the fcene of thofe con-ferences, in which the treaty of the Pyrenees between France and Spain, and the marriage of this Princefs with the King of France, were concluded. " Ifle " pacifique où fe doivent terminer les differends de deux grands empires à qui " tu fers de limites : ifle eternellement memorable par les conferences de deux " grands miniftres.——Augufte journée où deux fieres nations, long tems en- " nemis, et alors reconciliées par Marie Therefe s'avançent fur leur confins, " leur rois à leur tête, non plus pour fe combattre, mais pour s'embraffer.— " Fêtes facrées, mariage fortuné, voile nuptial, benediction, facrifice, puis- " je meler aujourdhui vos ceremonies, et vos pompes, avec ces pompes fu- " nebres, & le comble des grandeurs avec leur ruines !" In the funeral ora-tion of Henrietta, Queen of England (which is perhaps the nobleft of all his compofitions), after recounting all fhe had done to fupport her unfortunate hufband, he concludes with this beautiful Apoftrophe : " O mère ! O femme ! " O reine admirable & digne d'une meilleure fortune, fi les fortunes de la terre " étoient quelque chofe ! Enfin il faut ceder à votre fort. Vous avez affez " foutenu l'état, qui eft attaqué, par une force invincible et divine. Il ne refte " plus deformais, fi non que vous teniez ferme parmi fes ruines."

APOSTROPHE is a figure fo much of the fame kind, that it will not require many words.   It is an addrefs to a real perfon; but one who is either abfent or dead, as if he were prefent, and liftening to us.   It is fo much allied to an addrefs to inanimate objects perfonified, that both thefe figures are fometimes called apoftrophes.   However, the proper Apoftrophe is in boldnefs one degree lower than the addrefs to perfonified objects; for it certainly requires a lefs effort of imagination to fuppofe perfons prefent who are dead or abfent, than to animate infenfible beings, and direct our difcourfe to them.   Both figures are fubject to the fame rule of being prompted by paffion, in order to render them natural; for both are the language of paffion or ftrong emotions only. Among the poets Apoftrophe is frequent; as in Virgil:

—— Pereunt Hypanifque Dymafque
Confixi a fociis; nec te, tua plurima, Pantheu
Labentem pietas, nec Apollinis infula texit * !

The poems of Offian are full of the moft beautiful inftances of this figure : " Weep on the rocks of roaring winds, O maid " of Iniftore ! bend thy fair head over the waves, thou fairer " than the ghoft of the hills, when it moves in a funbeam at " noon over the filence of Morven ! He is fallen ! Thy youth " is low ; pale beneath the fword of Cuchullin ! †"   Quinctilian affords us a very fine example in profe ; when in the beginning of his fixth book, deploring the untimely death of his fon,

* Nor Pantheus ! thee, thy mitre, nor the bands
  Of awful Phœbus fav'd from impious hands.   DRYDEN.
† Fingal. B. I.

which

which had happened during the courfe of the work, he makes a very moving and tender Apoftrophe to him. "Nam quo " ille animo, qua medicorum admiratione, menfium octo vale- " tudinem tulit? ut me in fupremis confolatus eft? quam etiam " jam deficiens, jamque non nofter, ipfum illum alienatæ men- " tis errorem circa folas literas habuit? Tuofne ergo, O meæ " fpes inanes! labentes oculos, tuum fugientem fpiritum vidi? " Tuum corpus frigidum, exangue complexus, animam recipere, " auramque communem haurire amplius potui? Tene, confulari " nuper adoptione ad omnium fpes honorum patris admotum, " te, avunculo prætori generum deftinatum; te, omnium fpe At- " ticæ eloquentiæ candidatum, parens fuperftes tantum ad pœnas " amifi * !" In this paffage, Quinctilian fhews the true genius of an orator, as much as he does elfewhere that of the critic.

FOR fuch bold figures of difcourfe as ftrong Perfonifications, addreffes to perfonified objects, and Apoftrophes, the glowing imagination of the ancient Oriental nations was particularly fitted. Hence, in the facred fcriptures, we find fome very re- markable inftances: " O thou fword of the Lord! how long " will it be ere thou be quiet? put thyfelf up into thy fcabbard, " reft and be ftill! How can it be quiet, feeing the Lord hath " given it a charge againft Afhkelon, and againft the fea- " fhore?

* " With what fpirit, and how much to the admiration of the phyficians " did he bear throughout eight months his lingering diftrefs? With what " tender attention did he ftudy, even in the laft extremity, to comfort me? And, " when no longer himfelf, how affecting was it to behold the difordered efforts " of his wandering mind, wholly employed on fubjects of literature? Ah! " my fruftrated and fallen hopes! Have I then beheld your clofing eyes, and " heard the laft groan iffue from your lips? After having embraced your cold

" and

" fhore ? there hath he appointed it *." There is one paffage in particular, which I muft not omit to mention, becaufe it contains a greater affemblage of fublime ideas, of bold and daring figures, than is perhaps any where to be met with. It is in the fourteenth chapter of Ifaiah, where the prophet thus defcribes the fall of the Affyrian empire : " Thou fhalt take up this pro-
" verb againft the king of Babylon, and fay, how hath the op-
" preffor ceafed ! the golden city ceafed ! The Lord hath broken
" the ftaff of the wicked, and the fceptre of the rulers. He
" who fmote the people in wrath with a continual ftroke : he
" that ruled the nations in anger, is perfecuted, and none hin-
" dereth. The whole earth is at reft, and is quiet : they break
" forth into finging. Yea, the fir-trees rejoice at thee, and the
" cedars of Lebanon, faying, fince thou art laid down, no feller
" is come up againft us. Hell from beneath is moved for thee
" to meet thee at thy coming : it ftirreth up the dead for thee,
" even all the chief ones of the earth : it hath raifed up from
" their thrones all the kings of the nations. All they fhall fpeak,
" and fay unto thee, art thou alfo become weak as we ? art thou
" become like unto us ? Thy pomp is brought down to the
" grave, and the noife of thy viols : the worm is fpread under
" thee, and the worms cover thee. How art thou fallen from
" Heaven, O Lucifer, fon of the morning ! how art thou cut
" down to the ground, which didft weaken the nations ! For thou

" and breathlefs body, how was it in my power to draw the vital air, or con-
" tinue to drag a miferable life ? When I had juft beheld you raifed by confular
" adoption to the profpect of all your father's honours, deftined to be fon-in-law
" to your uncle the Prætor, pointed out by general expectation as the fuccefsful
" candidate for the prize of Attic eloquence, in this moment of your opening
" honours, muft I lofe you for ever, and remain an unhappy parent, furviving
" only to fuffer woe ?"

* Jer. xlvii. 6, 7.

" haft

" haft faid in thine heart, I will afcend into Heaven, I will exalt
" my throne above the ftars of God: I will fit alfo upon the
" mount of the congregation, in the fides of the north.   I will
" afcend above the heights of the clouds, I will be like the Moft
" High.   Yet thou fhalt be brought down to Hell, to the fides
" of the pit.   They that fee thee fhall narrowly look upon
" thee, and confider thee, faying, Is this the man that made
" the earth to tremble, that did fhake kingdoms ? That made
" the world as a wildernefs, and deftroyed the cities thereof?
" that opened not the houfe of his prifoners? All the Kings of
" the nations, even all of them lie in glory, every one in his
" own houfe.   But thou art caft out of thy grave, like an abo-
" minable branch : and as the raiment of thofe that are flain,
" thruft through-with a fword, that go down to the ftones of
" the pit, as a carcafe trodden under feet." This whole paffage is full of fublimity.   Every object is animated ; a variety
of perfonages are introduced : we hear the Jews, the fir-trees,
and cedars of Lebanon, the ghofts of departed Kings, the King
of Babylon himfelf, and thofe who look upon his body, all
fpeaking in their order, and acting their different parts without
confufion.

LECTURE XVII.

COMPARISON, ANTITHESIS, INTERROGA-TION, EXCLAMATION, AND OTHER FIGURES OF SPEECH.

WE are ftill engaged in the confideration of figures of fpeech; which, as they add much to the beauty of ftyle when properly employed, and are at the fame time liable to be greatly abufed, require a careful difcuffion. As it would be tedious to dwell on all the variety of figurative expreffions which rhetoricians have enumerated, I chofe to felect the capital figures, fuch as occur moft frequently, and to make my remarks on thefe; the principles and rules laid down concerning them, will fufficiently direct as to the ufe of the reft, either in profe or poetry. Of Metaphor, which is the moft common of them all, I treated fully; and in the laft Lecture I difcourfed of Hyperbole, Perfonification, and Apoftrophe. This Lecture will nearly finifh what remains on the head of Figures.

COM-

COMPARISON, or fimile, is what I am to treat of firft : a Figure frequently employed both by Poets and Profe writers, for the ornament of Compofition. In a former Lecture, I explained fully the difference betwixt this and Metaphor. A Metaphor is a comparifon implied, but not expreffed as fuch ; as when I fay, " Achilles is a Lion," meaning, that he refembles one in courage or ftrength. A Comparifon is, when the refemblance between two objects is expreffed in form, and generally purfued more fully than the nature of a Metaphor admits ; as when I fay, " The actions of princes are like thofe great ri- " vers, the courfe of which every one beholds, but their fprings " have been feen by few." This flight inftance will fhow, that a happy Comparifon is a kind of fparkling ornament, which adds not a little luftre and beauty to difcourfe ; and hence fuch figures are termed by Cicero, " Orationis lumina."

THE pleafure we take in comparifons is juft and natural. We may remark three different fources whence it arifes. Firft, from the pleafure which nature has annexed to that act of the mind by which we compare any two objects together, trace refemblances among thofe that are different, and differences among thofe that refemble each other; a pleafure, the final caufe of which is, to prompt us to remark and obferve, and thereby to make us advance in ufeful knowledge. This operation of the mind is naturally and univerfally agreeable ; as appears from the delight which even children have in comparing things together, as foon as they are capable of attending to the objects that furround them. Secondly, The pleafure of Comparifon arifes from the illuftration which the fimile employed gives to the principal object ; from the clearer view of it which it prefents ;

I   or or the more ſtrong impreſſion of it which it ſtamps upon the mind : and, thirdly, It ariſes from the introduction of a new, and commonly a ſplendid object, aſſociated to the principal one of which we treat ; and from the agreeable picture which that object preſents to the fancy; new ſcenes being thereby brought into view, which, without the aſſiſtance of this figure, we could not have enjoyed.

ALL Compariſons whatever may be reduced under two heads, *Explaining* and *Embelliſhing* Compariſons. For when a writer likens the object of which he treats to any other thing, it always is, or at leaſt always ſhould be, with a view either to make us underſtand that object more diſtinctly, or to dreſs it up, and adorn it. All manner of ſubjects admit of Explaining Compariſons. Let an author be reaſoning ever ſo ſtrictly, or treating the moſt abſtruſe point in philoſophy, he may very properly introduce a Compariſon, merely with a view to make his ſubject be better underſtood. Of this nature, is the following in Mr. Harris's Hermes, employed to explain a very abſtract point, the diſtinction between the powers of ſenſe and imagination in the human mind. " As wax," ſays he, " would " not be adequate to the purpoſe of ſignature, if it had not " the power to retain as well as to receive the impreſſion, the " ſame holds of the ſoul with reſpect to ſenſe and imagination. " Senſe is its receptive power ; imagination its retentive. Had " it ſenſe without imagination, it would not be as wax, but as " water, where, though all impreſſions be inſtantly made, yet " as ſoon as they are made, they are inſtantly loſt." In Compariſons of this nature, the underſtanding is concerned much more than the fancy: and therefore the only rules to be ob-

ſerved,

ferved, with refpect to them, are, that they be clear, and that they be ufeful ; that they tend to render our conception of the principal object more diftinct ; and that they do not lead our view afide, and bewilder it with any falfe light.

But embellifhing Comparifons, introduced not fo much with a view to inform and inftruct, as to adorn the fubject of which we treat, are thofe with which we are chiefly concerned at prefent, as figures of fpeech ; and thofe, indeed, which moft frequently occur. Refemblance, as I before mentioned, is the foundation of this Figure. We muft not, however, take Refemblance, in too ftrict a fenfe, for actual fimilitude or likenefs of appearance. Two objects may fometimes be very happily compared to one another, though they refemble each other, ftrictly fpeaking, in nothing ; only, becaufe they agree in the effects which they produce upon the mind ; becaufe they raife a train of fimilar, or, what may be called, concordant ideas ; fo that the remembrance of the one, when recalled, ferves to ftrengthen the impreffion made by the other. For example, to defcribe the nature of foft and melancholy mufic, Offian fays, " The mufic of Carryl was, like the memory of joys that are " paft, pleafant and mournful to the foul." This is happy and delicate. Yet, furely, no kind of mufic has any refemblance to a feeling of the mind, fuch as the memory of paft joys. Had it been compared to the voice of the nightingale, or the murmur of the ftream, as it would have been by fome ordinary poet, the likenefs would have been more ftrict ; but, by founding his fimile upon the effect which Carryl's mufic produced, the Poet, while he conveys a very tender image, gives us, at the fame time, a much ftronger impreffion of the nature and ftrain

of that mufic : " Like the memory of joys that are paft, plea-
" fant and mournful to the foul."

IN general, whether Comparifons be founded on the fimilitude of the two objects compared, or on fome analogy and
agreement in their effects, the fundamental requifite of a comparifon is, that it fhall ferve to illuftrate the object, for the fake
of which it is introduced, and to give us a ftronger conception
of it. Some little excurfions of Fancy may be permitted, in
purfuing the fimile ; but they muft never deviate far from the
principal object. If it be a great and noble one, every circumftance in the comparifon muft tend to aggrandife it ; if it be a
beautiful one, to render it more amiable ; if terrible, to fill us
with more awe. But to be a little more particular : The rules
to be given concerning Comparifons, refpect chiefly two articles ; the propriety of their introduction, and the nature of the
objects whence they are taken.

FIRST, the propriety of their introduction. From what has
been already faid of Comparifons, it appears, that they are not,
like the Figures of which I treated in the laft Lecture, the language of ftrong paffion. No ; they are the language of imagination rather than of paffion ; of an imagination fprightly,
indeed, and warmed ; but undifturbed by any violent or agitat-
ing emotion. Strong paffion is too fevere to admit this play of
Fancy. It has no leifure to caft about for refembling objects ;
it dwells on that object which has feized and taken poffeffion of
the foul. It is too much occupied and filled by it, to turn its
view afide, or to fix its attention on any other thing. An author, therefore, can fcarcely commit a greater fault, than, in the
midft

midſt of paſſion, to introduce a Simile. Metaphorical expreſſion may be allowable in ſuch a ſituation; though even this
may be carried too far: but the pomp and ſolemnity of a formal Compariſon is altogether a ſtranger to paſſion. It changes
the key in a moment; relaxes and brings down the mind; and
ſhews us a writer perfectly at his eaſe, while he is perſonating
ſome other, who is ſuppoſed to be under the torment of agitation. Our writers of tragedies are very apt to err here. In
ſome of Mr. Rowe's plays, theſe flowers of ſimiles have been
ſtrewed unſeaſonably. Mr. Addiſon's Cato, too, is juſtly cen-
ſurable in this reſpect; as, when Portius, juſt after Lucia had
bid him farewel for ever, and when he ſhould naturally have
been repreſented as in the moſt violent anguiſh, makes his reply
in a ſtudied and affected compariſon:

> Thus o'er the dying lamp th' unſteady flame
> Hangs quiv'ring on a point, leaps off by fits,
> And falls again, as loth to quit its hold.
> Thou muſt not go; my ſoul ſtill hovers o'er thee,
> And can't get looſe.

Every one muſt be ſenſible, that this is quite remote from the
language of Nature on ſuch occaſions.

HOWEVER, as Compariſon is not the ſtyle of ſtrong paſſion,
ſo neither, when employed for embelliſhment, is it the language of a mind wholly unmoved. It is a figure of dignity,
and always requires ſome elevation in the ſubject, in order to
make it proper: for it ſuppoſes the imagination to be uncommonly enlivened, though the heart be not agitated by paſſion.
In a word, the proper place of compariſons lies in the middle

region,

region between the highly pathetic, and the very humble ftyle. This is a wide field, and gives ample range to the Figure. But even this field we muft take care not to overſtock with it. For, as was before faid, it is a fparkling ornament; and all things that fparkle, dazzle and fatigue, if they recur too often. Similies fhould, even in poetry, be ufed with moderation; but, in profe writings, much more: otherwife, the ftyle will become difguftingly lufcious, and the ornament lofe its virtue and effect.

I PROCEED, next, to the rules that relate to objects, whence Comparifons fhould be drawn; fuppofing them introduced in their proper place.

IN the firft place, they muft not be drawn from things, which have too near and obvious a refemblance to the object with which we compare them. The great pleafure of the act of comparing lies, in difcovering likeneffes among things of different fpecies, where we would not, at the firft glance, expect a refemblance. There is little art or ingenuity in pointing out the refemblance of two objects, that are fo much a-kin, or lie fo near to one another in nature, that every one fees they muft be like. When Milton compares Satan's appearance, after his fall, to that of the Sun fuffering an eclipfe, and affrighting the nations with portentous darknefs, we are ftruck with the happinefs and the dignity of the fimilitude. But, when he compares Eve's bower in Paradife, to the arbour of Pomona; or Eve herfelf, to a Dryad, or Wood-nymph, we receive little entertainment: as every one fees, that one arbour muft, of

courfe,

courſe, in ſeveral reſpects, reſemble another arbour, and one beautiful woman another beautiful woman.

AMONG Similies faulty through too great obviouſneſs of the likeneſs, we muſt likewiſe rank thoſe which are taken from objects become trite and familiar in poetical Language. Such are the Similies of a hero to a lion, of a perſon in ſorrow to a flower drooping its head, of violent paſſion to a tempeſt, of chaſtity to ſnow, of virtue to the ſun or the ſtars, and many more of this kind, with which we are ſure to find modern writers, of ſecond rate genius, abounding plentifully; handed down from every writer of verſes to another, as by hereditary right. Theſe compariſons were, at firſt, perhaps, very proper for the purpoſes to which they are applied. In the antient original poets, who took them directly from nature, not from their predeceſſors, they had beauty. But they are now beaten; our ears are ſo accuſtomed to them, that they give no amuſement to the fancy. There is, indeed, no mark by which we can more readily diſtinguiſh a poet of true genius, from one of a barren imagination, than by the ſtrain of their compariſons. All who call themſelves poets affect them : but, whereas a mere verſifier ʿcopies no new image from nature, which appears, to his uninventive genius, exhauſted by thoſe who have gone before him, and, therefore, contents himſelf with humbly fol‐ lowing their tract; to an author of real fancy, nature ſeems to unlock, ſpontaneouſly, her hidden ſtores; and the eye " quick " glancing from earth to heaven," diſcovers new ſhapes and forms, new likeneſſes between objects unobſerved before, which render his Similies original, expreſſive, and lively.

BUT,

But, in the fecond place, as Comparifons ought not to be found ed on likeneffes too obvious, ftill lefs ought they to be founded on thofe which are too faint and remote. For thefe, in place of affifting, ftrain the fancy to comprehend them, and throw no light upon the fubject. It is alfo to be obferved, that a Comparifon which, in the principal circumftances, carries a fufficiently near refemblance, may become unnatural and obfcure, if pufhed too far. Nothing is more oppofite to the defign of this figure, than to hunt after a great number of coincidences in minute points, merely to fhow how far the poet's wit can ftretch the refemblance. This is Mr. Cowley's common fault; whofe comparifons generally run out fo far, as to become rather a ftudied exercife of wit, than an illuftration of the principal object. We need only open his works, his odes efpecially, to find inftances every where.

In the third place, the object from which a Comparifon is drawn, fhould never be an unknown object, or one of which few people can form clear ideas: " Ad inferendam rebus " lucem," fays Quinctilian, " repertæ funt fimilitudines. " Præcipuè, igitur, eft cuftodiendum ne id quod fimilitudinis " gratiâ afcivimus, aut obfcurum fit, aut ignotum. Debet " enim id quod illuftrandæ alterius rei gratiâ affumitur, ipfum " effe clarius eo quod illuminatur *." Comparifons, therefore,

---

* " Comparifons have been introduced into difcourfe, for the fake of throw-
" ing light on the fubject. We muft, therefore, be much on our guard, not
" to employ, as the ground of our Simile, any object which is either obfcure or
" unknown. That, furely, which is ufed for the purpofe of illuftrating fome
" other thing, ought to be more obvious and plain, than the thing intended to
" be illuftrated."

founded on philofophical difcoveries, or on any thing with which perfons of a certain trade only, or a certain profeffion, are converfant, attain not their proper effect. They fhould be taken from thofe illuftrious, noted objects, which moft of the readers either have feen, or can ftrongly conceive. This leads me to remark a fault of which modern poets are very apt to be guilty. The antients took their fimilies from that face of nature, and that clafs of objects, with which they and their readers were acquainted. Hence lions, and wolves, and ferpents, were fruitful, and very proper fources of Similies amongft them ; and thefe having become a fort of confecrated, claffical images, are very commonly adopted by the moderns ; injudicioufly however, for the propriety of them is now in a great meafure loft. It is only at fecond hand, and by defcription, that we are acquainted with many of thofe objects ; and, to moft readers of poetry, it were more to the purpofe, to defcribe lions, or ferpents, by Similies taken from men, than to defcribe men by lions. Now-a-days, we can much eafier form the conception of a fierce combat between two men, than between a bull and a tyger. Every country has a fcenery peculiar to itfelf ; and the imagery of every good poet will exhibit it. The introduction of unknown objects, or of a foreign fcenery, betrays a poet copying, not after nature, but from other writers. I have only to obferve further,

In the fourth place, that, in compofitions of a ferious or elevated kind, Similies fhould never be taken from low or mean objects. Thefe are degrading ; whereas, Similies are commonly intended to embellifh, and to dignify : and, therefore, unlefs in burlefque writings, or where Similies are introduced

8   purpofely

purpofely to vilify and diminifh an object, mean ideas fhould never be prefented to us. Some of Homer's Comparifons have been taxed without reafon, on this account. For it is to be remembered, that the meannefs or dignity of objects, depends, in a great degree, on the ideas and manners of the age wherein we live. Many Similies, therefore, drawn from the incidents of rural life, which appear low to us, had abundance of dignity in thofe fimpler ages of antiquity.

I HAVE now confidered fuch of the figures of Speech as feemed moft to merit a full and particular difcuffion: Metaphor, Hyperbole, Perfonification, Apoftrophe, and Comparifon. A few more yet remain to be mentioned; the proper ufe and conduct of which will be eafily underftood from the principles already laid down.

As Comparifon is founded on the refemblance, fo Antithefis on the contraft or oppofition of two objects. Contraft has always this effect, to make each of the contrafted objects appear in the ftronger light. White, for inftance, never appears fo bright as when it is oppofed to black; and when both are viewed together. Antithefis, therefore, may, on many occafions, be employed to advantage, in order to ftrengthen the impreffion which we intend that any object fhould make. Thus Cicero, in his oration for Milo, reprefenting the improbability of Milo's forming a defign to take away the life of Clodius, at a time when all circumftances were unfavourable to fuch a defign, and after he had let other opportunities flip when he could have executed the fame defign, if he had formed it, with much more eafe and fafety, heightens our conviction

of

of this improbability by a fkilful ufe of this figure: " Quem " igitur cum omnium gratiâ interficere noluit, hunc voluit cum " aliquorum querelâ? Quem jure, quem loco, quem tempore, " quem impune, non eft aufus, hunc injuriâ, iniquo loco, " alieno tempore, periculo capitis, non dubitavit occidere * ?" In order to render an Antithefis more complete, it is always of advantage, that the words and members of the fentence, ex- preffing the contrafted objects, be, as in this inftance of Cicero's, fimilarly conftructed, and made to correfpond to each other. This leads us to remark the contraft more, by fetting the things which we oppofe more clearly over againft each other; in the fame manner as when we contraft a black and a white object, in order to perceive the full difference of their colour, we would chufe to have both objects of the fame bulk, and placed in the fame light. Their refemblance to each other, in certain circumftances, makes their difagreement in others more palpable.

At the fame time, I muft obferve, that the frequent ufe of Antithefis, efpecially where the oppofition in the words is nice and quaint, is apt to render ftyle difagreeable. Such a fentence as the following, from Seneca, does very well, where it ftands alone : " Si quem volueris effe divitem, non eft quod augeas

* " Is it credible that, when he declined putting Clodius to death with " the confent of all, he would chufe to do it with the difapprobation of many ? " Can you believe that the perfon whom he fcrupled to flay, when he might " have done fo with full juftice; in a convenient place, at a proper time, with " fecure impunity, he made no fcruple to murder againft juftice, in an un- " favourable place, at an unfeafonable time, and at the rifque of capital con- " demnation ?"

" divitias, fed minuas cupiditates *." Or this : " Si ad na-
" turam vives, nunquam eris pauper; fi ad opinionem, nun-
" quam dives †." A maxim, or moral faying, properly enough
receives this form ; both becaufe it is fuppofed to be the fruit
of meditation, and becaufe it is defigned to be engraven on
the memory, which recalls it more eafily by the help of fuch
contrafted expreffions. But where a ftring of fuch fentences
fucceed each other ; where this becomes an author's favourite
and prevailing manner of expreffing himfelf, his ftyle is faulty ;
and it is upon this account Seneca has been often, and juftly,
cenfured. Such a ftyle appears too ftudied and laboured ; it
gives us the impreffion of an author attending more to his
manner of faying things, than to the things themfelves which
he fays. Dr. Young, though a writer of real genius, was too
fond of Antithefes. In his Eftimate of Human Life, we find
whole pages that run in fuch a ftrain as this : " The peafant
" complains aloud ; the courtier in fecret repines. In want,
" what diftrefs ? in affluence, what fatiety ? The great are
" under as much difficulty to expend with pleafure, as the
" mean to labour with fuccefs. The ignorant, through ill-
" grounded hope, are difappointed ; the knowing, through
" knowledge, defpond. Ignorance, occafions miftake ; miftake,
" difappointment ; and difappointment is mifery. Know-
" ledge, on the other hand, gives true judgment ; and true
" judgment of human things, gives a demonftration of their

---

* " If you feek to make one rich, ftudy not to increafe his ftores, but to
" diminifh his defires."

† " If you regulate your defires according to the ftandard of nature, you
" will never be poor; if according to the ftandard of opinion, you will never
" be rich."

I

" infufficiency

" infufficiency to our peace." There is too much glitter in fuch a ftyle as this to pleafe long. We are fatigued, by attending to fuch quaint and artificial fentences often repeated.

THERE is another fort of Antithefis, the beauty of which confifts, in furprifing us by the unexpected contrafts of things which it brings together. Much wit may be fhewn in this; but it belongs wholly to pieces of profeffed wit and humour, and can find no place in grave compofitions. Mr. Pope, who is remarkably fond of Antithefis, is often happy in this ufe of the figure. So, in his Rape of the Lock :

> Whether the nymph fhall break Diana's law,
> Or fome frail china jar receive a flaw;
> Or ftain her honour, or her new brocade ;
> Forget her prayers, or mifs a mafquerade;
> Or lofe her heart, or necklace, at a ball,
> Or whether heaven has doomed that Shock muft fall.

What is called the point of an epigram, confifts, for moft part, in fome Antithefis of this kind; furprifing us with the fmart and unexpected turn, which it gives to the thought; and in the fewer words it is brought out, it is always the happier.

COMPARISONS and Antithefes are figures of a cool nature ; the productions of imagination, not of paffion. Interrogations and Exclamations, of which I am next to fpeak, are paffionate figures. They are, indeed, on fo many occafions, the native language of paffion, that their ufe is extremely frequent; and, in ordinary converfation, when men are heated, they prevail as much as in the moft fublime oratory. The unfigured, literal ufe of Interrogation, is, to afk a queftion; but when men are

Z z 2

prompted

prompted by paffion, whatever they would affirm, or deny, with great vehemence, they naturally put in the form of a queftion; expreffing thereby the ftrongeft confidence of the truth of their own fentiment, and appealing to their hearers for the impoffibility of the contrary. Thus, in Scripture: " God is not a man that he fhould lie, neither the fon of man " that he fhould repent. Hath he faid it? And fhall he not do " it? Hath he fpoken it? and fhall he not make it good *?" So Demofthenes, addreffing himfelf to the Athenians: " Tell " me, will you ftill go about and afk one another, what news? " What can be more aftonifhing news than this, that the man " of Macedon makes war upon the Athenians, and difpofes of " the affairs of Greece?—Is Philip dead? No, but he is fick. " What fignifies it to you whether he be dead or alive? For, if " any thing happens to this Philip, you will immediately raife " up another." All this delivered without interrogation, had been faint and ineffectual; but the warmth and eagernefs which this queftioning method expreffes, awakens the hearers, and ftrikes them with much greater force.

INTERROGATIONS may often be employed with propriety, in the courfe of no higher emotions than naturally arife in pur-fuing fome clofe and earneft reafoning. But Exclamations be-long only to ftronger emotions of the mind; to furprife, ad-miration, anger, joy, grief, and the like:

Heu pietas! heu prifca fides! invictaque bello
Dextera!

---

* Numbers, chap. xxiii. ver. 19.

Both

Both Interrogation and Exclamation, and, indeed, all paffionate figures of fpeech, operate upon us by means of fympathy. Sympathy is a very powerful and extenfive principle in our nature, difpofing us to enter into every feeling and paffion, which we behold expreffed by others. Hence, a fingle perfon coming into company with ftrong marks, either of melancholy or joy, upon his countenance, will diffufe that paffion, in a moment, through the whole circle. Hence, in a great crowd, paffions are fo eafily caught, and fo faft fpread, by that powerful contagion which the animated looks, cries, and geftures of a multitude never fail to carry. Now, Interrogations and Exclamations, being natural figns of a moved and agitated mind, always, when they are properly ufed, difpofe us to fympathife with the difpofitions of thofe who ufe them, and to feel as they feel.

FROM this it follows, that the great rule with regard to the conduct of fuch figures is, that the writer attend to the manner in which nature dictates to us to exprefs any emotion or paffion, and that he give his language that turn, and no other; above all, that he never affect the ftyle of a paffion which he does not feel. With Interrogations he may ufe a good deal of free-dom ; thefe, as above obferved, falling in fo much with the ordinary courfe of language and reafoning, even when no great vehemence is fuppofed to have place in the mind. But, with refpect to Exclamations, he muft be more referved. No-thing has a worfe effect than the frequent and unfeafonable ufe of them. Raw, juvenile writers imagine, that, by pouring them forth often, they render their compofitions warm and animated. Whereas quite the contrary follows. They render
it

it frigid to excefs. When an author is always calling upon us to enter into tranfports which he has faid nothing to infpire, we are both difgufted and enraged at him. He raifes no fympathy, for he gives us no paffion of his own, in which we can take part. He gives us words, and not paffion; and of courfe, can raife no paffion, unlefs that of indignation. Hence, I incline to think, he was not much miftaken, who faid, that when, on looking into a book, he found the pages thick befpangled with the point which is called, " Punctum admirationis," he judged this to be a fufficient reafon for his laying it afide. And, indeed, were it not for the help of this " punctum ad- " mirationis," with which many writers of the rapturous kind fo much abound, one would be often at a lofs to difcover, whether or not it was Exclamation which they aimed at. For, it has now become a fafhion, among thefe writers, to fubjoin points of admiration to fentences, which contain nothing but fimple affirmations, or propofitions; as if, by an affected method of pointing, they could transform them in the reader's mind into high figures of eloquence. Much a-kin to this, is another con- trivance practifed by fome writers, of feparating, almoft all the members of their fentences from each other, by blank lines; as if, by fetting them thus afunder, they beftowed fome fpecial importance upon them; and required us, in going along, to make a paufe at every other word, and weigh it well. This, I think, may be called a Typographical Figure of Speech. Neither, indeed, fince we have been led to mention the arts of writers for increafing the importance of their words, does another cuftom, which prevailed very much fome time ago, feem worthy of imitation; I mean that of diftinguifhing the fignificant words, in every fentence, by Italick characters. On

fome

ſome occaſions, it is very proper to uſe ſuch diſtinctions. But when we carry them ſo far, as to mark with them every ſuppoſed emphatical word, theſe words are apt to multiply ſo faſt in the author's imagination, that every page is crowded with Italicks ; which can produce no effect whatever, but to hurt the eye, and create confuſion.   Indeed, if the ſenſe point not out the moſt emphatical expreſſions, a variation in the type, eſpecially when occurring ſo frequently, will give ſmall aid. And, accordingly, the moſt maſterly writers, of late, have, with good reaſon, laid aſide all thoſe feeble props of ſignificancy, and truſted wholly to the weight of their ſentiments for commanding attention.   But to return from this digreſſion :

ANOTHER Figure of Speech, proper only to animated and warm Compoſition, is what ſome critical writers call Viſion ; when, in place of relating ſomething that is paſt, we uſe the preſent tenſe, and deſcribe it as actually paſſing before our eyes. Thus Cicero, in his fourth oration againſt Catiline : " Videor " enim mihi hanc urbem videre, lucem orbis terrarum atque " arcem omnium gentium, ſubito uno incendio concidentem ; " cerno animo ſepulta in patria miſeros atque inſepultos acervos " civium ; verſatur mihi ante oculos aſpectus Cethegi, et furor, in " veſtra cæde bacchantis *."   This manner of deſcription ſuppoſes a ſort of enthuſiaſm, which carries the perſon who deſcribes in ſome meaſure out of himſelf; and, when well exe-

---

* " I ſeem to myſelf to behold this city, the ornament of the earth, and the " capital of all nations, ſuddenly involved on one conflagration. I ſee before " me the ſlaughtered heaps of citizens lying unburied in the midſt of their " ruined country. The furious countenance of Cethegus riſes to my view, " while with a ſavage joy he is triumphing in your miſeries."

cuted,

cuted, muſt needs impreſs the reader or hearer ſtrongly, by the
force of that ſympathy which I have before explained.   But,
in order to a ſucceſsful execution, it requires an uncommonly
warm imagination, and ſuch a happy ſelection of circumſtances,
as ſhall make us think we ſee before our eyes the ſcene that is
deſcribed.   Otherwiſe, it ſhares the ſame fate with all feeble attempts towards paſſionate figures ; that of throwing ridicule
upon the author, and leaving the reader more cool and unin-
tereſted than he was before.   The ſame obſervations are to be
applied to Repetition, Suſpenſion, Correction, and many more
of thoſe figurative forms of Speech, which rhetoricians have
enumerated among the Beauties of Eloquence. They are beautiful, or not, exactly in proportion as they are native expreſſions of
the ſentiment or paſſion intended to be heightened by them.
Let nature and paſſion always ſpeak their own language, and
they will ſuggeſt figures in abundance.   But when we ſeek to
counterfeit a warmth which we do not feel, no figures will
either ſupply the defect, or conceal the impoſture.

THERE is one Figure (and I ſhall mention no more) of frequent uſe among all public ſpeakers, particularly at the bar,
which Quinctilian inſiſts upon conſiderably, and calls Amplification.   It conſiſts in an artful exaggeration of all the circumſtances of ſome object or action which we want to place in a
ſtrong light, either a good or a bad one.   It is not ſo properly
one Figure, as the ſkilful management of ſeveral which we
make to tend to one point.   It may be carried on by a proper
uſe of magnifying or extenuating terms, by a regular enumeration of particulars, or by throwing together, as into one maſs,
a crowd of circumſtances ; by ſuggeſting compariſons alſo with

9   things

things of a like nature. But the principal inftrument by which
it works, is by a Climax, or a gradual rife of one circumftance
above another, till our idea be raifed to the utmoft. I fpoke
formerly of a Climax in found ; a Climax in fenfe, when well
carried on, is a figure which never fails to amplify ftrongly.
The common example of this, is that noted paffage in Cicero
which every fchoolboy knows : " Facinus eft vincire civem Ro-
" manum ; fcelus verberare, prope parricidium, necare ; quid
" dicam in crucem tollere * ?" I fhall give an inftance from a
printed pleading of a famous Scotch Lawyer, Sir George
M'Kenzie. It is in a charge to the jury, in the cafe of a woman accufed of murdering her own child. " Gentlemen, if
" one man had any how flain another, if an adverfary had killed
" his oppofer, or a woman occafioned the death of her enemy,
" even thefe criminals would have been capitally punifhed by
" the Cornelian law : but, if this guiltlefs infant, who could
" make no enemy, had been murdered by its own nurfe, What
" punifhments would not then the mother have demanded ?
" With what cries and exclamations would fhe have ftunned
" your ears ? What fhall we fay then, when a woman, guilty of
" homicide, a mother, of the murder of her innocent child,
" hath comprifed all thofe mifdeeds in one fingle crime ; a
" crime, in its own nature, deteftable ; in a woman, prodigious ;
" in a mother, incredible ; and perpetrated againft one whofe
" age called for compaffion, whofe near relation claimed affec-
" tion, and whofe innocence deferved the higheft favour ?" I
muft take notice, however, that fuch regular Climaxes as thefe,

* " It is a crime to put a Roman citizen in bonds : it is the height of
" guilt to fcourge him ; little lefs than parricide to put him to death. What
" name then fhall I give to crucifying him ?"

though they have confiderable beauty, have, at the fame time, no fmall appearance of art and ftudy; and, therefore, though they may be admitted into formal harangues, yet they fpeak not the language of great earneftnefs and paffion, which feldom proceed by fteps fo regular. Nor, indeed, for the purpofes of effectual perfuafion, are they likely to be fo fuccefsful, as an arrangement of circumftances in a lefs artificial order. For, when much art appears, we are always put on our guard againft the deceits of eloquence; but when a fpeaker has reafoned ftrongly, and, by force of argument, has made good his main point, he may then, taking advantage of the favourable bent of our minds, make ufe of fuch artificial figures to confirm our belief, and to warm our minds.

L E C T U R E XVIII.

FIGURATIVE LANGUAGE—GENERAL CHA-
RACTERS OF STYLE—DIFFUSE, CONCISE—
FEEBLE, NERVOUS—DRY, PLAIN, NEAT,
ELEGANT, FLOWERY.

HAVING treated, at confiderable length, of the Figures
of Speech, of their origin, of their nature, and of the
management of fuch of them as are important enough to require a particular difcuffion, before finally difmiffing this fubject,
I think it incumbent on me, to make fome obfervations concerning the proper ufe of Figurative Language in general.
Thefe, indeed, I have, in part, already anticipated. But, as great
errors are often committed in this part of Style, efpecially
by young writers, it may be of ufe that I bring together,
under one view, the moft material directions on this head.

I BEGIN with repeating an obfervation, formerly made, that
neither all the beauties, nor even the chief beauties of compofi-

3 A 2   tion,

tion, depend upon Tropes and Figures. Some of the moſt ſublime and moſt pathetic paſſages of the moſt admired authors, both in proſe and poetry, are expreſſed in the moſt ſimple Style, without any figure at all; inſtances of which I have before given. On the other hand, a compoſition may abound with theſe ſtudied ornaments; the language may be artful, ſplendid, and highly figured, and yet the compoſition be on the whole frigid and unaffecting. Not to ſpeak of ſentiment and thought, which conſtitute the real and laſting merit of any work, if the ſtyle be ſtiff and affected, if it be deficient in perſpicuity or preciſion, or in eaſe and neatneſs, all the Figures that can be employed will never render it agreeable: they may dazzle a vulgar, but will never pleaſe a judicious, eye.

In the ſecond place, Figures, in order to be beautiful, muſt always riſe naturally from the ſubject. I have ſhown that all of them are the language either of Imagination, or of Paſſion; ſome of them ſuggeſted by Imagination, when it is awakened and ſprightly, ſuch as Metaphors and Compariſons; others by Paſſion or more heated emotion, ſuch as Perſonifications and Apoſtrophes. Of courſe they are beautiful then only, when they are prompted by fancy, or by paſſion. They muſt riſe of their own accord; they muſt flow from a mind warmed by the object which it ſeeks to deſcribe; we ſhould never interrupt the courſe of thought to caſt about for Figures. If they be ſought after coolly, and faſtened on as deſigned ornaments, they will have a a miſerable effect. It is a very erroneous idea, which many have of the ornaments of Style, as if they were things detached from the ſubject, and that could be ſtuck to it, like lace upon a coat: this is indeed,

Purpureus

Purpureus late qui fplendeat unus aut alter
Affuitur pannus *. ———   Ars Poet.

And it is this falfe idea which has often brought attention to the beauties of writing into difrepute. Whereas, the real and proper ornaments of Style are wrought into the fubftance of it. They flow in the fame ftream with the current of thought. A writer of genius conceives his fubject ftrongly; his imagination is filled and impreffed with it; and pours itfelf forth in that Figurative Language which Imagination naturally fpeaks. He puts on no emotion which his fubject does not raife in him; he fpeaks as he feels; but his ftyle will be beautiful, becaufe his feelings are lively. On occafions, when fancy is languid, or finds nothing to roufe it, we fhould never attempt to hunt for figures. We then work, as it is faid, " invitâ Minervâ;" fuppofing figures invented, they will have the appearance of being forced; and in this cafe, they had much better be wanted.

In the third place, even when Imagination prompts, and the fubject naturally gives rife to Figures, they muft, however, not be employed too frequently. In all beauty, " fimplex mundi- " tiis;" is a capital quality. Nothing derogates more from the weight and dignity of any compofition, than too great attention to ornament. When the ornaments coft labour, that labour always appears; though they fhould coft us none, ftill the reader or hearer may be furfeited -with them; and when they come too thick, they give the impreffion of a light and frothy genius,

---

* " Shreds of purple with broad luftre fhine,
   " Sew'd on your poem."   Francis.

that,

that evaporates in fhew, rather than brings forth what is folid. The directions of the ancient critics, on this head, are full of good fenfe, and deferve careful attention. "Voluptatibus "maximis," fays Cicero, de Orat. L. iii. "faftidium finitimum "eft in rebus omnibus; quo hoc minus in oratione miremur. "In qua vel ex poëtis, vel oratoribus poffumus judicare, con- "cinnam, ornatam, feftivam fine intermiffione, quamvis claris "fit coloribus picta, vel poëfis, vel oratio, non poffe in delecta- "tione effe diuturnâ. Quare, bene et præclare, quamvis nobis "fæpe dicatur, belle et feftive nimium fæpe nolo *." To the fame purpofe, are the excellent directions with which Quinctilian concludes his difcourfe concerning Figures, L. ix. C. 3. "Ego illud de iis figuris quæ vere fiunt, adjiciam breviter, "ficut ornant orationem opportunæ pofitæ, ita ineptiffimas effe "cum immodice petuntur. Sunt, qui neglecto rerum pondere "et viribus fententiarum, fi vel inania verba in hos modos de- "pravarunt, fummos fe judicant artifices; ideoque non definunt "eas nectere; quas fine fententia fectare, tam eft ridiculum "quam quærere habitum geftumque fine corpore. Ne hæ "quidem quæ rectæ fiunt, denfandæ funt nimis. Sciendum im- "primis quid quifque poftulet locus, quid perfona, quid tem- "pus. Major enim pars harum figurarum pofita eft in delec- "tatione. Ubi vero, atrocitate, invidiâ, miferatione pug- "nandum eft; quis ferat verbis contrapofitis, et confimilibus,

---

* "In all human things, difguft borders fo nearly on the moft lively plea- "fures, that we need not be furprized to find this hold in eloquence. From "reading either poets or orators we may eafily fatisfy ourfelves, that neither a "poem nor an oration, which, without intermiffion is fhowy and fparkling, "can pleafe us long —Wherefore, though we may wifh for the frequent praife "of having expreffed ourfelves well and properly, we fhould not covet repeated "applaufe, for being bright and fplendid."

5

"& pa-

" & pariter cadentibus, irafcentem, flentem, rogantem? Cum in
" his rebus, cura verborum deroget affectibus fidem ; et ubi-
" cunque ars oftentatur, veritas abeffe videatur *." After thefe
judicious and ufeful obfervations, I have no more to add, on
this fubject, except this admonition.

In the fourth place, that without a genius for Figurative
Language, none fhould attempt it. Imagination is a power not
to be acquired ; it muft be derived from nature. Its redundancies we may prune, its deviations we may correct, its fphere we
may enlarge ; but the faculty itfelf we cannot create : and all
efforts towards a metaphorical ornamented ftyle, if we are deftitute of the proper genius for it, will prove awkward and difgufting. Let us fatisfy ourfelves, however, by confidering, that
without this talent, or at leaft with a very fmall meafure of it,

---

* " I muft add, concerning thofe figures which are proper in themfelves,
" that as they beautify a compofition when they are feafonably introduced, fo
" they deform it greatly, if too frequently fought after. There are fome, who,
" neglecting ftrength of fentiment and weight of matter, if they can only force
" their empty words into a Figurative Style, imagine themfelves great writers ;
" and therefore continually ftring together fuch ornaments ; which is juft as
" ridiculous, where there is no fentiment to fupport them, as to contrive gef-
" tures and dreffes for what wants a body. Even thofe figures which a fubject
" admits, muft not come too thick. We muft begin, with confidering what
" the occafion, the time, and the perfon who fpeaks, render proper. For the
" object aimed at by the greater part of thefe figures, is entertainment. But
" when the fubject becomes deeply ferious, and ftrong paffions are to be moved,
" who can bear the orator, who, in affected language and balanced phrafes, en-
" deavours to exprefs wrath, commiferation, or earneft intreaty ? On all fuch
" occafions, a folicitous attention to words weakens paffion ; and when fo
" much art is fhown, there is fufpected to be little fincerity."

ideas,

we may both write and fpeak to advantage.   Good fenfe, clear
ideas, perfpicuity of language, and proper arrangement of
words and thoughts, will always command attention.   Thefe
are indeed the foundations of all folid merit, both in fpeaking
and writing.   Many fubjects require nothing more; and thofe
which admit of ornament, admit it only as a fecondary requifite.   To ftudy and to know our own genius well; to follow
nature; to feek to improve, but not to force it, are directions
which cannot be too often given to thofe who defire to excell in
the liberal arts.

WHEN I entered on the confideration of Style, I obferved
that words being the copies of our ideas, there muft always be
a very intimate connection between the manner in which every
writer employs words, and his manner of thinking; and that,
from the peculiarity of thought and expreffion which belongs to
him, there is a certain character imprinted on his Style, which
may be denominated his manner; commonly expreffed by fuch
general terms, as ftrong, weak, dry, fimple, affected, or the
like.   Thefe diftinctions carry, in general, fome reference to
an author's manner of thinking, but refer chiefly to his mode of
expreffion.   They arife from the whole tenour of his language;
and comprehend the effect produced by all thofe parts of Style
which we have already confidered; the choice which he makes
of fingle words; his arrangement of thefe in fentences; the
degree of his precifion; and his embellifhment, by means of
mufical cadence, figures, or other arts of fpeech.   Of fuch general Characters of Style, therefore, it remains now to fpeak, as
the refult of thofe underparts of which I have hitherto treated.

THAT

THAT different fubjects require to be treated of in different forts of Style, is a pofition fo obvious, that I fhall not ftay to illuftrate it. Every one fees that Treatifes of Philofophy, for inftance, ought not to be compofed in the fame ftyle with orations. Every one fees alfo, that different parts of the fame compofition require a variation in the ftyle and manner. In a fermon, for inftance, or any harangue, the application or percration admits more ornament, and requires more warmth, than the didactic part. But what I mean at prefent to remark is, that amidft this variety, we ftill expect to find, in the compofitions of any one man, fome degree of uniformity or confiftency with himfelf in manner; we expect to find fome predominant character of Style impreffed on all his writings, which fhall be fuited to, and fhall mark, his particular genius, and turn of mind. The orations in Livy differ much in Style, as they ought to do, from the reft of his hiftory. The fame is the cafe with thofe in Tacitus. Yet both in Livy's orations, and in thofe of Tacitus, we are able clearly to trace the diftinguifhing manner of each hiftorian; the magnificent fullnefs of the one, and the fententious concifenefs of the other. The " Lettres " Perfanes," and " L'Efprit de Loix," are the works of the fame author. They required very different compofition furely, and accordingly they differ widely; yet ftill we fee the fame hand. Wherever there is real and native genius, it gives a determination to one kind of Style rather than another. Where nothing of this appears; where there is no marked nor peculiar character in the compofitions of any author, we are apt to infer, not without reafon, that he is a vulgar and trivial author, who writes from imitation, and not from the impulfe of original genius. As the moft celebrated painters are known by their hand, fo the beft and moft original writers are known and diftinguifhed, throughout all their works, by their Style and peculiar manner. This will be found to hold almoft without exception.

THE ancient Critics attended to thefe general charaƈters of Style which we are now to confider. Dionyfius of Halicarnaffus divides them into three kinds; and calls them the Auftere, the Florid, and the Middle. By the Auftere, he means a Style diftinguifhed for ftrength and firmnefs, with a negleƈt of fmoothnefs and ornament; for examples of which, he gives Pindar and Æfchylus among the Poets, and Thucydides among the Profe writers. By the Florid, he means, as the name indicates, a Style ornamented, flowing, and fweet; refting more upon numbers and grace, than ftrength; he inftances Hefiod, Sappho, Anacreon, Euripides, and principally Ifocrates. The Middle kind is the juft mean between thefe, and comprehends the beauties of both; in which clafs he places Homer and Sophocles among the Poets; in Profe, Herodotus, Demofthenes, Plato, and (what feems ftrange) Ariftotle. This muft be a very wide clafs indeed, which comprehends Plato and Ariftotle under one article as to Style *. Cicero and Quinƈtilian make alfo a threefold divifion of Style, though with refpeƈt to different qualities of it; in which they are followed by moft of the modern writers on Rhetoric; the *Simplex*, *Tenue*, or *Subtile;* the *Grave* or *Vehemens*; and the *Medium*, or, *temperatum genus dicendi.* But thefe divifions, and the illuftrations they give of them, are fo loofe and general, that they cannot advance us much in our

* De Compofitione Verborum, Cap. 25.

ideas

ideas of Style. I ſhall endeavour to be a little more particular in what I have to ſay on this ſubject.

ONE of the firſt and moſt obvious diſtinctions of the different kinds of Style, is what ariſes from an author's ſpreading out his thoughts more or leſs. This diſtinction forms, what are called the Diffuſe and the Conciſe Styles. A conciſe writer compreſſes his thought into the feweſt poſſible words ; he ſeeks to employ none but ſuch as are moſt expreſſive ; he lops off, as redundant, every expreſſion which does not add ſomething material to the ſenſe. Ornament he does not reject ; he may be lively and figured ; but his ornament is intended for the ſake of force, rather than grace. He never gives you the ſame thought twice. He places it in the light which appears to him the moſt ſtriking ; but if you do not apprehend it well in that light, you need not expect to find it in any other. His ſentences are arranged with compactneſs and ſtrength, rather than with cadence and harmony. The utmoſt preciſion is ſtudied in them ; and they are commonly deſigned to ſuggeſt more to the reader's imagination than they directly expreſs.

A DIFFUSE writer unfolds his thought fully. He places it in a variety of lights, and gives the reader every poſſible aſſiſtance for underſtanding it completely. He is not very careful to expreſs it at firſt in its full ſtrength ; becauſe he is to repeat the impreſſion ; and what he wants in ſtrength, he propoſes to ſupply by copiouſneſs. Writers of this character generally love magnificence and amplification. Their periods naturally run out into ſome length, and having room for ornament of every kind, they admit it freely.

3 B 2 EACH

EACH of thefe manners has its peculiar advantages; and each becomes faulty when carried to the extreme. The extreme of concifenefs becomes abrupt and obfcure; it is apt alfo to lead into a Style too pointed, and bordering on the epigrammatic. The extreme of diffufenefs becomes weak and languid, and tires the reader. However, to one or other of thefe two manners, a writer may lean according as his genius prompts him: and under the general character of a concife, or of a more open and diffufe Style, may poffefs much beauty in his compofition.

FOR illuftrations of thefe general characters, I can only refer to the writers who are examples of them. It is not fo much from detached paffages, fuch as I was wont formerly to quote for inftances, as from the current of an author's Style, that we are to collect the idea of a formed manner of writing. The two moft remarkable examples that I know, of concifenefs carried as far as propriety will allow, perhaps in fome cafes farther, are Tacitus the Hiftorian, and the Prefident Montefquieu in "L'Efprit de Loix." Ariftotle too holds an eminent rank among didactic writers for his brevity. Perhaps no writer in the world was ever fo frugal of his words as Ariftotle; but this frugality of expreffion frequently darkens his meaning. Of a beautiful and magnificent diffufenefs, Cicero is, beyond doubt, the moft illuftrious inftance that can be given. Addifon alfo, and Sir William Temple, come in fome degree under this clafs.

IN judging when it is proper to lean to the concife, and when to the diffufe manner, we muft be directed by the nature of the Compofition. Difcourfes that are to be fpoken, require

a more

a more copious Style, than books that are to be read. When
the whole meaning muſt be catched from the mouth of the
ſpeaker, without the advantage which books afford of pauſing
at pleaſure, and reviewing what appears obſcure, great conciſeneſs is always to be avoided. We ſhould never preſume too
much on the quickneſs of our hearer's underſtanding; but our
Style ought to be ſuch, that the bulk of men can go along with
us eaſily, and without effort. A flowing copious Style, therefore, is required in all public ſpeakers; guarding, at the ſame
time, againſt ſuch a degree of diffuſion, as renders them languid
and tireſome; which will always prove the caſe, when they
inculcate too much, and preſent the ſame thought under too
many different views.

IN written Compoſitions, a certain degree of conciſeneſs poſſeſſes great advantages. It is more lively; keeps up attention;
makes a briſker and ſtronger impreſſion; and gratifies the mind
by ſupplying more exerciſe to a reader's own thought. A ſentiment, which, expreſſed diffuſely, will barely be admitted to be
juſt, expreſſed conciſely, will be admired as ſpirited. Deſcription, when we want to have it vivid and animated, ſhould be
in a conciſe ſtrain. This is different from the common opinion;
moſt perſons being ready to ſuppoſe, that upon deſcription a writer
may dwell more ſafely than upon other things, and that by a full
and extended Style, it is rendered more rich and expreſſive. I
apprehend, on the contrary, that a diffuſe manner generally weakens it. Any redundant words or circumſtances
encumber the fancy, and make the object we preſent to it, appear confuſed and indiſtinct. Accordingly, the moſt maſterly
deſcribers, Homer, Tacitus, Milton, are almoſt always conciſe

3   in

in their defcriptions. They fhew us more of an object at one glance, than a feeble diffufe writer can fhow, by turning it round and round in a variety of lights. The ftrength and vivacity of defcription, whether in profe or poetry, depend much more upon the happy choice of one or two ftriking circumftances, than upon the multiplication of them.

Addresses to the paffions, likewife, ought to be in the concife, rather than the diffufe manner. In thefe, it is dangerous to be diffufe, becaufe it is very difficult to fupport proper warmth for any length of time. When we become prolix, we are always in hazard of cooling the reader. The heart, too, and the fancy run faft; and if once we can put them in motion, they fupply many particulars to greater advantage than an author can difplay them. The cafe is different, when we addrefs ourfelves to the underftanding; as in all matters of reafoning, explication, and inftruction. There I would prefer a more free and diffufe manner. When you are to ftrike the fancy, or to move the heart, be concife; when you are to inform the underftanding, which moves more flowly, and requires the affiftance of a guide, it is better to be full. Hiftorical narration may be beautiful, either in a concife or a diffufe manner, according to the writer's genius. Livy and Herodotus are diffufe; Thucydides and Salluft are fuccinct; yet all of them are agreeable.

I observed that a diffufe ftyle inclines moft to long periods; and a concife writer, it is certain, will often employ fhort fentences. It is not, however, to be inferred from this, that long or fhort fentences are fully characteriftical of the one or the other manner. It is very poffible for one to compofe always in fhort fentences, and to be withal extremely diffufe, if a fmall meafure

4

of

of fentiment be fpread through many of thefe fentences. Seneca
is a remarkable example. By the fhortnefs and quaintnefs of his
fentences, he may appear at firft view very concife; yet he is
far from being fo. He transfigures the fame thought into many
different forms. He makes it pafs for a new one, only by
giving it a new turn. So alfo, moft of the French writers compofe in fhort fentences; though their ftyle, in general, is not
concife; commonly lefs fo than the bulk of Englifh writers,
whofe fentences are much longer. A French author breaks
down into two or three fentences, that portion of thought which
an Englifh author crowds into one. The direct effect of fhort
fentences, is to render the Style brifk and lively, but not always
concife. By the quick fucceffive impulfes which they make on
the mind, they keep it awake; and give to Compofition more
of a fpirited character. Long periods, like Lord Clarendon's,
are grave and ftately; but, like all grave things, they are in hazard of becoming dull. An intermixture of both long and fhort
ones is requifite, when we would fupport folemnity, together
with vivacity; leaning more to the one or the other, according
as propriety requires, that the folemn or the fprightly fhould
be predominant in our compofition. But of long and fhort fentences, I had occafion, formerly, to treat under the head of the
conftruction of periods.

THE Nervous and the Feeble, are generally held to be characters of Style, of the fame import with the Concife and the
Diffufe. They do indeed very often coincide. Diffufe writers
have for the moft part fome degree of feeblenefs; and nervous
writers will generally be inclined to a concife expreffion. This,
however, does not always hold; and there are inftances of
writers,

writers, who, in the midſt of a full and ample Style, have maintained a great degree of ſtrength. Livy is an example; and in the Engliſh language, Dr. Barrow. Barrow's Style has many faults. It is unequal, incorrect and redundant; but withal, for force and expreſſiveneſs uncommonly diſtinguiſhed. On every ſubject, he multiplies words with an overflowing co-piouſneſs; but it is always a torrent of ſtrong ideas and ſignificant expreſſions which he pours forth. Indeed, the foundations of a nervous or a weak Style are laid in an author's manner of thinking. If he conceives an object ſtrongly, he will expreſs it with energy: but, if he has only an indiſtinct view of his ſubject; if his ideas be looſe and wavering; if his genius be ſuch, or, at the time of his writing, ſo careleſsly exerted, that he has no firm hold of the conception which he would communicate to us; the marks of all this will clearly appear in his Style. Several unmeaning words and looſe epithets will be found; his expreſſions will be vague and general; his arrangement indiſtinct and feeble; we ſhall conceive ſomewhat of his meaning, but our conception will be faint. Whereas a nervous writer, whether he employs an extended or a conciſe Style, gives us always a ſtrong impreſſion of his meaning; his mind is full of his ſubject, and his words are all expreſſive; every phraſe and every figure which he uſes, tends to render the picture, which he would ſet before us, more lively and complete.

I OBSERVED, under the head of Diffuſe and Conciſe Style, that an author might lean either to the one or to the other, and yet be beautiful. This is not the caſe with reſpect to the nervous and the feeble. Every author, in every compoſition, ought to ſtudy to expreſs himſelf with ſome ſtrength, and, in proportion

proportion, as he approaches to the feeble, he becomes a bad writer. In all kinds of writing, however, the fame degree of ftrength is not demanded. But the more grave and weighty any compofition is, the more fhould a character of ftrength predominate in the Style. Hence in hiftory, philofophy, and folemn difcourfes, it is expected moft. One of the moft complete models of a nervous Style, is Demofthenes in his orations.

As every good quality in Style has an extreme, when purfued to which it becomes faulty, this holds of the Nervous Style as well as others. Too great a ftudy of ftrength, to the neglect of the other qualities of Style, is found to betray writers into a harfh manner. Harfhnefs arifes from unufual words, from forced inverfions in the conftruction of a Sentence, and too much neglect of fmoothnefs and eafe. This is reckoned the fault of fome of our earlieft claffics in the Englifh language; fuch as Sir Walter Raleigh, Sir Francis Bacon, Hooker, Chillingworth, Milton in his profe works, Harrington, Cudworth, and other writers of confiderable note in the days of Queen Elizabeth, James I. and Charles I. Thefe writers had nerves and ftrength in a high degree, and are to this day eminent for that quality in Style. But the language in their hands was exceedingly different from what it is now, and was indeed entirely formed upon the idiom and conftruction of the Latin in the arrangement of Sentences. Hooker, for inftance, begins the Preface to his celebrated work of Ecclefiaftical Polity, with the following Sentence: " Though for no other caufe, yet for " this, that pofterity may know we have not loofely, through " filence, permitted things to pafs away as in dream, there

3 C

" fhall be, for men's information, extant this much, concern-
" ing the prefent ftate of the church of God eftablifhed
" amongft us, and their careful endeavours which would have
" upheld the fame." Such a fentence now founds harfh in our
ears. Yet fome advantages certainly attended this fort of Style;
and whether we have gained, or loft, upon the whole, by
departing from it, may bear a queftion. By the freedom of
arrangement, which it permitted, it rendered the Language
fufceptible of more ftrength, of more variety of collocation,
and more harmony of period. But however this be, fuch
a ftyle is now obfolete ; and no modern writer could adopt it
without the cenfure of harfhnefs and affectation. The prefent
form which the Language has affumed, has, in fome meafure,
facrificed the ftudy of ftrength to that of perfpicuity and eafe.
Our arrangement of words has become lefs forcible, perhaps,
but more plain and natural : and this is now underftood to be
the genius of our Language.

THE reftoration of King Charles II. feems to be the æra of
the formation of our prefent ftyle. Lord Clarendon was one of
the firft who laid afide thofe frequent inverfions which prevailed
among writers of the former age. After him, Sir William
Temple, polifhed the Language ftill more. But the author,
who, by the number and reputation of his works, formed it
more than any one, into its prefent ftate, is Dryden. Dryden
began to write at the Reftoration, and continued long an author both in poetry and profe. He had made the language
his ftudy ; and though . he wrote haftily, and often incor-
rectly, and his ftyle is not free from faults, yet there is a
richnefs in his diction, a copioufnefs, eafe, and variety in his
expreffion,

**

expreſſion, which has not been ſurpaſſed by any who have come after him *. Since his time, conſiderable attention has been paid to Purity and Elegance of Style: But it is Elegance, rather than Strength, that forms the diſtinguiſhing quality of moſt of the good Engliſh writers. Some of them compoſe in a more manly and nervous manner than others; but, whether it be from the genius of our Language, or from whatever other cauſe, it appears to me, that we are far from the ſtrength of ſeveral of the Greek and Roman authors.

HITHERTO we have conſidered Style under thoſe characters that reſpect its expreſſiveneſs of an author's meaning. Let us now proceed to conſider it in another view, with reſpect to the degree of ornament employed tò beautify it. Here, the Style of different authors ſeems to raiſe, in the following gradation: a Dry, a Plain, a Neat, an Elegant, a Flowery manner. Of each of theſe in their order.

FIRST, a Dry manner. This excludes all ornament of every kind. Content with being underſtood, it has not the leaſt aim to pleaſe, either the fancy or the ear. This is tolerable only in pure didactic writing; and even there, to make us bear it,

* Dr. Johnſon, in his life of Dryden, gives the following character of his proſe ſtyle: " His prefaces have not the formality of a ſettled ſtyle, in which " the firſt half of the ſentence betrays the other. The clauſes are never " balanced, nor the periods modelled; every word ſeems to drop by chance, " though it falls into its proper place. Nothing is cold or languid; the whole " is airy, animated, and vigorous; what is little, is gay; what is great, is " ſplendid. Though all is eaſy, nothing is feeble; though all ſeems careleſs, " there is nothing harſh; and though, ſince his earlier works, more than a " century has paſſed, they have nothing yet uncouth or obſolete."

great

great weight and folidity of matter is requifite; and entire perfpicuity of Language. Ariftotle is the thorough example of a
Dry Style. Never, perhaps, was there any author who ad-
hered fo rigidly to the ftrictnefs of a didactic manner, throughout all his writings, and conveyed fo much inftruction without
the leaft approach to ornament. With the moft profound
genius, and extenfive views, he writes like a pure intelligence,
who addreffes himfelf folely to the underftanding, without
making any ufe of the channel of the imagination. But this
is a manner which deferves not to be imitated. For, although
the goodnefs of the matter may compenfate the drynefs or
harfhnefs of the Style, yet is that drynefs a confiderable defect;
as it fatigues attention, and conveys our fentiments, with difadvantage, to the reader or hearer.

A PLAIN Style rifes one degree above a Dry one. A writer
of this character, employs very little ornament of any kind,
and refts, almoft, entirely upon his fenfe. But, if he is at no
pains to engage us by the employment of figures, mufical arrangement, or any other art of writing, he ftudies, however,
to avoid difgufting us like a dry and a harfh writer. Befides Perfpicuity, he purfues Propriety, Purity, and Precifion, in his
Language; which form one degree, and no inconfiderable one, of
beauty. Livelinefs too, and force, may be confiftent with a
very Plain Style: and, therefore, fuch an author, if his fentiments be good, may be abundantly agreeable. The difference
between a dry and plain writer, is, that the former is incapable
of ornament, and feems not to know what it is; the latter
feeks not after it. He gives us his meaning, in good language,
diftinct and pure; any further ornament he gives himfelf no

trouble

trouble about; either, becaufe he thinks it unneceffary to his fubject; or, becaufe his genius does not lead him to delight in it; or, becaufe it leads him to defpife it *.

THIS laft was the cafe with Dean Swift, who may be placed at the head of thofe that have employed the Plain Style. Few writers have difcovered more capacity. He treats every fubject which he handles, whether ferious or ludicrous, in a mafterly manner. He knew, almoft, beyond any man, the Purity, the Extent, the Precifion of the Englifh Language; and, therefore, to fuch as wifh to attain a pure and correct Style, he is one of the moft ufeful models. But we muft not look for much ornament and grace in his Language. His haughty and morofe genius, made him defpife any embellifhment of this kind as beneath his dignity. He delivers his fentiments in a plain, downright, pofitive manner, like one who is fure he is in the right; and is very indifferent whether you be pleafed or not. His fentences are commonly negligently arranged; diftinctly enough as to the fenfe; but, without any regard to fmoothnefs of found; often without much regard to compactnefs, or elegance. If a metaphor, or any other figure, chanced to render his fatire more poignant, he would, perhaps, vouchfafe to adopt it, when it came in his way; but if it tended only to embelifh and illuftrate, he would rather throw it afide. Hence, in his ferious pieces, his ftyle often borders upon the

* On this head, of the General Characters of Style, particularly, the Plain and the Simple, and the characters of thofe Englifh authors who are claffed under them, in this, and the following Lecture, feveral ideas have been taken from a manufcript treatife on rhetoric, part of which was fhewn to me, many years ago, by the learned and ingenious Author, Dr. Adam Smith; and which, it is hoped, will be given by him to the Public.

dry

dry and unpleaſing; in his humourous ones, the plainneſs of his manner gives his wit a ſingular edge, and ſets it off to the higheſt advantage. There is no froth, nor affectation in it; it flows without any ſtudied preparation; and while he hardly appears to ſmile himſelf, he makes his reader laugh heartily. To a writer of ſuch a genius as Dean Swift, the Plain Style was moſt admirably fitted. Among our philoſophical writers, Mr. Locke comes under this claſs; perſpicuous and pure, but almoſt without any ornament whatever. In works which admit, or require, ever ſo much ornament, there are parts where the plain manner ought to predominate. But we muſt remember, that when this is the character which a writer affects throughout his whole compoſition, great weight of matter, and great force of ſentiment, are required, in order to keep up the reader's attention, and prevent him from tiring of the author.

WHAT is called a Neat Style comes next in order; and here we are got into the region of ornament; but that ornament not of the higheſt or moſt ſparkling kind. A writer of this cha-racter ſhows, that he does not deſpiſe the beauty of Language. It is an object of his attention. But his attention is ſhown in the choice of his words, and in a graceful collocation of them; rather than in any high efforts of imagination, or eloquence. His ſentences are always clean, and free from the incumbrance of ſuperfluous words; of a moderate length; rather inclining to brevity, than a ſwelling ſtructure; cloſing with propriety; without any tails, or adjections dragging after the proper cloſe. His cadence is varied; but not of the ſtudied muſical kind. His figures, if he uſes any, are ſhort and correct; rather than bold

and

and glowing. Such a Style as this, may be attained by a writer who has no great powers of fancy or genius; by induſtry merely, and careful attention to the rules of writing; and it is a Style always agreeable. It imprints a character of moderate elevation on our compoſition, and carries a decent degree of ornament, which is not unſuitable to any ſubject whatever. A familiar letter, or a law paper, on the drieſt ſubject, may be written with neatneſs; and a ſermon, or a philoſophical treatiſe, in a Neat Style, will be read with pleaſure.

AN Elegant Style is a character, expreſſing a higher degree of ornament than a neat one; and, indeed, is the term uſually applied to Style, when poſſeſſing all the virtues of ornament, without any of its exceſſes or defects. From what has been formerly delivered, it will eaſily be underſtood, that complete Elegance implies great perſpicuity and propriety; purity in the choice of words, and care and dexterity in their harmonious and happy arrangement. It implies, farther, the grace and beauty of Imagination ſpread over Style, as far as the ſubject admits it; and all the illuſtration which Figurative Language adds, when properly employed. In a word, an elegant writer is one who pleaſes the fancy and the ear, while he informs the underſtanding; and who gives us his ideas clothed with all the beauty of expreſſion, but not overcharged with any of its miſplaced finery. In this claſs, therefore, we place only the firſt rate writers in the Language; ſuch as, Addiſon, Dryden, Pope, Temple, Bolingbroke, Atterbury, and a few more: writers who differ widely from one another in many of the attributes of Style, but whom we now claſs together, under the denomination

denomination of Elegant, as in the fcale of Ornament, poffeffing nearly the fame place.

WHEN the ornaments, applied to Style, are too rich and
gaudy in proportion to the fubject; when they return upon us
too faft, and ftrike us either with a dazzling luftre, or a falfe
brilliancy, this forms what is called a Florid Style; a term commonly ufed to fignify the excefs of ornament. In a young
compofer this is very pardonable. Perhaps, it is even a pro-
mifing fymptom in young people, that their Style fhould incline
to the Florid and Luxuriant: " Volo fe efferat in adolofcente
" fæcunditas," fays Quinctilian, " multum inde decoquent
" anni, multum ratio limabit, aliquid velut ufu ipfo deteretur;
" fit modo unde excidi poffit quid et exculpi.—Audeat hæc ætas
" plura, et inveniat et inventis gaudeat; fint licet illa non fatis in-
" terim ficca et fevera. Facile remedium eft ubertatis: fterilia
" nullo labore vincuntur *." But, although the Florid Style may
be allowed to youth, in their firft effays, it muft not receive
the fame indulgence from writers of maturer years. It is to be
expected, that judgment, as it ripens, fhould chaften imagination, and reject, as juvenile, all fuch ornaments as are redundant, unfuitable to the fubject, or not conducive to illuftrate
it. Nothing can be more contemptible than that tinfel fplendor
of Language, which fome writers perpetually affect. It were

---

* " In youth, I wifh to fee luxuriancy of fancy appear. Much of it will
" be diminifhed by years; much will be corrected by ripening judgment;
" fome of it, by the mere practice of compofition, will be worn away. Let
" there be only fufficient matter, at firft, that can bear fome pruning and lop-
" ping off. At this time of life, let genius be bold and inventive, and pride
" itfelf in its efforts, though thefe fhould not, as yet, be correct. Luxuri-
" ancy can eafily be cured; but for barrennefs there is no remedy."

well,

well, if this could be afcribed to the real overflowing of a rich imagination. We fhould then have fomething to amufe us, at leaft, if we found little to inftruct us. But the worft is, that with thofe frothy writers, it is a luxuriancy of words, not of fancy. We fee a laboured attempt to rife to a fplendour of compofition, of which they have formed to themfelves fome loofe idea; but having no ftrength of genius for attaining it, they endeavour to fupply the defect by poetical words, by cold exclamations, by common place figures, and every thing that has the appearance of pomp and magnificence. It has efcaped thefe writers, that fobriety in ornament, is one great fecret for rendering it pleafing; and that, without a foundation of good fenfe and folid thought, the moft Florid Style is but a childifh impofition on the Public. The Public, however, are but too apt to be fo impofed on; at leaft, the mob of Readers, who are very ready to be caught, at firft, with whatever is dazzling and gaudy.

I CANNOT help thinking, that it reflects more honour on the religious turn, and good difpofitions of the prefent age, than on the public tafte, that Mr. Harvey's Meditations have had fo great a currency. The pious and benevolent heart, which is always difplayed in them, and the lively fancy which, on fome occafions, appears, juftly merited applaufe: but the perpetual glitter of expreffion, the fwoln imagery, and ftrained defcription which abound in them, are ornaments of a falfe kind. I would, therefore, advife ftudents of oratory to imitate Mr. Harvey's piety, rather than his Style; and, in all compofitions of a ferious kind, to turn their attention, as Mr. Pope fays, " from founds to things, from fancy to the heart." Admonitions of this kind, I have already had occasion to give, and may hereafter repeat them; as I conceive nothing more incumbent on me in this course of Lectures, than to take every opportunity of cautioning my Readers against the affected and frivolous use of ornament; and, instead of that slight and superficial taste in writing, which I apprehend to be at present too fashionable, to introduce, as far as my endeavours can avail, a taste for more solid thought, and more manly Simplicity in Style.

LECTURE XIX.

GENERAL CHARACTERS OF STYLE—SIMPLE, AFFECTED, VEHEMENT—DIRECTIONS FOR FORMING A PROPER STYLE.

HAVING entered in the laſt Lecture on the conſideration of the general Characters of Style, I treated of the conciſe and diffuſe, the nervous and feeble manner. I conſidered Style alſo, with relation to the different degrees of ornament employed to beautify it; in which view, the manner of different authors riſes according to the following gradation: Dry, Plain, Neat, Elegant, Flowery.

I AM next to treat of Style under another character, one of great importance in writing, and which requires to be accurately examined, that of Simplicity, or a Natural Style, as diſtinguiſhed from Affectation. Simplicity, applied to writing, is a term very frequently uſed; but, like many other critical terms often uſed looſely, and without preciſion. This has been owing chiefly

to

to the different meanings given to the word Simplicity, which, therefore, it will be neceſſary here to diſtinguiſh; and to ſhew in what ſenſe it is a proper attribute of Style. We may remark four different acceptations in which it is taken.

THE firſt is, Simplicity of Compoſition, as oppoſed to too great a variety of parts. Horace's precept refers to this:

Denique ſit quod vis ſimplex duntaxat et unum *.

THIS is the Simplicity of plan in a tragedy, as diſtinguiſhed from double plots, and crowded incidents; the Simplicity of the Iliad, or Æneid, in oppoſition to the digreſſions of Lucan, and the ſcattered tales of Arioſto; the Simplicity of Grecian architecture, in oppoſition to the irregular variety of the Gothic. In this ſenſe, Simplicity is the ſame with Unity.

THE ſecond ſenſe is, Simplicity of Thought, as oppoſed to Refinement. Simple thoughts are what ariſe naturally; what the occaſion, or the ſubject ſuggeſt unſought; and what, when once ſuggeſted, are eaſily apprehended by all. Refinement in writing, expreſſes a leſs natural and obvious train of thought, and which it required a peculiar turn of genius to purſue; within certain bounds very beautiful; but when carried too far, approaching to intricacy, and hurting us by the appearance of being *recherché*, or far ſought. Thus, we would naturally ſay, that Mr. Parnell is a poet of far greater Simplicity, in his turn of thought, than Mr. Cowley: Cicero's thoughts on moral

---

* " Then learn the wand'ring humour to controul,
" And keep one equal tenor through the whole."   FRANCIS.

9   ſubjects

subjects are natural; Seneca's too refined and laboured. In
these two senses of Simplicity, when it is oppofed, either to
variety of parts, or to refinement of thought, it has no proper
relation to Style.

THERE is a third fenfe of Simplicity, in which it has refpect
to Style; and ftands oppofed to too much ornament, or pomp
of Language; as when we fay, Mr. Locke is a fimple, Mr.
Harvey a florid, writer; and it is in this fenfe, that the
" *fimplex*," the " *tenue*," or " *fubtile genus dicendi*," is underftood by Cicero and Quinctilian. The Simple Style, in this
fenfe, coincides with the Plain or the Neat Style, which I
before mentioned; and, therefore, requires no farther illuftration.

BUT there is a fourth fenfe of Simplicity, alfo refpecting
Style; but not refpecting the degree of ornament employed,
fo much as the eafy and natural manner in which our Language expreffes our thoughts. This is quite different from the
former fenfe of the word juft now mentioned, in which Simplicity was equivalent to Plainnefs: whereas, in this fenfe, it is
compatible with the higheft ornament. Homer, for inftance,
poffeffes this Simplicity in the greateft perfection; and yet no
writer has more Ornament and Beauty. This Simplicity, which
is what we are now to confider, ftands oppofed, not to Ornament, but to Affectation of Ornament, or appearance of labour about our Style; and it is a diftinguifhing excellency in
writing.

A WRITER

A WRITER of Simplicity expresses himself in such a manner, that every one thinks he could have written in the same way; Horace describes it,

> ——————— ——————— ————ut sibi quivis
> Speret idem, sudet multum, frustraque laboret
> Ausus idem *.

There are no marks of art in his expression; it seems the very language of nature; you see in the Style, not the writer and his labour, but the man, in his own natural character. He may be rich in his expression; he may be full of figures, and of fancy; but these flow from him without effort; and he appears to write in this manner, not because he has studied it, but because it is the manner of expression most natural to him. A certain degree of negligence, also, is not inconsistent with this character of Style, and even not ungraceful in it; for too minute an attention to words is foreign to it: " Habeat ille," says Cicero, (Orat. No. 77.) " molle quiddam, et quod indicet non ingra-
" tam negligentiam hominis, de re magis quàm de verbo la-
" borantis †." This is the great advantage of Simplicity of Style, that, like simplicity of manners, it shows us a man's sentiments and turn of mind laid open without disguise. More studied and artificial manners of writing, however beautiful,

---

* " From well-known tales such fictions would I raise,
" As all might hope to imitate with ease;
" Yet, while they strive the same success to gain,
" Should find their labours, and their hopes in vain."   FRANCIS.

† " Let this Style have a certain softness and ease, which shall characterise
" a negligence, not unpleasing in an author, who appears to be more sollicitous
" about the thought than the expression."

2

have

have always this difadvantage, that they exhibit an author in form, like a man at court, where the fplendour of drefs, and the ceremonial of behaviour, conceal thofe peculiarities which diftinguifh one man from another. But reading an author of Simplicity, is like converfing with a perfon of diftinction at home, and with eafe, where we find natural manners, and a marked character.

THE higheft degree of this Simplicity, is expreffed by a French term, to which we have none that fully anfwers in our Language, *naïveté*. It is not eafy to give a precife idea of the import of this word. It always expreffes a difcovery of character. I believe the beft account of it is given by a French critic, M. Marmontel, who explains it thus : That fort of amiable ingenuity, or undifguifed opennefs, which feems to give us fome degree of fuperiority over the perfon who fhows it; a certain infantine Simplicity, which we love in our hearts, but which difplays fome features of the character that we think we could have art enough to hide ; and which, therefore, always leads us to fmile at the perfon who difcovers this character. La Fontaine, in his Fables, is given as the great example of fuch *naïveté*. This, however, is to be underftood, as defcriptive of a particular fpecies only of Simplicity.

WITH refpect to Simplicity, in general, we may remark, that the antient original writers are always the moft eminent for it. This happens from a plain reafon, that they wrote from the dictates of natural genius, and were not formed upon the labours and writings of others, which is always in hazard of

producing

producing Affectation. Hence, among the Greek writers, we have more models of a beautiful Simplicity than among the Roman. Homer, Hefiod, Anâcreon, Theocritus, Herodotus, and Xenophon, are all diftinguifhed for it. Among the Romans alfo, we have fome writers of this character, particularly Terence, Lucretius, Phœdrus, and Julius Cæfar. The following paffage of Terence's Andria, is a beautiful inftance of Simplicity of manner in defcription :

Funus interim
Procedit ; fequimur ; ad fepulchrum venimus ;
In ignem impofita eft ; fletur ; interea hæc foror
Quam dixi, ad flammam acceffit imprudentius
Satis cum periculo. Ibi tum exanimatus Pamphilus,
Bene diffimulatum amorem, & celatum indicat ;
Occurrit præceps, mulierem ab igne retrahit,
Mea Glycerium, inquit, quid agis ? Cur te is perditum ?
Tum illa, ut confuetum facile amorem cerneres,
Rejecit fe in eum, flens quam familiariter *.

Act. I. Sc. 1.

All

---

* " Meanwhile the funeral proceeds ; we follow ;
" Come to the fepulchre : the body's placed
" Upon the pile ; lamented ; whereupon
" This fifter, I was fpeaking of, all wild,
" Ran to the flames with peril of her life.
" There ! there ! the frighted Pamphilus betrays
" His well diffembled and long hidden love ;
" Runs up, and takes her round the waift, and cries,
" Oh ! my Glycerium ! what is it you do ?
" Why, why, endeavour to deftroy yourfelf ?

" Then

All the words here are remarkably happy and elegant; and
convey a moſt lively picture of the ſcene deſcribed: while, at the ſame time, the Style appears wholly artleſs and unlaboured. Let us, next, conſider ſome Engliſh writers who come under this claſs.

SIMPLICITY is the great beauty of Archiſhop Tillotſon's manner. Tillotſon has long been admired as an eloquent writer, and a model for preaching. But his eloquence, if we can call it ſuch, has been often miſunderſtood. For, if we include, in the idea of eloquence, vehemence and ſtrength, picturefque deſcription, glowing figures, or correct arrangement of ſentences, in all theſe parts of oratory the Archbiſhop is exceedingly deficient. His Style is always pure, indeed, and perſpicuous, but careleſs and remiſs, too often feeble and languid; little beauty in the conſtruction of his ſentences, which are frequently ſuffered to drag unharmoniouſly; ſeldom any attempt towards ſtrength or ſublimity. But, notwithſtanding theſe defects, ſuch a conſtant vein of good ſenſe and piety runs through his works, ſuch an earneſt and ſerious manner, and ſo much uſeful inſtruction conveyed in a Style ſo pure, natural, and unaffected, as will juſtly recommend him to high regard, as long as the Engliſh Language remains; not, indeed, as a model of the higheſt eloquence, but as a ſimple and amiable writer, whoſe manner is ſtrongly expreſſive of great goodneſs and worth. I obſerved before, that Simplicity of manner

---

" Then ſhe in ſuch a manner, that you thence
" Might eaſily perceive their long long love,
" Threw herſelf back into his arms, and wept,
" Oh! how familiarly! COLMAN.

may be confiſtent with ſome degree of negligence in Style; and it is only the beauty of that Simplicity which makes the negligence of ſuch writers ſeem graceful. But, as appears in the Archbiſhop, negligence may ſometimes be carried ſo far as to impair the beauty of Simplicity, and make it border on a flat and languid manner.

Sir William Temple is another remarkable writer in the Style of Simplicity. In point of ornament and correctneſs, he riſes a degree above Tillotſon; though, for correctneſs, he is not in the higheſt rank. All is eaſy and flowing in him; he is exceedingly harmonious; ſmoothneſs, and what may be called amænity, are the diſtinguiſhing characters of his manner; relaxing, ſometimes, as ſuch a manner will naturally do, into a prolix and remiſs Style. No writer whatever has ſtamped upon his Style a more lively impreſſion of his own character. In reading his works, we ſeem engaged in converſation with him; we become thoroughly acquainted with him, not merely as an author, but as a man; and contract a friendſhip for him. He may be claſſed as ſtanding in the middle, between a negligent Simplicity, and the higheſt degree of Ornament, which this character of Style admits.

Of the latter of theſe, the higheſt, moſt correct, and ornamented degree of the ſimple manner, Mr. Addiſon, is, beyond doubt, in the Engliſh Language, the moſt perfect example: and, therefore, though not without ſome faults, he is, on the whole, the ſafeſt model for imitation, and the freeſt from conſiderable defects, which the Language affords. Perſpicuous and pure he is in the higheſt degree; his preciſion, indeed, not
very

very great; yet nearly as great as the fubjects which he treats of require: the conftruction of his fentences eafy, agreeable, and commonly very mufical; carrying a character of fmoothnefs, more than of ftrength. In Figurative Language, he is rich; particularly, in fimilies and metaphors; which are fo employed, as to render his Style fplendid without being gaudy. There is not the leaft Affectation in his manner; we fee no marks of labour; nothing forced or conftrained; but great elegance joined with great eafe and fimplicity. He is, in particular, diftinguifhed by a character of modefty, and of politenefs, which appears in all his writings. No author has a more popular and infinuating manner; and the great regard which he every where fhews for virtue and religion, recommends him highly. If he fails in any thing, it is in want of ftrength and precifion, which renders his manner, though perfectly fuited to fuch effays as he writes in the Spectator, not altogether a proper model for any of the higher and more elaborate kinds of compofition. Though the public have ever done much juftice to his merit, yet the nature of his merit has not always been feen in its true light: for, though his poetry be elegant, he certainly bears a higher rank among the profe writers, than he is intitled to among the poets; and, in profe, his humour is of a much higher, and more original ftrain, than his philofophy. The character of Sir Roger de Coverley difcovers more genius than the critique on Milton.

Such authors as thofe, whofe characters I have been giving, one never tires of reading. There is nothing in their manner that ftrains or fatigues our thoughts: we are pleafed, without being dazzled by their luftre. So powerful is the charm of

Simplicity

Simplicity in an author of real genius, that it atones for many defects, and reconciles us to many a carelefs expreffion. Hence, in all the moft excellent authors, both in profe and verfe, the fimple and natural manner may be always remarked; although other beauties being predominant, this form not their peculiar and diftinguifhing character. Thus Milton is fimple in the midft of all his grandeur; and Demofthenes in the midft of all his vehemence. To grave and folemn writings, Simplicity of manner adds the more venerable air. Accordingly, this has often been remarked as the prevailing character throughout all the facred Scriptures: and indeed no other character of Style was fo much fuited to the dignity of infpiration.

Of authors, who, notwithftanding many excellencies, have rendered their Style much lefs beautiful by want of Simplicity, I cannot give a more remarkable example than Lord Shaftfbury. This is an author on whom I have made obfervations feveral times before, and fhall now take leave of him, with giving his general character under this head. Confiderable merit, doubtlefs, he has. His works might be read with profit for the moral philofophy which they contain, had he not filled them with fo many oblique and invidious infinuations againft the Chriftian Religion; thrown out, too, with fo much fpleen and fatire, as do no honour to his memory, either as an author or a man. His language has many beauties. It is firm, and fupported in an uncommon degree: it is rich and mufical. No Englifh author, as I formerly fhewed, has attended fo much to the regular conftruction of his fentences, both with refpect to propriety, and with refpect to cadence. All this gives fo much elegance and pomp to his language, that there is no wonder it fhould

5　　　　　　　　　　　　　　　have

have been fometimes highly admired. It is greatly hurt, however, by perpetual ftiffnefs and affectation. This is its capital
fault. His lordfhip can exprefs nothing with Simplicity. He
feems to have confidered it as vulgar, and beneath the dignity
of a man of quality, to fpeak like other men. Hence he is ever
in bufkins; full of circumlocutions and artificial elegance. In
every fentence, we fee the marks of labour and art; nothing of
that eafe, which expreffes a fentiment coming natural and warm
from the heart. Of figures and ornament of every kind, he is
exceedingly fond; fometimes happy in them; but his fondnefs
for them is too vifible; and having once laid hold of fome metaphor or allufion that pleafed him, he knows not how to part
with it. What is moft wonderful, he was a profeffed admirer
of Simplicity; is always extolling it in the ancients, and cenfuring the moderns for the want of it; though he departs from
it himfelf as far as any one modern whatever. Lord Shaftfbury
poffeffed delicacy and refinement of tafte, to a degree that we
may call exceffive and fickly; but he had little warmth of paffion; few ftrong or vigorous feelings: and the coldnefs of his
character led him to that artificial and ftately manner which appears in his writings. He was fonder of nothing than of wit
and raillery; but he is far from being happy in it. He attempts it often, but always awkwardly; he is ftiff, even in his
pleafantry; and laughs in form, like an author, and not like a
man *.

FROM

* It may perhaps be not unworthy of being mentioned, that the firft edition of
his Enquiry into Virtue was publifhed, furreptitioufly I believe, in a feparate
form, in the year 1699; and is fometimes to be met with; by comparing which,
with the corrected edition of the fame treatife, as it now ftands among his works,
we

FROM the account which I have given of Lord Shaftſbury's manner, it may eaſily be imagined, that he would miſlead many who blindly admired him. Nothing is more dangerous to the tribe of imitators, than an author, who, with many impoſing beauties, has alſo ſome very conſiderable blemiſhes. This is fully exemplified in Mr. Blackwall of Aberdeen, the author of the Life of Homer, the Letters on Mythology, and the Court of Auguſtus; a writer of conſiderable learning, and of ingenuity alſo; but infected with an extravagant love of an artificial Style, and of that parade of language which diſtinguiſhes the Shaftſburean manner.

HAVING now ſaid ſo much to recommend Simplicity, or the eaſy and natural manner of writing, and having pointed out the defects of an oppoſite manner; in order to prevent miſtakes on this ſubject, it is neceſſary for me to obſerve, that it is very poſſible for an author to write ſimply, and yet not beautifully. One may be free from affectation, and not have merit. The beautiful Simplicity ſuppoſes an author to poſſeſs real genius; to write with ſolidity, purity, and livelineſs of imagination. In this caſe, the ſimplicity or unaffectedneſs of his manner, is the crowning ornament; it heightens every other beauty; it is the dreſs of nature, without which, all beauties are imperfect. But if mere unaffectedneſs were ſufficient to conſtitute the beauty of Style, weak, trifling, and dull writers might often lay claim to this beauty. And, accordingly, we frequently meet with pretended critics, who extol the dulleſt writers on account

we ſee one of the moſt curious and uſeful examples that I know, of what is called *Limæ labor*; the art of poliſhing language, breaking long ſentences, and working up an imperfect draught into a highly finiſhed performance.

                                    **

                                                                        of

of what they call the " Chaſte Simplicity of their manneɪ;" which, in truth, is no other than the abſence of every ornament, through the mere want of genius and imagination. We muſt diſtinguiſh, therefore, between that Simplicity which accompanies true genius, and which is perfectly compatible with every proper ornament of Style, and that which is no other than a careleſs and ſlovenly manner. Indeed, the diſtinction is eaſily made from the effect produced. The one never fails to intereſt the Reader; the other is inſipid and tireſome.

I PROCEED to mention one other manner or character of Style, different from any that I have yet ſpoken of; which may be diſtinguiſhed by the name of the Vehement. This always implies ſtrength; and is not, by any means, inconſiſtent with Simplicity: but in its predominant character is diſtinguiſhable from either the ſtrong or the ſimple manner. It has a peculiar ardour; it is a glowing Style; the language of a man, whoſe imagination and paſſions are heated, and ſtrongly affected by what he writes; who is therefore negligent of leſſer graces, but pours himſelf forth with the rapidity and fulneſs of a torrent. It belongs to the higher kinds of oratory; and indeed is rather expected from a man who is ſpeaking, than from one who is writing in his cloſet. The orations of Demoſthenes furniſh the full and perfect example of this ſpecies of Style.

AMONG Engliſh writers, the one who has moſt of this character, though mixed, indeed, with ſeveral defects, is Lord Bolingbroke. Bolingbroke was formed by nature to be a factious leader; the demagogue of a popular aſſembly. Accordingly, the Style that runs through all his political writings, is that of

one

one declaiming with heat, rather than writing with deliberation. He abounds in Rhetorical Figures ; and pours himſelf forth with great impetuoſity. He is copious to a fault ; places the ſame thought before us in many different views ; but generally with life and ardour. He is bold, rather than correct ; a torrent that flows ſtrong, but often muddy. His ſentences are varied as to length and ſhortneſs ; inclining, however, moſt to long periods, ſometimes including parentheſes, and frequently crowding and heaping a multitude of things upon one another, as naturally happens in the warmth of ſpeaking. In the choice of his words, there is great felicity and preciſion. In exact conſtruction of ſentences, he is much inferior to Lord Shaftſbury ; but greatly ſuperior to him in life and eaſe. Upon the whole, his merit, as a writer, would have been very conſiderable, if his matter had equalled his Style. But whilſt we find many things to commend in the latter, in the former, as I before remarked, we can hardly find any thing to commend. In his reaſonings, for moſt part, he is flimſy and falſe ; in his political writings, factious ; in what he calls his philoſophical ones, irreligious and ſophiſtical in the higheſt degree.

I SHALL inſiſt no longer on the different manners of Writers, or the general Characters of Style. Some other, beſides thoſe which I have mentioned, might be pointed out ; but I am ſenſible, that it is very difficult to ſeparate ſuch general conſiderations of the Style of authors from their peculiar turn of ſentiment, which it is not my buſineſs, at preſent, to criticiſe. Conceited Writers, for inſtance, diſcover their ſpirit ſo much in their compoſition, that it imprints on their Style a character of pertneſs ; though I confeſs it is difficult to ſay, whether this can

be

be claſſed among the attributes of Style, or rather is to be aſcribed entirely to the thought. In whatever claſs we rank it, all appearances of it ought to be avoided with care, as a moſt diſguſting blemiſh in writing. Under thoſe general heads, which I have conſidered, I have taken an opportunity of giving the character of many of the eminent claſſics in the Engliſh language.

FROM what I have ſaid on this ſubject, it may be inferred, that to determine among all thoſe different manners of writing, what is preciſely the beſt, is neither eaſy, nor neceſſary. Style is a field that admits of great latitude. Its qualities in different authors may be very different; and yet in them all beautiful. Room muſt be left here for genius; for that particular determination which every one receives from nature to one manner of expreſſion more than another. Some general qualities, indeed, there are of ſuch importance, as ſhould always, in every kind of compoſition, be kept in view; and ſome defects we ſhould always ſtudy to avoid. An oſtentatious, a feeble, a harſh, or an obſcure Style, for inſtance, are always faults; and Perſpicuity, Strength, Neatneſs, and Simplicity, are beauties to be always aimed at. But as to the mixture of all, or the degree of predominancy of any one of theſe good qualities, for forming our peculiar diſtinguiſhing manner, no preciſe rules can be given; nor will I venture to point out any one model as abſolutely perfect.

IT will be more to the purpoſe, that I conclude theſe diſſertations upon Style, with a few directions concerning the proper method of attaining a good Style in general; leaving the particular character of that Style to be either formed by the fubject on which we write, or prompted by the bent of genius.

THE firft direction which I give for this purpofe, is, to ftudy clear ideas on the fubject concerning which we are to write or fpeak. This is a direction which may at firft appear to have fmall relation to Style. Its relation to it, however, is extremely clofe. The foundation of all good Style, is good fenfe accompanied with a lively imagination. The Style and thoughts of a writer are fo intimately connected, that, as I have feveral times hinted, it is frequently hard to diftinguifh them. Wherever the impreffions of things upon our minds are faint and indiftinct, or perplexed and confufed, our Style in treating of fuch things will infallibly be fo too. Whereas, what we conceive clearly and feel ftrongly, we will naturally exprefs with clearnefs and with ftrength. This, then, we may be affured, is a capital rule as to Style, to think clofely of the fubject, till we have attained a full and diftinct view of the matter which we are to clothe in words, till we become warm and interefted in it; then, and not till then, fhall we find expreffion begin to flow. Generally fpeaking, the beft and moft proper expreffions, are thofe which a clear view of the fubject fuggefts, without much labour or enquiry after them. This is Quinctilian's obfervation, Lib. viii. c. i. " Plerumque optima verba rebus cohærent, et " cernuntur fuo lumine. At nos quærimus illa, tanquam la- " teant feque fubducant. Ita nunquam putamus verba effe circa " id de quo dicendum eft ; fed ex aliis locis petimus, et in- " ventis vim afferimus *."

IN

---

* " The moft proper words for the moft part adhere to the thoughts which " are to be expreffed by them, and may be difcovered as by their own light. But

" we

In the fecond place, in order to form a good Style, the frequent practice of compofing is indifpenfibly neceffary. Many rules concerning Style I have delivered; but no rules will anfwer the end without exercife and habit. At the fame time, it is not every fort of compofing that will improve Style. This is fo far from being the cafe, that by frequent, carelefs, and hafty compofition, we fhall acquire certainly a very bad Style; we fhall have more trouble afterwards in unlearning faults, and correcting negligences, than if we had not been accuftomed to compofition at all. In the beginning therefore, we ought to write flowly, and with much care. Let the facility and fpeed of writing, be the fruit of longer practice. " Moram et folicitu-" dinem," fays Quinctilian with the greateft reafon, L. x. c. 3, " initiis impero. Nam primum hoc conftituendum ac obti-" nendum eft, ut quam optime fcribamus: celeritatem dabit " confuetudo. Paulatim res facilius fe oftendent, verba re-" fpondebunt, compofitio profequetur. Cuncta denique ut " in familiâ bene inftitutâ in officio erunt. Summa hæc eft " rei; cito fcribendo non fit ut bene fcribatur; bene fcribendo, " fit ut cito *."

" hunt after them, as if they were hidden, and only to be found in a corner.
" Hence, inftead of conceiving the words to lie near the fubject, we go in queft
" of them to fome other quarter, and endeavour to give force to the expref-
" fions we have found out."

* " I enjoin that fuch as are beginning the practice of compofition, write
" flowly, and with anxious deliberation. Their great object at firft fhould be,
" to write as well as poffible; practice will enable them to write fpeedily. By
" degrees matter will offer itfelf ftill more readily; words will be at hand;
" compofition will flow; every thing, as in the arrangement of a well-ordered
" family, will prefent itfelf in its proper place. The fum of the whole is this;
" by hafty compofition, we fhall never acquire the art of compofing well; by
" writing well, we fhall come to write fpeedily."

We

WE muft obferve, however, that there may be an extreme, in too great and anxious a care about words. We muft not retard the courfe of thought, nor cool the heat of imagination, by paufing too long on every word we employ. There is, on certain occafions, a glow of compofition which fhould be kept up, if we hope to exprefs ourfelves happily, though at the expence of allowing fome inadvertencies to pafs. A more fevere examination of thefe muft be left to be the work of correction. For, if the practice of compofition be ufeful, the laborious work of correcting is no lefs fo; is indeed abfolutely neceffary to our reaping any benefit from the habit of compofition. What we have written, fhould be laid by for fome little time, till the ardour of compofition be paft, till the fondnefs for the expreffions we have ufed be worn off, and the expreffions themfelves be forgotten; and then reviewing our work with a cool and critical eye, as if it were the performance of another, we fhall difcern many imperfections which at firft efcaped us. Then is the feafon for pruning redundancies; for weighing the arrangement of fentences; for attending to the juncture and connecting particles; and bringing Style into a regular, correct, and fupported form. This " *Limæ Labor*," muft be fubmitted to by all who would communicate their thoughts with proper advantage to others; and fome practice in it will foon fharpen their eye to the moft neceffary objects of attention, and render it a much more eafy and practicable work than might at firft be imagined.

IN the third place, with refpect to the affiftance that is to be gained from the writings of others, it is obvious, that we ought to render ourfelves well acquainted with the Style of the beft

2   authors.

authors. This is requisite, both in order to form a just taste in
Style, and to supply us with a full stock of words on every subject.
In reading authors, with a view to Style, attention should be
given to the peculiarities of their different manners; and in
this, and former Lectures, I have endeavoured to suggest several
things that may be useful in this view. I know no exercise
that will be found more useful for acquiring a proper Style, than
to translate some passage from an eminent English author,
into our own words. What I mean is, to take, for instance,
some page of one of Mr. Addison's Spectators, and read it carefully over two or three times, till we have got a firm hold of
the thoughts contained in it; then to lay aside the book; to
attempt to write out the passage from memory, in the best way
we can; and having done so, next to open the book, and
compare what we have written, with the Style of the author.
Such an exercise will, by comparison, shew us where the defects of our Style lie; will lead us to the proper attentions for
rectifying them; and, among the different ways in which the
same thought may be expressed, will make us perceive that
which is the most beautiful. But,

In the fourth place, I must caution, at the same time, against
a servile imitation of any one author whatever. This is always
dangerous. It hampers genius; it is likely to produce a stiff
manner; and those who are given to close imitation, generally
imitate an author's faults as well as his beauties. No man will
ever become a good writer, or speaker, who has not some degree of confidence to follow his own genius. We ought to
beware, in particular, of adopting any author's noted phrases, or
transcribing passages from him. Such a habit will prove fatal to
all

all genuine compofition.   Infinitely better it is to have fomething that is our own, though of moderate beauty, than to
affeÄ to ſhine in borrowed ornaments, which will, at laſt,
betray the utter poverty of our genius.   On theſe heads of com-
poſing, correÄing, reading, and imitating, I advife every
ſtudent of oratory to conſult what QuinÄilian has delivered in
the Xth book of his Inſtitutions, where he will find a variety
of excellent obſervations and direÄions, that well deferve attention.

In the fifth place, it is an obvious, but material rule, with
refpeÄ to Style, that we always ſtudy to adapt it to the ſubjeÄ,
and alſo to the capacity of our hearers, if we are to ſpeak in
public.   Nothing merits the name of eloquent or beautiful,
which is not ſuited to the occaſion, and to the perſons to whom
it is addreffed.   It is to the laſt degree awkward and abſurd, to
attempt a poetical florid Style, on occaſions, when it ſhould be
our buſineſs only to argue and reaſon ; or to ſpeak with elaborate pomp of expreſſion, before perſons who comprehend nothing of it, and who can only ſtare at our unfeaſonable magnificence.   Theſe are defeÄs not ſo much in point of Style, as,
what is much worſe, in point of common ſenſe. When we begin to
write or ſpeak, we ought previouſly to fix in our minds a clear
conception of the end to be aimed at; to keep this ſteadily in
our view, and to ſuit our Style to it.   If we do not ſacrifice to
this great objeÄ, every ill-timed ornament that may occur to
our fancy, we are unpardonable; and though children and fools
may admire, men of ſenſe will laugh at us and our Style.

In

IN the laſt place, I cannot conclude the ſubject without this
admonition, that, in any caſe, and on any occaſion, attention
to Style muſt not engroſs us ſo much, as to detract from a
higher degree of attention to the thoughts: " Curam verbo-
" rum," ſays the great Roman Critic, " rerum volo eſſe ſoli-
" citudinem *." A direction the more neceſſary, that the preſent taſte of the age in writing, ſeems to lean more to Style
than to thought. It is much eaſier to dreſs up trivial and common ſentiments with ſome beauty of expreſſion, than to afford a
fund of vigorous, ingenious, and uſeful thoughts. The latter,
requires true genius ; the former, may be attained by induſtry,
with the help of very ſuperficial parts. Hence, we find ſo
many writers frivolouſly rich in Style, but wretchedly poor in
Sentiment. The public ear is now ſo much accuſtomed to a
correct and ornamented Style, that no writer can, with ſafety,
neglect the ſtudy of it. But he is a contemptible one who does
not look to ſomething beyond it ; who does not lay the chief
ſtreſs upon his matter, and employ ſuch ornaments of Style to
recommend it, as are manly, not foppiſh : " Majore animo,"
ſays the writer whom I have ſo often quoted, " aggredienda eſt
" eloquentia ; quæ ſi toto corpore valet, ungues polire et capil-
" lum componere, non exiſtimabit ad curam ſuam pertinere.
" Ornatus et virilis et fortis, et ſanctus ſit ; nec effeminatam
" levitatem, et fuco ementitum colorem amet ; ſanguine et viri-
" bus niteat †.

---

* " To your expreſſion be attentive ; but about your matter be ſolicitous."

† " A higher ſpirit ought to animate thoſe who ſtudy eloquence. They ought
" to conſult the health and foundneſs of the whole body, rather than bend
" their attention to ſuch trifling objects as paring the nails, and dreſſing the
" hair. Let ornament be manly and chaſte, without effeminate gaiety, or
" artificial colouring ; let it ſhine with the glow of health and ſtrength."

LECTURE XX.

CRITICAL EXAMINATION OF THE STYLE OF MR. ADDISON, IN Nº 411. OF THE SPECTATOR.

I HAVE infifted fully on the fubject of Language and Style, both becaufe it is, in itfelf, of great importance, and becaufe it is more capable of being afcertained by precife rule, than feveral other parts of compofition. A critical analyfis of the Style of fome good author will tend further to illuftrate the fubject; as it will fuggeft obfervations which I have not had occafion to make, and will fhow, in the moft practical light, the ufe of thofe which I have made.

MR. ADDISON is the author whom I have chofen for this purpofe. The Spectator, of which his papers are the chief ornament, is a book which is in the hands of every one, and which cannot be praifed too highly. The good fenfe, and good writing, the ufeful morality, and the admirable vein of humour which abound in it, render it one of thofe ftandard

books

books which have done the greateſt honour to the Engliſh **L E C T.**
nation. I have formerly given the general character of Mr. **XX.**
Addiſon's Style and manner, as natural and unaffected, eaſy
and polite, and full of thoſe graces which a flowery imagination
diffuſes over writing. At the ſame time, though one of the
moſt beautiful writers in the Language, he is not the moſt correct ; a circumſtance which renders his compoſition the more
proper to be the ſubject of our preſent criticiſm. The free
and flowing manner of this amiable writer ſometimes led him
into inaccuracies, which the more ſtudied circumſpection and
care of far inferior writers have taught them to avoid. Remarking his beauties, therefore, which I ſhall have frequent
occaſion to do as I proceed, I muſt alſo point out his negligences and defects. Without a free, impartial diſcuſſion of
both the faults and beauties which occur in his compoſition, it
is evident, this piece of criticiſm would be of no ſervice : and,
from the freedom which I uſe in criticiſing Mr. Addiſon's Style,
none can imagine, that I mean to depreciate his writings,
after having repeatedly declared the high opinion which I entertain of them. The beauties of this author are ſo many, and
the general character of his Style is ſo elegant and eſtimable, that
the minute imperfections I ſhall have occaſion to point out, are
but like thoſe ſpots in the ſun, which may be diſcovered by the
aſſiſtance of art, but which have no effect in obſcuring its luſtre.
It is, indeed, my judgment, that what Quinctilian applies to
Cicero, " Ille ſe profeciſſe ſciat, cui Cicero valde placebit,"
may, with juſtice, be applied to Mr. Addiſon; that to be highly
pleaſed with his manner of writing, is the criterion of one's
having acquired a good taſte in Engliſh Style. The paper on
which we are now to enter, is No. 411. the firſt of his cele-

brated Effays on the Pleafures of the Imagination, in the Sixth Volume of the Spectator. It begins thus:

Our fight is the moft perfect, and moft delightful of all our fenfes.

THIS is an excellent introductory fentence. It is clear, precife, and fimple. The author lays down, in a few plain words, the propofition which he is going to illuftrate throughout the reft of the paragraph. In this manner we fhould always fet out. A firft fentence fhould feldom be a long, and never an intricate one.

HE might have faid, *Our fight is the moft perfect, and the moft delightful.*—But he has judged better, in omitting to repeat the article, *the.* For the repetition of it is proper, chiefly when we intend to point out the objects of which we fpeak, as diftinguifhed from, or contrafted with, each other; and when we want that the reader's attention fhould reft on that diftinction. For inftance; had Mr. Addifon intended to fay, That our fight is at once the moft *delightful,* and the moft *ufeful,* of all our fenfes, the article might then have been repeated with propriety, as a clear and ftrong diftinction would have been conveyed. But as between *perfect* and *delightful,* there is lefs contraft, there was no occafion for fuch repetition. It would have had no other effect, but to add a word unneceffarily to the fentence. He proceeds:

It fills the mind with the largeft variety of ideas, converfes with its objects at the greateft diftance, and continues the longeft

5

in

in action, without being tired or satiated with its proper enjoy-ments.

THIS sentence deserves attention, as remarkably harmonious, and well constructed. It possesses, indeed, almost all the properties of a perfect sentence. It is entirely perspicuous. It is loaded with no superfluous or unnecessary words. For, *tired or satiated*, towards the end of the sentence, are not used for synonymous terms. They convey distinct ideas, and refer to different members of the period; that this sense *continues the longest in action without being tired*, that is, without being fatigued with its action; and also, without being *satiated with its proper enjoyments*. That quality of a good sentence which I termed its unity, is here perfectly preserved. It is *our sight* of which he speaks. This is the object carried through the sentence, and presented to us, in every member of it, by those verbs, *fills, converses, continues*, to each of which, it is clearly the nominative. Those capital words are disposed of in the most proper places; and that uniformity is maintained in the construction of the sentence, which suits the unity of the object.

OBSERVE too, the music of the period; consisting of three members, each of which, agreeably to a rule I formerly mentioned, grows, and rises above the other in sound, till the sentence is conducted, at last, to one of the most melodious closes which our Language admits; *without being tired or satiated with its proper enjoyments. Enjoyments*, is a word of length and dignity, exceedingly proper for a close which is designed to be a musical one. The harmony is the more happy, that this disposition of the members of the period which suits the sound

fo

fo well, is no lefs juft and proper with refpect to the fenfe. It follows the order of nature. Firft, we have the variety of objects mentioned, which fight furnifhes to the mind; next, we have the action of fight on thofe objects; and laftly, we have the time and continuance of its action. No order could be more natural or happy.

THIS fentence has ftill another beauty. It is figurative, without being too much fo for the fubject. A metaphor runs through it. The fenfe of fight is, in fome degree, perfonified. We are told of its *converfing* with its objects; and of its not being *tired* or *fatiated* with its *enjoyments*; all which expreffions are plain allufions to the actions and feelings of men. This is that flight fort of Perfonification, which, without any appearance of boldnefs, and without elevating the fancy much above its ordinary ftate, renders difcourfe picturefque, and leads us to conceive the author's meaning more diftinctly, by clothing abftract ideas, in fome degree, with fenfible colours. Mr. Addifon abounds with this beauty of Style beyond moft authors; and the fentence which we have been confidering, is very expreffive of his manner of writing. There is no blemifh in it whatever, unlefs that a ftrict Critic might perhaps object, that the epithet *large*, which he applies to *variety,—the largeft variety of ideas*, is an epithet more commonly applied to extent than to number. It is plain, that he here employed it to avoid the repetition of the word *great*, which occurs immediately afterwards.

The fenfe of feeling can, indeed, give us a notion of extenfion, fhape, and all other ideas that enter at the eye, except colours;
but,

but, at the same time, it is very much straitened and confined in its operations, to the number, bulk, and distance of its particular objects.

THIS sentence is by no means so happy as the former. It is, indeed, neither clear nor elegant. *Extension and shape* can, with no propriety, be called *ideas*; they are properties of matter. Neither is it accurate, even according to Mr. Locke's philosophy (with which our Author seems here to have puzzled himself), to speak of any sense *giving us a notion of ideas;* our senses give us the ideas themselves. The meaning would have been much more clear, if the Author had expressed himself thus: " The sense of feeling can, indeed, give us the idea of " extension, figure, and all the other properties of matter " which are perceived by the eye, except colours."

THE latter part of the sentence is still more embarrassed. For what meaning can we make of the sense of feeling being *confined, in its operations, to the number, bulk, and distance, of its particular objects?* Surely, every sense is confined, as much as the sense of feeling, to the number, bulk, and distance of its own objects. Sight and feeling are, in this respect, perfectly on a level; neither of them can extend beyond their own objects. The turn of expression is so inaccurate here, that one would be apt to suspect two words to have been omitted in the printing, which were originally in Mr. Addison's manuscript; because the insertion of them would render the sense much more intelligible and clear. These two words are, *with regard :—— it is very much straitened, and confined, in its operations, with regard to the number, bulk, and distance of its particular objects.*

9   The

The meaning then would be, that feeling is more limited than fight *in this respect*; that it is confined to a narrower circle, to a smaller number of objects.

THE epithet *particular*, applied to *objects*, in the conclusion of the sentence, is redundant, and conveys no meaning whatever. Mr. Addison seems to have used it in place of *peculiar*, as indeed he does often in other passages of his writings. But *particular* and *peculiar*, though they are too often confounded, are words of different import from each other. *Particular* stands opposed to *general*; *peculiar* stands opposed, to what is possessed in *common with others*. *Particular* expresses what in the logical Style is called *Species*; *peculiar*, what is called *differentia*.—*Its peculiar objects* would have signified in this place, the objects of the sense of feeling, as distinguished from the objects of any other sense; and would have had more meaning than *its particular objects*. Though, in truth, neither the one nor the other epithet was requisite. It was sufficient to have said simply, *its objects*.

Our sight seems designed to supply all these defects, and may be considered as a more delicate and diffusive kind of touch, that spreads itself over an infinite multitude of bodies, comprehends the largest figures, and brings into our reach some of the most remote parts of the universe.

HERE again the author's Style returns upon us in all its beauty. This is a sentence distinct, graceful, well arranged, and highly musical. In the latter part of it, it is constructed with three members, which are formed much in the same manner

ner with thofe of the fecond fentence, on which I beftowed fo much praife.   The conftruction is fo fimilar, that if it had followed immediately after it, we fhould have been fenfible of a faulty monotony.   But the interpofition of another fentence between them, prevents this effect.

It is this fenfe which furnifhes the imagination with its ideas ; fo that by the pleafures of the Imagination or Fancy (which I fhall ufe promifcuoufly), I here mean fuch as arife from vifible objects, either when we have them actually in our view ; or when we call up their ideas into our minds by paintings, ftatues, defcriptions, or any the like occafion.

In place of, *It is this fenfe which furnifhes*—the author might have faid more fhortly, *This fenfe furnifhes.*   But the mode of expreffion which he has ufed, is here more proper.   This fort of full and ample affertion, *it is this which,* is fit to be ufed when a propofition of importance is laid down, to which we feek to call the reader's attention.   It is like pointing with the hand at the object of which we fpeak.   The parenthefis in the middle of the fentence, *which I fhall ufe promifcuoufly,* is not clear.   He ought to have faid, *terms which I fhall ufe promifcuoufly* ; as the verb *ufe* relates not to the pleafures of the imagination, but to the terms of fancy and imagination, which he was to employ as fynonymous.   *Any the like occafion*—to call a painting or a ftatue *an occafion* is not a happy expreffion, nor is it very proper to fpeak of *calling up ideas by occafions.*   The common phrafe, *any fuch means,* would have been more natural.

We

LECT.
XX.

We cannot indeed have a single image in the fancy, that did not make its first entrance through the sight ; but we have the power of retaining, altering, and compounding those images which we have once received, into all the varieties of picture and vision that are most agreeable to the imagination ; for, by this faculty, a man in a dungeon is capable of entertaining himself with scenes and landscapes more beautiful than any that can be found in the whole compass of nature.

It may be of use to remark, that in one member of this sentence there is an inaccuracy in syntax. It is very proper to say, *altering and compounding those images which we have once received, into all the varieties of picture and vision.* But we can with no propriety say, *retaining them into all the varieties ;* and yet, according to the manner in which the words are ranged, this construction is unavoidable. For *retaining*, *altering*, and *compounding*, are participles, each of which equally refers to, and governs the subsequent noun, *those images* ; and that noun again is necessarily connected with the following preposition, *into*. This instance shows the importance of carefully attending to the rules of Grammar and Syntax ; when so pure a writer as Mr. Addison could, through inadvertence, be guilty of such an error. The construction might easily have been rectified, by disjoining the participle *retaining* from the other two participles in this way : " We have the power of retaining those images " which we have once received ; and of altering and com- " pounding them into all the varieties of picture and vision ;" or better perhaps thus : " We have the power of retaining, al- " tering, and compounding those images which we have once " received ; and of forming them into all the varieties of pic-
" ture

" ture and vifion."—The latter part of the fentence is clear
and elegant.

There are few words in the Englifh Language, which are em-
ployed in a more loofe and uncircumfcribed fenfe than thofe of the
Fancy and the Imagination.

There are few words—which are employed.—It had been
better, if our author here had faid more fimply—*Few words in*
the Englifh language are employed.—Mr. Addifon, whofe Style
is of the free and full, rather than the nervous kind, deals, on
all occafions, in this extended fort of phrafeology.   But it
is proper only when fome affertion of confequence is advanced, and which can bear an emphafis; fuch as that in
the firft fentence of the former paragraph.   On other occafions, thefe little words *it is,* and *there are,* ought to be
avoided as redundant and enfeebling—*thofe of the Fancy and the*
Imagination.   The article ought to have been omitted here.   As
he does not mean the powers of *the Fancy and the Imagination,*
but the words only, the article certainly had no proper place ;
neither, indeed, was there any occafion for other two words,
thofe of.   Better, if the fentence had run thus : " Few words
" in the Englifh language are employed in a more loofe and
" uncircumfcribed fenfe, than Fancy and Imagination."

I therefore thought it neceffary to fix and determine the notion of
thefe two words, as I intend to make ufe of them in the thread of
my following fpeculations, that the reader may conceive rightly
what is the fubject which I proceed upon.

LECT.
XX.

THOUGH *fix* and *determine* may appear fynonymous words, yet a difference between them may be remarked, and they may be viewed, as applied here, with peculiar delicacy. The author had juft faid, that the words of which he is fpeaking were *loofe* and *uncircumfcribed*. *Fix* relates to the firft of thefe, *determine* to the laft. We *fix* what is *loofe* ; that is, we confine the word to its proper place, that it may not fluctuate in our imagination, and pafs from one idea to another; and we *determine* what is *uncircumfcribed*, that is, we afcertain its *termini* or limits, we draw the circle round it, that we may fee its boundaries. For we cannot conceive the meaning of a word, nor indeed of any other thing clearly, till we fee its limits, and know how far it extends. Thefe two words, therefore, have grace and beauty as they are here applied ; though a writer, more frugal of words than Mr. Addifon, would have preferred the fingle word *afcertain*, which conveys, without any metaphor, the import of them both.

THE *notion of thefe words* is fomewhat of a harfh phrafe, at leaft not fo commonly ufed, as the *meaning of thefe words——as I intend to make ufe of them in the thread of my fpeculations* ; this is plainly faulty. A fort of metaphor is improperly mixed with words in the literal fenfe. He might very well have faid, *as I intend to make ufe of them in my following fpeculations.* —— This was plain language; but if he chofe to borrow an allufion from *thread*, that allufion ought to have been fupported ; for there is no confiftency in *making ufe of them in the thread of fpeculations* ; and, indeed, in exprefling any thing fo fimple and familiar as this is, plain language is always to be preferred to metaphorical——*the fubject which I proceed upon,*

upon, is an ungraceful close of a sentence; better, *the subject* L E C T.
upon which I proceed.   XX.

*I must therefore desire him to remember, that by the pleasures of
the Imagination, I mean only such pleasures as arise originally from
sight, and that I divide these pleasures into two kinds.*

As the last sentence began with—*I therefore thought it neceffary to fix*, it is carelefs to begin this fentence in a manner fo
very fimilar, *I must therefore defire him to remember*; efpecially,
as the fmall variation of ufing, *on this account*, or, *for this reafon*, in place of *therefore*, would have amended the Style.——
When he fays—*I mean only fuch pleafures*—it may be remarked,
that the adverb *only* is not in its proper place.   It is not intended
here to qualify the verb *mean*, but *fuch pleafures*; and therefore fhould have been placed in as clofe connection as poffible
with the word which it limits or qualifies.   The Style becomes
more clear and neat, when the words are arranged thus: " by
" the pleafures of the Imagination, I mean fuch pleafures only
" as arife from fight."

*My defign being, first of all, to difcourfe of thofe primary plea-
fures of the imagination, which entirely proceed from fuch objects
as are before our eyes; and, in the next place, to fpeak of thofe fecondary pleafures of the Imagination, which flow from the ideas
of vifible objects, when the objects are not actually before the eye,
but are called up into our memories, or formed into agreeable vifions of things, that are either abfent or fictitious.*

3 H 2   IT

IT is a great rule in laying down the divifion of a fubject, to ftudy neatnefs and brevity as much as poffible. The divifions are then more diftinctly apprehended, and more eafily remembered. This fentence is not perfectly happy in that refpect. It is fomewhat clogged by a tedious phrafeology. *My defign being firft of all to difcourfe—in the next place to fpeak of—fuch objects as are before our eyes—things that are either abfent or fictitious.* Several words might have been fpared here; and the Style made more neat and compact.

The pleafures of the Imagination, taken in their full extent, are not fo grofs as thofe of fenfe, nor fo refined as thofe of the underftanding.

This fentence is diftinct and elegant.

The laft are indeed more preferable, becaufe they are founded on fome new knowledge or improvement in the mind of man : Yet it muft be confeffed, that thofe of the Imagination are as great and as tranfporting as the other.

IN the beginning of this fentence, the phrafe, *more preferable,* is fuch a plain inaccuracy, that one wonders how Mr. Addifon fhould have fallen into it; feeing *preferable* of itfelf, expreffes the comparative degree, and is the fame with more eligible, or more excellent.

I MUST obferve farther, that the propofition contained in the laft member of this fentence, is neither clear nor neatly expreffed—

9

expreſſed—*it muſt be confeſſed, that thoſe of the imagination are as great, and as tranſporting as the other.*—In the former ſentence, he had compared three things together; the pleaſures of the Imagination, thoſe of ſenſe, and thoſe of the underſtanding. In the beginning of this ſentence, he had called the pleaſures of the underſtanding *the laſt:* and he ends the ſentence, with obſerving, that thoſe of the Imagination are as great and tranſporting *as the other.* Now, beſides that *the other* makes not a proper contraſt with *the laſt,* he leaves it ambiguous, whether, by *the other,* he meant the pleaſures of the Underſtanding, or the pleaſures of Senſe; for it may refer to either by the conſtruction; though, undoubtedly, he intended that it ſhould refer to the pleaſures of the Underſtanding only. The propoſition reduced to perſpicuous language, runs thus: " Yet it muſt be confeſſed, that the pleaſures of the
" Imagination, when compared with thoſe of the Underſtand-
" ing, are no leſs great and tranſporting.'

A beautiful proſpect delights the ſoul as much as a demonſtration ; and a deſcription in Homer has charmed more readers than a chapter in Ariſtotle.

THIS is a good illuſtration of what he had been aſſerting, and is expreſſed with that happy and elegant turn, for which our author is very remarkable.

Beſides, the pleaſures of the Imagination have this advantage above thoſe of the Underſtanding, that they are more obvious, and more eaſy to be acquired.

THIS

THIS is alſo an unexceptionable ſentence.

It is but opening the eye, and the ſcene enters.

THIS ſentence is lively and picturefque.   By the gaiety and briſkneſs which it gives the Style, it ſhows the advantage of intermixing ſuch a ſhort ſentence as this amidſt a run of longer ones, which never fails to have a happy effect.   I muſt remark, however, a ſmall inaccuracy.   A *ſcene* cannot be ſaid to *enter;* an *actor* enters ; but a ſcene *appears*, or *preſents itſelf.*

The colours paint themſelves on the fancy, with very little attention of thought or application of mind in the beholder.

THIS is ſtill beautiful illuſtration ; carried on with that agreeable flowerineſs of fancy and ſtyle, which is ſo well ſuited to thoſe pleaſures of the Imagination, of which the author is treating.

We are ſtruck, we know not how, with the ſymmetry of any thing we ſee, and immediately aſſent to the beauty of an object, without enquiring into the particular cauſes and occaſions of it.

THERE is a falling off here from the elegance of the former ſentences.   We *aſſent* to the truth of a propoſition ; but cannot ſo well be ſaid *to aſſent to the beauty of an object.   Acknowledge* would have expreſſed the ſenſe with more propriety.   The cloſe of the ſentence too is heavy and ungraceful—*the particular cauſes and occaſions of it*—both *particular*, and *occaſions*, are words quite ſuperfluous; and the pronoun *it* is in ſome meaſure ambiguous,

biguous, whether it refers to beauty or to object. It would

have been fome amendment to the Style to have run thus :
" we immediately acknowledge the beauty of an object, with-
" out enquiring into the caufe of that beauty."

*A man of a polite imagination is let into a great many pleafures,
that the vulgar are not capable of receiving.*

Polite is a term more commonly applied to manners or behaviour, than to the mind or imagination. There is nothing
farther to be obferved on this fentence, unlefs the ufe of *that*
for a relative pronoun, inftead of *which ;* an ufage which is too
frequent with Mr. Addifon. *Which* is a much more definite
word than *that*, being never employed in any other way than
as a relative ; whereas *that* is a word of many fenfes ; fometimes a demonftrative pronoun, often a conjunction. In fome
cafes we are indeed obliged to ufe *that* for a relative, in order to
avoid the ungraceful repetition of *which* in the fame fentence.
But when we are laid under no neceffity of this kind, *which* is
always the preferable word, and certainly was fo in this fentence—*Pleafures which the vulgar are not capable of receiving,*
is much better than *pleafures that the vulgar, &c.*

*He can converfe with a picture, and find an agreeable compa-
nion in a ftatue. He meets with a fecret refrefhment in a defcription ; and often feels a greater fatisfaction in the profpect of fields
and meadows, than another does in the poffeffion. It gives him,
indeed, a kind of property in every thing he fees ; and makes the
moft rude uncultivated parts of nature adminifter to his pleafures :
fo that he looks upon the world, as it were, in another light, and
disfovers.*

8

difcovers in it a multitude of charms that conceal themfelves from the generality of mankind.

ALL this is very beautiful. The illuftration is happy; and the Style runs with the greateft eafe and harmony. We fee no labour, no ftiffnefs, or affectation; but an author writing from the native flow of a gay and pleafing imagination. This predominant character of Mr. Addifon's manner, far more than compenfates all thofe little negligences which we are now remarking. Two of thefe occur in this paragraph. The firft, in the fentence which begins with, *It gives him indeed a kind of property*—To this *it*, there is no proper antecedent in the whole paragraph. In order to gather the meaning, we muft look back as far as to the third fentence before, the firft of the paragraph, which begins with, *A man of a polite imagination.* This phrafe, *polite imagination*, is the only antecedent to which this *it* can refer; and even that is an improper antecedent, as it ftands in the genitive cafe, as the qualification only of *a man.*

THE other inftance of negligence, is towards the end of the paragraph—*So that he looks upon the world, as it were, in another light.*—*By another* light, Mr. Addifon means, a light different from that in which other men view the world. But though this expreffion clearly conveyed this meaning to himfelf when writing, it conveys it very indiftinctly to others; and is an inftance of that fort of inaccuracy, into which, in the warmth of compofition, every writer of a lively imagination is apt to fall; and which can only be remedied by a cool, fubfequent review.—*As it were*—is upon moft occafions no more than an ungraceful palliative, and here there was not the leaft occafion

for

for it, as he was not about to fay any thing which required a foftening of this kind. To fay the truth, this laft fentence, *fo that he looks upon the world*, and what follows, had better been wanting altogether. It is no more than an unneceffary recapitulation of what had gone before; a feeble adjection to the lively picture he had given of the pleafures of the imagination. The paragraph would have ended with more fpirit at the words immediately preceding; *the uncultivated parts of nature adminifter to his pleafures.*

There are, indeed, but very few who know how to be idle and innocent, or have a relifh of any pleafures that are not criminal; every diverfion they take, is at the expence of fome one virtue or another, and their very firft ftep out of bufinefs is into vice or folly.

Nothing can be more elegant, or more finely turned, than this fentence. It is neat, clear, and mufical. We could hardly alter one word, or difarrange one member, without fpoiling it. Few fentences are to be found more finifhed, or more happy.

A man fhould endeavour, therefore, to make the fphere of his innocent pleafures as wide as poffible, that he may retire into them with fafety, and find in them, fuch a fatisfaction as a wife man would not blufh to take.

This alfo is a good fentence, and gives occafion to no material remark.

Of this nature are those of the imagination, which do not require such a bent of thought as is necessary to our more serious employments, nor, at the same time, suffer the mind to sink into that indolence and remissness, which are apt to accompany our more sensual delights ; but, like a gentle exercise to the faculties, awaken them from sloth and idleness, without putting them upon any labour or difficulty.

THE beginning of this sentence is not correct, and affords an instance of a period too loosely connected with the preceding one. *Of this nature,* says he, *are those of the imagination.* We might ask of what nature? For it had not been the scope of the preceding sentence to describe the nature of any set of pleasures. He had said, that it was every man's duty to make the sphere of his innocent pleasures as wide as possible, in order that, within that sphere, he might find a safe retreat, and a laudable satisfaction. The transition is loosely made, by beginning the next sentence with saying, *Of this nature are those of the imagination.* It had been better, if, keeping in view the governing object of the preceding sentence, he had said, " This " advantage we gain," or, " This satisfaction we enjoy, by " means of the pleasures of imagination." The rest of the sentence is abundantly correct.

We might here add, that the pleasures of the fancy are more conducive to health than those of the understanding, which are worked out by dint of thinking, and attended with too violent a labour of the brain.

ON this sentence, nothing occurs deserving of remark, except that *worked out by dint of thinking,* is a phrase which

borders

borders too much on vulgar and colloquial language, to be
proper for being employed in a polifhed compofition.

Delightful fcenes, whether in nature, painting, or poetry, have a kindly influence on the body, as well as the mind, and not only ferve to clear and brighten the imagination, but are able to difperfe grief and melancholy, aud to fet the animal fpirits in pleafing and agreeable motions. For this reafon Sir Francis Bacon, in his Effay upon Health, has not thought it improper to prefcribe to his reader a poem, or a profpeƐt, where he particularly diffuades him from knotty and fubtile difquifitions, and advifes him to purfue ftudies that fill the mind with fplendid and illuftrious objeƐts, as hiftories, fables, and contemplations of nature.

In the latter of thefe two fentences, a member of the period is altogether out of its place; which gives the whole fentence a harfh and disjointed caft, and ferves to illuftrate the rules I formerly gave concerning arrangement. The wrong-placed member which I point at, is this; *where he particularly diffuades him from knotty and fubtile difquifitions ;*—thefe words fhould, undoubtedly, have been placed not where they ftand, but thus: *Sir Francis Bacon, in his Effay upon Health, where he particularly diffuades the reader from knotty and fubtile fpeculations, has not thought it improper to prefcribe to him, &c.* This arrangement reduces every thing into proper order.

I have, in this Paper, by way of introduƐion, fettled the notion of thofe pleafures of the imagination, which are the fubjeƐt of my prefent undertaking, and endeavoured, by feveral confiderations, to recommend to my readers the purfuit of thofe pleafures ; I fhall,

*in my next Paper examine the feveral fources from whence thefe
pleafures are derived.*

THESE two concluding fentences afford examples of the proper collocation of circumftances in a period. I formerly fhowed,
that it is often a matter of difficulty to difpofe of them in fuch a
manner, as that they fhall not embarrafs the principal fubject of
the fentence. In the fentences before us, feveral of thefe inci-
dental circumftances neceffarily come in—*By way of introduction—by feveral confiderations—in this Paper—in the next Paper.*
All which are, with great propriety, managed by our author.
It will be found, upon trial, that there were no other parts of
the fentence, in which they could have been placed to equal
advantage. Had he faid, for inftance, " I have fettled the
" notion, (rather, *the meaning*) — of thofe pleafures of
" the imagination, which are the fubject of my prefent
" undertaking, by way of introduction, in this paper, and
" endeavoured to recommend the purfuit of thofe plea-
" fures to my readers by feveral confiderations," we muft
be fenfible, that the fentence, thus clogged with circumftances
in the wrong place, would neither have been fo neat nor fo
clear, as it is by the prefent conftruction

LECTURE XXI.

CRITICAL EXAMINATION OF THE STYLE IN N° 412 OF THE SPECTATOR.

THE obfervations which have occurred in reviewing that paper of Mr. Addifon's, which was the fubject of the laft Lecture, fufficiently fhow, that, in the writings of an author of the moft happy genius, and diftinguifhed talents, inaccuracies may fometimes be found. Though fuch inaccuracies may be overbalanced by fo many beauties, as render Style highly plea-fing and agreeable upon the whole, yet it muft be defirable to every writer to avoid, as far as he can, inaccuracy of any kind. As the fubject therefore is of importance, I have thought it might be ufeful to carry on this criticifm throughout two or three fubfequent Papers of the Spectator. At the fame time I muft intimate, that the Lectures on thefe Papers are folely intended for fuch as are applying themfelves to the ftudy of Englifh Style. I pretend not to give inftruction to thofe who are already well acquainted with the powers of language. To them my remarks may prove unedifying; to fome they may

feem

LECT.
XXI.

feem tedious and minute : but to fuch as have not yet made all the proficiency which they defire in elegance of Style, ftrict attention to the compofition and ftructure of fentences cannot fail to prove of confiderable benefit : and though my remarks on Mr. Addifon fhould, in any inftance, be thought ill-founded, they will, at leaft, ferve the purpofe of leading them into the train of making proper remarks for themfelves *. I proceed, therefore, to the examination of the fubfequent paper N°. 412.

I fhall firft confider thofe pleafures of the imagination, which arife from the actual view and furvey of outward objects : and thefe, I think, all proceed from the fight of what is great, uncommon, or beautiful.

THIS fentence gives occafion for no material remark. It is fimple and diftinct. The two words which he here ufes, *view* and *furvey*, are not altogether fynonymous : as the former may be fuppofed to import mere infpection; the latter more deli-

---

* If there be readers who think any farther apology requifite for my adventuring to criticife the fentences of fo eminent an author as Mr. Addifon, I muft take notice, that I was naturally led to it by the circumftances of that part of the kingdom where thefe Lectures were read; where the ordinary fpoken language often differs much from what is ufed by good Englifh authors. Hence it occurred to me, as a proper method of correcting any peculiarities of dialect, to direct ftudents of eloquence, to analize and examine, with particular attention, the ftructure of Mr. Addifon's fentences. Thofe Papers of the Spectator, which are the fubject of the following Lectures, were accordingly given out in exercife to ftudents, to be thus examined and analized ; and feveral of the obfervations which follow, both on the beauties and blemifhes of this Author, were fuggefted, by the obfervations given to me in confequence of the exercife prefcribed.

berate

berate examination. Yet they lie fo near to one another in
meaning, that, in the prefent cafe, any one of them, perhaps,
would have been fufficient. The epithet *actual*, is introduced,
in order to mark more ftrongly the diftinction between what
our author calls the primary pleafures of imagination, which
arife from immediate view, and the fecondary, which arife from
remembrance or defcription.

There may, indeed, be fomething fo terrible or offenfive, that
the horror, or loathfomenefs of an object, may overbear the pleafure
which refults from its novelty, greatnefs, or beauty; but ftill there
will be fuch a mixture of delight in the very difguft it gives us,
as any of thefe three qualifications are moft confpicuous and
prevailing.

THIS fentence muft be acknowledged to be an unfortunate
one. The fenfe is obfcure and embarraffed, and the expreffion
loofe and irregular. The beginning of it is perplexed by the
wrong pofition of the words *fomething* and *object*. The natural
arrangement would have been, *There may, indeed, be fomething*
in an object fo terrible or offenfive, that the horror or loathfomenefs
of it may overbear.—Thefe two epithets, *horror* or *loathfome-*
nefs, are awkwardly joined together. *Loathfomenefs* is, indeed,
a quality which may be afcribed to an object; but *horror* is
not; it is a feeling excited in the mind. The Language would
have been much more correct, had our Author faid, *There may,*
indeed, be fomething in an object fo terrible or offenfive, that the
horror or difguft which it excites may overbear.—The firft two
epithets, *terrible* or *offenfive*, would then have expreffed the
qualities of an object; the latter, *horror* or *difguft*, the correfponding

responding fentiments which thefe qualities produce in us. *Loathfomenefs* was the moft unhappy word he could have chofen : for to be *loathfome*, is to be odious, and feems totally to exclude any *mixture of delight*, which he afterwards fuppofes may be found in the object.

In the latter part of the fentence there are feveral inaccuracies. When he fays, *there will be fuch a mixture of delight in the very difguft it gives us, as any of thefe three qualifications are moft confpicuous.* The conftruction is defective, and feems hardly grammatical. He meant affuredly to fay, *fuch a mixture of delight as is proportioned to the degree in which any of thefe three qualifications are moft confpicuous.*—We know, that there may be a mixture of pleafant and of difagreeable feelings excited by the fame object ; yet it appears inaccurate to fay, that there is any *delight in the very difguft.*—The plural verb *are*, is improperly joined to *any of thefe three qualifications* ; for as *any* is here ufed diftributively, and means *any one of thefe three qualifications*, the correfponding verb ought to have been fingular. The order in which the two laft words are placed, fhould have been reverfed, and made to ftand, *prevailing and confpicuous.* They are *confpicuous*, becaufe they *prevail.*

By greatnefs, I do not only mean the bulk of any fingle object, but the largenefs of a whole view, confidered as one entire piece.

In a former Lecture, when treating of the Structure of Sentences, I quoted this fentence as an inftance of the carelefs manner in which adverbs are fometimes interjected in the midft of a period. *Only*, as it is here placed, appears to be a limita-

3   tion

tion of the following verb, *mean*. The queftion might be put, What more does he than only mean? as the author, undoubtedly, intended it to refer to the *bulk of a fingle object*, it would have been placed, with more propriety, after thefe words :—*I do not mean the bulk of any fingle object only, but the largenefs of a whole view.*—As the following phrafe, *confidered as one entire piece*, feems to be fomewhat deficient, both in dignity and propriety, perhaps this adjection might have been altogether omitted, and the fentence have clofed with fully as much advantage at the word *view*.

Such are the profpects of an open champaign country, a vaft uncultivated defert, of huge heaps of mountains, high rocks and precipices, or a wide expanfe of waters, where we are not ftruck with the novelty, or beauty of the fight, but with that rude kind of magnificence which appears in many of thefe ftupendous works of nature.

THIS fentence, in the main, is beautiful. The objects prefented are all of them noble, felected with judgment, arranged with propriety, and accompanied with proper epithets. We muft, however, obferve, that the fentence is too loofely, and not very grammatically, connected with the preceding one. He fays,—*fuch are the profpects ;*—*fuch*, fignifies, of that nature or quality ; which neceffarily prefuppofes fome adjective, or word defcriptive of a quality going before, to which it refers. But, in the foregoing fentence, there is no fuch adjective. He had fpoken of *greatnefs* in the abftract only; and, therefore, *fuch* has no diftinct antecedent to which we can refer it. The fentence would have been introduced with more grammatical propriety, by faying, *To this clafs belong,* or, *under this head are ranged, the profpects, &c.*—The *of,* which is prefixed to *huge heaps of mountains,* is mifplaced, and has, perhaps, been an error in the printing; as, either all the particulars here enumerated fhould have had this mark of the genitive, or it fhould have been prefixed to none but the firft.—When, in the clofe of the fentence, the Author fpeaks of that *rude magnificence, which appears in many of thefe ftupendous works of nature,* he had better have omitted the word *many,* which feems to except fome of them. Whereas, in his general propofition, he undoubtedly meant to include all the ftupendous works he had enumerated; and there is no queftion that, in all of them, a rude magnificence appears.

Our imagination loves to be filled with an object, or to grafp at any thing that is too big for its capacity. We are flung into a pleafing aftonifhment at fuch unbounded views; and feel a delightful ftillnefs and amazement in the foul, at the apprehenfion of them.

THE Language here is elegant, and feveral of the expreffions remarkably happy. There is nothing which requires any animadverfion except the clofe, *at the apprehenfion of them.* Not only is this a languid enfeebling conclufion of a fentence, otherwife beautiful, but *the apprehenfion of views,* is a phrafe deftitute of all propriety, and, indeed, fcarcely intelligible. Had this adjection been entirely omitted, and the fentence been allowed to clofe with *ftillnefs and amazement in the foul,* it would have been a great improvement. Nothing is frequently more

6

hurtful

hurtful to the grace or vivacity of a period, than fuperfluons dragging words at the conclufion.

The mind of man naturally hates every thing that looks like a reftraint upon it, and is apt to fancy itfelf under a fort of confine-ment, when the fight is pent up in a narrow compafs, and fhortened on every fide by the neighbourhood of walls or mountains. On the contrary, a fpacious horizon is an image of liberty, where the eye has room to range abroad, to expatiate at large on the immenfity of its views, and to lofe itfelf amidft the variety of objects that offer themfelves to its obfervation. Such wide and undetermined profpects are as pleafing to the fancy, as the fpeculations of eternity, or infinitude, are to the underftanding.

Our Author's Style appears, here, in all that native beauty which cannot be too much praifed. The numbers flow fmooth-ly, and with a graceful harmony. The words which he has chofen, carry a certain amplitude and fulnefs, well fuited to the nature of the fubject; and the members of the periods rife in a gradation, accommodated to the rife of the thought. The eye firft *ranges abroad*; then *expatiates at large on the immenfity of its views*; and, at laft, *lofes itfelf amidft the variety of objects that offer themfelves to its obfervation.* The *fancy* is elegantly con-trafted with the *underftanding*, *profpects* with *fpeculations*, and *wide and undetermined profpects*, with *fpeculations of eternity and infinitude.*

But if there be a beauty or uncommonnefs joined with this gran-deur, as in a troubled ocean, a heaven adorned with ftars and meteors, or a fpacious landfcape cut out into rivers, woods, rocks,

3 K 2   *and*

and meadows, the pleasure still grows upon us, as it arises from more than a single principle.

THE article prefixed to *beauty*, in the beginning of this sentence, might have been omitted, and the Style have run, perhaps, to more advantage thus: *But if beauty, or uncommonness, be joined to this grandeur—A landscape cut out into rivers, woods,* &c. seems unseasonably to imply an artificial formation, and had better have been expressed by, *diversified with rivers, woods,* &c.

Every thing that is new or uncommon, raises a pleasure in the imagination, because it fills the soul with an agreeable surprise, gratifies its curiosity, and gives it an idea of which it was not before possessed. We are, indeed, so often conversant with one set of objects, and tired out with so many repeated shows of the same things, that whatever is new or uncommon contributes a little to vary human life, and to divert our minds, for a while, with the strangeness of its appearance. It serves us for a kind of refreshment, and takes off from that satiety we are apt to complain of in our usual and ordinary entertainments.

THE Style in these Sentences flows in an easy and agreeable manner. A severe critic might point out some expressions that would bear being retrenched. But this would alter the genius and character of Mr. Addison's Style. We must always remember, that good composition admits of being carried on under many different forms. Style must not be reduced to one precise standard. One writer may be as agreeable, by a pleasing diffuseness, when the subject bears, and his genius prompts it, as another by a concise and forcible manner. It is fit, how-

8

ever,

ever, to obferve, that, in the beginning of thofe Sentences
which we have at prefent before us, the phrafe, *raifes a plea-*
fure in the imagination, is unqueftionably too flat and feeble,
and might eafily be amended, by faying, *affords pleafure to the*
imagination ; and towards the end, there are two *of*'s, which
grate harfhly on the ear, in that phrafe, *takes off from that*
fatiety we are apt to complain of; where the correction is as eafily
made as in the other cafe, by fubftituting, *diminifhes that fatiety*
of which we are apt to complain. Such inftances fhow the advantage of frequent reviews of what we have written, in order
to give proper correctnefs and polifh to our Language.

It is this which beftows charms on a monfter, and makes even
the imperfections of nature pleafe us. It is this that recommends
variety where the mind is every inftant called off to fomething
new, and the attention not fuffered to dwell too long, and wafte
itfelf, on any particular object. It is this likewife, that improves
what is great or beautiful, and makes it afford the mind a double
entertainment.

Still the Style proceeds with perfpicuity, grace, and harmony. The full and ample affertion, with which each of thefe
Sentences is introduced, frequent, on many occafions, with our
Author, is here proper and feafonable ; as it was his intention
to magnify, as much as poffible, the effects of novelty and
variety, and to draw our attention to them. His frequent ufe
of *that*, inftead of *which*, is another peculiarity of his Style;
but, on this occafion in particular, cannot be much com-
mended, as, *it is this which*, feems, in every view, to be better
than, *it is this that*, three times repeated. I muft, likewife,
take

LECT.
XXI.

take notice, that the antecedent to, *it is this*, when critically confidered, is not altogether proper. It refers, as we difcover by the fenfe, to *whatever is new or uncommon*. But as it is not good language to fay, *whatever is new beftows charms on a monfter*, one cannot avoid thinking that our Author had done better to have begun the firft of thefe three Sentences, with faying, *It is novelty which beftows charms on a monfter, &c.*

Groves, fields, and meadows, are at any feafon of the year pleafant to look upon; but never fo much as in the opening of the Spring, when they are all new and frefh, with their firft glofs upon them, and not yet too much accuftomed and familiar to the eye.

IN this expreffion, *never fo much as in the opening of the Spring*, there appears to be a fmall error in grammar; for when the conftruction is filled up, it muft be read, *never fo much pleafant.* Had he, to avoid this, faid, *never fo much fo*, the grammatical error would have been prevented, but the language would have been awkward. Better to have faid, *but never fo agreeable as in the opening of the Spring.* We readily fay, the eye is accuftomed to objects, but to fay, as our Author has done at the clofe of the Sentence, that objects are *accuftomed to the eye*, can fcarcely be allowed in a profe compofition.

For this reafon, there is nothing that more enlivens a profpect than rivers, jetteaus, or falls of water, where the fcene is perpetually fhifting and entertaining the fight, every moment, with fomething that is new. We are quickly tired with looking at hills and vallies, where every thing continues fixed and fettled in the fame

place

place and posture, but find our thoughts a little agitated and re-
lieved at the fight of fuch objects as are ever in motion, and fliding
away from beneath the eye of the beholder.

THE firft of thefe fentences is connected in too loofe a manner with that which immediately preceded it. When he fays,
For this reafon, there is nothing that more enlivens, &c. we are
entitled to look for the *reafon* in what he had juft before faid.
But there we find no *reafon* for what he is now going to affert,
except that groves and meadows are moft pleafant in the Spring.
We know that he has been fpeaking of the pleafure produced
by Novelty and Variety, and our minds naturally recur to this,
as the reafon here alluded to ; but his language does not properly exprefs it. It is, indeed, one of the defects of this amiable
writer, that his fentences are often too negligently connected
with one another. His meaning, upon the whole, we gather
with eafe from the tenour of his difcourfe. Yet this negligence
prevents his fenfe from ftriking us with that force and evidence,
which a more accurate juncture of parts would have produced.
Bating this inaccuracy, thefe two fentences, efpecially the latter,
are remarkably elegant and beautiful. The clofe, in particular,
is uncommonly fine, and carries as much expreffive harmony
as the language can admit. It feems to paint, what he is defcribing, at once to the eye and the ear.—*Such objects as are
ever in motion, and fliding away from beneath the eye of the beholder.*—Indeed, notwithftanding thofe fmall errors, which the
ftrictnefs of critical examination obliges me to point out, it may
be fafely pronounced, that the two paragraphs which we have
now confidered in this paper, the one concerning greatnefs, and
the other concerning novelty, are extremely worthy of Mr. Addifon,

L E C T.
XXI.

difon, and exhibit a Style, which they who can fuccefsfully imitate, may efteem themfelves happy.

But there is nothing that makes its way more directly to the foul than Beauty, which immediately diffufes a fecret fatisfaction and complacency through the imagination, and gives a finifhing to any thing that is great or uncommon. The very firft difcovery of it ftrikes the mind with an inward joy, and fpreads a cheerfulnefs and delight through all its faculties.

Some degree of verbofity may be here difcovered, and phrafes repeated, which are little more than the echo of one another ; fuch as—*diffufing fatisfaction and complacency through the imagination—ftriking the mind with inward joy—fpreading cheerfulnefs and delight through all its faculties.* At the fame time, I readily admit that this full and flowing Style, even though it carry fome redundancy, is not unfuitable to the gaiety of the fubject on which the author is entering, and is more allowable here, than it would have been on fome other oc-cafions.

There is not, perhaps, any real beauty or deformity more in one piece of matter than another; becaufe we might have been fo made, that whatever now appears loathfome to us, might have fhewn itfelf agreeable ; but we find, by experience, that there are feveral modifications of matter, which the mind, without any previous confideration, pronounces at firft fight beautiful or deformed.

In this fentence there is nothing remarkable, in any view, to draw our attention. We may obferve only, that the word *more*, towards the beginning, is not in its proper place, and that

the

the prepofition *in* is wanting before *another*.　The phrafe ought
to have ftood thus—*Beauty or deformity in one piece of matter,*
more than in another.

Thus we fee, that every different fpecies of fenfible creatures has
its different notions of Beauty, and that each of them is moft affected
with the beauties of its own kind.　This is nowhere more re-
markable, than in birds of the fame fhape and proportion, when
we often fee the male determined in his courtfhip by the fingle grain
or tincture of a feather, and never difcovering any charms but in
the colour of its fpecies.

NEITHER is there here any particular elegance or felicity of
language.—*Different fenfe of Beauty* would have been a more
proper expreffion to have been applied to irrational creatures,
than as it ftands, *different notions of Beauty*.　In the clofe of the
fecond Sentence, when the Author fays, *colour of its fpecies,* he
is guilty of a confiderable inaccuracy in changing the gender, as
he had faid in the fame Sentence, that the *male was determined*
in his courtfhip.

There is a fecond kind of Beauty, that we find in the feveral
products of art and nature, which does not work in the imagina-
tion with that warmth and violence, as the beauty that appears in
our proper fpecies, but is apt, however, to raife in us a fecret de-
light, and a kind of fondnefs for the places or objects in which we
difcover it.

STILL, I am forry to fay, we find little to praife.　As in his
enunciation of the fubject, when beginning the former paragraph, he appeared to have been treating of Beauty in general,

in diſtinction from greatneſs or novelty; this *ſecond kind of Beauty* of which he here ſpeaks, comes upon us in a ſort of ſurprize, and it is only by degrees we learn, that formerly he had no more in view than the Beauty which the different ſpecies of ſenſible creatures find in one another. This *ſecond kind of Beauty*, he ſays, *we find in the ſeveral products of art and nature.* He undoubtedly means, not in all, but *in ſeveral of the products of art and nature;* and ought ſo to have expreſſed himſelf; and in the place of *products*, to have uſed alſo the more proper word, *productions.* When he adds, that this kind of Beauty *does not work in the imagination with that warmth and violence as the beauty that appears in our proper ſpecies;* the language would certainly have been more pure and elegant, if he had ſaid, that it *does not work upon the imagination with ſuch warmth and violence, as the beauty that appears in our own ſpecies.*

This conſiſts either in the gaiety or variety of colours, in the ſymmetry and proportion of parts, in the arrangement and diſpoſition of bodies, or in a juſt mixture and concurrence of all together. Among theſe ſeveral kinds of Beauty, the eye takes moſt delight in colours.

To the language here, I ſee no objection that can be made.

We no where meet with a more glorious or pleaſing ſhow in nature, than what appears in the heavens at the riſing and ſetting of the Sun, which is wholly made up of thoſe different ſtains of light, that ſhow themſelves in clouds of a different ſituation.

THE chief ground of criticiſm on this Sentence, is the disjointed ſituation of the relative *which.* Grammatically, it refers

fers to *the rifing and fetting of the Sun.* But the Author meant, that it fhould refer *to the fhow* which appears in the heavens at that time. It is too common among Authors, when they are writing without much care, to make fuch particles as *this*, and *which*, refer not to any particular antecedent word, but to the tenour of fome phrafe, or perhaps the fcope of fome whole Sentence, which has gone before. This practice faves them trouble in marfhaling their words, and arranging a period: but, though it may leave their meaning intelligible, yet it renders that meaning much lefs perfpicuous, determined, and precife, than it might otherwife have been. The error I have pointed out, might have been avoided by a fmall alteration in the conftruction of the Sentence, after fome fuch manner as this : *We no where meet with a more glorious and pleafing fhow in nature, than what is formed in the heavens at the rifing and fetting of the Sun, by the different ftains of light which fhow themfelves in clouds of different fituations.* Our Author writes, *in clouds of a different fituation*, by which he means, clouds that differ in fituation from each other. But, as this is neither the obvious nor grammatical meaning of his words, it was neceffary to change the expreffion, as I have done, into the plural number.

For this reafon, we find the poets, who are always addreffing themfelves to the imagination, borrowing more of their epithets from colours than from any other topic.

On this Sentence nothing occurs, except a remark fimilar to what was made before, of loofe connection with the Sentence which precedes. For, though he begins with faying, *For this reafon*, the foregoing Sentence, which was employed about the

clouds

LECT.
XXI.

clouds and *the Sun*, gives no reason for the general proposition he now lays down. The *reason* to which he refers, was given two Sentences before, when he observed, that the eye takes more delight in colours than in any other beauty; and it was with that Sentence that the present one should have stood immediately connected.

As the Fancy delights in every thing that is great, strange, or beautiful, and is still more pleased, the more it finds of these perfections in the same object, so it is capable of receiving a new satisfaction by the assistance of another sense.

Another sense here, means grammatically, *another sense than Fancy.* For there is no other thing in the period to which this expression, *another sense,* can at all be opposed. He had not for some time made mention of any *sense* whatever. He forgot to add, what was undoubtedly in his thoughts, *another sense than that of sight.*

Thus any continued sound, as the music of birds, or a fall of water, awakens every moment the mind of the beholder, and makes him more attentive to the several beauties of the place which lie before him. Thus, if there arises a fragrancy of smells or perfumes, they heighten the pleasures of the imagination, and make even the colours and verdure of the landscape appear more agreeable; for the ideas of both senses recommend each other, and are pleasanter together, than when they enter the mind separately; as the different colours of a picture, when they are well-disposed, set off one another, and receive an additional beauty from the advantage of their situation.

WHETHER

WHETHER Mr. Addifon's theory here be juft or not, may L E C T. be queftioned.   A continued found, fuch as that of a fall of XXI. water, is fo far from *awakening*, *every moment*, *the mind of the beholder*, that nothing is more likely to lull him afleep.   It may, indeed, pleafe the imagination, and heighten the beauties of the fcene; but it produces this effect, by a foothing, not by an awakening influence.   With regard to the Style, nothing appears exceptionable.   The flow, both of language and of ideas, is very agreeable.   The Author continues, to the end, the fame pleafing train of thought, which had run through the reft of the Paper: and leaves us agreeably employed in comparing together different degrees of Beauty.

LECTURE XXII.

CRITICAL EXAMINATION OF THE STYLE IN N°. 413. OF THE SPECTATOR.

THOUGH in yesterday's Paper we considered how every thing that is great, new, or beautiful, is apt to affect the imagination with pleasure, we must own, that it is impossible for us to assign the necessary cause of this pleasure, because we know neither the nature of an idea, nor the substance of a human soul, which might help us to discover the conformity or disagreeableness of the one to the other; and, therefore, for want of such a light, all that we can do in speculations of this kind, is, to reflect on those operations of the soul that are most agreeable, and to range, under their proper heads, what is pleasing or displeasing to the mind, without being able to trace out the several necessary and efficient causes from whence the pleasure or displeasure arises.

THIS Sentence, considered as an introductory one, must be acknowledged to be very faulty. An introductory Sentence should fhould never contain any thing that can in any degree fatigue or puzzle the reader. When an Author is entering on a new branch of his fubject, informing us of what he has done, and what he purpofes farther to do, we naturally expect that he fhould exprefs himfelf in the fimpleft and moft perfpicuous manner poffible. But the Sentence now before us is crowded and indiftinct ; containing three feparate propofitions, which, as I fhall afterwards fhow, required feparate Sentences to have un- folded them. Mr. Addifon's chief excellency, as a writer, lay in defcribing and painting. There he is great; but in method- ifing and reafoning, he is not fo eminent. As, befides the general fault of prolixity and indiftinctnefs, this Sentence contains fe- veral inaccuracies, I will be obliged to enter into a minute dif- cuffion of its ftructure and parts ; a difcuffion, which to many readers will appear tedious, and which therefore they will natu- rally pafs over ; but which, to thofe who are ftudying compo- fition, I hope may prove of fome benefit.

Though in yefterday's Paper we confidered—The import of *though* is, *notwithftanding that.* When it appears in the beginning of a Sentence, its relative generally is *yet :* and it is employed to warn us, after we have been informed of fome truth, that we are not to infer from it fome other thing which we might per- haps have expected to follow : as, " Though virtue be the " only road to happinefs, yet it does not permit the unlimited ". gratification of our defires." Now it is plain, that there was no fuch oppofition between the fubject of yefterday's Paper, and what the Author is now going to fay, between his afferting a fact, and his not being able to affign the caufe of that fact, as rendered the ufe of this adverfative particle *though*, either ne- ceffary ceſſary or proper in the introduction.—*We conſidered how every thing that is great, new, or beautiful, is apt to affect the imagination with pleaſure.*—The adverb *how* ſignifies, either the means by which, or the manner in which, ſomething is done. But, in truth, neither one nor other of theſe had been conſidered by our Author. He had illuſtrated the fact alone, that they do affect the imagination with pleaſure; and, with reſpect to the *quomodo*, or the *how*, he is ſo far from having conſidered it, that he is juſt now going to ſhow that it cannot be explained, and that we muſt reſt contented with the knowledge of the fact alone, and of its purpoſe or final cauſe.—*We muſt own, that it is impoſſible for us to aſſign the neceſſary cauſe* (he means, what is more commonly called the *efficient cauſe*) *of this pleaſure, becauſe we know neither the nature of an idea, nor the ſubſtance of a human ſoul.*—*The ſubſtance of a human ſoul* is certainly a very uncouth expreſſion, and there appears no reaſon why he ſhould have varied from the word *nature*, which would have equally applied to *idea* and to *ſoul*.

Which might help us, our Author proceeds, *to diſcover the conformity or diſagreeableneſs of the one to the other* —The *which*, at the beginning of this member of the period, is ſurely ungrammatical, as it is a relative, without any antecedent in all the Sentence. It refers, by the conſtruction, to *the nature of an idea, or the ſubſtance of a human ſoul;* but this is by no means the reference which the Author intended. His meaning is, that *our knowing* the nature of an idea, and the ſubſtance of a human ſoul, might help us to diſcover the conformity or diſagreeableneſs of the one to the other: and therefore the ſyntax abſolutely required the word *knowledge* to have been inſerted as the ante-

cedent

cedent to *which*. I have before remarked, and the remark deferves to be repeated, that nothing is a more certain fign of carelefs compofition than to make fuch relatives as *which*, not refer to any precife expreffion, but carry a loofe and vague relation to the general ftrain of what had gone before. When our fentences run into this form, we may be affured there is fomething in the conftruction of them that requires alteration. The phrafe of difcovering *the conformity or difagreeablenefs of the one to the other* is likewife exceptionable; for *difagreeablenefs* neither forms a proper contraft to the other word, *conformity*, nor expreffes what the author meant here (as far as any meaning can be gathered from his words), that is, a certain unfuitablenefs or want of conformity to the nature of the foul. To fay the truth, this member of the fentence had much better have been omitted altogether. *The conformity or difagreeablenefs of an idea to the fubftance of a human foul,* is a phrafe which conveys to the mind no diftinct nor intelligible conception whatever. The author had before given a fufficient reafon for his not affigning the efficient caufe of thofe pleafures of the imagination, becaufe we neither know the nature of our own ideas nor of the foul: and this farther difcuffion about the conformity or difagreeablenefs of the nature of the one, to the fubftance of the other, affords no clear nor ufeful illuftration.

And therefore, the fentence goes on, *for want of fuch a light, all that we can do in fpeculations of this kind, is to reflect on thofe operations of the foul that are moft agreeable, and to range under their proper heads what is pleafing or difpleafing to the mind.*——— The two expreffions in the beginning of this member, *therefore*, and *for want of fuch a light*, evidently refer to the fame thing, and are quite fynonymous. One or other of them, therefore, had better have been omitted. Inftead of *to range under their proper heads*, the language would have been fmoother, if *their* had been left out ;—*without being able to trace out the feveral neceffary and efficient caufes from whence the pleafure or difpleafure arifes.* The expreffion, *from whence*, though feemingly juftified by very frequent ufage, is taxed by Dr. Johnfon as a vicious mode of fpeech ; feeing *whence* alone, has all the power of *from whence*, which therefore appears an unneceffary reduplication. I am inclined to think, that the whole of this laft member of the fentence had better have been dropped. The period might have clofed with full propriety, at the words, *pleafing or difpleafing to the mind.* All that follows, fuggefts no idea that had not been fully conveyed in the preceding part of the fentence. It is a mere expletive adjection which might be omitted, not only without injury to the meaning, but to the great relief of a fentence already labouring under the multitude of words.

Having now finifhed the analyfis of this long fentence, I am inclined to be of opinion, that if, on any occafion, we can adventure to alter Mr. Addifon's Style, it may be done to advantage here, by breaking down this period in the following manner: " In " yefterday's paper, we have fhown that every thing which is " great, new, or beautiful, is apt to affect the imagination with " pleafure. We muft own, that it is impoffible for us to affign " the efficient caufe of this pleafure, becaufe we know not the " nature either of an idea, or of the human foul. All that we " can do, therefore, in fpeculations of this kind, is to reflect on " the operations of the foul, which are moft agreeable, and to

" range

" range under proper heads, what is pleasing or displeasing to
" the mind."—We proceed now to the examination of the following sentences.

Final causes lie more bare and open to our observation, as there
are often a great variety that belong to the same effect; and these,
though they are not altogether so satisfactory, are generally more
useful than the other, as they give us greater occasion of admiring
the goodness and wisdom of the first contriver.

THOUGH some difference might be traced between the sense
of *bare* and *open,* yet as they are here employed, they are so
nearly synonymous, that one of them was sufficient. It would
have been enough to have said, *Final causes lie more open to ob-*
servation.—One can scarcely help observing here, that the ob-
viousness of final causes does not proceed, as Mr. Addison
supposes, from a variety of them concurring in the same
effect, which is often not the case; but from our being able to
ascertain more clearly, from our own experience, the congruity
of a final cause with the circumstances of our condition;
whereas the constituent parts of subjects, whence efficient causes
proceed, lie for most part beyond the reach of our faculties.
But as this remark respects the thought more than the style, it
is sufficient for us to observe, that when he says, *a great variety*
that belong to the same effect, the expression, strictly considered, is
not altogether proper. The accessory is properly said to belong to
the principal; not the principal to the accessory. Now an effect
is considered as the accessory or consequence of its cause; and
therefore, though we might well say a variety of effects belong

to the fame caufe, it feems not fo proper to fay, that a variety of caufes belong to the fame effect.

One of the final caufes of our delight in any thing that is great may be this : The Supreme Author of our being has fo formed the foul of man, that nothing but himfelf can be its laft, adequate, and proper happinefs. Becaufe, therefore, a great part of our happinefs muft arife from the contemplation of his being, that he might give our fouls a juft relifh of fuch a contemplation, he has made them naturally delight in the apprehenfion of what is great or unlimited.

THE concurrence of two conjunctions, *becaufe, therefore,* forms rather a harfh and unpleafing beginning of the laft of thefe Sentences; and, in the clofe, one would think, that the Author might have devifed a happier word than *apprehenfion,* to be applied to what is *unlimited.* But that I may not be thought hypercritical, I fhall make no farther obfervation on thefe Sentences.

Our admiration, which is a very pleafing motion of the mind, immediately rifes at the confideration of any object that takes up a good deal of room in the fancy, and, by confequence, will improve into the higheft pitch of aftonifhment and devotion, when we contemplate his nature, that is neither circumfcribed by time nor place, nor to be comprehended by the largeft capacity of a created being.

HERE, our Author's Style rifes beautifully along with the thought. However inaccurate he may fometimes be when coolly philofophifing, yet, whenever his fancy is awakened by defcription,

defcription, or his mind, as here, warmed with fome glowing fentiment, he prefently becomes great, and difcovers, in his language, the hand of a mafter. Every one muft obferve, with what felicity this period is conftructed. The words are long and majeftic. The members rife one above another, and conduct the fentence, at laft, to that full and harmonious clofe, which leaves upon the mind fuch an impreffion, as the author intended to leave, of fomething uncommonly great, awful, and magnificent.

He has annexed a fecret pleafure to the idea of any thing that is new or uncommon, that he might encourage us in the purfuit of knowledge, and engage us to fearch into the wonders of creation; for every new idea brings fuch a pleafure along with it, as rewards the pains we have taken in its acquifition, and, confequently, ferves as a motive to put us upon frefh difcoveries.

The Language, in this Sentence, is clear and precife: only, we cannot but obferve, in this, and the two following Sentences, which are conftructed in the fame manner, a ftrong proof of Mr. Addifon's unreafonable partiality to the particle *that*, in preference to *which—annexed a fecret pleafure to the idea of any thing that is new or uncommon, that he might encourage us.*—Here the firft *that*, ftands for a relative pronoun, and the next *that*, at the diftance only of four words, is a conjunction. This confufion of founds ferves to embarrafs Style. Much better, fure, to have faid, *the idea of any thing which is new or uncommon, that he might encourage.*—The expreffion with which the fentence concludes—*a motive to put us upon frefh difcoveries*—is flat, and, in fome degree, improper. He fhould
have

LECT.
XXII.
have said, *put us upon making fresh discoveries—or rather, serves as a motive inciting us to make fresh discoveries.*

He has made every thing that is beautiful in our own species, pleasant, that all creatures might be tempted to multiply their kind, and fill the world with inhabitants; for, 'tis very remarkable, that wherever nature is crost in the production of a monster (the result of any unnatural mixture) the breed is incapable of propagating its likeness, and of founding a new order of creatures; so that, unless all animals were allured by the beauty of their own species, generation would be at an end, and the earth unpeopled.

HERE we muſt, however reluctantly, return to the employment of cenſure: for this is among the worſt Sentences our Author ever wrote; and contains a variety of blemiſhes. Taken as a whole, it is extremely deficient in unity. Inſtead of a complete propoſition, it contains a ſort of chain of reaſoning, the links of which are ſo ill put together, that it is with difficulty we can trace the connection; and, unleſs we take the trouble of peruſing it ſeveral times, it will leave nothing on the mind but an indiſtinct and obſcure impreſſion.

BESIDES this general fault, reſpecting the meaning, it contains ſome great inaccuracies in Language. Firſt, God's having made every thing which *is beautiful in our own species* (that is in the human ſpecies) *pleaſant*, is certainly no motive for *all creatures*, for beaſts, and birds, and fiſhes, *to multiply their kind*. What the Author meant to ſay, though he has expreſſed himſelf in ſo erroneous a manner, undoubtedly was, " In all
" the

" the different orders of creatures, he has made every thing,
" which is beautiful, in their own fpecies, pleafant, that all
" creatures might be tempted to multiply their kind." The
fecond member of the Sentence is ftill worfe. *For, it is very
remarkable, that wherever nature is croft in the production of a
monfter, &c.* The reafon which he here gives, for the preceding affertion, intimated by the cafual particle *for*, is far from
being obvious. The connection of thought is not readily apparent, and would have required an intermediate ftep, to render
it diftinct. But, what does he mean, by *nature being croft in the
production of a monfter?* One might underftand him to mean,
" difappointed in its intention of producing a monfter," as
when we fay, one is croft in his purfuits, we mean, that he is
difappointed in accomplifhing the end which he intended. Had
he faid, *croft by the production of a monfter*, the fenfe would
have been more intelligible. But the proper rectification of
the expreffion would be to infert the adverb *as*, before the prepofition *in*, after this manner—*wherever nature is croft, as in
the production of a monfter*,—the infertion of this particle *as*,
throws fo much light on the conftruction of this member of the
fentence, that I am very much inclined to believe, it had ftood
thus, originally, in our Author's manufcript ; and that the prefent reading is a typographical error, which, having crept into
the firft edition of the Spectator, ran through all the fubfequent ones.

*In the laft place, he has made every thing that is beautiful, in
all other objects, pleafant, or rather has made fo many objects appear beautiful, that he might render the whole creation more gay
and delightful. He has given, almoft, every thing about us the*

I   *power*

power of raiſing an agreeable idea in the imagination ; ſo that it is impoſſible for us to behold his works with coldneſs or indiffe-rence, and to ſurvey ſo many beauties without a ſecret ſatisfaction and complacency.

THE idea, here, is ſo juſt, and the Language ſo clear, flowing, and agreeable, that, to remark any diffuſeneſs which may be attributed to theſe ſentences, would be juſtly eſteemed hypercritical.

Things would make but a poor appearance to the eye, if we ſaw them only in their proper figures and motions : and what rea-ſon can we aſſign for their exciting, in us, many of thoſe ideas which are different from any thing that exiſts in the objects them-ſelves (for ſuch are light and colours), were it not to add ſuper-numerary ornaments to the univerſe, and make it more agreeable to the imagination ?

OUR Author is now entering on a theory, which he is about to illuſtrate, if not with much philoſophical accuracy, yet, with great beauty of fancy, and glow of expreſſion. A ſtrong inſtance of his want of accuracy, appears in the manner in which he opens the ſubject. For what meaning is there in things *exciting in us many of thoſe ideas which are different from any thing that exiſts in the objects ?* No one, ſure, ever imagined, that our ideas exiſt in the objects. Ideas, it is agreed on all hands, can exiſt no where but in the mind. What Mr. Locke's philoſophy teaches, and what our Author ſhould have ſaid, is, *exciting in us many ideas of qualities which are different from any thing that exiſts in the objects.* The ungraceful parentheſis

7

which

which follows, *for such are light and colours*, had far better have been avoided, and incorporated with the reft of the Sentence, in this manner :—" exciting in us many ideas of quali-" ties, fuch as light and colours, which are different from any " thing that exifts in the objects."

We are every where entertained with pleafing fhows, and ap-paritions. We difcover imaginary glories in the heavens, and in the earth, and fee fome of this vifionary beauty poured out upon the whole creation; but what a rough unfightly fketch of nature fhould we be entertained with, did all her colouring difappear, and the feveral diftinctions of light and fhade vanifh? In fhort, our fouls are delightfully loft and bewildered in a pleafing delufion; and we walk about like the enchanted hero of a romance, who fees beautiful caftles, woods, and meadows; and, at the fame time, hears the warbling of birds, and the purling of ftreams; but, upon the finifhing of fome fecret fpell, the fantaftic fcene breaks up, and the difconfolate knight finds himfelf on a barren heath, or in a folitary defert.

AFTER having been obliged to point out feveral inaccuracies, I return with much more pleafure to the difplay of beauties, for which we have now full fcope; for thefe two Sentences are fuch as do the higheft honour to Mr. Addifon's talents as a writer. Warmed with the idea he had laid hold of, his delicate fenfibility to the beauty of nature, is finely difplayed in the illuftration of it. The Style is flowing and full, without being too diffufe. It is flowery, but not gaudy; elevated, but not oftentatious.

AMIDST this blaze of beauties, it is neceſſary for us to re-mark one or two inaccuracies. When it is ſaid, towards the cloſe of the firſt of thoſe Sentences, *what a rough unſightly ſketch of nature ſhould we be entertained with*, the prepoſition *with*, ſhould have been placed at the beginning, rather than at the end of this member; and the word *entertained*, is both improperly applied here, and careleſsly repeated from the former part of the Sentence. It was there employed according to its more common uſe, as relating to agreeable objeƈts. *We are every where entertained with pleaſing ſhows.* Here, it would have been more proper to have changed the phraſe, and ſaid, *with what a rough unſightly ſketch of nature ſhould we be preſented.*— At the cloſe of the ſecond Sentence, where it is ſaid, *the fan-taſtic ſcene breaks up*, the expreſſion is lively, but not alto-gether juſtifiable. An aſſembly *breaks up*; a ſcene *cloſes* or *diſ-appears*.

BATING theſe two ſlight inaccuracies, the Style, here, is not only correƈt, but perfeƈtly elegant. The moſt ſtriking beauty of the paſſage ariſes from the happy ſimile which the Author employs, and the fine illuſtration which it gives to the thought. The *enchanted hero*, the *beautiful caſtles*, the *fantaſtic ſcene*, the *ſecret ſpell*, the *diſconſolate knight*, are terms choſen with the utmoſt felicity, and ſtrongly recal all thoſe romantic ideas with which he intended to amuſe our imagination. Few authors are more ſuccefsful in their imagery than Mr. Addiſon; and few paſſages in his works, or in thoſe of any author, are more beautiful and piƈtureſque, than that on which we have been com-menting.

It

It is not improbable, that something like this may be the state of L E C T.
XXII.
the soul after its first separation, in respect of the images it will
receive from matter ; though, indeed, the ideas of colours are so
pleasing and beautiful in the imagination, that it is possible the soul
will not be deprived of them, but, perhaps, find them excited by
some other occasional cause, as they are, at present, by the different
impressions of the subtile matter on the organ of sight.

As all human things, after having attained the summit, begin to decline, we must acknowledge, that, in this Sentence,
there is a sensible falling of from the beauty of what went
before. It is broken, and deficient in unity. Its parts are not
sufficiently compacted. It contains, besides, some faulty expressions. When it is said, *something like this may be the state of*
the soul, to the pronoun *this,* there is no determined antecedent ; it refers to the general import of the preceding description, which, as I have several times remarked, always
renders Style clumsy and inelegant, if not obscure—*the state of*
the soul after its first separation, appears to be an incomplete
phrase, and *first,* seems an useless, and even an improper word.
More distinct if he had said,—*state of the soul immediately on its*
separation from the body—the adverb *perhaps,* is redundant, after
having just before said, *it is possible.*

I have here supposed, that my reader is acquainted with that
great modern discovery, which is, at present, universally acknow-
ledged by all the enquirers into natural philosophy ; namely, that
light and colours, as apprehended by the imagination, are only
ideas in the mind, and not qualities that have any existence in mat-
ter. As this is a truth which has been proved incontestibly by

many modern philosophers, and is, indeed, one of the finest specu-
lations in that science, if the English Reader would see the notion
explained at large, he may find it in the eighth chapter of the
second book of Mr. Locke's Essay on the Human Understanding.

IN these two concluding Sentences, the Author, haftening to
finish, appears to write rather carelessly. In the first of them,
a manifest tautology occurs, when he speaks of what is *uni-*
versally acknowledged by all enquirers. In the second, when he
calls *a truth which has been incontestibly proved*; first, a *specula-*
tion, and afterwards, *a notion*, the Language surely is not
very accurate. When he adds, *one of the finest speculations in*
that science, it does not, at first, appear what science he means.
One would imagine, he meant to refer to *modern philosophers*;
for *natural philosophy* (to which, doubtless, he refers) stands
at much too great a distance to be the proper or obvious antecedent to the pronoun *that.* The circumstance towards the
close, *if the English Reader would see the notion explained at*
large, he may find it, is properly taken notice of by the Author
of the Elements of Criticism, as wrong arranged; and is rectified thus: *the English Reader, if he would see the notion ex-*
plained at large, may find it, &c.

IN concluding the Examination of this Paper, we may obferve, that, though not a very long one, it exhibits a striking
view both of the beauties, and the defects, of Mr. Addison's
Style. It contains some of the best, and some of the worst
Sentences, that are to be found in his works. But, upon the
whole, it is an agreeable and elegant Essay.

L E C T U R E   XXIII.

CRITICAL EXAMINATION OF THE STYLE
IN Nº 414. OF THE SPECTATOR.

*IF we confider the works of Nature and Art, as they are qua-
lified to entertain the imagination, we fhall find the laft very
defective in comparifon of the former; for though they may fometimes appear as beautiful or ftrange, they can have nothing in them
of that vaftnefs and immenfity which afford fo great an entertainment to the mind of the beholder.*

I HAD occafion formerly to obferve, that an introductory
Sentence fhould always be fhort and fimple, and contain no
more matter than is neceffary for opening the fubject. This
fentence leads to a repetition of this obfervation, as it contains
both an affertion and the proof of that affertion; two things
which, for the moft part, but efpecially at firft fetting out, are
with more advantage kept feparate. It would certainly have
been better, if this Sentence had contained only the affertion,
ending with the word *former;* and if a new one had then be-

gun,

gun, entering on the proofs of Nature's fuperiority over Art, which is the fubject continued to the end of the paragraph. The proper divifion of the period I fhall point out, after having firft made a few obfervations which occur on different parts of it.

If we confider the works—Perhaps it might have been preferable, if our Author had begun, with faying, *When we confider the works.*—Difcourfe ought always to begin, when it is poffible, with a clear propofition. The *if*, which is here employed, converts the Sentence into a fuppofition, which is always in fome degree entangling, and proper to be ufed only when the courfe of reafoning renders it neceffary. As this obfervation however may, perhaps, be confidered as over-refined, and as the fenfe would have remained the fame in either form of expreffion, I do not mean to charge our Author with any error on this account. We cannot abfolve him from inaccuracy in what immediately follows—*the works of Nature and Art.* It is the fcope of the Author throughout this whole Paper, to compare Nature and Art together, and to oppofe them in feveral views to each other. Certainly therefore, in the beginning, he ought to have kept them as diftinct as poffible, by interpofing the prepofition, and faying *the works of Nature, and of Art.* As the words ftand at prefent, they would lead us to think that he is going to treat of thefe works, not as contrafted, but as connected; as united in forming one whole. When I fpeak of Body and Soul as united in the Human Nature, I would interpofe neither article nor prepofition between them; " Man is " compounded of Soul and Body." But the cafe is altered, if I mean to diftinguifh them from each other; then I reprefent them as

6   feparate;

separate; and say, " I am to treat of the interests of the Soul,
" and of the Body."

Though they may sometimes appear as beautiful or strange—I
cannot help considering this as a loose member of the period.
It does not clearly appear at first what the antecedent is to *they*.
In reading onwards, we see the works of Art to be meant; but
from the structure of the Sentence, *they* might be understood to
refer to *the former*, as well as to *the last*.   In what follows,
there is a greater ambiguity—*may sometimes appear as beautiful
or strange*.   It is very doubtful in what sense we are to understand *as*, in this passage.   For, according as it is accented in
reading, it may signify, that *they appear equally beautiful or
strange*, to wit, with the works of Nature; and then it has the
force of the Latin *tam:* or it may signify no more than that
they *appear in the light of beautiful and strange*; and then it has
the force of the Latin *tanquam*, without importing any comparison.   An expression so ambiguous, is always faulty; and it is
doubly so here; because, if the Author intended the former
sense, and meant (as seems most probable) to employ *as* for a
mark of *comparison*, it was necessary to have mentioned both
the compared objects; whereas only one member of the comparison is here mentioned, viz. the works of Art; and if he intended the latter sense, *as* was in that case superfluous and en-
cumbering, and he had better have said simply, *appear beautiful
or strange*.—The epithet *strange*, which Mr. Addison applies to
the works of Art, cannot be praised.   *Strange works*, appears
not by any means a happy expression to signify what he here
intends, which is new or uncommon.

                                                THE

THE fentence concludes with much harmony and dignity— *they can have nothing in them of that vaftnefs and immenfity which afford fo great an entertainment to the mind of the beholder.* There is here a fulnefs and grandeur of expreffion well fuited to the fubject; though, perhaps, *entertainment* is not quite the proper word for expreffing the effect which vaftnefs and immenfity have upon the mind. Reviewing the obfervations that have been made on this period, it might, I think, with advantage, be refolved into two Sentences fome-what after this manner: " When we confider the works of Na-" ture and of Art, as they are qualified to entertain the imagi-" tion, we fhall find the latter very defective in comparifon of " the former. The works of Art may fometimes appear no " lefs beautiful or uncommon than thofe of Nature; but they " can have nothing of that vaftnefs and immenfity which fo " highly tranfport the mind of the beholder."

The one, proceeds our Author in the next Sentence, *may be as polite and delicate as the other; but can never fhew herfelf fo auguft and magnificent in the defign.*

THE *one* and the *other,* in the firft part of this Sentence, muft unqueftionably refer to the *works of Nature and of Art.* For of thefe he had been fpeaking immediately before; and with reference to the plural word, *works,* had employed the plural pronoun *they.* But in the courfe of the Sentence, he drops this conftruction; and paffes very incongruoufly to the perfonification of Art—*can never fhew herfelf*—To render his ftyle confiftent, *Art,* and not *the works of Art,* fhould have been made the nominative in this Sentence.—*Art may be as po-*

lite

lite and delicate as Nature, but can never shew herself—Polite is a
term oftener applied to persons and to manners, than to things;
and is employed to signify their being highly civilized. Polished, or refined, was the idea which the Author had in view.
Though the general turn of this Sentence be elegant, yet, in
order to render it perfect, I must observe, that the concluding
words, *in the design*, should either have been altogether omitted,
or something should have been properly opposed to them in the
preceding member of the period, thus: " Art may, in the exe-
" cution, be as polished and delicate as Nature; but, in the de-
" sign, can never shew herself so august and magnificent."

*There is something more bold and masterly in the rough, careless
strokes of Nature, than in the nice touches and embellishments of
Art.*

THIS Sentence is perfectly happy and elegant; and carries, in
all the expressions, that *curiosa felicitas*, for which Mr. Addison
is so often remarkable. *Bold and masterly*, are words applied with
the utmost propriety. The *strokes of Nature* are finely opposed
to *the touches of art*; and the *rough strokes* to the *nice touches*;
the former painting the freedom and ease of Nature, and the
other, the diminutive exactness of art; while both are introduced before us as different performers, and their respective
merits in execution very justly contrasted with each other.

*The beauties of the most stately garden or palace lie in a narrow
compass, the imagination immediately runs them over, and requires
something else to gratify her; but in the wide fields of Nature, the*

fight wanders up and down with confinement, and is fed with an infinite variety of images, without any certain stint or number.

THIS Sentence is not altogether so correct and elegant as the former.   It carries, however, in the main, the character of our Author's style ; not strictly accurate, but agreeable, easy, and unaffected ; enlivened too with a slight personification of the imagination, which gives a gaiety to the period.   Perhaps it had been better, if this personification of the imagination, with which the Sentence is introduced, had been continued throughout, and not changed unnecessarily, and even improperly, into *fight*, in the second member, which is contrary both to unity and elegance.   It might have stood thus—*the imagination immediately runs them over, and requires something else to gratify her ; but in the wide fields of Nature, she wanders up and down without confinement.*—The epithet *stately*, which the author uses in the beginning of the sentence, applies with more propriety to *palaces*, than to *gardens*.   The close of the sentence, *without any certain stint or number*, may be objected to, as both superfluous and ungraceful.   It might perhaps have terminated better in this manner—*she is fed with an infinite variety of images, and wanders up and down without confinement.*

For this reason, we always find the Poet in love with a country life, where Nature appears in the greatest perfection, and furnishes out all those scenes that are most apt to delight the imagination.

THERE is nothing in this Sentence to attract particular attention.   One would think it was rather the *country*, than a *coun-*

try

try life, on which the remark here made fhould reft.   A *country*
life may be productive of fimplicity of manners, and of other
virtues ; but it is to *the country* itfelf, that the properties here
mentioned belong, of difplaying the beauties of Nature, and
furnifhing thofe fcenes which delight the imagination.

But though there are feveral of thefe wild fcenes that are more
delightful than any artificial fhows, yet we find the works of Na-
ture ftill more pleafant, the more they refemble thofe of art ; for in
this cafe, our pleafure rifes from a double principle ; from the
agreeablenefs of the objects to the eye, and from their fimilitude to
other objects : we are pleafed, as well with comparing their beau-
ties, as with furveying them, and can reprefent them to our minds
either as copies or as originals.   Hence it is, that we take delight
in a profpect which is well laid out, and diverfified with fields and
meadows, woods and rivers ; in thofe accidental landfcapes of trees,
clouds, and cities, that are fometimes found in the veins of marble,
in the curious fretwork of rocks and grottos ; and, in a word, in
any thing that hath fuch a degree of variety and regularity as may
feem the effect of defign, in what we call the works of chance.

THE Style in the two Sentences, which compofe this paragraph, is fmooth and perfpicuous.   It lies open in fome places
to criticifm ; but left the reader fhould tire of what he may confider as petty remarks, I fhall pafs over any which thefe Sentences fuggeft ; the rather too, as the idea which they prefent
to us, of Nature's refembling Art, of Art's being confidered as an
original, and Nature as a copy, feems not very diftinct nor well
brought out, nor indeed very material to our Author's purpofe.

*If the products of Nature rise in value, according as they more
or less resemble those of Art, we may be sure that artificial works
receive a greater advantage from the resemblance of such as are
natural ; because here the similitude is not only pleasant, but the
pattern more perfect.*

IT is necessary to our present design, to point out two
considerable inaccuracies which occur in this Sentence. *If the
products* (he had better have said the *productions*) *of Nature rise
in value, according as they more or less resemble those of Art.*——
Does he mean, that these productions *rise in value,* both according as they *more resemble,* and as they *less resemble,* those of Art ?
His meaning undoubtedly is, that they rise in value only, according as they *more resemble* them : and therefore, either these
words, *or less,* must be struck out, or the Sentence must run
thus—*productions of Nature rise or sink in value, according as they
more or less resemble.*—The present construction of the Sentence
has plainly been owing to hasty and careless writing.

THE other inaccuracy is toward the end of the Sentence, and
serves to illustrate a rule which I formerly gave, concerning the
position of adverbs.   The Author says,—*because here, the similitude is not only pleasant, but the pattern more perfect.*   Here,
by the position of the adverb *only,* we are led to imagine that
he is going to give some other property of the similitude, that
it is *not only pleasant,* as he says, but more than pleasant ; it is
useful, or, on some account or other, valuable.   Whereas, he is
going to oppose another thing to the *similitude* itself, and not to
this property of its being *pleasant ;* and therefore, the right collocation, beyond doubt, was, *because here, not only the similitude*

is

is pleasant, but the pattern more perfect : the contrast lying, not between *pleasant* and *more perfect*, but between *similitude* and *pattern.*—Much of the clearness and neatness of Style depends on such attentions as these.

The prettiest landscape I ever saw, was one drawn on the walls of a dark room, which stood opposite on one side to a navigable river, and, on the other, to a park. The experiment is very common in optics.

In the description of the landscape which follows, Mr. Addison is abundantly happy; but in this introduction to it, he is obscure and indistinct. One who had not seen the experiment of the Camera Obscura, could comprehend nothing of what he meant. And even, after we understand what he points at, we are at some loss, whether to understand his description as of one continued landscape, or of two different ones, produced by the projection of two Camera Obscuras on opposite walls. The scene, which I am inclined to think Mr. Addison here refers to, is Greenwich Park, with the prospect of the Thames, as seen by a Camera Obscura, which is placed in a small room in the upper story of the Observatory; where I remember to have seen, many years ago, the whole scene here described, corresponding so much to Mr. Addison's account of it in this passage, that, at the time, it recalled it to my memory. As the Observatory stands in the middle of the Park, it overlooks, from one side, both the river and the park; and the objects afterwards mentioned, the ships, the trees, and the deer, are presented in one view, without needing any assistance from opposite walls. Put into plainer language, the Sentence might run thus: " The

" prettiest

" prettieſt landſcape I ever ſaw, was one formed by a Camera
" Obſcura, a common optical inſtrument, on the wall of a dark
" room, which overlooked a navigable river and a park."

*Here you might diſcover the waves and fluctuations of the water
in ſtrong and proper colours, with the picture of a ſhip entering at
one end, and ſailing by degrees through the whole piece. On
another, there appeared the green ſhadows of trees, waving to
and fro with the wind, and herds of deer among them in minia-
ture, leaping about upon the wall.*

Bating one or two ſmall inaccuracies, this is beautiful and
lively painting. The principal inaccuracy lies in the connection of the two Sentences, *Here*, and *On another*. I ſuppoſe
the Author meant, on *one ſide*, and *on another ſide*. As it ſtands,
another is ungrammatical, having nothing to which it refers. But
the fluctuations of the water, the ſhip entering and ſailing on by
degrees, the trees waving in the wind, and the herds of deer
among them leaping about, is all very elegant, and gives a
beautiful conception of the ſcene meant to be deſcribed.

*I muſt confeſs the novelty of ſuch a ſight, may be one occaſion of
its pleaſantneſs to the imagination ; but certainly the chief reaſon, is
its near reſemblance to Nature ; as it does not only, like other pictures, give the colour and figure, but the motions of the things it
repreſents.*

In this Sentence there is nothing remarkable, either to be
praiſed or blamed. In the concluſion, inſtead of *the things it
repreſents*, the regularity of correct Style requires *the things
which it repreſents*. In the beginning, as *one occaſion* and the
chief

9

chief reaſon are oppoſed to one another, I ſhould think it better to have repeated the ſame word—*one reaſon of its pleaſantneſs to the imagination, but certainly the chief reaſon is, &c.*

We have before obſerved, that there is generally, in Nature, ſomething more grand and auguſt than what we meet with in the curioſities of Art. When, therefore, we ſee this imitated in any meaſure, it gives us a nobler and more exalted kind of pleaſure, than what we receive from the nicer and more accurate productions of Art.

It would have been better to have avoided terminating theſe two Sentences in a manner ſo ſimilar to each other; *curioſities of Art—productions of Art.*

On this account, our Engliſh gardens are not ſo entertaining to the fancy as thoſe in France and Italy, where we ſee a large extent of ground covered over with an agreeable mixture of garden and foreſt, which repreſent every where an artificial rudeneſs, much more charming than that neatneſs and elegance which we meet with in thoſe of our own country.

THE expreſſion *repreſent every where an artificial rudeneſs,* is ſo inaccurate, that I am inclined to think, what ſtood in Mr. Addiſon's manuſcript muſt have been—*preſent every where.* —For the mixture of garden and foreſt does not *repreſent,* but actually *exhibits* or *preſents,* artificial rudeneſs. That mixture *repreſents* indeed *natural rudeneſs,* that is, is deſigned to imitate it; but it in reality *is,* and *preſents, artificial rudeneſs.*

It

It might indeed be of ill confequence to the public, as well as unprofitable to private perfons, to alienate fo much ground from pafturage and the plough, in many parts of a country that is fo well peopled and cultivated to a far greater advantage. But why may not a whole eftate be thrown into a kind of garden by frequent plantations, that may turn as much to the profit as the pleafure of the owner? A marfh overgrown with willows, or a mountain fhaded with oaks, are not only more beautiful, but more beneficial, than when they lie bare and unadorned. Fields of corn make a pleafant profpect; and if the walks were a little taken care of that lie between them, and the natural embroidery of the meadows were helped and improved by fome fmall additions of art, and the feveral rows of hedges were fet off by trees and flowers that the foil was capable of receiving, a man might make a pretty landfcape of his own poffeffions.

THE ideas here are juft, and the Style is eafy and perfpicuous, though in fome places bordering on the carelefs. In that paffage, for inftance, *if the walks were a little taken care of that lie between them*—one member is clearly out of its place, and the turn of the phrafe, *a little taken care of*, is vulgar and colloquial. Much better, if it had run thus—*if a little care were beftowed on the walks that lie between them.*

Writers who have given us an account of China, tell us, the inhabitants of that country laugh at the plantations of our Europeans, which are laid out by the rule and the line; becaufe, they fay, any one may place trees in equal rows and uniform figures. They chufe rather to fhow a genius in works of this nature, and therefore always conceal the art by which they direct themfelves.

felves. They have a word, it feems, in their Language, by which they exprefs the particular beauty of a plantation, that thus ftrikes the imagination at firft fight, without difcovering what it is that has fo agreeable an effect.

THESE Sentences furnifh occafion for no remark, except that in the laft of them, *particular* is improperly ufed inftead of *peculiar*—*the peculiar beauty of a plantation that thus ftrikes the imagination*, was the phrafe to have conveyed the idea which the Author meant ; namely, the beauty which diftinguifhes it from plantations of another kind.

Our Britifh gardeners, on the contrary, inftead of humouring nature, love to deviate from it as much as poffible. Our trees rife in cones, globes, and pyramids. We fee the marks of the fciffars on every plant and bufh.

THESE Sentences are lively and elegant. They make an agreeable diverfity from the ftrain of thofe which went before; and are marked with the hand of Mr. Addifon. I have to remark only, that, in the phrafe, *inftead of humouring nature, love to deviate from it*—*humouring* and *deviating*, are terms not properly oppofed to each other; a fort of perfonification of nature is begun in the firft of them, which is not fupported in the fecond.—To *humouring*, was to have been oppofed, *thwarting*—or if *deviating* was kept, *following*, or *going along with nature*, was to have been ufed.

I do not know whether I am fingular in my opinion, but, for my own part, I would rather look upon a tree, in all its luxu-

riancy and diffusion of boughs and branches, than when it is thus cut and trimmed into a mathematical figure ; and cannot but fancy that an orchard, in flower, looks infinitely more delightful, than all the little labyrinths of the most finished parterre.

THIS Sentence is extremely harmonious, and every way beautiful. It carries all the characteristics of our Author's natural, graceful, and flowing Language.—A tree, in *all its luxuriancy and diffusion of boughs and branches*, is a remarkably happy expression. The Author seems to become luxuriant in describing an object which is so, and thereby renders the sound a perfect echo to the sense.

But as our great modellers of gardens have their magazines of plants to dispose of, it is very natural in them, to tear up all the beautiful plantations of fruit trees, and contrive a plan that may most turn to their profit, in taking off their evergreens, and the like moveable plants, with which their shops are plentifully stocked.

AN author should always study to conclude, when it is in his power, with grace and dignity. It is somewhat unfortunate, that this Paper did not end, as it might very well have done, with the former beautiful period. The impression left on the mind by the beauties of nature, with which he had been entertaining us, would then have been more agreeable. But in this Sentence there is a great falling off; and we return with pain from those pleasing objects, to the insignificant contents of a nursery-man's shop.

LECTURE XXIV.

CRITICAL EXAMINATION OF THE STYLE IN A PASSAGE OF DEAN SWIFT's WRITINGS.

MY defign, in the four preceding Lectures, was not merely to appretiate the merit of Mr. Addifon's Style, by pointing out the faults and the beauties that are mingled in the writings of that great Author. They were not compofed with any view to gain the reputation of a Critic; but intended for the affiftance of fuch as are defirous of ftudying the moft proper and elegant conftruction of Sentences in the Englifh Language. To fuch, it is hoped, they may be of advantage; as the proper application of rules refpecting Style, will always be beft learned by means of the illuftration which examples afford. I conceived that examples, taken from the writings of an Author fo juftly efteemed, would, on that account, not only be more attended to, but would alfo produce this good effect, of familiarifing thofe who ftudy compofition with the Style of a writer,

3 P 2

from

from whom they may, upon the whole, derive great benefit.
With the fame view, I fhall, in this Lecture, give one critical
exercife more of the fame kind, upon the Style of an Author
of a different character, Dean Swift ; repeating the intimation
I gave formerly, that fuch as ftand in need of no affiftance of
this kind, and who, therefore, will naturally confider fuch
minute difcuffions concerning the propriety of words, and
ftructure of Sentences, as beneath their attention, had beft pafs
over what will feem to them a tedious part of the work.

I FORMERLY gave the general character of Dean Swift's
Style.   He is efteemed one of our moft correct writers.   His
Style is of the plain and fimple kind; free of all affectation, and
all fuperfluity; perfpicuous, manly, and pure.   Thefe are its
advantages.   But we are not to look for much ornament and
grace in it *.   On the contrary, Dean Swift feems to have
flighted and defpifed the ornaments of Language, rather than
to have ftudied them.   His arrangement is often loofe and
negligent.   In elegant, mufical, and figurative Language, he
is much inferior to Mr. Addifon.   His manner of writing
carries in it the character of one who refts altogether upon his
fenfe, and aims at no more than giving his meaning in a clear
and concife manner.

* I am glad to find, that, in my judgment concerning this Author's compofition, I have coincided with the opinion of a very able critic : " This eafy
" and fafe conveyance of meaning, it was Swift's defire to attain, and for
" having attained, he certainly deferves praife, though, perhaps, not the
" higheft praife.   For purpofes merely didactic, when fomething is to be told
" that was not known before, it is in the higheft degree proper : but againft
" that inattention by which known truths are fuffered to be neglected, it
" makes no provifion , it inftructs, but does not perfuade."   Johnfon's Lives
of the Poets; in Swift.

3   THAT

THAT part of his writings, which I ſhall now examine, is the beginning of his treatiſe, entitled, " A Propoſal for correcting, " improving, and aſcertaining the Engliſh Tongue," in a Letter addreſſed to the Earl of Oxford, then Lord High Treaſurer. I was led, by the nature of the ſubject, to chooſe this treatiſe : but, in juſtice to the Dean, I muſt obſerve, that, after having examined it, I do not eſteem it one of his moſt correct productions ; but am apt to think it has been more haſtily compoſed than ſome other of them. It bears the title and form of a Letter ; but it is, however, in truth, a Treatiſe deſigned for the Public : and, therefore, in examining it, we cannot proceed upon the indulgence due to an epiſtolary correſpondence. When a man addreſſes himſelf to a Friend only, it is ſufficient if he makes himſelf fully underſtood by him ; but when an Author writes for the Public, whether he aſſume the form of an Epiſtle or not, we are always entitled to expect, that he ſhall expreſs himſelf with accuracy and care. Our Author begins thus :

What I had the honour of mentioning to your Lordſhip, ſometime ago, in converſation, was not a new thought, juſt then ſtarted by accident or occaſion, but the reſult of long reflection ; and I have been confirmed in my ſentiments by the opinion of ſome very judicious perſons with whom I conſulted.

THE diſpoſition of circumſtances in a Sentence, ſuch as ſerve to limit or to qualify ſome aſſertion, or to denote time and place, I formerly ſhowed to be a matter of nicety ; and I obſerved, that it ought to be always held a rule, not to crowd ſuch circumſtances together, but rather to intermix them with more

capital

capital words, in such different parts of the Sentence as can admit them naturally. Here are two circumstances of this kind placed together, which had better have been separated, *Some time ago, in conversation*---better thus :---*What I had the honour, sometime ago, of mentioning to your Lordship in conversation— was not a new thought*, proceeds our Author, *started by accident or occasion :* the different meaning of these two words may not, at first, occur. They have, however, a distinct meaning, and are properly used : for it is one very laudable property of our Author's Style, that it is seldom incumbered with superfluous, synonymous words. *Started by accident*, is, fortuitously, or at random ; started *by occasion;* is, by some incident, which at that time gave birth to it. His meaning is, that it was not a new thought which either casually sprung up in his mind, or was suggested to him, for the first time, by the train of the discourse : but, as he adds, *was the result of long reflection.*—He proceeds :

They all agreed, that nothing would be of greater use towards the improvement of knowledge and politeness, than some effectual method, for correcting, enlarging, and ascertaining our Language ; and they think it a work very possible to be compassed under the protection of a prince, the countenance and encouragement of a ministry, and the care of proper persons chosen for such an undertaking.

THIS is an excellent Sentence ; clear, and elegant. The words are all simple, well chosen, and expressive ; and arranged in the most proper order. It is a harmonious period too, which is a beauty not frequent in our Author. The last part of it

consists

confifts of three members, which gradually rife and fwell above one another, without any affected or unfuitable pomp;—*under the protection of a prince, the countenance and encouragement of a miniftry, and the care of proper perfons chofen for fuch an undertaking.* We may remark, in the beginning of the Sentence, the proper ufe of the prepofition *towards*—*greater ufe towards the improvement of knowledge and politenefs*—importing the pointing or tendency of any thing to a certain end; which could not have been fo well expreffed by the prepofition *for*, commonly employed in place of *towards*, by Authors who are lefs attentive, than Dean Swift was, to the force of words.

ONE fault might, perhaps, be found, both with this and the former Sentence, confidered as introductory ones. We expect, that an introduction is to unfold, clearly and directly, the fubject that is to be treated of. In the firft Sentence, our Author had told us, of a thought he mentioned to his Lordfhip, in converfation, which had been the refult of long reflection, and concerning which he had confulted judicious perfons. But what that thought was, we are never told directly. We gather it indeed from the fecond fentence, wherein he informs us, in what thefe judicious perfons agreed; namely, that fome method for improving the language was both ufeful and practicable. But this indirect method of opening the fubject, would have been very faulty in a regular treatife; though the eafe of the epiftolary form, which our Author here affumes in addreffing his patron, may excufe it in the prefent cafe.

I was glad to find your Lordfhip's anfwer in fo different a ftyle from what hath commonly been made ufe of, on the like occafions, for

fome

fome years paft ; " That all fuch thoughts muft be deferred to a time of peace ;" a topic which fome have carried fo far, that they would not have us, by any means, think of preferving our civil and religious conftitution, becaufe we are engaged in a war abroad.

THIS Sentence alfo is clear and elegant; only there is one inaccuracy, when he fpeaks of his Lordfhip's *anfwer* being in fo different a ftyle from what had formerly been ufed. His *anfwer* to what? or to whom? For from any thing going before, it does not appear that any application or addrefs had been made to his Lordfhip by thofe perfons, whofe opinion was mentioned in the preceding Sentence; and to whom the anfwer, here fpoken of, naturally refers. There is a little indiftinctnefs, as I before obferved, in our Author's manner of introducing his fubject here.—We may obferve too, that the phrafe —*glad to find your anfwer in fo different a ftyle*—though abundantly fuited to the language of converfation, or of a familiar letter, yet, in regular compofition, requires an additional word—*glad to find your anfwer run in fo different a ftyle.*

It will be among the diftinguifhing marks of your miniftry, my Lord, that you have a genius above all fuch regards, and that no reafonable propofal, for the honour, the advantage, or ornament of your country, however foreign to your immediate office, was ever neglected by you.

THE phrafe—*a genius above all fuch regards,* both feems fomewhat harfh, and does not clearly exprefs what the Author means, namely, the *confined views* of thofe who neglected every thing that belonged to the arts of peace in the time of war.— Bating this expreffion, there is nothing that can be fubject to
the

the leaft reprehenfion in this Sentence, nor in all that follows, L E C T. XXIV.
to the end of the paragraph.

I confefs, the merit of this candor and condefcenfion is very much leffened, becaufe your Lordfhip hardly leaves us room to offer our good wifhes; removing all our difficulties, and fupplying our wants, fafter than the moft vifionary projeƐor can adjuft his fchemes. And therefore, my Lord, the defign of this paper is not fo much to offer you ways and means, as to complain of a grievance, the redreffing of which is to be your own work, as much as that of paying the nation's debts, or opening a trade into the South Sea; and, though not of fuch immediate benefit as either of thefe, or any other of your glorious aƐions, yet, perhaps, in future ages not lefs to your honour.

THE compliments which the Dean here pays to his patron, are very high and ftrained; and fhow, that, with all his furlinefs, he was as capable, on fome occafions, of making his court to a great man by flattery, as other writers. However, with refpeƐt to the Style, which is the fole objeƐ of our prefent confideration, every thing here, as far as appears to me, is faultlefs. In thefe Sentences, and, indeed, throughout this paragraph, in general, which we have now ended, our Author's Style appears to great advantage. We fee that eafe and fimplicity, that correƐnefs and diftinƐnefs, which particularly charaƐerife it. It is very remarkable, how few Latinifed words Dean Swift employs. No writer, in our Language, is fo purely Englifh as he is, or borrows fo little affiftance from words of foreign derivation. From none can we take a better model of the choice and proper fignificancy of words. It is remarkable, in the Sentences we have now before us, how plain all the expreſſions are, and yet, at the ſame time, how ſignificant; and, in the midſt of that high ſtrain of compliment into which he riſes, how little there is of pomp, or glare of expreſſion. How very few writers can preſerve this manly temperance of Style; or would think a compliment of this nature ſupported with ſufficient dignity, unleſs they had embelliſhed it with ſome of thoſe high ſounding words, whoſe chief effect is no other than to give their Language a ſtiff and forced appearance?

My Lord, I do here, in the name of all the learned and polite perſons of the nation, complain to your Lordſhip, as Firſt Miniſter, that our Language is extremely imperfect; that its daily improvements are by no means in proportion to its daily corruptions; that the pretenders to poliſh and refine it, have chiefly multiplied abuſes and abſurdities; and that, in many inſtances, it offends againſt every part of grammar.

The turn of this Sentence is extremely elegant. He had ſpoken before of a grievance for which he ſought redreſs, and he carries on the alluſion, by entering, here, directly on his ſubject, in the Style of a public repreſentation preſented to the Miniſter of State. One imperfection, however, there is in this Sentence, which, luckily for our purpoſe, ſerves to illuſtrate a rule before given, concerning the poſition of adverbs, ſo as to avoid ambiguity. It is in the middle of the Sentence;—*that the pretenders to poliſh and refine it, have chiefly multiplied abuſes and abſurdities.*—Now, concerning the import of this adverb, *chiefly*, I aſk, whether it ſignifies that theſe pretenders to poliſh the Language, have been the *chief perſons* who have multiplied

7   its

its abufes, in diftinction *from others*; or, that the *chief thing* which thefe pretenders have done, is to multiply the abufes of our Language, in oppofition to their *doing any thing to refine it?* Thefe two meanings are really different; and yet, by the pofition which the word *chiefly* has in the Sentence, we are left at a lofs in which to underftand it. The conftruction would lead us rather to the latter fenfe; that the chief thing which thefe pretenders have done, is to multiply the abufes of our Language. But it is more than probable, that the former fenfe was what the Dean intended, as it carries more of his ufual fatirical edge; " that the pretended refiners of our Lan-" guage were, in fact, its chief corruptors;" on which fup-pofition, his words ought to have run thus: *that the pretenders to polifh and refine it, have been the chief perfons to multiply its abufes and abfurdities;* which would have rendered the fenfe perfectly clear.

PERHAPS, too, there might be ground for obferving farther upon this Sentence, that as Language is the object with which it fets out; *that our Language is extremely imperfect*; and then follows an enumeration concerning Language, in three parti-culars, it had been better if Language had been kept the ruling word, or the nominative to every verb, without changing the fcene; by making *pretenders* the ruling word, as is done in the fecond member of the enumeration, and then, in the third, re-turning again to the former word, *Language—That the pre-tenders to polifh—and that, in many inftances, it offend*—I am perfuaded, that the ftructure of the Sentence would have been more neat and happy, and its unity more complete, if the members of it had been arranged thus: " That our Language

" is

" is extremely imperfect; that its daily improvements are by
" no means in proportion to its daily corruptions; that, in
" many instances, it offends against every part of grammar;
" and that the pretenders to polish and refine it, have been the
" chief persons to multiply its abuses and absurdities."—This
degree of attention seemed proper to be bestowed on such a
Sentence as this, in order to show how it might have been
conducted after the most perfect manner.   Our Author, after
having said,

*Lest your Lordship should think my censure too severe, I shall
take leave to be more particular;* proceeds in the following
paragraph :

*I believe your Lordship will agree with me, in the reason why
our Language is less refined than those of Italy, Spain, or
France.*

I AM sorry to say, that now we shall have less to commend
in our Author.   For the whole of this paragraph, on which
we are entering, is, in truth, perplexed and inaccurate.   Even,
in this short Sentence, we may discern an inaccuracy—*why our
Language is less refined than those of Italy, Spain, and France;*
putting the pronoun *those* in the plural, when the antecedent
substantive to which it refers is in the singular, *our Language.*
Instances of this kind may sometimes be found in English
authors; but they found harsh to the ear, and are certainly
contrary to the purity of grammar.   By a very little attention,
this inaccuracy could have been remedied; and the Sentence
have been made to run much better in this way; " why

" our

" our Language is lefs refined than the Italian, Spanifh, or
" French."

It is plain, that the Latin Tongue, in its purity, was never in this ifland; towards the conqueft of which, few or no attempts were made till the time of Claudius; neither was that Language ever fo vulgar in Britain, as it is known to have been in Gaul and Spain.

To fay, that *the Latin Tongue, in its purity, was never in this ifland,* is very carelefs Style; it ought to have been, *was never fpoken in this ifland.* In the progrefs of the Sentence, he means to give a reafon why the Latin was never fpoken in its purity amongft us, becaufe our ifland was not conquered by the Romans till after the purity of their Tongue began to decline. But this reafon ought to have been brought out more clearly. This might eafily have been done, and the relation of the feveral parts of the Sentence to each other much better pointed out by means of a fmall variation; thus: " It is plain, " that the Latin Tongue, in its purity, was never fpoken in " this ifland, as few or no attempts towards the conqueft of " it were made till the time of Claudius." He adds, *Neither was that Language ever fo vulgar in Britain.—Vulgar* was one of the worft words he could have chofen for expreffing what he means here; namely, that the Latin Tongue was at no time fo *general,* or fo much in *common ufe,* in Britain, as it is known to have been in Gaul and Spain.—*Vulgar,* when applied to Language, commonly fignifies impure, or debafed Language, fuch as is fpoken by the low people, which is quite oppofite to the Author's fenfe here; for, in place of meaning to fay, that
the

the Latin fpoken in Britain was not fo debafed, as what was fpoken in Gaul and Spain; he means juft the contrary, and had been telling us, that we never were acquainted with the Latin at all, till its purity began to be corrupted.

Further, we find that the Roman legions here were at length all recalled to help their country againft the Goths, and other barbarous invaders.

THE chief fcope of this Sentence is, to give a reafon why the Latin Tongue did not ftrike any deep root in this ifland, on account of the fhort continuance of the Romans in it. He goes on:

Meantime the Britons, left to fhift for themfelves, and daily haraffed by cruel inroads from the Picts, were forced to call in the Saxons for their defence; who, confequently, reduced the greateft part of the ifland to their own power, drove the Britons into the moft remote and mountainous parts, and the reft of the country, in cuftoms, religion, and language, became wholly Saxon.

THIS is a very exceptionable fentence. Firft, the phrafe *left to fhift for themfelves,* is rather a low phrafe, and too much in the familiar Style to be proper in a grave treatife. Next, as the Sentence advances—*forced to call in the Saxons for their defence, who, confequently, reduced the greateft part of the ifland to their own power.*—What is the meaning of *confequently* here? if it means " afterwards," or " in progrefs of time," this, certainly, is not a fenfe in which *confequently* is often taken; and therefore the expreffion is chargeable with obfcurity. The adverb, *confequently,* in its moft common acceptation, denotes one
                                                                    thing

thing following from another, as an effect from a caufe. If he ufes it in this fenfe, and means that the Britons being fubdued by the Saxons, was a neceffary confequence of their having called in thefe Saxons to their affiftance, this confequence is drawn too abruptly, and needed more explanation. For though it has often happened, that nations have been fubdued by their own auxiliaries, yet this is not a confequence of fuch a nature that it can be affumed, as feems here to be done, for a firft and felf-evident principle.—But further, what fhall we fay to this phrafe, *reduced the greateft part of the ifland to their own power?* we fay *reduce to rule, reduce to practice*—we can fay, that *one nation reduces another to fubjection*—But when *dominion* or *power* is ufed, we always, as far as I know, fay, *reduce under their power.* *Reduce to their power,* is fo harfh and uncommon an expreffion, that, though Dean Swift's authority in language be very great, yet, in the ufe of this phrafe, I am of opinion, that it would not be fafe to follow his example.

BESIDES thefe particular inaccuracies, this Sentence is charge-able with want of unity in the compofition of the whole. The perfons and the fcene are too often changed upon us—Firft, the Britons are mentioned, who are haraffed by inroads from the Picts; next, the Saxons appear, who fubdue the greateft part of the ifland, and drive the Britons into the mountains; and, laftly, the reft of the country is introduced, and a defcrip-tion given of the change made upon it. All this forms a groupe of various objects, prefented in fuch quick fucceffion, that the mind finds it difficult to comprehend them under one view. Accordingly, it is quoted in the *Elements of Criticifm,* as an in-ftance of a fentence rendered faulty by the breach of unity.

This

*This I take to be the reafon why there are more Latin words re-
maining in the Britiſh than the old Saxon; which, excepting ſome
few variations in the orthography, is the ſame in moſt original
words with our preſent Engliſh, as well as with the German and
other northern dialects.*

THIS Sentence is faulty, ſomewhat in the ſame manner with
the laſt.   It is looſe in the connection of its parts; and, beſides
this, it is alſo too looſely connected with the preceding ſentence.
What he had there ſaid, concerning the Saxons expelling the
Britons, and changing the cuſtoms, the religion, and the language of the country, is a clear and good reaſon for our preſent language being Saxon rather than Britiſh.   This is the inference which we would naturally expect him to draw from the
premiſes juſt before laid down : But when he tells us, that
*this is the reaſon why there are more Latin words remaining in
the Britiſh tongue than in the old Saxon*, we are preſently at a
ſtand.   No reaſon for this inference appears.   If it can be gathered at all from the foregoing deduction, it is gathered only
imperfectly.   For, as he had told us, that the Britons had
ſome connection with the Romans, he ſhould have alſo told us,
in order to make out his inference, that the Saxons never had
any.   The truth is, the whole of this paragraph concerning the
influence of the Latin tongue upon ours, is careleſs, perplexed,
and obſcure.   His argument required to have been more fully
unfolded, in order to make it be diſtinctly apprehended, and
to give it its due force.   In the next paragraph, he proceeds
to diſcourſe concerning the influence of the French tongue upon
our language.   The Style becomes more clear, though not remarkable for great beauty or elegance.

Edward

Edward the Confessor having lived long in France, appears to be the first who introduced any mixture of the French tongue with the Saxon; the court affecting what the Prince was fond of, and others taking it up for a fashion, as it is now with us. William the Conqueror proceeded much further, bringing over with him vast numbers of that nation, scattering them in every monastery, giving them great quantities of land, directing all pleadings to be in that language, and endeavouring to make it universal in the kingdom.

On these two Sentences, I have nothing of moment to observe. The sense is brought out clearly, and in simple, unaffected language.

This, at least, is the opinion generally received; but your Lordship hath fully convinced me, that the French tongue made yet a greater progress here under Harry the Second, who had large territories on that continent both from his father and his wife; made frequent journeys and expeditions thither; and was always attended with a number of his countrymen, retainers at court.

In the beginning of this Sentence, our Author states an opposition between an opinion generally received, and that of his Lordship; and, in compliment to his patron, he tells us, that his Lordship had convinced him of somewhat that differed from the general opinion. Thus one must naturally understand his words: *This, at least, is the opinion generally received; but your Lordship hath fully convinced me*—Now here there must be an inaccuracy of expression. For, on examining what went before, there appears no sort of opposition betwixt the generally received opinion, and that of the Author's patron. The general opinion was, that William the Conqueror had proceeded much farther than Edward the Confeſſor, in propagating the French language, and had endeavoured to make it univerſal. Lord Oxford's opinion was, that the French tongue had gone on to make a yet greater progreſs under Harry the Second, than it had done under his predeceſſor William: which two opinions are as entirely conſiſtent with one another, as any can be; and therefore the oppoſition here affected to be ſtated between them, by the adverſative particle *but,* was improper and groundleſs.

For ſome centuries after, there was a conſtant intercourſe between France and England by the dominions we poſſeſſed there, and the conqueſts we made; ſo that our language, between two and three hundred years ago, ſeems to have had a greater mixture with French than at preſent; many words having been afterwards rejected, and ſome ſince the days of Spenſer; although we have ſtill retained not a few, which have been long antiquated in France.

THIS is a Sentence too long and intricate, and liable to the ſame objection that was made to a former one, of the want of unity. It conſiſts of four members, each divided from the ſubſequent by a ſemicolon. In going along, we naturally expect the Sentence is to end at the ſecond of theſe, or, at fartheſt, at the third; when, to our ſurpriſe, a new member pops out upon us, and fatigues our attention in joining all the parts together. Such a ſtructure of a Sentence is always the mark of careleſs writing. In the firſt member of the Sentence, *a conſtant intercourſe between France and England, by the dominions we poſſeſſed there, and the conqueſts we made,* the conſtruction is not ſufficiently

ciently filled up. In place of *intercourse by the dominions we possessed*, it should have been—*by reason of the dominions we possessed*—or—*occasioned by the dominions we possessed*—and in place of—*the dominions we possessed there, and the conquests we made*, the regular Style is—*the dominions which we possessed there, and the conquests which we made*. The relative pronoun *which*, is indeed in phrases of this kind sometimes omitted : But, when it is omitted, the Style becomes elliptic ; and though in conversation, or in the very light and easy kinds of writing, such elliptic Style may not be improper, yet in grave and regular writing, it is better to fill up the construction, and insert the relative pronoun.—After having said—*I could produce several instances of both kinds, if it were of any use or entertainment*—our Author begins the next paragraph thus :

To examine into the several circumstances by which the language of a country may be altered, would force me to enter into a wide field.

There is nothing remarkable in this Sentence, unless that here occurs the first instance of a metaphor since the beginning of this treatise ; *entering into a wide field*, being put for beginning an extensive subject. Few writers deal less in figurative language than Swift. I before observed, that he appears to despise ornaments of this kind ; and though this renders his Style somewhat dry on serious subjects, yet his plainness and simplicity, I must not forbear to remind my readers, is far preferable to an ostentatious and affected parade of ornament.

I shall only observe, that the Latin, the French, and the English, seem to have undergone the same fortune. The first from the

3 R 2

days

LECT.
XXIV.

days of Romulus, to those of Julius Cæsar, suffered perpetual changes; and by what we meet in those Authors who occasionally speak on that subject, as well as from certain fragments of old laws, it is manifest that the Latin, three hundred years before Tully, was as unintelligible in his time, as the French and English of the same period are now; and these two have changed as much since William the Conqueror (which is but little less than 700 years), as the Latin appears to have done in the like term.

THE Dean plainly appears to be writing negligently here. This Sentence is one of that involved and intricate kind, of which some instances have occurred before; but none worse than this. It requires a very distinct head to comprehend the whole meaning of the period at first reading. In one part of it we find extreme carelessness of expression. He says, *it is manifest that the Latin, 300 years before Tully, was as unintelligible in his time, as the English and French of the same period are now.* By the English and French *of the same period,* must naturally be understood, *the English and French that were spoken three hundred years before Tully.* This is the only grammatical meaning his words will bear; and yet assuredly what he means, and what it would have been easy for him to have expressed with more precision, is, *the English and French that were spoken 300 years ago;* or at a period equally distant from our age, as the old Latin, which he had mentioned, was from the age of Tully. But when an author writes hastily, and does not review with proper care what he has written, many such inaccuracies will be apt to creep into his Style.

Whether our Language or the French will decline as fast as the Roman did, is a question that would perhaps admit more debate

4

than

than it is worth. There were many reasons for the corruptions of the last; as the change of their government to a tyranny, which ruined the study of eloquence, there being no further use or encouragement for popular orators; their giving not only the freedom of the city, but capacity for employments, to several towns in Gaul, Spain, and Germany, and other distant parts, as far Asia, which brought a great number of foreign pretenders to Rome; the slavish disposition of the Senate and people, by which the wit and eloquence of the age were wholly turned into panegyric, the most barren of all subjects; the great corruption of manners, and introduction of foreign luxury, with foreign terms to express it, with several others that might be assigned; not to mention the invasion from the Goths and Vandals, which are too obvious to insist on.

In the enumeration here made of the causes contributing towards the corruption of the Roman Language, there are many inaccuracies—*The change of their government to a tyranny*—of whose government? He had indeed been speaking of the Roman language, and therefore we guess at his meaning; but the Style is ungrammatical; for he had not mentioned the Romans themselves; and therefore, when he says *their government*, there is no antecedent in the Sentence to which the pronoun, *their*, can refer with any propriety—*Giving the capacity for employments to several towns in Gaul*, is a questionable expression. For though towns are sometimes put for the people who inhabit them, yet to give a town *the capacity for employments*, sounds harsh and uncouth.—*The wit and eloquence of the age wholly turned into panegyric*, is a phrase which does not well express the meaning. Neither wit nor eloquence can be turned into panegyric;

gyric; but they may be turned *towards panegyric*, or, *employed in panegyric*, which was the fenfe the Author had in view.

THE conclufion of the enumeration is vifibly incorrect—*The great corruption of manners, and introduction of foreign luxury, with foreign terms to exprefs it, with feveral others that might be affigned*—He means, *with feveral other reafons.* The word *reafons*, had indeed been mentioned before; but as it ftands at the diftance of thirteen lines backward, the repetition of it here became indifpenfable, in order to avoid ambiguity. *Not to mention*, he adds, *the invafions from the Goths and Vandals, which are too obvious to infift on.* One would imagine him to mean, that the invafions from the Goths and Vandals, are *hiftorical facts* too well known and obvious to be infifted on. But he means quite a different thing, though he has not taken the proper method of expreffing it, through his hafte, probably, to finifh the paragraph; namely, that thefe invafions from the Goths and Vandals *were caufes of the corruption of the Roman Language too obvious to be infifted on.*

I SHALL not purfue this criticifm any further. I have been obliged to point out many inaccuracies in the paffage which we have confidered. But, in order that my obfervations may not be conftructed as meant to depreciate the Style or the Writings of Dean Swift below their juft value, there are two remarks, which I judge it neceffary to make before concluding this Lecture. One is, That it were unfair to eftimate an Author's Style on the whole, by fome paffage in his writings, which chances to be compofed in a carelefs manner. This is the cafe with refpect to this treatife, which has much the appearance of a hafty pro-

3   duction;

duction; though, as I before obferved, it was by no means on that account that I pitched upon it for the fubject of this exercife. But after having examined it, I am fenfible that, in many other of his writings, the Dean is more accurate.

My other obfervation, which applies equally to Dean Swift and Mr. Addifon, is, that there may be writers much freer of fuch inaccuracies, as I have had occafion to point out in thefe two, whofe Style, however, upon the whole, may not have half their merit. Refinement in Language has, of late years, begun to be much attended to. In feveral modern productions of very fmall value, I fhould find it difficult to point out many errors in Language. The words might, probably, be all proper words, correctly and clearly arranged ; and the turn of the fentence fonorous and mufical ; whilft yet the Style, upon the whole, might deferve no praife. The fault often lies in what may be called the general caft, or complexion of the Style ; which a perfon of a good tafte difcerns to be vicious; to be feeble, for inftance, and diffufe ; flimfy or affected ; petulant or oftentatious ; though the faults cannot be fo eafily pointed out and particularifed, as when they lie in fome erroneous, or negligent conftruction of a fentence. Whereas, fuch writers as Addifon and Swift, carry always thofe general characters of good Style, which, in the midft of their occafional negligences, every perfon of good tafte muft difcern and approve. We fee their faults overbalanced by higher beauties. We fee a writer of fenfe and reflection expreffing his fentiments without affectation, attentive to thoughts as well as to words ; and, in the main current of his Language, elegant and beautiful ; and, therefore, the only proper ufe to be made of the blemifhes

which

L E C T.
XXIV.

which occur in the writings of such authors, is to point out to those who apply themselves to the study of composition, some of the rules which they ought to observe for avoiding such errors; and to render them sensible of the necessity of strict attention to Language and to Style. Let them imitate the ease and simplicity of those great authors; let them study to be always natural, and, as far as they can, always correct in their expressions; let them endeavour to be, at some times, lively and striking; but carefully avoid being at any time ostentatious and affected.

END OF THE FIRST VOLUME.